Gary Numan is one of Britain's most important and respected musical artists. He has been lauded by everyone from Prince ('His album *Replicas* never left my turntable . . . There are people still trying to work out what a genius he was') through the Foo Fighters and Nine Inch Nails to Lady Gaga ('[He] proves music has always been really inventive for the masses'). Born in Hammersmith in 1958, Gary was the frontman of Tubeway Army before embarking on a successful solo career. His #1 singles 'Are "Friends" Electric?' and 'Cars', both released in 1979, are cult classics and his 2017 album *Savage* entered the UK charts at #2. Gary is considered a pioneer of electronic music and, in 2017, he received the Ivor Novello Inspiration Award for song writing. He lives in California with his wife and three daughters.

(R)evolution

GARY NUMAN

The Autobiography

CONSTABLE

CONSTABLE

First published in Great Britain in 2020 by Constable
This paperback edition published in 2021 by Constable

1 3 5 7 9 10 8 6 4 2

A CIP catalogue record for this book
is available from the British Library.

ISBN: 978-1-47213-463-9

Typeset in Bembo by Hewer Text UK Ltd, Edinburgh
Printed and bound in Great Britain by Clays Ltd, Elcograf, S.p.A.

Papers used by Constable are from well-managed
forests and other responsible sources

MIX
Paper from
responsible sources
FSC
www.fsc.org   FSC® C104740

Constable
An imprint of
Little, Brown Book Group
Carmelite House
50 Victoria Embankment
London EC4Y 0DZ

An Hachette UK Company
www.hachette.co.uk

www.littlebrown.co.uk

I dedicate this book, as I do my life, to my wife Gemma, and my children Raven, Persia and Echo, to Beryl and Tony Webb, my mum and dad, who gave me that life to live and every opportunity to live it well, and to my brother John.

Contents

Chapter One

1958

I wasn't born Gary Numan. I was born Gary Anthony James Webb, in Hammersmith Hospital, London, 8 March 1958. At 10.30 p.m. to be precise. The only child my mum would ever give birth to, although luckily not the only child she would ever be a mother to.

My mum Beryl had worked as a dressmaker before falling pregnant with me, and she was still only twenty years old when I arrived. My dad, Anthony David Webb, although everyone knows him as Tony, was about a year and a half older than my mum, and by the time they got married I was only a few months away from being born. A situation somewhat frowned upon back in those days. Dad was employed as a paint sprayer at the time but had also worked as a merchant seaman and had spent two years in Germany doing his National Service with the Army.

I have traits of both parents when it comes to the way I look, but my character seems to have come very much from my dad. Like him I can be stubborn, argumentative and opinionated, although we've both mellowed a lot as we've got older. But, also like him, I am honest. Brutally honest, in fact. Like him, I'm fiercely loyal to my family, generous with time, with love, with anything I have. My parents always made me feel special, as though anything was possible if you just tried. No dream was ever put down as stupid or childish, no matter how unlikely it might have seemed. I was brought up to believe that I could be whatever I wanted to be, knowing they would always help me in any way they could. I couldn't have asked for a more loving or supportive family, and I know for certain that without them my life would have been very different.

It's been said at times that I'm something of a perfectionist, but I don't believe that's true. I'm obsessive, and that's not the same thing at all. I want to be as good as I can be, but I'm not searching for perfection, nor do I expect it from anyone else. I'm competitive, but I don't get upset if I lose. I want the best for people I care for. I don't need to be in charge, but it helps get things done the way I want them done. I found early on that running a band works best when you don't have to debate every decision, so, when it comes to my career, the buck stops with me. That works for creative projects as well. Too much input from other people just slows everything down and dilutes the finished result. I'm happy to come up with the ideas, make all the decisions and sink or swim on what I end up with. It brings a lot of pressure, and it doesn't always work out well, but I'm not one to blame other people for my mistakes. So, not a perfectionist, but very much in charge of my own direction and future. My obsessive nature has been a powerful force with my music career, but it's also helped in many of the other things I've been involved in, flying aeroplanes being one.

My mother came from a very close family, and as soon as she had a child of her own did everything she could to make sure we were safe and looked after. Although quite small in size, she could be a formidable woman. Fiery and protective, nothing came before family. If she took to you, though, she was warm and friendly, always ready to listen and to help.

Around the time I was born my parents were renting a room in a bungalow in Ashford, Middlesex, but not long after I came along we were forced out by the landlady. Apparently she accused my mum of washing the walls so much the paint had started to come off. Knowing my mum and her obsession with keeping a clean house, especially with a new baby, I suspect that may have been true. The next place we went to had a different kind of landlord problem. This one seemed to be more interested in looking at my mum than the walls, so we moved on again.

My dad and his brother Lionel decided to rent a house that the two families would share. We took the upper floor and Lionel, his wife Val and their two children, Clive and Garry, took the ground floor. Garry, another Garry Webb, was born about twenty days after me, so there were two babies in the house at the same time. Not an easy situation for either family I'd guess.

I've often talked about being spoiled as a child but not in the way people think. My parents had no money, so I wasn't showered with expensive toys, and I certainly didn't get whatever I asked for – far from it. I was spoiled with love, kindness and caring. I was made to feel I was the most important thing in the world as far as my mum and dad were concerned. I felt safe, protected and important. For the first few years of my life I didn't see my dad much; he worked constantly to try and pull us up from our poor beginnings. He has always had a phenomenal work ethic, and there was, and still is, nothing he wouldn't do to help his family. But it's true to say that money was in short supply for much of my early childhood.

I've always been interested in machines and technology, even as a small child. The kind that move mostly, but not exclusively. One of the best presents my parents ever got for me was a home-made control panel my dad had put together out of wood and various old dials and switches he'd found in his shed. That panel allowed me to be whoever and whatever I wanted. I was a pilot, a ship's captain, an explorer on a spaceship far out in space — anything my imagination could think of. That small wooden control panel allowed me to explore the universe from the safety of my bedroom, to control huge, powerful machines that had yet to be invented, to wage war, to win races, to do anything I wanted. It was the perfect gift, made with love and understanding by parents who knew me inside out. It was exactly what I needed. Many years later I would have some of those same adventures but for real.

Around the age of four I saw something on television that would have a huge effect on my life. I saw a guitar player called Hank Marvin performing on a TV show, and I was captivated. Not by the music, but by the guitar he was playing. It was electric. It had a switch and dials and a lead that went to an amplifier that had yet more dials and switches. It was one of the most exciting things I'd ever seen, and I desperately wanted one. Electric guitars were out of the question, of course, but I was lucky enough to get an acoustic guitar. I tied some string to it to make it look like it had a lead and taught myself a few chords. I wasn't hugely interested in music itself at that point, although we did often play records as a family — it was the sounds I was interested in. But it was the first steps in what would become my entire life.

4

The most exciting machines for me as a youngster were aeroplanes. I loved everything about them. They were beautiful, sleek, fast, noisy, powerful and complex. People that could fly aeroplanes seemed like gods and I would ask my parents to take me to watch them coming and going at the airport every chance I got. When I was five, or thereabouts, they took me to a small local airfield called Fairoaks to look at some light aircraft. You could get a bit closer to the planes than you could at the airport, so it was very exciting, but I was amazed when they said I could walk out to one and have a really close look. I was absolutely staggered when a pilot came out and asked if I wanted a ride. I didn't know it at the time, but my mum and dad had booked a small pleasure flight for us all. It was an incredible experience, and I loved every second of it. I was allowed to sit at the front next to the pilot and I marvelled at his skills as he flew this little plane across the sky, pointing out things along the way. It had a huge, lasting effect on me. I desperately wanted to be a pilot, to know as much about aviation as I possibly could.

For years afterwards, planes were my biggest passion, but music was never too far away from my thoughts. I spent countless days at my grandparents' (Nan and Poppa), lying out in their back garden watching the airliners fly over. They had a house not too far from the end of the runway at Heathrow, and it was exhilarating to hear the thunder of the jets as the planes got closer. When they came over the house, they were so low you could see every detail. It was my favourite thing to do. They were like dragons, huge and dangerous, fast and powerful, beautiful but menacing, and I thought it must surely take someone magical to tame them.

As I said, Dad worked so hard I barely saw him for the first few years of my life. Most of the day-to-day upbringing my mum did alone. When I was born, she also developed epilepsy, so the strain on her must have been enormous, but I was bliss-fully unaware of the hardships she was going through. Part of that is probably just down to me being a child, but my mum endured a lot throughout her life and yet never made it a burden for the family. She was incredibly strong in so many ways.

Most of my dad's early jobs were driving. He drove buses, lorries, coaches, vans, all sorts of things. Many of my early memories involve sitting in between my mum and dad in some vehicle or other. I have one clear memory of us running out of fuel on a foggy night out in the country somewhere and watch-ing my dad walking away, disappearing into the dark night with a petrol can in hand. Sitting there with my mum waiting for him to come back was one of the most nerve-racking experi-ences of my young life.

My mum was always telling me stories of my dad's upbring-ing. One time she had gone to his house early on in their rela-tionship and was waiting for him in the front room when he suddenly burst through the wall, having a fierce fight with one of his brothers. The walls were made of asbestos, and they had hit it so hard they'd shattered it and gone straight through. My dad once told me that as a kid he and his brothers had gone out and dragged home a fallen tree trunk, placed one end in the fire in their house and set it on fire. They would slide the trunk further into the fire as the end burnt away. They couldn't afford to buy wood or coal to burn. Mum said this was why my dad was so determined to work hard and do what he could for us, so that we never had to live the way he had.

6

Things got a little better for us when we were able to move out of the shared house and into a council house – 53 St Anne's Avenue, Stanwell, Middlesex, a three-bedroom semi, became our new home. A three-bedroom semi felt like a palace to us. Strangely enough, Lionel and his family moved into number 55 right next door. Our garden backed on to the playing fields of my school, Town Farm, so getting to school was easy.

The British government began a study of all children born in England, Scotland and Wales between 3 and 9 March 1958. About 17,000 children in all, including me. The National Child Development Study has followed us throughout our lives and, along with other similar studies, has been able to help build a greater understanding of how our experiences as children affected how we turned out as adults, how different areas of our lives, such as health, wealth, family, education and employment are linked, and how these aspects of life vary for people from different backgrounds. Essentially, how our natural abilities can be affected by environment and upbringing. I loved being a part of the study, to be honest. It made me feel special, although I think that was more to do with the way it was explained to me by my mum. She told me it was for gifted children, which wasn't true. For me it just seemed like regular questionnaires, cognitive assessments, clinical assessments and other measurements. It was through these extra tests and assessments that it was discovered I had an above average IQ – in the gifted level, apparently. That may have been why Mum said it was for gifted children, of course. Whatever, it made Mum and Dad very happy.

Although I was considered bright at school, in my pre-teen years I was also pretty shy, reluctant to take part in anything that would put the spotlight on me. School plays, reading out loud, anything like that were a nightmare for me. I did have my fair share of confrontations, though. A short temper coupled with an absolute lack of patience with stupidity or ignorance saw me in fights more than once. I took offence too easily at times. One time someone called my cousin Garry 'Spider', which seems an incredibly childish thing to be angry about now. Garry didn't hear but I did and that was enough. I punched Spider man in the face, and he immediately opened his mouth and started crying. His broken Spangle sweet fell out, which seemed pretty funny to me at the time. Within seconds Spider man's friends got involved, so I had to make a run for it. I was running as fast as I could, but my wellington boots were too big and kept slipping off. Luckily, as I ran out of the school gates, my dad was waiting for me, and I dived into his car safe and sound. It really was lucky. My dad hardly ever picked me up from school, as our house was so close.

When I was seven, my dad's brother John died. I remember seeing my dad cry for just a brief moment, something I'd not seen before and have never seen again. Soon after that John's children were sent out to various family members to look after, and one of them, Donovan, came to us. I can't truly remember the ins and outs of what went on back then, but Donovan was in a sorry condition when he came to us, so my mum and dad decided to adopt him. It took a while, but eventually Donovan became John, and John became my brother, whom I have loved with all my heart from the day he arrived. I've heard so many comments over the years about how I must have been jealous of a new baby coming into the family, or how I must have resented him, going from being an only child to having a baby brother. I never had any of those feelings. Not one. Ever.

After several years in St Anne's Avenue, we moved again, this time to 615 London Road, Ashford, Middlesex. But this move meant a great deal to my mum and dad. This time we were moving not to a rented house, but to one they owned. All my dad's hard work, all my mum's sacrifices, had come good. They were now homeowners. Although I wasn't too aware of what that meant at the time, I recognised that it was an important step for them, and I knew they were proud.

It was here that I met two boys that would become lifelong friends, although things started badly. Nicky and Garry Robson lived in the next street, so, according to kids' law, we were enemies. Our meetings were usually a series of threats and shoves until one day we just started giggling at the pointless stupidity of it all, and that was that. Friends for life. It was Garry who many years later would trace around my face on a single cover and come up with an outline that would become the most recognisable Numan symbol. Nicky would become an award-winning video editor and helped me out more than once during some of my leaner career years. Nicky eventually emigrated to the USA and wrote a book about the experience. I actually bought a copy when I made my own move to California in 2012, without realising at first it was the same Nicky Robson whom I'd grown up with.

Garry and I had very similar tastes in music and spent many an evening talking about fame and fortune and all the things we were going to do when we grew up. Before that, though, I had a different set of friends, boys from my own street. We were all mad fans of The Monkees, so we put together what we laughingly called a band and started doing 'shows' in people's houses up and down the street. We were called The Monkee Juniors, and our show consisted of putting on a Monkees record and miming enthusiastically to one song. On a good day we'd earn enough money to get some chocolate from the corner shop. I didn't realise it at the time, but it was perfect practice for when I would eventually appear on *Top of the Pops* many years later. My friend Chris insisted on being the handsome singer Davy Jones, and as I had a guitar, still with string attached, I was Mike Nesmith. The real Mike Nesmith used to wear a green bobble hat, without the bobble, so my mum made me one just like it. I think it added to my performance.

The first thing I ever bought with my own pocket money should have been a Monkees album. I'd wanted it for ages, but when I got to the record shop, I saw a country album by Hank Williams Junior. I knew my mum liked country music, so I bought that instead and hurried home. She cried when I gave it to her, and I saw how much it meant. Not the album itself, but the thought behind it. It seemed such a small thing, but it was the first real present I'd ever got for her, and she treasured it for years. It was also a lesson for me in the power of kindness and how making someone else happy makes you happy as well.

Chapter Two

1970

In my final year at primary school, I sat my Eleven Plus exam. The Eleven Plus decided who would go on to the grammar school and who would go the secondary-school route. Grammar-school education was generally seen as being for the brighter children, but I'm not sure it worked that well in practice. I think the year I took it only eight of us got through to grammar school, so Mum and Dad were very proud. A first-rate education followed by a steady job seemed a certainty, and it must have felt good to them, parenting job almost done so to speak. Things were definitely going in the right direction. Many years later, though, I read reports from my primary school and found that I was considered rebellious with a vivid imagination, and that I was strong-minded. I was surprised at that. I really didn't think I'd done much to be noticed at all, and I certainly didn't see myself as rebellious.

I started grammar school in Ashford, Middlesex, in 1970 when I was twelve. I wasn't looking forward to it. I would be one of the youngest in the school, and I felt small and insignificant. Nervous of being bullied, nervous of the teachers, nervous of the unknown. My cousin Clive had been at the school for a few years already, so I at least had someone there whom I knew. I hoped he would look out for me. As it turned out, it wasn't too bad at all, and I settled in fairly quickly. Everything was bigger, of course – the school itself, the older children – but I found my feet soon enough.

Around that time, my dad bought a go-kart, a 210 Villiers. We drove it around a track at the back of Blackbushe airfield in Camberley a few times until I blew a hole in the engine. I didn't know how to change gears, so I went round in second gear for a few laps until I revved it to death. Undeterred, my dad sold it and bought a single-gear 100cc go-kart, mainly for me, I think. I loved it, and we went to tracks every weekend for a while. I eventually got my competition licence, but I wasn't really interested in racing other people. I only cared about improving my own times, beating myself. I was fearless in that little kart, though, and had some spectacular accidents. I loved becoming at one with the machine. After my disaster with the Villiers, I took far greater notice of what was happening. Machines talk to you, and if you listen carefully, they can tell you a great deal about how they feel. They usually tell you a problem is coming, and if you're listening, you'll have time to do something about it. Years later, when I was flying planes, that mechanical sympathy would save me more than once.

I joined the Air Training Corps when I was thirteen, I think, 94 Feltham Squadron. I'd assumed that you would get to fly in aeroplanes fairly often, but I was in it for nearly a year and only flew once, so it was somewhat disappointing. We did do lots of marching, though, and I even fired a gun once. Mostly the time was spent building a go-kart. I obviously had nothing against go-karts, but I joined the ATC because I liked aeroplanes, and aeroplanes seemed to a have very little to do with what went on there. No one else even seemed that interested in them. While I was a member, I went on an adventure to get the Duke of Edinburgh Bronze Award. In groups of three, you had to hike across a moor for a day or two, navigate your way from checkpoint to checkpoint, camp overnight, cook your own meals over a campfire, that sort of thing. As luck would have it, it was the wettest weekend of the year, so the conditions were pretty harsh. I remember one of the other boys had taken a shine to my mum and talked endlessly about what he wanted to do to her. We got electrocuted climbing over a farmer's fence, made even more unpleasant by being soaking wet, but eventually finished at the right place. I'd lied about my age as you had to be fourteen to enter, and I was still a few months away from that. Funnily enough, I never did receive my Bronze certificate . . .

Back at school, some of the classrooms looked out over the school field, and in the distance you could see Heathrow Airport. This was a problem. As my time at the school unfolded, I found it harder and harder to concentrate, and I would drift off looking at the planes coming and going. I still wanted to be a pilot, but the idea of a musical career was also really beginning to take shape. I spent more time daydreaming, with thoughts of being in a band or flying airliners around the world, and school started to feel more like an obstacle than a necessary step towards adulthood. I became intolerant of authority when it was applied badly. I became difficult. My school work began to suffer, as did my behaviour, and at one point I was taken to see the headmaster, who pointed out that in his twenty-one years of teaching I was the most disruptive pupil he'd ever had to deal with. I was actually proud of that at the time, which shows just how childish I still was. Horrified now of course. I was showing off, causing trouble, not doing the work. I discovered that the strictest punishment the school would give was Headmaster's Detention after school, or 'Bod's Own' as we called it, and if you didn't go, they just gave it to you again, so you didn't go again, and nothing actually happened. There was nothing to stop an idiot being an idiot, so there I was, in full flow. I was also becoming interested in girls and sex, and that definitely added another layer of teenage bravado and anxiety to the mix.

I was put on Headmaster's Report for most of my third year, when I had to have a report filled in on a sheet by the teachers after every lesson. It eventually got so bad that I was made to change class and had to redo the entire third year. I was considered arrogant and troublesome. Doing a year again was meant to be a humiliating wake-up call. It was definitely humiliating, but, unfortunately, it didn't wake me up to my stupidity. My behaviour continued to slide ever downwards. To be fair, I think the school gave me every chance they could. I obviously upset a lot of teachers, and some of them decided I wasn't worth the trouble and our relationships deteriorated badly. With some it became openly hostile. But, the school did recognise that there was something more going on than just the standard behaviour of a wayward teenager and they recommended I see a child psychologist.

My interest in music had been growing stronger throughout all the turmoil at school. I've never been sure whether that interest was driven by an enthusiasm for music itself or the lifestyle it could bring. Both probably. I was a big T-Rex fan by now, and Marc Bolan always seemed to project a life of rich glamour – increasingly, I wanted that life. The kids at school, probably prompted by their parents, were talking a lot about what they wanted to do with their lives, and the options seemed relentlessly boring. With the exception of becoming a pilot, nothing seemed exciting, nothing offered the life I was looking for. But a rock star? They seemed to have everything you could ever wish for. More and more my thoughts were turning to what I needed to do to get the life I wanted, and more and more school was getting in the way.

At home I constantly wrote poetry and short stories. I was not a social child at all. I had a few friends in the street – and Garry and Nicky, of course – but I was just as happy, if not more so, being alone, when I could dream my dreams and make my plans. I'd started to write songs, or bits of songs, but very much poor attempts at the sort of thing Marc Bolan was doing. My mum and dad had by now bought me an electric guitar, an odd one, if I'm honest, and I was spending a lot of time not exactly playing it but plugging it into a variety of effects pedals and making noises. I was, even then, more interested in the sounds that instruments could make than I was learning scales and becoming proficient as a player.

My cousin Richard, several years older than me, had a beautiful Rickenbacker guitar, and for a while I spent a lot of time with him. He introduced me to lots of obscure music I'd not heard before, and he taught me a few more chord shapes which was fun, but I just wasn't that interested in learning how to be an accomplished musician.

Marc Bolan used to play a guitar called a Gibson Les Paul, so that became top of my wish list. At that time, I didn't realise that lots of companies made Les Paul-shaped guitars, so when I saw one advertised for just £37, I told my parents, and they agreed to buy it for me. I travelled to Shaftesbury Avenue in

London with Garry Robson and was surprised to see it had Columbus written on it and not Gibson. The man in the shop explained that Columbus was an offshoot of Gibson, and that's why it was cheaper. Underneath, he said, it's a real Gibson. Total liar. It only cost a tenth of a real Gibson because it was only a tenth as good, and not one splinter of it was anything to do with Gibson. I still loved it, though.

I'd started dying my hair, even got a spiky haircut that was meant to be like David Bowie's, but was far from it, in truth. It dawned on me that I didn't have the gaunt, angular face I wanted; I tended to look more like a peanut. It was quite a setback to my rock-star dreaming. I had my ear pierced by a clearly bored man in a shop in Staines high street when I was fourteen. He didn't ask which ear, just sat me down on a chair pushed against a wall so only my right ear was facing him, and that's the one he pierced. Then the older kids at school decided that if you had your right ear pierced you were gay, although you weren't gay with the left pierced apparently. I'm not gay, not that it matters, but it caused a few more confrontations, which didn't help my situation at school. The hair dye didn't help either.

My troubles at school were obviously a huge disappointment to my mum and dad. I'm sure my argument that I was going to be a pop star so school didn't matter felt as stupidly unrealistic to them then as it does when I say it out loud now. I can't believe how patient they were, and kind. They didn't let me get away with anything, though. I was told off and punished often for what I was doing at school, but they never put down the dream itself. The attitude was always that being a pop star would be great, but, just in case it didn't work out, I should still try hard at school while I was there.

On the school's recommendation, my mum took me to see a child psychologist, a Dr Vorster. I spent many a session with him. He seemed to have a permanent cold and would hawk up phlegm every few minutes, spit it onto a tissue and then deposit said tissue into a bin next to his desk, where I was sitting. It was pretty gross, to be honest, and massively distracting. We discussed my behaviour and a whole range of other things that presumably he felt might be playing a part. Eventually he admitted that I needed more specialist help and referred me to St Thomas's hospital in London. My memory is that we went to the child-psychiatry department, but I can't be sure. I was seen by a lovely lady doctor who specialised in children with issues like mine. Unfortunately, I saw the trips to St Thomas's as little more than a way of getting out of school, so I paid scant attention to what was said at the time, which I very much regret now. But I do clearly remember that it was at one of those sessions she mentioned Asperger's syndrome for the first time. I was put on two drugs, Nardil and Valium, which I stayed on for about a year. I've since read that the diagnostic criteria for Asperger's weren't really arrived at until several years after my trips to St Thomas's, so I've always been unsure about claiming that I was ever officially diagnosed. I've just always accepted that I have it. Again, my memory of that period is far from complete, but I have a strong feeling that my mum was not pleased with the Asperger's verdict, that she saw it as a slight on her parenting skills. It wasn't, of course, but I think any suggestion that I had mental-health issues was not taken at all well by her. I don't think we went to many more sessions after that, but I did keep taking the drugs. They kept me calm. My explosive temper was kept very much in check while I was on them, which was a good thing, but they didn't seem to be the real answer to my behaviour issues.

Peer pressure is a very powerful thing, never more so than when you're a teenager, but for some reason, almost certainly due to my Asperger's, peer pressure has never really touched me. I am not swayed by any feelings of shame, or guilt, or a need to belong, nothing. When my friends would say you can't hang out with us if you don't smoke, I would move on. If they said you can't hang out with us if you don't drink, I'd move on. Whatever it was, if I didn't want to do it, I didn't. I don't do dares. A dare is just doing something stupid to amuse other people. Why would I want to do that? To belong? I don't need to belong. I dare myself. I set my own challenges. Challenges that have meaning, that have purpose. I was therefore something of a loner. I followed my own path. I did things because I wanted to, or needed to, all part of a longer journey.

I sipped an alcoholic drink once, didn't like it, saw no reason to persevere. I was witness to so many horrible examples of why drinking at a young age was not a good thing, or cool, that I had no interest in trying to 'get a taste' for it. Same with smoking. A kid at school used to smoke, in the most exaggerated way, and he always looked to me like a little boy trying desperately too hard to be a man. It looked pathetic, and I never wanted to look desperate like that, to pretend to be something I wasn't. Actually be the thing you want to be, don't pretend.

During my last year at the grammar school, a careers lecturer made the point, incorrectly as it turned out, that 'for those of you that dream of being a pilot, only one in a thousand ever achieve it'. The school had around a thousand pupils, and I was not the most academically accomplished, not by a long way, so with that terribly inaccurate career statement still ringing in my ear, I abandoned all thoughts of becoming a pilot. As far as I was concerned, the only thing left for me was being a pop star, and school had just become an even bigger obstacle.

For a while, after the Asperger's revelation, I became very interested in trying to understand more about how the mind works, mine in particular. I read various books about mental-health issues and, wherever possible, tried to find connections between the way I behaved, or felt, and the conditions I read about. I think part of it was a genuine interest in trying to understand what was going on, but a part of it was also a desire to simply believe that I was different. I wanted to be unique. It seemed necessary. I read about a thing called the disembodied self, a condition that means people are able to adopt an entirely different personality from one day to another. I tried that for a while and genuinely felt that I could do it. I would decide each morning what my personality was going to be for that day and be it. I wonder now, of course, if anyone else ever noticed, but it felt very real at the time. I also wonder why. What was the point? What was I hoping to achieve, whether I was successful or not? I tend to think it was just one rather odd way of trying to figure out what my personality really was, because I do believe it can be shaped, up to a point, while we're still young.

At the end of my second try at the third year, I was expelled from Ashford Grammar and moved to Stanwell Secondary School, where, quite by accident, things got off to a very bad start. On my first day, trying to set a good impression, I arrived early and was one of the first into the assembly hall. I noticed a row of chairs at the back and genuinely thought it was a first-come-first-served situation so sat down on a chair. But no, I'd committed a grave offence and was promptly marched away and given the cane. Before my first lesson had even started! Every thought of keeping a lower profile was abandoned, and my time at Stanwell was a disaster from day one. But, this time, I don't feel I was entirely to blame. Caning me, when I clearly had yet to learn the rules, was simply the school making a statement that they would take no shit from the newly arrived troublemaker. I understand their thinking now, but back then it was the worst thing they could have done and virtually guaranteed my time there would be filled with problems. My resistance to what I saw as unfairly handled authority, even at school level, became stronger. For example, the school uniform required a white shirt but, on one particular day, I didn't have a clean one. Not my fault. I chose the closest I had, a pale blue shirt, and went to school. During assembly, a teacher shouted at me, in front of everyone, 'Look at the state of you, boy.' I took great offence at that. I was clean, my clothes were fresh and ironed, and his comment seemed an insult to my mum, who made sure I at least arrived at school tidy. What made it worse, the teacher doing the shouting looked like a crumpled ragamuffin. So, with temper flaring, I replied, 'Fuck me, look at the state of you,' or something like that, and I was caned again. Sometimes, though, I was treated harshly through no fault of my own. As an example, our computer studies teacher failed to show up for one lesson, and the deputy headmistress came in and told us to get out our maths books. I raised my hand and told her it was a computer studies lesson. I honestly thought I was being helpful, but I got caned for that as well.

The thing that did bother me was the disappointment I saw in my parents when I was expelled from Ashford Grammar and the worry that my continued troubles at Stanwell caused them. I had been the bright shining star going towards a bright shining future when I started at grammar school, and I'd ruined it. Their pride in my grammar-school place had turned to a quiet embarrassment, coupled with a real concern about how I was progressing. But even through all that disappointment, they allowed me to talk endlessly about my pop-star future, although I doubt they shared my confidence that it was guaranteed to happen. Looking back, the way I used to feel about it, speaking about it with such confidence, is a little embarrassing now. Today I'm far more aware, as my parents probably were back then, just how incredibly unlikely it is to ever achieve chart success, number 1 especially. But I think when you are younger, you do tend to look at your future as an endless opportunity, where all things are possible. I know I did. Again, I thank my parents for that. They made me feel that anything was possible – you just had to try, have faith in yourself and persevere.

I made regular trips into London, usually with Garry Robson, to hang out in music shops mostly, look at gear, buy tickets for shows, that sort of thing. On one trip we had a scare that has stayed with us our entire lives. We always travelled on the Underground, as we were still too young to drive – a bus to Hounslow and the Piccadilly line train from there into London. Usually we'd get off at Piccadilly Circus and spend the day walking up and down Shaftesbury Avenue and around that general area. As a rule, the front and rear carriages of those trains tended to have fewer people on them, so that's where we'd aim for. One day we'd done just that, so as we got off at Piccadilly and started to make our long way up to the street exit, we were two of the last in that stream of passengers. As usual, we were excited and chatting to each other intently about teenager things, not really taking much notice of the people around us, just following the people ahead. I was aware of a group of girls behind us, who seemed to be the last people off the train – the bulk of the passengers were up ahead, and there was an old man directly in front of us. Everything was normal. There was nothing at all to indicate something strange was about to happen: no creeping coldness; no hairs standing up on the back of your neck. Nothing. As we reached the top of a long escalator the old man in front, who I was vaguely aware was dressed with more than a hint of the 1940s about him, including a hat, turned left. Garry and I turned left, still thinking we were following the flow of passengers from our train. But no. Within a few feet, ten at the most, we came hard up against a wall. No way through, no old man. For a moment I was startled, and my attention was now fully on what had happened to that man. I turned to Garry and said, 'Were you following the old man in the grey coat?' 'Yes,' he said. 'Where did he go?' In the few seconds it had taken us to turn, stop and talk, the group of girls behind us had got off the escalator, turned right and were now out of sight, and we were suddenly quite alone and terrified. Without a word we ran and didn't stop running until we burst out of the station into the daylight and noise of Piccadilly Circus.

Ghost stories are two a penny, and I have no doubt that mine is no more believable to most people than others are to me. I really don't care. I have no interest in whether it's believed or not. I know what happened. I have a witness who saw exactly the same thing, and our conviction has never wavered. The only thing that has changed over time is that my memory of it has now become more a memory of the story of it, rather than the moment itself. For example, at the time there was nothing unusual in any way about the man apart from his slightly outdated sense of dress. Now I only see him as grey. True, he was wearing all grey at the time, but now I see grey skin, and I know that wasn't the case. It had a huge effect on me. I've used the image of that man on many occasions, including on two album covers (*Dance* and *I, Assassin*) and elsewhere.

During the period I was at Stanwell, my mum and dad bought me a Gibson Les Paul. Not a copy, a real Gibson Les Paul. I remember driving to a shop called Tempo's in Ealing with my dad and choosing it, a strikingly good-looking guitar with a sunburst finish. As I recall, my dad paid £395 for it, which was a fortune. I was the envy of all my friends, many of whom played and had their own dreams of a career in music. One such friend, Gary Stevenson, who would later become a world-class music producer, was reading a book called *The Gibson Story*, which included a bit about guitars called 'Seconds'. These were guitars that, apparently, played perfectly well but had some cosmetic defect. I've never actually read the book, but that's what I was told. 'Wouldn't it be funny if your guitar was a Second,' he said, laughing. As soon as school was over, I rushed home to check, confident that my guitar was perfect in every way. A Second had the number two stamped on it at the top of the neck, after the final varnish. I checked mine over carefully, and, I couldn't believe it, found a very clear number two right there. It actually made me love it all the more. My beautiful guitar was a reject, imperfect. I spent hours going over every square inch of it, but I didn't find any imperfection. I still have that guitar forty-five years later. I still tour with it and use it on my albums, and I have never found any manufacturing imperfections. It has a thousand other imperfections now, of course, as it's toured the world more times than I can remember. Broken in half, rebuilt, split, rebuilt – it's had a hard, hard life, and I absolutely love it still, more than ever. That guitar is the only thing I've ever owned in my entire life that I couldn't bear to lose.

One of the last things I sat through at Stanwell was another careers talk. This was a much more intimate affair than the one at Ashford. It was a one-on-one meeting with one of the few teachers I liked, and he asked me straight away what sort of job I wanted. I explained that I couldn't say what sort of job I wanted; I could only explain what I wanted from it, the atmosphere I needed it to have. I wanted something that was constantly changing and endlessly challenging. Something that involved travel and excitement. Something unpredictable, fast-moving, creative. I couldn't think of any normal job that could give me that sort of life. School seemed to be tailored towards a very limited number of opportunities. Things like accounting, banking and the like. My bedroom looked out over the busy London Road, and each morning and evening I would sit in my room and watch the traffic crawling by. I couldn't imagine doing that day in, day out, for the rest of my life. I'm sure that one of the biggest factors that made me want to try a music career was my dread of ending up in a mundane job for the rest of my life. More than anything I didn't want my life to be predictable. I wanted to do something where the opportunity to achieve great things genuinely existed, no matter how unlikely it might still be. I had to be a pop star.

I wasn't expelled from Stanwell, but I was asked to leave, which I thought was pretty decent of them. I still had one more year of school to get through, so, partly to make amends to my parents, I agreed to go to Brooklands Technical College in Weybridge. I was to do a course that, when completed, should give me five O-level qualifications. So, nothing special academically, but not a complete disaster. My dad would drop me at the train station in Ashford each morning, and I would make my way to Brooklands. The five O-level courses I had decided on were English language, English literature, maths, music and another I no longer remember, but things began to go wrong almost straight away. My first day in maths started with a slight altercation with the teacher that really bothered me. As the lesson started the teacher announced, rather cockily I thought, 'No one will know the answer to this, but what number does this represent?' He then wrote a series of zeros and ones on the board. Binary. Now I actually knew binary, so, rather pleased with myself and thinking that this would be a great way to kick things off, I put up my hand and gave the answer, which was nineteen. I can only assume that I deflated his ego somehow, because he quickly wiped it off the board, said I was wrong and then said some things that made me feel pretty small, in front of a class of total strangers. I was both mortified and angry and never went back. It seemed to me at the time that a teacher who was more interested in looking clever, and was willing to humiliate someone to do it, than actually teaching was a complete knob, and I wanted no part of it. Something of an overreaction, of course, but not unexpected given my history.

I did my best with English language for a while. English lit was stunningly boring, and I stopped going at some point during the first term. Whatever the fifth subject was I don't think I lasted at too long, but the one I did persevere with was music, until one particular incident. We were tasked with writing a four-part piece of music, on paper, something I was far from good at. But I could write a tune, so I was pretty happy with my offering. One by one the teacher played the various pieces of music written by the class, and then he played mine. It sounded very pretty to me. 'You can't have that,' he said. I can't remember now exactly what he thought was wrong with it, but it was something to do with the written notes on paper being unacceptable for some reason, even though he'd just played it as it was written, and it sounded perfectly OK. So I countered with, 'But it sounds all right, doesn't it?' To which he replied, 'That's not the point.' I couldn't believe it. We're talking about music, and the teacher's saying it doesn't matter what it sounds like. As far as I was concerned, then and now, the *only* thing that matters in music is what it sounds like. I realised then and there that a formal music education was not for me. Anything so wrapped up in such a rigid, set way of doing things, that ignored the music itself, was never going to work for me. So that was music gone as well. Many years later, a band mate, classically trained, told me that if I'd presented one of my number 1 songs – 'Are "Friends" Electric?', I think – to a musical examination board I would have failed because it would have been considered 'unattractive' in classical circles. Sometimes not knowing the 'right' way to do something is a good thing.

I enjoyed being at the college, but I wasn't really going to many lessons after the first term, and hardly any at all in the second. My dad had been dropping me off at the station every morning so was shocked to receive a letter from the college asking why I hadn't been attending. The letter also let him know that I hadn't been to enough lectures to qualify for the third term, so I was out, and that was my schooling over. The sum total of my school achievements was a twenty-five-yard swimming certificate. In my defence, I can honestly say I never failed an exam, because I never took any. I seemed to fall through the cracks in the British education system. In a strange way, though, it all fed into the fact that I started my quest for pop stardom with absolutely nothing to fall back on, and so absolutely nothing to lose.

Chapter Three

1973

The first band I ever went to see was Nazareth, a heavy-rock band. They'd released a single called 'This Flight Tonight' that I'd really liked, but I didn't know much else about them. I went to see them with a friend at the Rainbow Theatre in Finsbury Park, a regular venue in those days for the bigger bands of the time. I think it's some kind of church these days. We were early so saw the full set of the support band as well, Silverhead, who I thought were brilliant. The bass player was Nigel Harrison, who would end up playing in Blondie years later, but the real focal point was the singer, Michael Des Barres. I was completely mesmerised by him, the first frontman I'd ever seen in the flesh. He had such a great voice, and he just controlled the stage. I was totally impressed. So much so that I went out the next day and bought their album *16 and Savage*. Michael would go on to be the front man for Power Station at one point. I met him in Los Angeles recently when he was the host of a radio show I was interviewed on. He was lovely, great to talk to, and I was able to tell him how big an impression he'd made on me all those years ago.

Nazareth were good too, although I think I was just enjoying being at my first gig, feeling the crowd, the volume, the excitement of it all. I did find myself looking at other things, though, even during Silverhead. At almost every gig I went to, even now to be honest, I spend a lot of time looking at the lights, watching how they work with the music, studying how the band interact with the crowd. You can learn so much from watching other people. I learned at the Nazareth gig that a frequency exists that makes me instantly fall over. During the chorus of one particular song, the guitarist hit a note and allowed the guitar to feed back. Whatever frequency that was had an immediate effect on me, as though a switch had been thrown and I'd been turned off. It happened three times, only during that song, and never since, but each time I would go down as though my legs had vanished.

I spent a great deal of my time at home talking to my mum and dad about how I was going to be famous. They had always gently indulged me and offered words of encouragement, until one day when my dad did neither. He said, 'Unless you get off your arse and do something about it, nothing's ever going to happen.' I felt betrayed, for a moment, and then real-ised that he was absolutely right. Dreaming about these things is all well and good, but at some point you have to start doing something about it. Dreams need to become plans. I bought a copy of *Melody Maker* the next day and started looking for bands in need of a guitar player. Not cool bands touring the world; local bands playing at weddings and social clubs. I still had much to learn.

The first band I joined was called Crimson Lake and I played a few tiny gigs with them, mainly in pubs and working men's clubs. I remember the main guitar player only had three fingers and played his guitar upside down like Jimi Hendrix. I'm pretty sure I only got into the band because I had a decent guitar.

I then moved on to another band called Black Gold. Much the same thing, playing in much the same places. I hated the music, just endless cover versions of old songs like 'Tie a Yellow Ribbon', 'Proud Mary' and 'Route 66'. I thought it would be useful experience, but it didn't take me too long to realise that playing in those sorts of bands was not going to get me where I wanted to be.

I went back to *Melody Maker* and started to look for bands that were heading in a direction that would be more useful. I was still trying to gain experience so didn't see any of this as a serious step on the ladder to success, but just being in a band, playing proper gigs, would, I thought, teach me valuable lessons. I was still cripplingly shy, and the thought of moving to the front and playing my own songs was still too much to deal with. I was happy to push that part of my ambition back a little for now. I finally got an audition for a band based in Woking. I turned up at a terraced house, carried my amp, pedals and guitar in, and met the two men whose band I was hoping to join. I had no idea what their music was like, but, as I say, I was just looking for experience, so at that point it didn't matter too much. One of them seemed to be more in charge, and the other looked a bit sleepy, but they were nice. I plugged in my pedals, turned on the amp distortion and away I went. I'll be the first to admit that the pedals and distortion hid my lack of ability quite effectively, so when they asked if I could play without all the effects, I was done for. I did my best, but I was given a very polite 'We'll let you know', and I packed up the gear and left. They never did let me know, but a year or so later I was watching The Jam on *Top of the Pops* and there they were. I'm positive it was the two I'd met – Paul Weller and Bruce Foxton, plus a drummer. The Jam. I'd failed an audition for The Jam, and when I heard their music, I understood why. My wailing, distorted guitar sound was never going to fit.

By now I was a fully devoted Bowie fan and finally got to see him live when he played Wembley Arena on his *Station to Station* tour. His apparent conflict with Marc Bolan, and my loyalty to Bolan and T-Rex, meant that I was late to the Bowie phenomenon, so I missed the Ziggy Stardust and Aladdin Sane periods. By the time I'd got into him he'd already retired Ziggy and moved on. But I would get to see 'The Thin White Duke'. I dressed up as best I could, white shirt, waistcoat, slicked-back blonde and orange hair, I even had a packet of Gitanes cigarettes in my pocket. Unsmoked, of course.

I was with a fairly big group of friends. Our seats had a great view of the stage but were on the raised level around the side of the arena, not too far from the front but not on the main floor. This made getting to the front somewhat problematic. The gig was amazing, and although my friends and I were standing up and screaming, the crowd around us seemed a tad more subdued. Eventually we badgered enough of them and they slowly began to stand and get more involved. Getting from our raised level to the floor below wasn't that far down. I felt sure we could make the jump without injuring ourselves. The only obstacle was a fairly old arena employee guarding the balcony edge. As the main set finished and the crowd were going crazy we made our move and rushed the old man, sweeping past him and leaping from our level onto the main arena floor below. As the crowd were standing, the way through to the front appeared blocked, so we ran along the seats themselves and miraculously found ourselves at the very front, just in time for Bowie's return to the stage for the encore. At that point in my life I don't think I'd ever been more excited and pumped up. The band launched into 'The Jean Genie', one of my favourite Bowie songs, and I could barely contain myself. I threw my green glow stick at him, although for the life of me I can't imagine why. But it hit him on the chest and then he bent down, picked it up and held it in his hand as he sang the song. I couldn't believe it. Best thing ever.

It was slightly ruined at the end when I was waiting by the stage to try and get it back from the road crew when I saw one of them hand it to a girl further along. I was so angry and disappointed. I made a rather unpleasant fuss, unfortunately, and so had to be bundled out before it turned nasty. Amazing night, though. The next day I read an article in the *Daily Mirror* about the 'Riot at David Bowie concert', started by people jumping from the upper level. That was me, I started that.

It was always safer to travel in large groups when you looked the way we did. This was before I could drive, so we used the train to get about, mostly to London. Just getting in and out of the city was always difficult in those days, and violence towards us was never far away. But we were able to find a club in Wardour Street called Crackers that was safe. We even managed to persuade the club owners to start a Bowie night every Saturday, so that became a regular thing for us for quite a while. Another place safe for us, not too far from Poland Street, was a club called Louise's. Louise's was a gay club, but they let us in anyway. When you knocked on the door, a small flap would open, and they would look you over first before opening the door and letting you in. The way we looked caused us trouble in most places but definitely opened the door at Louise's. It really was one of the friendliest clubs I've ever been to, and when that door opened it felt like a sanctuary. No violence, no threats, no insults, no fear.

Soon after I learned to drive, I went with my girlfriend at the time, Jo Casey, to see a band at the Marquee club in Wardour Street, not too far from Crackers. Jo was lagging behind me slightly, and I'd turned round to take something from her, a roll of film I think, and as I looked forward again a fist hit me in the face. He must have started to swing the punch while I was still looking behind, because when I looked forward it was only an inch away. There were about five of them, and for the next few seconds all I could see were boots and fists flying towards me. I remember thinking, So this is what it feels like to get beaten up. I'd always wondered, always been terrified of it happening, and here it was. I saw a gap and tried to run, but I ran into the side of a parked car and fell across the bonnet, with them still punching and kicking. I looked to my left and saw one of them raise his umbrella and stab it down towards my face. It was a common thing at that time for yobs to sharpen the metal points of umbrellas, and this one had done exactly that. I could see it clearly in that moment. I turned my face away, but it hit me in the side of the head and went into my ear, cutting as it went. I managed to push away from the car and ran across the road into what I'd always thought was a police station – I'd seen policemen coming out of it many times before. But when I got to the desk, I found out it wasn't a police station at all, it was a gym. That seemed to drain all my energy and I slumped onto the desk. It was then I realised I was bleeding badly. Blood was pooling onto the desk and running down the front onto the floor.

I'm not sure what happened next, but eventually two policemen arrived, and I was taken to hospital in an ambulance. Jo was still with me, having clumped as many of the attackers as she could. I don't know which hospital I was taken to, and I can't remember too much about it, but I do remember I was stitched up and the doctor telling me how lucky I was. The cut stopped just a fraction of an inch from my eardrum. With that done we left the hospital but had no idea where we were, so we called a taxi and made our way back to the Marquee club. As we got out of the cab another yob on the other side of the street pointed at me and shouted out to his friends to come and give me another beating. I couldn't believe it. From what I could see, his friends were already busy attacking someone else, so I managed to get into the relative safety of the Marquee and meet up with my own friends.

My mum and dad were very upset when I got home. I had scuff marks and bruises all over my face, my body looked battered, I had blood all over my clothes, and stiches on the side of my head and into my ear. It looked pretty bad. I remember my dad asking if I'd managed to get a punch in, but it hadn't even occurred to me.

Then punk happened. With largely the same group of friends I went out to see The Clash and a range of lesser punk bands. We even managed to see The Sex Pistols at Notre Dame Hall in London in November of '76. As I was walking to the gig Billy Idol shouted out and asked for directions. At that time Billy was well known in the punk scene but nothing like the huge star he would become. If I'm honest, punk music was never really for me, apart from the Pistols, who I loved. But the energy of it, the excitement, the look, the attitude, I was taken with all of it.

Not surprising, then, that from my group of friends, now expanding somewhat as we got closer to people we met through our travels in London, we decided to start our own band. The band consisted of a school friend of mine on the drums, a David Bowie lookalike on bass, a coke fiend on guitar, and me, also on guitar and singer. I was the only one who wrote songs, so our set would be made up of my songs and an assortment of Lou Reed and Iggy Pop covers. We played three gigs, the first at my old Ashford Grammar School strangely enough, another at Crackers and the third I can't remember. Each gig the band had a different name because it seemed impossible to find one that suited everyone. I think we were called Riot, Heroin and Stiletto. Friction was part of the band pretty much from day one. At one point they grumbled because we were only playing my songs, which seemed a bit unfair, as I was the only one who had written any. It came to an end for me when I turned up to a rehearsal in Chelsea after our third gig only to hear someone else singing. I gathered I was no longer in the band.

What followed was a series of strange and unhappy experiences where I was to find out that not only was I no longer in the band, I was no longer wanted at all, even as a friend. It became horribly clear one evening when I drove round to each of their houses to pick them up. We were supposed to be going into town that night to see a band in Covent Garden. At each house I was told my friends had already left, but, strange as that was, I made my way to London to meet up with them there. When I arrived, I saw them all gathered outside the venue and went over to say hello, only for them to walk away without a word. At first I didn't get it and followed them. It was only when one of the girlfriends came up to me and said they didn't want me around any more that it finally sank in. It was so incredibly spineless I could barely believe it. Some of these people I'd known for years, and now I wasn't even worth talking to. I was completely shunned, by pretty much every friend I had, new and old. You would think it would have been a crushing experience for me. I think for most people it would be, but this is one of the many examples why I think my Asperger's is a gift. It certainly hurt for a while, but I was able to wrap that horrible feeling into a neat box and move it to one side. I kept just a small amount with me, though. Not enough to make me bitter and twisted; just enough to fuel the fire of my determination. It quickly became little more than a sidestep along the way. It was like throwing a switch. I simply turned them off, and the hurt with them. I would need to do that many, many times as my life unfolded.

Apparently, me being the frontman was a significant cause of the ill feeling that pushed me out. It's hard to imagine people feeling jealous about something as small as a new, completely unknown band, but as the rumours slowly filtered back to me, that's what it seemed to be. With that in mind I went back to the *Melody Maker* ads to look for a new band. Once again I decided I'd stay in the background for a while and gain what experience I could. I was asked to audition for a band called The Lasers. The audition went OK. Although they only did cover versions of other people's songs, they were quite punky and certainly not part of the weddings and working men's club circuit. They were looking for a lead guitar player to join what was at that point a three-piece line-up. A drummer, a guitarist called Wayne Kerr and a bass player called Paul Gardiner, who was also the singer. I immediately got on well with Paul, who was a lovely, modest, easy-going man. To be honest, I was not a lead guitarist so not really what they were looking for. Thanks to Paul, though, I was allowed to join the band. I'm pretty sure the other two were less keen.

We had our first rehearsal in a small room at my mum and dad's house in Wraysbury, and it went well enough. I had to learn all the songs they were playing, all cover versions. By the end, I asked why they didn't play any of their own songs. They said they didn't write songs, so I said, 'I do.' For the next hour or so I played them all of the songs I'd written for the previous band, including one called 'My Shadow In Vain'. Paul loved them but admitted he wouldn't be able to sing them. So, by the end of that first rehearsal, the band were playing all my songs, and I was the singer. Plus, my songs don't really have guitar solos, so I didn't even need to keep pretending I was a lead guitarist. I also asked them about the band name. It seemed to me that every band was called The something. 'Wouldn't it be good to have a name that wasn't The something?' I said. Again, it was Paul who seemed the most interested and asked what ideas I had. I was writing lots of short stories at that time, and I'd written something after a newspaper article I'd read about a gang that would travel on the London Underground and, when the train stopped at a station, jump out and attack whoever was there, get back on the train and leave. I called my story 'Tubeway Army', and that became the new name of the band. So much for staying in the background. But without Paul's enthusiasm, I doubt any of it would have happened. The other two were pushed along as much by him as they were by me.

Soon after I was at The Roxy club in Covent Garden, look-ing for gigs for the band, and got talking to the owner. My previous band had now renamed themselves Meanstreet, and I noticed they were booked to play as support a few days later. I told the owner the story of my removal from the band, and he thought it would be fun to put us on the same bill. So, a few days later, I found myself sitting out on the street in front of the club waiting to load in when who should walk up but the Meanstreet singer. The same one who had effectively pushed me out of the band. I expected him to be somewhat abashed and apologetic. Surprisingly, rather than showing any signs of guilt, he was actually off with me, and, after a bit of toing and froing, said, 'I don't like liars,' and huffed off. To this day I have no idea what he was talking about.

The gig went as well as I'd hoped. We were OK, Meanstreet were awful and I never saw them again. Over the next few months, and a handful of small gigs, I gradually turned Tubeway Army into a more punk-sounding band. We were still not the fast, thrashing, typical punk band, but I did my best to lean us in that direction. One of the things that set us apart, and I believe eventually won us a record deal, is that our songs had melodies and were sung rather than shouted or screamed. We were merging a different sensibility with the energy of punk, so arguably straddled the fence between pop and punk a little. In truth, though, Tubeway Army was never truly a punk band. It was a work in progress, a vehicle taking me towards somewhere as yet unknown. I knew punk, or my version of it, was not the future I wanted musically. But punk was opening doors for so many new bands in the late seventies. New record labels were springing up everywhere, and existing labels were all looking for their token punk band. It seemed as if there was opportunity on every street corner, and I felt a burning desire to take advantage of it as soon as possible.

I was an avid science-fiction reader for most of my early years. I loved all the robot books of Asimov, a lot of J. G. Ballard, and especially Fred Saberhagen and his Berserker series, but my favourite sci-fi writer was Philip K. Dick. I'd read his book *Do Androids Dream of Electric Sheep* when I was still at Ashford Grammar, and it was hugely influential on the songs I was writing, and would be for several years yet. I was fascinated by the near future, how things would change in my lifetime, how society would evolve and how technology would play a part in that. My own short stories became increasingly focused on this obsession with the near future and what answers we might find to the many problems I saw growing daily. It was fertile time for me creatively, and night after night I would be at home writing. Writing songs, writing stories and writing poems.

But I was also studying. I read everything I could about the music business, about every label, every band. To get your foot in the door you need to know where the doors are. But what door to open? Not all of them had what you wanted or needed, or required what you were offering. You had to know where to aim. I'd said often, to anyone who would listen, that no matter how talented you are, you would always need luck. If you sat in the bath singing loudly with the window open, you would need a vast amount of luck to be discovered. But you could narrow down the amount of luck you needed by learning about the business as much as possible. What venues were important, what magazines or papers had influence, what labels had a slot to fill in their roster. If you took your band to the venues that were often in the gig reviews, you had a better chance of being seen by people who mattered, and so on and so on. You would always need luck, but there was still so much you could do to minimise how lucky you needed to be. I made it my mission to learn what I could do to make my own luck.

When I left Weybridge College, I went to work and started a series of pretty mundane jobs while I plotted and schemed how to start my music career. I fitted air-conditioning units in office buildings for a while, but after a fight with another worker, and then getting trapped by a huge metal core pipe that rolled onto me in a basement of a bank, I moved on. I worked for an air-freight company called United Marine (1939) Ltd as an export clerk for a while. I enjoyed that. The manager was quite young and a Bowie fan. We would spend much of the day listening to music, and he even allowed me to take my guitar and amp in and play at times. He would often set up a track in the warehouse out of old wooden pallets, and we would have races seeing who could get around it the quickest in the forklift. I wasn't there too long before I was transferred to their import department in another building. That was less fun. I have a real problem talking on the phone, don't really like it, and so I would avoid talking to the customers if at all possible. As I was supposed to be importing their goods and clearing them through customs, it was pretty essential that I talked to them, so I lost that job after a while.

Foolishly, perhaps, I got another job, doing much the same thing, at a company called Mercury Airfreight. This one was even worse. A group of more petty-minded people I have yet to meet. There were five on the group of tables I sat at. The man opposite would threaten to punch me if my curly phone cord went onto his desk. The man I sat beside threatened to slash my tyres because I put a piece of paper into his waste-paper bin, and I was putting up with all of this for just £18 a week. It was while I was at Mercury that I accidentally ran someone over, the same man that threatened to slash my tyres strangely enough. We used to park our cars at the back of the building and exit via an outside ramp that ran around one end of it. It was winter, snow had fallen and it was freezing cold. I saw the car ahead of me go onto the ramp and head down, and I followed some way behind. Halfway down, the ramp turned slightly to the right, following the shape of the building, but the car in front didn't. The ramp had completely iced over and, out of control, he'd slid into the wall and stopped. I pushed lightly on my own brakes, but the wheels just locked, and I started my own slide down the ramp. To my utter amazement, my knife-threatening workmate, having just experienced the same loss of control himself, instead of getting out of the way ran around to the back of his car and put his hands up telling me to stop. As if I could do anything about it. I waved at him to get out of the way, but he didn't. My car slid into him pretty hard, and I saw him fly up into the air, then I hit his car, which seemed to fly up and sideways, hitting the side of the building and nearly knocking over a lady on the ramp walkway. I'm pretty sure I ran the man over again when another car came down the ramp and crashed into mine. Not my fault. I can't remember much after that, but I do know he ended up in hospital with two broken legs and expected me to pay for his car damage. I left soon after and started what would be the last proper job I ever had.

I did have other incidents in that car. One of them wasn't a crash, but something else entirely. Near where I lived was an area called Laleham. During the day it was a pretty spot by the river that families would picnic and relax in. In the evening, though, it turned into a place where young couples would head to for fumbling sexual encounters in their cars. I was there one evening when the girl I was with let out a scream. I looked out of the rather steamy window and saw a man standing there looking in, with what looked like a stocking pulled over his face. He looked more like a bank robber than a peeping Tom. As soon as he was discovered he ran, got quickly into his own car and sped off. Now I am not a fighting person but I saw an opportunity here to impress the girl I was with, with my rugged manliness, and so sped off in hot pursuit, not intending for one second to actually catch him and have a fight. For a while it all went quite nicely to plan. She was crying and asking me to stop and I was the steely eyed vigilante on a mission. Unfortunately the peeper decided he'd run away long enough and pulled over, and my bluff was called. So, it was at that moment that I pretended to finally listen to the pleading of my girlfriend and let the man off with a stern glare as I drove past and disappeared into the safety of the night.

Chapter Four

1977

If Tubeway Army were ever going to attract the interest of a record company, we needed a demo. I'd found a studio in Cambridge called Spaceward that offered a great rate for a full day. Thanks yet again to my mum and dad, who paid for the session, we were able to go there in October of '77 and record three songs: 'That's Too Bad', 'Oh Didn't I Say' and 'O. D. Receiver'. The line-up of the band had changed a little. Wayne and the original drummer had gone, and I think it was my uncle Jess who played drums on those sessions. With demo in hand, Paul and I did the rounds of the record labels, giving out our cassette to each one we thought might be interested. One or two felt too intimidating, and we were too scared to even go through the door, but it was an exciting time. Derek, the man who ran the rehearsal room we now practised in, also took some cassettes and did his best to drum up interest for us. It was Derek who, while sitting in the office of one of the more well-known punk labels, had to suffer the humiliation of the record exec ejecting our cassette from his machine, throwing it out of the door and being told to fuck off. Things had not gone well.

It was at this point that the luck I always knew we would need really showed itself. Paul Gardiner needed some money, so he took some of his records to a Beggars Banquet record store. Beggars used to buy second-hand albums, and it was a good way of making some quick cash. Paul struck up a conversation with the man behind the counter, Steve Webbon, and was told that the two men who owned Beggars Banquet had started their own record label. Steve promised to pass our demo cassette to them. Some time later, we got a call from one of the label owners, Martin Mills, who said he liked 'That's Too Bad' but wanted to see us live. We had no gigs planned, so Martin arranged for us to play at The Vortex club in Wardour Street. The Vortex used to be Crackers, which had been such a big part of my life not that long ago. It felt amazing to actually be playing a gig there with a record label watching. We were to support another band already signed to Beggars called The Doll. I was sick with nerves. I was, in fact, nervous at all of the gigs I'd played up to that point. It was quite a problem. I was so nervous before a gig I could barely hold a conversation at times, sometimes for a few days before the gig even happened. Overcoming that fear was the hardest part of performing.

As soon as we walked on, though, everything changed. I felt different, the nerves vanished and whether we had a good night or bad I was comfortable. The gig at The Vortex for Beggars was a good one, and afterwards we waited eagerly for what Martin and the label's co-owner Nick Austin would say. It was exactly what we wanted to hear. They said we put on a really good show and that I 'had an excellent command of the audience'. There wasn't much of an audience, to be honest, but it was a lovely comment at just the right time. This was also the first gig we'd done with our new drummer Bob Simmons. My uncle Jess, who'd played on the demo, had gone back to concentrate on his own band Shadowfax.

The following day Martin Mills called and said that Beggars were interested in signing us and releasing 'That's Too Bad' as a single, but there was a problem. Beggars had a strict plan they were working to and a budget – a certain number of bands and a certain amount of money spent – and they already had the bands, and they'd already spent the money. I explained that we didn't need any money to record the song – we'd already done that. We didn't need musical equipment – we already had everything we needed. We even had our own modest PA system, thanks yet again to my mum and dad. More than that, we even had our own van. I was driving around in a Ford Transit at that point, which had become the band van. So, all they needed to do was pay for the pressing and the sleeve, and with that Beggars offered us a deal, and I was on my way. It was a terrible deal, and it would stay terrible for a very long time, but we had one, and that was all that mattered.

I had no real idea at the time just how much my mum and dad had done for me. I knew about everything they'd bought of course, and I knew it was hard for them, and I was hugely grateful, but I didn't know how far they'd actually gone until much later. I found out that buying me all those things had used almost every penny of their life savings. I get upset when I think of that even now. What an extraordinary thing to do. They had no idea whether I was any good or not. I didn't know, so how could they? I very much doubt they truly liked the music and saw a bright road to fame and fortune in it. It wasn't an investment for the future; it was simply to help me to achieve my dream, and they gave everything they had. I talk about needing luck, about creating my own, but the luckiest thing that ever happened to me was my mum and dad, and I remain eternally grateful.

I loved being with Beggars. They were small but friendly and it felt more like a family than a business. Their main office in those days was at the back of their shop on Hogarth Road in Earls Court. I spent a lot of time there, just hanging around, soaking up the atmosphere and revelling in the fact that I was a signed artist. Although I was only on the very first rung of the ladder, it felt as though I was already halfway up it.

I'm not sure exactly what day I signed the contract with Beggars, but 'That's Too Bad' was released on 10 February 1978, four days before my mum's fortieth birthday. It was also the day I stopped working at WH Smith, my last proper job, and it's the day I've always considered as the true start of my career. I remember seeing the sleeve for the first time, listening to the vinyl record for the first time. It was such an amazing feeling. I was nineteen, I had a record deal and I'd released my first single. It sold about four thousand copies, nothing at all really, but it felt like a huge number at the time. Four thousand people had bought one of my records, listened to my songs – actually liked them, presumably. Four thousand people! That would have been about five full assembly halls at Ashford Grammar. That was just huge to me.

The music press didn't really like it, unfortunately. They had nothing good to say about it, or me, in fact. With my bleached blonde hair, they said I either looked like Steve Severin from Siouxsie and the Banshees or Billy Idol. I wasn't known as Gary Numan at that point. I was still struggling to find a name that felt right and was more 'rock starry' than Webb. I called myself Valeriun on the sleeve of 'That's Too Bad'. I'd seen it written on a wall somewhere and thought it had a nice flow to it. That was definitely a mistake.

Surprisingly, Paul had done most of the early pushing with Beggars. It was Paul who had chased them up regularly and badgered them to listen to the demo, for example. But once the single was out, I increasingly took the lead. We needed gigs, so I pushed Beggars to get us on stage wherever they could. We would usually be the support for the other bands on the label, but I was OK with that. It's never really mattered to me where you are in a line-up. It's being seen at all that matters. I know so many bands that make such a big deal about being a 'head-liner'. I honestly don't care that much, never have.

I had no money, so I signed on the dole and, if I remember correctly, qualified for £12 a week. The unemployment officer was very kind. When he asked me what work I wanted, I said, 'I want to be a pop star.' He replied, 'I can't help you with that,' signed me up and sent me on my way. He said I should do whatever I needed to do to make that happen. Usually they would insist you went to job interviews regularly and that you proved you were trying to get work. Luckily, I wasn't expected to do any of that. I was left alone to sort my own ambitions out, which I was already getting on with pretty well. I was very grateful to him. Thanks to him I was free to work exclusively on the band and my songwriting for several months, until I lost my nerve and signed off.

On 15 April 1978, we went into a studio called The Music Centre in Wembley to record our second single 'Bombers'. The Music Centre was nothing like the home-made vibe of Spaceward in Cambridge, which I'd really liked. It was big, incredibly well equipped and seriously professional. Just work-ing there felt like another step up the ladder. By now Bob Simmons had left and been replaced by a new drummer called

Barry Benn. I'm told Bob became a vicar eventually. I'd also added a second guitarist called Sean Burke. The reason for the second guitarist was misunderstood by Beggars. I didn't want him to play different parts to me, as they'd expected – I wanted him to play exactly the same parts. It was power I was looking for, not complexity.

With 'Bombers' I had my first taste of what I saw as interference. The song had a line that read 'All the junkies pull the needles from their arms and hope it lasts the night'. Nick Austin thought that having the word junkies in the lyric would prevent the song getting played on the radio. As it had about as much chance of being played on the radio as I had of flying to the moon, I didn't entirely see why it mattered. But he was the label, and I at least admired his optimism. I exchanged the word 'junkies' for 'nurses', which still made sense, and we finished the song. Even during the making of 'Bombers' I'd begun to feel that punk was over, and I really didn't want to be involved in it, even on the fringes as we were. Paul, as always, was firmly on my side and agreed that we needed to find a new direction, something that was a more genuine representation of what we were as a band. I had no idea what that was, but I knew it wasn't punk, not even our melodic version of it. I'd written punkish music to get the deal with Beggars, but my heart had never really been in it – it was always a means to an end. Now I could see so many signs that punk was dying, and I didn't want Tubeway Army to become known as a punk band and die with it. Within the band the arguments became more heated. Paul and I were all for moving on and changing; Sean and Barry were firmly of the opinion that punk was for ever and that's where we should stay.

'Bombers' had a particularly scathing review in one of the music papers which said 'Please give up gracefully, old chums. The market for this sort of heavyweight monotony has died. Never mind, you can sit and tell your grandchildren how you nearly made it.' I wrapped that comment up in Asperger's ribbon and put it to one side with all the others. But I didn't entirely disagree with him. In many ways, it backed up my own worries about where we were going musically.

Our first headline gig was at the Hope and Anchor pub in Islington, north London. I think we had three people in the audience, no exaggeration, and they were all from Beggars. It was totally empty. It was so embarrassing, especially with the label there. It could hold about 150 people, and I'd really hoped that having put out the singles we'd be able to pull in a decent crowd – at least half fill it. It's hard to get up and play to a crowd of three. The embarrassment, the disappointment, the vibeless atmosphere, the feeling of abject failure. But you have to, and we did, and we played our hearts out.

The last gig we ever played as Tubeway Army took place in July 1978 at the White Hart pub in Acton. It was supposed to be a support slot to a great band called The Skids, but somehow the bill got reversed, a printing error on the poster, I think, and so The Skids went on first and we followed. My dad came to almost every gig, helped with the gear, helped with everything. He would often say to me as the nerves became unbearable, 'Why do you do it if you hate it so much?' 'Because it's all I've ever wanted,' I'd reply. Before we went on at The White Hart I was suffering particularly badly with pre-show nerves, retching in the corner of our little room. He leaned over and said to me, 'If you can't find a way of dealing with this, this is not the career for you.' He was right, of course. The gig was horrendous. I can't remember whether the crowd liked us or not, but I don't think so. About halfway through our set, a huge fight broke out that was particularly vicious, the venue pulled the plug and that was that. I walked off the stage and told the band I would never play another gig like that again. I was done with punk, done with shithole venues and the violence. There had to be a better way. I started to think about what my dad had said – 'If you can't find a way' – so I began to find a way. When I played live again, it would be different. I would be different.

The gig was reviewed, and I was crucified for not handling the situation better, or at all, when the fight broke out. The review was stupid, unfair and it swept off me like water off a duck's back. I'd already decided that for the foreseeable future Tubeway Army would be a studio-only band. As we left the venue, I'd put a Tubeway Army sticker on a road sign outside the pub – it was still there years later. We had a band meeting, and I told them I was done with punk and had no intention of ever playing live again until things had improved and we could be sure of an audience, one that had come to see us. As far as I was concerned, if Sean and Barry wanted to carry on as a punk band, they were free to go and start one of their own. We had a huge row. They said I was burning my bridges – something about seeing people on the ladder again as we came back down, I think – lots of angry stuff anyway. But that was the end of that line-up, and it was back to me and Paul. Uncle Jess was called in once again to help us out on drums when we returned to Spaceward studio a few weeks later to record our first album.

The first Tubeway Army album was essentially meant to be the live set we'd been playing, but I had plenty of other songs as well. To start moving away from the punk style we would need some of those. It was an exciting time. Simply going to a studio to record our first album was a dream come true. When we arrived at Spaceward, I went in to say hello to the recording engineer Mike Kemp, who also owned the studio and had, I think, pretty much built it. While Paul and Jess were unloading the equipment from the van, I went into the control room with Mike and noticed a synthesiser on a desk in the corner. It was a MiniMoog. I'd never seen a real synth before, and it was a fascinating machine to look at. Dials and switches from one side to the other, the rear section tipped up like a portable control panel. In many ways it reminded me of the control panel my dad had made for me as a child, except this one looked incredibly high-tech. I'd always associated synths with prog-rock bands like Yes and ELP, and that sort of music had never really been of any interest to me. I'd liked some of what Kraftwerk had done, and really liked some of the things Bowie had done with Brian Eno, but none of it had ever made me think of synths as a way forward for me.

I was intrigued, though, so I asked Mike if I could have a go. After Mike had turned it on, the sound that came out of it when I pressed a key was just awesome, in the truest sense of the word. The room shook and you felt the sound as much as heard it. I had never experienced anything like it, and I was absolutely blown away. This was everything I'd been looking for. The sheer weight of the sound was shocking. It was like a huge bulldozer of noise, a vast wall of sound. It was a sonic assault on the ears. It felt unstoppable, immensely powerful and totally exhilarating. For me everything changed in that one moment. I was elated, grinning from ear to ear, excited and giggling. I felt as if I'd stumbled across something that only I knew about. That was ridiculous, obviously, but that's how it felt. I'd heard synths before, but I'd never heard them sound like that. This was the thing I'd been waiting for, the new direction I knew was out there. More than that, this was something that was perfectly suited to the way I'd always seen music – the sound itself came first.

By the time Paul and Jess had finished unloading the van and setting up the gear in the studio, I'd already changed everything in my head. I was already thinking about how we could adapt the songs from guitar-based to synth-based. Over the next few days we recorded a bunch of songs and reworked them with new synth parts, or often just replaced the guitar chugging with a synth pumping. It was an entirely different album to the one we had gone in there to record, and it was entirely different to the album Beggars Banquet expected, and that turned out to be quite a major problem.

Chapter Five

1978

W hen we played the first version of the album to Beggars, they were far from happy. They'd expected, I think, to get an album filled with polished pop–punk crossover versions of the songs we'd been playing live. Understandably, I suppose. I'd given them no hint at all that we were going to go in a very different direction. I didn't know myself until I got to the studio and tried the Moog. I was adamant, though, that the electronic music I'd come up with was what I wanted to do. More than that, I was absolutely positive that very soon everybody was going to be doing it. I honestly thought I'd discovered some-thing new, and I was terrified that someone else would also discover it and put out an electronic album before mine. I was passionate about the music itself and desperate to get the album out as quickly as possible – to be, as I thought, at the front of the pack. The meeting became more heated. At one point Nick Austin and I got to our feet and faced off, shouting our points of view. It was beginning to get out of hand, but it felt like the most important moment of my life to me. I can't remember too much about it beyond that, but at some point Martin quietly said that maybe they should give it a try.

As luck would have it, my mum and dad had bought me an old upright pub piano for about £20 and put it in a room in their house, the same room we'd had the first Lasers rehearsal in. I had no idea how to play a piano, but a tune is a tune, so I just played until things made sense and sounded as though they belonged together. Writing on the piano opened up a new world of possibilities, and soon I had several more songs that I was keen to add to the album. By now I had some idea of what the synth could do, and I felt these songs would translate to the synth even better than the guitar songs had before. Beggars allowed us to go back to the studio for another session and record some more songs that, although written on piano, were meant to be electronic from the outset. With that done, we finally had the album ready, and it was nothing like I would have imagined just a few weeks before.

In October I started to take flying lessons. My dad was part of a group at his work who had decided to all chip in some money to collectively buy a little second-hand light aeroplane. My dad didn't want to learn to fly it, so he said I should, knowing that I'd always been obsessed with planes. I started to take lessons at the Thee Counties Aero Club at Blackbushe Airport in Surrey. Progress was somewhat erratic due to the poor weather and the club having a large turnover of instructors, but I still managed to go solo after only seven hours of training, which was quick.

The next argument with Beggars was about the name of the band. I was keen to drop Tubeway Army. To me, although it had enjoyed little success, the band was seen as a punk band, and I wanted to move well away from that connection. The new music was radically different, and I wanted to move forward with it under my own name. By now I'd dropped Valeriun and after spending a considerable amount of time searching had eventually found a new name that I thought suited me perfectly. In the Beggars office, looking through their Earl's Court edition of the Yellow Pages phone book, I'd seen a company called Neumann Kitchen Appliances. The word Neumann really resonated with me. I had no problem with Germany, but I was English, a Londoner, and I didn't want a German-sounding name. I removed the 'e' and the second 'n' and there it was. Numan. It was perfect. I had no idea what I was looking for exactly, but I always thought I'd know it when I saw it, and there it was. I would be Gary Numan. I was happy. I felt complete. I'd found my musical direction, something new and unusual, I had my first album ready to go, a label ready to release it, and now I had my name. Everything had come together. Except that Beggars didn't want to drop the name Tubeway Army, and this was an argument I wasn't going to win. So, on 24 November 1978, the album was released, titled simply *Tubeway Army*.

The album did OK. I can't remember exactly what it sold, but I think it might have been around three thousand copies. Whatever the numbers were, the reviews for the album were somewhat mixed. Interestingly, though, they weren't the wave of negative comments we'd half expected. Beggars seemed very encouraged by that, and our move into electronic music was now seen in a better light. The uncertainty about the rights and wrongs of releasing the album evaporated.

I began to learn some startling truths, though. Far from being the first person to discover electronic music, I seemed to be one of the last. The more I looked into it the more electronic artists I found, people who had been doing it long before me. The Human League, Orchestral Manoeuvres in the Dark, Fad

Gadget, Daniel Miller and especially Ultravox, who were on their third album as I released my first. All of them already doing something I'd thought I'd discovered alone. I'd known about Kraftwerk, of course, but their music, although I liked much of it, had always seemed too synthetic somehow. That makes little sense, I know, but I saw a clear distinction between a band that seemed to be trying to remove the human element from the music almost completely and what I was doing, which was the opposite of that. I was using electronic music to search for an even greater emotional involvement than normal, more conventional forms of music.

Synthesisers were seen by many as cold, emotionless devices, very much the way that Kraftwerk seemed to project them. But I saw them completely differently. With a synth you don't just use the notes you play to express the emotion of the music, you can choose the very sound itself. A piano sounds like a piano, a guitar, in the main, sounds like a guitar, but a synth can create sounds the world has never heard before. I found it capable of creating moods and atmospheres that were impossible to find in conventional music, and the sound itself could evolve. By pressing one key you could unleash something never heard before and then, by simply holding that key down, you could manipulate the sound and allow it to change. I became a firm believer in the idea that sometimes one note is enough. Let the sound evolve – let that be the drama. No need for a thousand-notes-per-second guitar solos or the keyboard wizardry (that I never liked) of the prog-rock players. Just sound. Noises. One low, rumbly drone could create a sense of menace far more effectively than any number of discordant chords. It felt like a new way of thinking about how music could be put together. I began to see myself not as a musician, but as an arranger of noises.

I was now spending pretty much every minute of the day at the piano writing songs. If I wasn't at the piano, I was playing the guitar, although I was writing songs on the guitar less and less. The keyboard seemed to suit me much better as far as songwriting was concerned. I'm not a good player, not on the guitar or the piano. I can play well enough to write songs, and that's all I need. I have often wondered if being a skilled player has an undesirable side effect at times on the songs people like to write. So many gifted musicians seem to write songs more as vehicles to demonstrate their skill rather than as a beautiful melody. Anyway, whatever the truth of that, it's not a problem I'll ever have to deal with. As a player I am average at best, and I think that's being kind to myself.

I can write songs, though, and after the *Tubeway Army* album was recorded I did nothing else. I think it was soon after it was released Beggars booked the next recording session for me at a small sixteen-track studio in London's Chinatown called Gooseberry Studios. This was to record the second album *Replicas*. Gooseberry was primarily used by reggae bands, but it had everything I needed. It even had its own in-house synth, made by Roland. I can't remember the model now, but it had a series of tabs along the front that when lowered would replicate certain known sounds. But some of the tabs could also be a short cut to other, more unusual noises, and those were the ones I was interested in. The studio owners had drilled a hole through one end of it, threaded a heavy chain through the hole and locked it to the wall. They seemed rather intent on making sure it stayed in the studio.

Beggars also allowed me to rent a MiniMoog for a few hours each day for four of the five days we had booked in the studio. With an entire album to record in just a few days, and with limited availability of the Moog, I had precious little time to experiment. I had to find workable sounds, as well as layers of additional melodies, as quickly as possible. It was fun, but it added a noticeable amount of pressure. Not least because I still had only a vague idea what the various dials and switches on the synths did. I essentially twiddled things randomly until the Moog made a sound I liked and that could work for the part of the song we were working on. Once I had the sound, I'd quickly record that part, on the first take if at all possible, and then move straight on to the next sound or section. Sometimes, if a mistake was made but it wasn't too glaring, we had to leave it. We just didn't have the time to get everything perfect. It was all quite amateurish, I suppose, but it felt exciting and adventurous to me, and I was in my element. I was learning about studio techniques, about the equipment, about mixing, about so many things. Martin Mills and Nick Austin came to the studio often and heard for the first time the new batch of songs I'd written. Songs like 'Me, I Disconnect from You', 'Down in the Park', 'Praying to the Aliens' and 'Are "Friends" Electric?'. Everyone seemed very happy with the way *Replicas* was coming together. It was certainly a clear progression from the first album, even though it was only a few weeks since *Tubeway Army* had been released. I was writing so prolifically that songs were pouring out of me, and Beggars allowed us back into the studio for another session, so I was able to record a few more. Added to the original session we now had enough songs for a full album and several B-sides.

I'm not sure if I've ever mentioned this before but my brother John was key to me writing 'Me, I Disconnect From You'. I woke up one morning and heard him playing a short six note sequence on the piano downstairs. I loved it, so I jumped out of bed, grabbed some clothes and ran downstairs before he'd had a chance to move away from the piano and forget what he'd done. John was only 13 at the time and didn't spend too much time writing songs, although he does now. I got him to show me what he'd been playing, I added to more notes to the end of the sequence and that became the key part of the entire song that I'd finish off later that day. Without John coming up with that sequence I doubt I'd ever have written 'Me, I Disconnect From You'. He definitely deserved a song writing credit for that one and, to my great shame, I didn't even think of it. In my defence the world was beginning to come at me in an ever more rushed and chaotic way and it was not my intention to deny him, it just got lost in all the madness. Without a doubt I still owe him though.

Replicas was very much a science-fiction album. I'd been writing a series of short stories at the time about what I thought London might become in the next fifty years or so, the central idea being that control was handed over to a machine, a computer that, absent of political ideology and bias, would be better suited to fixing problems fairly and efficiently. But the machine realised that the biggest problem was people. Without people, London, and the world, would run smoothly and peacefully, so it devised a scheme that would allow for the systematic elimination of humans one by one. The stories featured machines called Machmen, which inspired the song 'The Machman' on the album, and 'Down in the Park' was taken from a bit about so-called criminals being hunted by machines, each one designed to kill or injure in a different way. There was far more to it than that, of course, including synthetic prostitutes, which led to 'Are "Friends" Electric?', but you get the idea. The writing of *Replicas* came together quickly because I already had all of those stories and characters. All I needed to do was adapt them into lyrics.

With the *Replicas* sleeve I was achieving two things. First, I was a visual representation of one of the characters sung about on the album, a Machman. I thought it was important that the sleeve gave people a clue as to what they might expect when they played the record, that it was an extension of the content. I have always thought that a musical career is very much like a machine. There are a lot of moving parts, all needing to work together smoothly for the machine as a whole to function. The music, the way you look, the way you sing and talk, the lyrics, and most definitely the sleeve, all play a part. Second, though, I'd been thinking about what my dad had said back at the White Hart pub in Acton, which already seemed like a lifetime ago but was only months: 'If you can't find a way of dealing with this, this is not the career for you.' I had found a way. I would become someone else. I would become a character from the album, and I would hide behind, or within, that image. With *Replicas* I created the first of many personas I would hide behind until, decades later, the need for them eventually faded away.

Replicas was released in April '79, still under the name Tubeway Army. I'd argued yet again to be allowed to drop the band name and be a solo artist, but Beggars would have none of it. Paul had no objections either way – he was happy to go along with me, wherever I was going. The first single from the album, 'Down in the Park', sold about 10,000 copies, which, again, was not great, but a huge leap forward from anything I'd done previously. 'Down in the Park' was a slow-paced, slow-building, doom-laden five-minute marathon of a song. It was as far from radio-friendly, or the pop music of the day, as you could get. Menacing and eerie, it remains to this day one of my favourite songs and has been covered by other artists countless times. Back then, though, it didn't seem to get noticed that much. It didn't come close to the Top 40, didn't get any radio play, but nonetheless I felt it had pushed us up a level. After all, 10,000 copies isn't a disaster for a new band with a new type of music. The single scraped in to the Top 200, number 198, I think, but I was happy with that. After all, that meant only 197 people were ahead of me. Considering the thousands of bands out there, that didn't seem too bad.

The album sold about the same number initially, which was also a big improvement over the first album but nothing special. My hopes for it were quite modest, in that I hoped it might get me to a level where I could play live again, but where I would be able to sell out the better clubs – places like the Marquee, for example. A level where I would have my own crowd, that came to see me, knew the music and wanted to listen without throwing bottles at me or starting a fight. It seemed to be going reasonably well from my point of view. I had absolutely no idea what was just around the corner.

We were invited to record a radio session for John Peel on Radio 1, which I saw as a fantastic opportunity. John Peel was a champion of music outside of the mainstream – countless successful bands owed him a nod of gratitude – and Radio 1 was huge. John had already given a few plays to a song or two off the first album, but this was a major step up from that. We recorded three songs, 'Me, I Disconnect from You', 'Down in the Park' and, for reasons I will never understand, I decided to play a song from the album called 'I Nearly Married a Human'. It's an odd song, to say the least, and an even odder choice when you could only play three songs on the session. I'm sure I was trying to impress upon the listeners just how different we were, but, really, playing that was probably a mistake. It went well, though, and I began to feel as though things were beginning to pick up. A little over a year after we'd signed to Beggars, we had two albums out, three singles, a Peel session and one or two people I spoke to had even heard of the band.

We began to make plans for a headlining club tour. However, my uncle Jess, about seven years older than me, had toured before and was not enthusiastic about doing so again. He had a good job and decided to stick with that. He did help us with the auditions for a new, hopefully permanent, drummer though. In addition, there was no way I could play the keyboards and guitar and sing at the same time, so I'd need a keyboard player as well, possibly two, and probably another guitarist. We auditioned at a rehearsal room under one of the Beggars shops in Fulham. I couldn't believe the standard of the people who turned up. It was awful. One man came straight from work at a building site with his boots still encrusted in concrete. He couldn't even clap in time. Another complained that the songs were too difficult, which is not the best way to get a job. Then Ced Sharpley turned up and everything seemed bright. He was amazing. A real drummer. Solid, inventive, energetic, he learned the songs straight away, added new flourishes and, most important of all, he was easy to get along with, likeable and good fun.

The keyboard player auditions were fairly straightforward. The first man to arrive came with some decent gear of his own, which was a good thing. He was French, spoke little English and seemed to be suffering from a stomach bug. Every few minutes he'd disappear to the toilet, so we'd wait for him to come back, get halfway through another song, only for him to shoot off to the toilet again. He seemed to have bad eyesight as well and played with his face a few inches away from the keyboard. He also couldn't play very well. The next man in was Chris Payne, who had no gear but could play anything I asked him to, with one hand, while chatting to me. He was definitely in. He assured me he knew all about synthesisers, which turned out to be a total lie, as he'd never even seen a synth before. I didn't find that out until much later, though. Like Ced, Chris was fun, extremely likeable and a great player. The new Tubeway Army was coming together.

On 4 May 1979 'Are "Friends" Electric?' was released. Initially they pressed 20,000 copies as a picture disc, and I can't begin to tell you how big a thing that was. Picture discs were relatively new at that time and used mainly for bigger bands to launch major singles. Beggars had by now come under the umbrella of a major label, WEA, and I have never discovered who suggested or approved the idea that they could press 20,000 picture-disc copies of my single. I don't know if it was someone at Beggars or WEA, but whoever it was changed my life. What a gamble that was. Twenty thousand very expensive copies of a strange song by an unknown band who had only sold half that number before. 'Are "Friends" Electric?' was five minutes fifteen seconds – way too long to get on the radio. It had no chorus as such, apart from two spoken-word sections. You couldn't dance to it, and it had a lyric that only really made sense if you knew it was about a robot pros-titute, which thankfully nobody did to begin with. It ticked none of the boxes for a hit single, and yet somebody had decided to make it an instant collectors' item by making it a limited-edition picture disc. It was an incredible decision, and it started to work immediately, jumping straight into the lower reaches of the chart. It also generated enough interest to get us a spot on TV. *The Old Grey Whistle Test* was a hugely influential programme at the time. It didn't have the vast audience and commercial sway of *Top of the Pops*, but it was the next best thing in the UK, and we were asked to play two songs live. I'd watched *Whistle Test* for years and seen some of my favourite artists appear on it. It was a huge, huge deal for me. This was an opportunity to be seen by a national audience that could, undeniably, make a real difference to our future. I would be standing on the same floor that legends had stood on, facing the same cameras they'd faced. This was the moment that could bring us serious attention and catapult us into the big league. I knew all of that, and the pressure was crushing.

Major opportunities for a fledgling band are extraordinarily hard to come by. You might only get one, if you're lucky. When you recognise that everything you've ever dreamed of could be won or lost in that one moment, you feel the enormity of that. In the years to come you might go on to do hundreds of TV shows or important events, but it's likely that nothing will ever be as stressful and frightening as the first. I was elated and terrified in equal measure. If it went well, we could be on our way to fame and fortune. If it didn't, we might never recover the lost ground. I knew one thing, though: we would definitely need another keyboard player, and that guitarist.

Since discovering Ultravox I'd become a huge fan. I thought

they were doing something very similar to what I was trying to do, only they were much better. The music was polished, refined, beautifully played and slickly produced. The singer was a fascinating, enigmatic character called John Foxx, with a unique voice to match his incredibly cool appearance. Ultravox had quickly become the yardstick I measured myself against, and I never came close to reaching the level they soared to so effortlessly. Sadly, the band had broken up not long before, so I dared to ask their keyboard player Billy Currie if he would join the band. Billy was, as far as I was concerned, a rock star, a hero of mine. He had already been through all the things that were now happening to me, and I was over the moon when he agreed to join.

I'm embarrassed to admit that my memory of the guitar player we used for our *Whistle Test* performance, Trevor Grant, is somewhat sketchy. As far as I can remember, Trevor only ever played with us that one time and must have been recommended by someone else, as I didn't know him before.

In the days leading up to our *Whistle Test* slot, I practised constantly. Not the music – the way I would move. I had no idea how to move. I couldn't dance if my life depended on it. I had no meaningful experience of being on stage bar a handful of gigs. What little experience I did have had been holding a guitar, but I was only going to sing on the show, so no guitar to hide behind. It was the hands and arms that were the biggest problem. I didn't know what to do with my hands and arms. So I practised. I worked out what I should do for each line of each song. Where I would look, when I would look away, when I would hold the mic, when I would put my arms out to one side, everything. Like a wooden puppet on strings. It was totally unnatural and contrived, but I could think of no other way.

I did have a few ideas. As I said, I'd watched the show for years, *Top of the Pops* as well. I'd noticed that bands were always lit up in bright colours, flashing away like a nightclub dance floor. I didn't want any of that. When we arrived, I asked if it would be possible to only have white light, no colours, and could they put some on the floor in front of us so the light was coming up, bleaching us out and creating unusual shadows. The TV crew were surprisingly agreeable and lit us exactly as I'd asked. I'd also noticed over the years that whenever bands appeared on TV, they would always be looking into whatever camera was on them, usually smiling. I thought that was a wasted opportunity. It gave the viewer that same happy face on view for the entire song, regardless of what it was about. I decided not to do that. I would look at the camera only when the lyric required an extra boost, when looking into the camera would deliver a lyric straight into the heart of the person watching. Apart from that I'd ignore the cameras completely and look forward as though I had a crowd in front of me. I also decided I wasn't going to smile. The songs were not happy songs, and the band would be dressed in black from top to bottom. I'd be dressed as a Machman, and I'd be singing 'Down in the Park', about 'rape machines' and 'kill by numbers'. Smiling wouldn't work at all. I'd be singing 'Are "Friends" Electric?' about loneliness, loss and robot sex. Definitely no smiling.

We arrived at the BBC studios early on 29 May and had a couple of unsettling things happen during the day. First of all, an enthusiastic fire officer at the BBC seemed to convince himself that the drape we had around our drum riser was a fire risk. He tried repeatedly to set it on fire in a variety of ways and held us up quite a bit. My nerves were already frayed, so I could have done without that. The second thing happened seconds before we were due to play – remember, this was a live performance on national TV, and our first. A camera, while changing position, collided with the PA system that would allow us to hear ourselves as we played and knocked it over. There was a mad scramble to get it back in place, and they only made it with seconds to spare. It was almost a disaster before it had even begun. It went very well and I was enormously relieved, and very happy, when it was over. I was ecstatic when I was told we'd been booked to appear on *Top of the Pops* the next day.

I couldn't believe it – none of us could. Mum and Dad could barely take it in. In many ways, just being on *Top of the Pops* meant you'd made it. You were a success just by appearing. It was a monumental, extraordinary moment and a second, epic opportunity to put the band firmly on the map. Two major TV shows in one week. We were flying.

I was told that the single had got up around the Top 80. I am absolutely convinced that, initially at least, it was due entirely to it being a picture disc. Collectors were buying it because it was collectable. I don't think many people even bothered to listen to it to begin with, but that's the power of marketing. At that time, *Top of the Pops* had a spot on the show called 'Bubbling Under'. They would pick a song outside the Top 40 that was of interest for whatever reason and have it on. That week, I'm told – no idea if it's true – it was between us and Simple Minds, and they choose us because they thought Tubeway Army was a more interesting name than Simple Minds. Whatever, we were on it. For *Top of The Pops* I asked my old friend Garry Robson to play guitar for us. We only had to mime for the show, and I thought it would be an amazing experience for him to take part. I couldn't count the number of times we'd sat at home as kids and watched the show, talking about what we'd do when it was our turn.

I wanted to do much the same thing with the lights on *Top of the Pops* as I'd done on *Whistle Test*, but I expected the crew there to be more difficult. The biggest stars in the world appeared on *Top of the Pops* every week, and they seemed to have a fairly set style, so I doubted the crew would be willing to change anything. I couldn't have been more wrong. They seemed surprised that someone was actually taking an interest in the way it looked and couldn't have been more helpful. I used the camera in exactly the same way as I had before. It was easier on *Top of the Pops*, as they had a small crowd moving from stage to stage.

The day was surreal, to say the least, but despite my nervousness, I couldn't have been happier. Just being at the BBC, walking into the studio, being given our own dressing room, being a part of such an iconic and influential TV show. Famous people walking here, there and everywhere. Most of all, though, knowing what it meant for me, for the band, for the label, for Mum and Dad. Everyone was excited. The performance itself was rehearsed a couple of times before the actual take so by the time we did it for real we were reasonably familiar with how it would go. It was terrifying and exhilarating in equal measure. If my career stopped right then, I could always say I'd been on *Top of the Pops*.

To be honest, proud as I was, as far as I was concerned this was only the beginning. It seemed that as each incredible thing happened, I was already thinking about what needed to happen next. It's been a feature of my life that I'm rarely able to live in the moment, to simply enjoy what's happening right now, no matter how rewarding or satisfying it should be. I'm always thinking ahead, always trying to figure out what it really means, where it might take me, what dangers are hidden within it, what I need to do to shape what comes next. *Top of the Pops* was no exception.

When the recording was over, we decided to go to a club Paul and I visited often called Blitz. It was run by Steve Strange and, on this night, he decided that, although Paul, Billy Currie and I could come in, he wasn't going to let in anyone else in our group. We had a bit of a row, but he was adamant and so what should have been a fantastic celebration of an amazing day was somewhat ruined. I was pretty angry at the small-minded pettiness of it. That first *Top of the Pops* appearance caused a huge surge in sales of the single. The picture discs had sold out, so they started to press conventional vinyl in a picture bag, and they began to sell in quite meaningful numbers. The next week the song went to 48, the week after to 27 and then to 20. At 20 I thought it had probably peaked. I could barely believe it had reached the Top 20. We were now a band with a chart single, and people knew who we were. The day after that first *Top of the Pops* I signed my first-ever autograph, for a road sweeper, as I left the Beggars office on Hogarth Road. I'd never been so proud, or so flattered. People were recognising me as I walked around. It was such an incredible feeling of accomplishment. But I was pretty sure that as far as 'Are "Friends" Electric?' was concerned we'd probably gone as far as we could go. When the next chart position was due, I sat glued to the radio. I listened intently to the placings from 40 to 20, and there was no mention of it. I was bitterly disappointed. It must have dropped right out of the Top 40. The countdown continued and as each number went by my heart sank a little further. I'd hoped that by some miracle it might have gone up again, but by the time it got to 14 I could have cried. There was no way it had gone up that much. It must have gone out completely. Then, at 13, I heard our name. I was ecstatic. It was the best day ever – up to then at least.

While the *Replicas* and 'Are "Friends" Electric?' drama was unfolding I was already back in the studio starting work on my next album, *The Pleasure Principle*. The day I recorded the demo for 'Cars', at a small studio behind the Strand in London, I remember walking back through the backstreets to the car and hearing 'Are "Friends" Electric?' coming out of an upper-floor apartment window. I stopped outside and looked up. I could see the shadow of a woman against a curtain moving to the song as she ironed her clothes. I stayed for a moment. It was such a surreal experience on so many levels. Not long ago, no one knew about me or my music, and here I was listening to the song being played in someone's apartment – I could see someone enjoying it. I even enjoyed the thought that she would never know I'd been standing outside her window watching her shadow as she listened to it. It was such a lovely feeling.

'Are "Friends" Electric?' wasn't being played on the radio, which was massively problematic. Pretty much every other record in the chart was being played several times a day on Radio 1, as well as the other vitally important stations around the UK, but not 'Are "Friends" Electric?'. No one was hearing the song, no one was listening to it throughout the day. It seemed so unfair, but although I didn't know it then, a lack of radio play was something destined to haunt me for ever more. It's incredibly difficult to make any impression on the chart without radio play. When you are fighting for the higher positions, it's almost unheard-of for a single to be able to climb the chart without radio support. However, the next week it unbelievably went to number 7, and the week after, against all the odds, it rose again to number 2. The feeling of being at number 2 is indescribable. The supreme joy of having got that far is equalled only by the realisation that you are just one place away from number 1, and the fear that you won't reach it suddenly hits you. It's an extraordinary melting pot of emotions. You tell yourself you've done better than you could have hoped for, that your dream has most definitely come true. Whatever happens next you really are a pop star. You've done it. You've absolutely done it, and yet you could actually go one further and be the biggest-selling artist in the country. The weight of what it would mean for that not to happen becomes almost unbearable. It seems utter madness that you could feel disappointed by 'only' getting to number 2. A few weeks ago, you'd have eaten your own head to be number 2. But not now. Now you know that it will be devastating to get so close and not make it. You keep telling yourself that the vast majority of people who have long and highly successful careers in music never get to number 1. You can be considered a great success without ever having a number 1, and yet . . . It's the holy grail. The pinnacle. The top of the mountain. Nothing better. It can never be taken away from you. It's in the history books. It just doesn't get any more special. So, you lie awake at night, counting down the days until the next chart is announced.

The next week I couldn't even bear to listen. The phone rang, I picked it up and heard Martin Mills say, 'You've done it. You're number 1.' And that was it. Mum and Dad were there, my brother John, it was the most extraordinary moment, but it was fleeting. I went back into the front room and carried on watching the TV. You know it's happened, you know it's extraordinary, but I looked around the room and everything was the same. It felt strangely unreal, an anticlimax almost. There was no fanfare, no ticker-tape parade, no trumpets and camera flashes. Nothing had changed. It takes a while for something as enormous as that to really start to sink in, I guess. I was about to learn that everything had, of course, changed for me. One thing was for sure: we wouldn't be playing a club tour. It was going to be a lot bigger than that.

We did another *Top of the Pops* as the number-1-selling band in the UK, which was a truly wonderful experience. This time the studio audience knew exactly who we were. Fans were gathered at the entrance to the BBC studios and screamed as we went in. We arrived in a limo. For a while 'Are "Friends" Electric?' was selling up to 40,000 copies a day. It was huge, phenomenal. A few weeks later, *Replicas* went to number 1 too, so, for that week at least, I was number 1 in both the album and singles charts. The single stayed at number 1 for four consecutive weeks, and I was indeed a pop star.

I learned over time that a lot of the other electronic bands in the UK that had been around before me were pretty upset that I'd come along, seemingly out of nowhere, and had so much success. I could understand that. If you've been breaking new ground musically but not getting anywhere, it must be very frustrating to see someone come along, discover something you've known about for some time and then within a few months have a double number 1 with it. I can only imagine how that must hurt. I was seen as a 'Johnny come lately', apparently. All I can say in my defence is I just wrote some songs, wrapped them in an image, gave them a persona and went for it. I didn't do anything that they couldn't have done before. Also, my success opened the floodgates for electronic music, and soon every label was signing up their token electronic band. It became something of a golden period for all those bands that had been struggling to get noticed, and some of them would go on to even greater heights than me.

Chapter Six

1979

The pop-star experience wasn't entirely what I expected. It was too much, too soon in many ways. A part of me felt like I knew exactly what I was doing, but another, far bigger, part felt like a fraud. The wrong man in the wrong job. In many ways I'd liken becoming successful to losing your virginity. You've thought about it for so long, dreamed about it, fantasised, planned, become a little obsessed perhaps. But, when it finally happens, it's nothing like you expected. So much so that it's almost a disappointment, and you realise that there is a whole world of things you need to learn, and quickly. You discover things to enjoy you had no idea existed, and things to avoid you had no idea were waiting for you. You suddenly find yourself trying to navigate a world you have no experience of whatsoever. People you've never met before faint when they see you; girls cry uncontrollably and grab for you. Huge stars shake your hand and call you by your first name as though you're now one of them. But you aren't, not in the slightest. You become aware of hostility you've never known before, and for reasons you can't begin to understand. After all, all you've done is write a song that lots of people like. How can that be a bad thing? How can people hate you for that? For every girl who screams, there are others that sneer and shout abuse. Men threaten you if you dare step outside your protected bubble for even a second. Letters pour in, a nice one here, a death threat there. For every nice comment there are a dozen that seem to see you and your song as the coming of the Devil. You are suddenly drowning in the most overwhelming wave of constantly changing experiences and emotions. You bounce off the walls of what had previously been the easily understood boundaries of what is acceptable and what isn't. It seems as though the world goes mad and you are the only sane one in it, adrift in a stormy sea, desperately trying not to sink and be lost for ever.

And yet, it's still an extraordinary, exciting journey. You just have to learn how to control it. How to enjoy what's good, how to avoid what's bad, and find a path through the things you don't understand. It takes time. It takes years. Many, many years. In that first rush you do find much that is enjoyable, that comes close to being what you'd hoped for. Not everyone is fake or hostile – there are plenty of sincere and kind people who help you along the way, in ways big and small. There is no shortage of advice, of course, most of which you ignore, and some of which perhaps you shouldn't have. The end result is that your life will never be the same again, and you either start to battle your way through or you get buried.

One of the things I learned almost straight away was that becoming successful is not the glorious end of the journey. It's just the start of a far harder, more brutal, more dangerous next step. Whereas before you had nothing to lose and all to gain, it's now the opposite. Now you can make mistakes that could cost you everything you've won. But isn't that exactly what you wanted? Didn't you say at that school careers meeting that you wanted something that was endlessly challenging? Welcome.

You have everything you wanted. Perhaps you should have been more careful what you wished for.

In many ways, it took me too long to fully understand how different things were for me. For example, the first thing I did was to rent a large holiday caravan at a campsite in Weymouth. As a child we'd gone there every year in my mum and dad's tiny touring caravan, and I always thought that the really rich people stayed in the bigger vans up the hill. I clearly had a very limited view of what rich and poor truly meant. Simon Le Bon bought a mega yacht and went to Montserrat. I rented a caravan at Littlesea Camp in Weymouth. Not that I was rich. It would take a long time before any meaningful money arrived. I had so much to learn, about music, about fame, about the entire world.

Becoming famous quickly, at a young age, especially when you are essentially a solo act, is not ideal. When you add Asperger's, you have an unfortunate mix that is almost guaranteed to lead to struggle. For many people, success comes slowly, and it's the best way by far. It builds over time, with each album doing a little better than the one before, until the big one finally arrives. You get used to the changes as you go through that gentle progression. You learn how to handle the press, you learn how to perform on bigger stages, how to write, how to record – you get used to the increasing pressure, demands and workload. In short, some careers as they build serve almost as a university course on music-career preparedness, preparing you for the big time if and when it ever comes. So, when it finally arrives, you know exactly what you're doing. You're older, wiser and more professional, so it's just another small step up to the top of the ladder. It couldn't have been more different for me. My rise was sudden, meteoric almost. I was totally unprepared for the reality of fame, and I had no experience of anything. I was young, naive and with a mental condition that, although I would never wish to change it, was crashing around in my head like a wounded elephant. I would not recommend the way I made it to anyone, not that we ever really have a choice. I'm amazed I survived, temporarily damaged undoubtedly, but relatively intact.

The reviews for 'Down in the Park', 'Are "Friends" Electric?' and *Replicas* had not been kind, to say the least. Despite its incredible success with the public, the music press seemed to view electronic music, or perhaps me in particular, as somehow unworthy. I read lots of spiteful comments, of course, but the ones that bothered me most were when people said it wasn't real music – that it was created by machines; that it was cold and lacking emotion. What made those sort of comments especially unfair, I felt, was that *Replicas* had guitar all over it. Some of the songs had virtually no keyboards whatsoever, a few had been written on the guitar and absolutely every note had been written by me.

Largely as a reaction to that criticism, I think, I decided to make *The Pleasure Principle* even more electronic. I would have no guitars on it at all. It would have drums, bass, keyboards obviously, even a viola, but no guitars. I wanted to prove that the guitar was not the be-all and end-all of music, and I wanted to show that electronic music was something very new. What better way to do that than remove the one instrument long considered absolutely essential. What people had considered 'real' music for so long needed to change.

The Pleasure Principle title came from a painting by the Belgian surrealist artist René Magritte. The sleeve was an adaptation of that painting but with a clear nod towards technology. Where Magritte had a rock on a desk, for example, I had a glowing purple Perspex pyramid. Lyrically the album continued with a smattering of sci-fi ideas, but it was not a theme album the way *Replicas* had been. The songs were more a collection of thoughts I'd had about the way technology was evolving and where it would take us. 'Metal', for example, was about a machine created to be human-like but very aware that it wasn't. It was sad, frightened of the engineers who made it and confused by the fact that it cried without really understanding why. It wanted to be human but knew it could never be and so could only look forward to a life of regret and disappointment. Another song 'M. E.', which stood for Mechanical Engineering, its model type, was about the thoughts of the last machine left alive. Long after the world was dead and humans were a thing of the past, this machine still lingered. For hundreds of years it waited, unable to die, utterly alone, but fully aware. So many songs I heard talked about the human condition, about love lost and found, but I wondered how a machine would feel. With so much talk of making machines self-aware in the future, I wondered about the kindness of that. It seemed horrific to me.

Not everything was sci-fi, of course. 'Cars' was about an incident I'd had while driving a few years before. I'd unintentionally angered two men in the car in front, and when we stopped in traffic, they got out intent on doing me harm. Shouting, kicking the car, trying to open the doors, which luckily I always kept locked – they tried everything to get to me. I was genuinely terrified. I saw a gap appear in the lane beside me, so I drove into that and then, panicking and desperate to get away, up onto the pavement. I drove along the pavement, pedestrians leaping out of the way, off into the next street and escaped. I felt then, and have done ever since, that a car is like a tank for civilians. It keeps us safe, separated from the outside world. In our metal shell we are able to travel wherever we need to go, safe and protected. 'Cars' is about that feeling and is one of only two songs I've ever written on a bass guitar. The irony that 'Cars', now considered one of the all-time classic electronic songs, was written on a bass guitar is not lost on me.

'Cars' came about because I wanted to learn how to play bass better. I went to London and bought a bass guitar, a Shergold Modulator. Back at my parents' house, and in the same room as the first ever Tubeway Army rehearsal, where I'd not long ago written 'Down in the Park' and 'Are "Friends" Electric?', I took the bass out and played it for the first time. The very first four notes were the four notes of the main 'Cars' bass riff. I liked that, so I played four different notes as an answer line, and 'Cars' was pretty much done, in less than a minute. Those eight notes are the song, exactly as I played them straight out of the case. A few minutes later, I had the third section of the song done, and about thirty minutes later I had the lyrics. I've never written a song more quickly than that. Without doubt that was the most productive few minutes of my entire life.

When we demoed 'Cars' at the studio behind the Strand, just before I saw the lady in the window swaying to 'Are "Friends" Electric?', I had another bit of luck. Thanks to Martin Mills, Beggars had now bought me a Poly Moog synth, and it had a sound in it called 'Vox Humana', an alternate string-type sound, but unlike anything I'd ever heard before. The song started, and I pressed a key on the Poly Moog and then waited for inspiration to strike. I held that high note for several bars before accepting that inspiration was nowhere in sight. Instead of just lifting off my finger, I ran down the keys randomly with no firm melody idea in mind. But it sounded perfect. That long sustain followed by the descending run of notes was the perfect way to start the song. It screamed. It was exciting. It was exactly what it needed. I firmly believe accidents are an integral part of making music. I absolutely rely on them happening at some point when I'm making an album.

Even 'Are "Friends" Electric?' was an accident. I'd been working on two songs, neither of which I could finish. One of them would become the main verse groove of 'Are "Friends" Electric?', the other the music behind the spoken-word section. On the day it all came together, I played the first song and, as usual, couldn't think where to take it, so, in a huff, went straight into the other song I was working on and realised that they worked together. On top of that, when I first wrote 'Are "Friends" Electric?', the notes of the main riff were slightly different – it was almost sad and lilting to begin with. I hit a wrong note when I was playing it one day, before we went to the studio to record it, and thought it sounded better. That mistake stayed. It's often assumed that pop stars consider themselves talented and special, and that we must be bigheaded because of that. Not true at all, not for me anyway. I have never forgotten that my first big single was two songs I couldn't finish stuck together, and it was a bad playing mistake that accidentally improved it. Nothing to get bigheaded about. More than that, it was the 20,000 picture discs of 'Are "Friends" Electric?' that first got us noticed, not the song, and it was someone for ever unknown at *Top of the Pops* who gave us our 'Bubbling Under' chance. So, talented? Maybe a little.

Lucky? Absolutely, and being lucky is nothing to be bigheaded about.

After the success of 'Are "Friends" Electric?' and *Replicas* I finally had enough leverage to get my way with the band name, and Tubeway Army was over. From now on all my albums would be as Gary Numan. I think at the time this was seen as a power grab by some people, that the band had some success and I immediately dumped it and went solo. But that wasn't it at all. I'd wanted to be a solo artist from the moment I discovered the synth, but it was only after 'Are "Friends" Electric?' that I had the power to finally get what I wanted. I think the perception of a power grab hung around, though, and I don't think it helped my already poor relationship with the music press.

'Cars' went to number 1 soon after it was released. *The Pleasure Principle* did the same in the album chart, so, for only the tenth time at that point, an artist had the double: a simultaneous number 1 single and album twice in the same year. I'd released three albums in just eleven months, which itself was pretty remarkable, and had two number 1 singles and two number 1 albums to show for it. I think of myself as pretty modest, but that was a stunning achievement, by any measure.

A few days before 'Cars' hit number 1, my first major tour began at the Glasgow Apollo in Scotland. The tour would run for sixteen shows and include two nights at the Hammersmith Odeon in London. The stage set was based on another of my *Replicas* short stories. In that one the buildings would glow as darkness fell, the idea being that there wouldn't be any dark areas and people would feel, and be, safer. I had a set built that looked like two glowing skyscrapers. The two keyboard players were positioned halfway up, one in each tower, the drummer on a tall riser in between with a huge triangle shape behind him. When I discussed the idea for buildings that glowed for the stage show, I learned that nothing like that existed – they would have to be designed and built. So, in the weeks leading up to the tour, we experimented with different types of light sources and fittings, different types of Perspex, and eventually a panel was built that could glow at various intensities and yet wasn't so bright it would blind the audience. By clamping a series of these panels to a metal framework over twenty-two feet high we created the two glowing towers. The result was spectacular, and the light show looked like nothing I'd ever seen before.

The small pyramid shape used on *The Pleasure Principle* sleeve had seemed to resonate with the fans, so we incorporated it into the show as much as possible. For example, I had two radio-controlled, pyramid-shaped machines built that would move around the stage during certain songs, controlled by a man from side stage. We rehearsed the show at an old theatre in London, and I clearly remember how amazing it felt to see my name stencilled onto the mass of flight cases. I marvelled at the sheer size of the stage show, the enormous number of lights, what seemed like miles of cable stretching this way and that, the number of crew milling about necessary to run a show that big. It was all so incredibly big-time, and it was all for me. Because of me. It felt good, I can't deny that, but the pressure to front it as a singer was enormous. I didn't rate my voice much – I never have, really, although I've grown more comfortable with it over the years. I know it's distinctive, that it has a unique sound, but that doesn't always work in your favour. I also knew I had little experience to draw from. I'd done a grand total of thirty-six little punk shows so far, all in tiny places, nothing that could remotely prepare me for what I was about to do. I felt hopelessly out of my depth.

One of the good things about being a solo artist is that you rarely have to debate anything. You make your own decisions. But when you write everything, produce your own albums, when you create everything that people see, when it's only you who's ever interviewed, when you're in charge of a huge operation, then everything falls to you. It should do, of course – this is not a grumble – but the responsibility of that, especially when you're feeling the full weight of it for the first time, is almost unbearable. Being effectively a one-man operation is lonely and worrying for much of the time, and never more so than when you're starting out. You have band mates, of course, but you pay them – they are not a part of the decision making, they don't share the fear and the worry, the burden of constant creativity or the embarrassment of failure. If a decision has to be made, you have to make it, and you sink or swim with that decision. I was now playing a major tour, I was a huge star, and yet remarkably I had no management, no team around me. In addition, it was as new to the record label as it was to me. We were all running blindly forward at breakneck speed, with just a flickering candle to guide the way. It was unbelievably exciting and, scared or not, I was loving most of it. If I needed advice, I'd ask my dad, who had no experience of the music business whatsoever. But I respected his intelligence and intuition enormously, and his calm advice helped me struggle through those early days more than anyone.

Before we'd got into rehearsals for the tour, I had to find a guitarist who would be a permanent fixture in the band. I don't remember auditioning anyone else other than Rrussell Bell. It may have been no one else came along. It may have been Rrussell was the first and was so obviously what we needed we didn't look at anyone else. I can't remember, but Rrussell was perfect. A great guitar player, he could also play the electric viola, which would be very useful when Chris was busy with keyboards during the set. He was smart, funny, enthusiastic and just slotted in seamlessly from the moment he walked through the door. I had the band, and I was very happy.

Next I needed a support band. I actually asked Richard Jobson from The Skids to begin with, after I'd played with them at my last-ever punk gig at the White Hart in Acton. Since then they'd had some success of their own, and I was quite a fan. Richard very politely declined, so I had a rethink and decided to go for a small electronic outfit that wouldn't need much stage space. As the stage-show ideas were coming together, it was becoming clear just how big the production was going to be and stage space would be at a premium. It was then that Orchestral Manoeuvres in the Dark came into the picture. I listened to their music, loved it and asked them if they wanted to join the tour. They said yes, and that was the support band confirmed. OMD were perfect. Two men and a tape recorder called Winston, easy to be with, great to watch, fun to be around. As I remember, money was a problem for them at the time, so I said we'd put their gear on our trucks and invited them to travel with us on our bus. The tour seemed to be a major step up for OMD, and I was very happy to see them sign a major deal and really take off the following year.

I named the tour *The Touring Principle*, and I wanted each concert to be more than just a show – I wanted it to be an event. Something so striking people would talk about it for a long time afterwards. My attitude was that if people found me uninterest-ing to watch, which I thought was highly possible, they could always look at the spectacle taking place behind me. The light show had to be special, far more than people would normally expect to see in the venues we were playing. I even had the PA painted white so that it became a visual part of the show.

Just arriving at the venue was exciting. Fans running up the street after the bus, police trying to control things. This was the pop-star dream I'd read about. Long before the show started, I could hear the fans inside the venue screaming and chanting. I was incredibly nervous but, strangely enough, nothing like as bad as I'd been when we played in those tiny pubs. I was a Machman now. I was a character from a story, and that charac-ter was confident and arrogant and scared of nothing. As I walked out onto the stage and the crowd went truly ballistic, I felt calmer than I could ever have thought possible. I'd found a way. The crowd was full of Gary Numan lookalikes. Everywhere I looked I saw my own image staring back at me, people singing along knowing every word to every song. People crying, some fainting and being carried out. The noise was loud enough to overpower the PA, and it was the best feeling I'd ever known, an immense experience from beginning to end. More than anything, standing on a stage with a crowd going crazy is the biggest, most rewarding thrill of all. Was then, is now. Unfortunately, back then that reward also came with a level of stress and worry that at times saw me walking on a knife edge mentally. I seemed to be flitting from elation to anger to desper-ation to easy-going from one minute to the next.

We had a few incidents here and there – keyboards breaking down, the pyramid robots having a mind of their own, stuff like that – but generally the tour ran pretty smoothly. It was only at the Coventry show that a couple of unfortunate things happened. While we were on stage, some people climbed up the scaffolding outside the building and managed to get into the dressing-room area. They stole quite a few things, including the jacket I used to wear for the encore, which was a bit upsetting. During the show, people in the crowd started to climb onto the stage, trying to get to me. Not a major problem, but I had an overly zealous security man who started hitting the backs of their legs with a mic stand. That seemed way over the top to me, so I stopped him, had a little rant at the crowd, as it was spoiling the show somewhat, and carried on. If I'm honest, it unsettled me quite a bit.

Every night of the tour was amazing (except maybe Coventry), but playing at Hammersmith Odeon was extra special. I was born in Hammersmith for one thing, and when Paul and I were making our many trips into London, long before we even had a record deal, we'd drive past the Odeon and say to each other 'One day'. Before I even knew Paul, I'd gone to see a band there, and I remembered the exact seat I sat in, three rows from the front, five in from the left. I'd gone to see Mott the Hoople, I think, with Queen supporting, and now here I was.

Before the soundcheck for the Hammersmith show, Beggars asked me to visit them at their office in Hogarth Road that afternoon. For some reason they asked me to stand with them outside on the pavement. After a few minutes not quite understanding what was going on, a white Corvette pulled into the street, right up to where we were standing. The Corvette was my favourite car at the time, and this one was beautiful. Everyone swarmed around it and then, unbelievably, I was handed the keys. It was a present from the label. This was my new car. What an amazing surprise. I remembered a conversation I'd had months before with Dave Dee from WEA. During the filming of the 'Cars' promo video, he'd sat down and asked me if everything was all right. I thought it was just a simple chat about things, as so much had happened recently. I did say that I was a little frustrated by not having any money. I was selling vast numbers of records, but I was still having to borrow my dad's car to go to interviews and rehearsals, even to the video that day, because I couldn't even afford an old second-hand one. Dave asked me what my favourite car was, so I told him: a white Corvette with red interior had always been my dream car. I honestly thought no more about it. I later found out that the whole thing was a ploy to encourage me to re-sign with Beggars/WEA. Apparently, while we were in the process of trying to renegotiate my Beggars deal, my lawyer was seen going into the offices of another label. It was assumed that I was therefore looking to sign with that other label. Dave had been sent to find out what I was thinking and what they could do to keep me. The car became a bribe, in that I would only get it if I agreed to re-sign with Beggars. I was unaware of all this at the time, as my dad had been looking after the negotiations for me. The funny thing was my lawyer hadn't gone to that other label for me, and my dad knew that. I had no intention of going anywhere else, so it was a completely unnecessary bribe. I loved that car.

When I arrived at the Odeon, in the Corvette, I went and found that same seat I'd sat in at the Mott the Hoople gig years before. I sat down and looked around at this huge building, with seats disappearing into the distance. I think that was the best moment of all for me throughout that entire, amazing year. Not the shows, not being on *Top of the Pops*, not the car, not even the number 1 phone call. It was sitting there, alone and quiet, in the seat I'd sat in as a fan. It was then that the true enormity of what had happened in the past few months really began to sink in.

After our two nights at the Hammersmith Odeon, Beggars put on a party at a nightclub in Kensington. Aftershow parties are annoying for the most part, and generally I dislike them enormously. It's impossible to talk to your friends, the people you actually want to celebrate with. You are pulled this way and that to shake hands and smile for people you've never met, it's loud, you can't really make out what people are shouting in your ear, your jaw aches with the constant smiling for photographs, and, as the evening progresses, people get drunk and can get rude and unpleasant. I lasted about as long as I could, and then I snuck out. As I was leaving, I saw some celebrities coming in, and Steve Strange was next in line. The man who had ruined my *Top of the Pops* celebration was trying to get in to my aftershow. I told the doorman he wasn't welcome and walked to my car. A few minutes later, I drove past the club entrance in the Corvette and heard Steve shout, 'You're a fucking bitch,' which made me smile for the next few miles. I might even have given him a reverse Churchill as I drove away. I guess we can all be petty.

The tour continued around the UK for another ten days or so, ending at the City Hall in Sheffield. It had so many dramas, big and small, and most of them revolved around my failing attempts to try to keep on an even keel. I had a drunk girlfriend of one of the crew tell me how shit I was, and then the wife of another tried to sneak into my room. One minute people were offering you sex that I wasn't even sure it was possible for a human being to perform, the next they were throwing bottles at you every time you stepped outside. It was all just conflicting madness and mayhem. I was constantly being talked about in the press as if I was the Devil himself, and I confess that, exciting as it was at times, it was all incredibly disorienting. A funnier incident occurred when one of the band – I think it was Billie Curry, but I can't be sure – having waited far too long for some room service one evening, walked into the hotel restaurant completely naked to ask where it was. Generally, though, I didn't take to touring the way I'd hoped. It pushed me out into an environment that I was extremely uncomfortable with, and it felt like the entire world was watching me stumbling.

In November, we released 'Complex', from *The Pleasure Principle*, as the next single. Very different to 'Cars', it was a slow, sad, ballad-type song. I was keen to show a different side to what I was doing, and I was also keen to show that electronic music could be emotional. I thought 'Complex', with it's pretty, lilting melodies, was the right choice to achieve both aims. When I look back now, though, I understand completely what I was aiming for, but I think momentum would have been better maintained by a different song. I now think 'Metal' should have been the next single to 'Cars', and 'Complex' was perhaps a mistake.

Although I was sharing the burden of business decisions with my dad, we were both very aware that I needed professional management going forward. We arranged a number of meetings with managers over the next few months but always came away with the same feeling of unease. Not one of them talked about what they could do for me. Every one of them, without exception, spent the entire meeting talking about what they wanted from it. What percentages they would take for this, that and the other and so on. I didn't feel comfortable with any of them. I had always thought of my dad as intelligent, honest and intuitive, and I trusted him more than anyone. If I could learn how to be a pop star, why couldn't he learn how to be a manager? So, I asked him to do it, and he agreed, but strictly on the condition that it was only until the right pro manager came along. That wouldn't be for another thirty years.

Chapter Seven

1980

In January 1980, I went into the studio to start recording the demo songs for my next album, *Telekon* – RAK studios at first, but then we moved to one closer to home, Rock City Studios, which was in the Shepperton film-studio complex. Around this time I was also presented with silver and gold discs for *Replicas*, *The Pleasure Principle*, 'Are "Friends" Electric?', 'Cars' and 'Complex'. The original *Tubeway Army* album was re-released as well, with a new sleeve, and this time it made it into the chart. I think I have a silver disc for that one somewhere. The extreme reaction to my arrival in the music world was never more obvious than the award categories in various publications at the end of the year. I can no longer remember exactly what they all were now, but I would win best album of the year and worst album of the year; best single and worst single; best concert and worst concert. I was the brightest new hope and the biggest disappointment. It showed me that opinion really doesn't mean much. All that mattered was looking after the people who supported you. A fanbase will always have a fanatical element that loves you one minute and then hates you the next. Nothing you can do about those people. But most fans really do want what's best for you, and I began to appreciate that more with each passing day. In the coming years, their loyalty and support would pick me up from the floor and put me back on track more times than I could count.

In early February, I began preparing for my first tour of North America, which would start at the Toronto Danforth Music Hall in Canada on the 18th of that month. I had the entire UK tour stage set flown out to Toronto, including the pyramid robots. It was astronomically expensive, but I didn't care. I should have, though. It's difficult to know where to start when explaining how flawed my thinking was about certain things, but this would be a good point when it came to touring. To be fair, I was now earning a lot of money from selling records, so I felt well off. I saw touring as a way of saying thank you to the fans for that support. I wanted the shows to be as spectacular as possible, which was hugely expensive, and I didn't want to charge high ticket prices to make the fans pay for my indulgence. I saw touring as an investment in the fanbase. I saw it as creating a partnership, generating fan loyalty that would build career longevity. It was pointed out to me time and again that I was losing a fortune every time I stepped on stage, even when I was selling out night after night in big venues, but it fell on deaf ears. Eventually, this would become a problem that even I couldn't ignore.

Before the tour began, we flew into New York to record two TV shows. One was as the music guest of *The Merv Griffin Show*, a hugely popular talk show of the day. The other was as the music guest of the legendary *Saturday Night Live*. *SNL* is still extremely popular today, but back then it had a live audience of around fifty million people, and you played live. No miming to a backing track on *SNL*. It was enormously influential in the USA, and the weight of that pressed heavily on me in the days leading up to it. A good *SNL* performance could launch me in America; a bad one could kill my chances before we'd barely started. They rehearsed early in the day, so we were able to get the sound adjusted correctly, and it was a useful rehearsal to calm the nerves. They then had a second rehearsal, with a full studio audience, which they filmed and would use as a fallback should anything go wrong during the live show that evening. When it came time to film the actual show, we felt well practised, and it wasn't quite the nerve-racking experience I'd been expecting. The *SNL* cast and crew were incredibly kind to us throughout the day, and included people like Bill Murray, Harry Shearer and Gilda Radner. The show host, the actor Elliot Gould, spoke to me during the day and, again, was extremely friendly, which did much to help calm the nerves. The show went very well, and the impact was instant. We'd driven from the airport to the TV studio the day before and no one knew who I was. The next day we drove back to the airport and it seemed as if everyone knew who I was. The power of those two shows was unbelievable, particularly *SNL*.

We rehearsed in Toronto for a short while before the tour started. We had a support band booked, whose name I can't remember, I'm afraid, but we didn't get to tour with them. A day or two before the tour began, we all went out for the evening and found ourselves walking past a club. There were some interesting sounds coming out of it, so we went in to investigate. What I saw was like nothing I'd ever seen before. On the small stage was a man completely covered in bandages, like the Invisible Man, with a white suit, a white top hat, playing a violin with some keyboards in front of him and a microphone. It was absolutely brilliant. I watched as he began a song and then held the keys of his keyboard down by squeezing thin packets of matches between them to make a chord. He'd then sing and play the violin over the top. It was genius. His name was Nash the Slash. I asked if he wanted to come out on tour with us, he said yes, and the next day he turned up at the Music Hall, and so it began.

We only played thirteen shows on that first North American tour, which isn't many. I believe the idea was to hit all the main cities as a taster experience and return for a much bigger tour later. I had my twenty-second birthday the night we played San Francisco, and the next night we ended the tour in Los Angeles. Being in Los Angeles was an amazing experience, and I loved it immediately. I've loved it ever since. The earlier TV appearances, plus the success of the tour, had an amazing effect on the popularity of 'Cars', helping it reach number 3 in the Billboard chart.

As the tour progressed I was introduced to various celebrities both before and after the shows. Some I'd heard of, some I hadn't. One of the biggest was Paul Stanley from Kiss, who came to see me when we played New York. In the US Kiss are like royalty but they were never really my cup of tea. Even so, whether I'm a fan or not, I always treat everyone with equal respect. The problem I had with Paul Stanley was that he arrived, with a friend, just a few minutes before we were due to go on, and I was extremely nervous. Not of meeting him – of the show itself. I did my best to chat and be sociable, not an easy thing for me at the best of times, but I don't think I did a very good job of it. I've always had the feeling I might not have come across as respectful as I could have, and almost certainly gave less than the reverence he was probably used to. I regret that. Someone taking the time to come out and see you play, to meet up with you, deserved better. Sometimes nerves can get the better of you.

At one point during the tour I was told I'd won the Best Male Singer award at the 1979 British Rock and Pop Awards (the then-equivalent of the BRITs). I was picked up straight from the airport, having not slept for about twenty-four hours, and driven to a studio somewhere where I was to appear live by satellite on TV in the UK to accept my award. I was put in front of a camera and an earpiece was placed in my ear, which didn't work. I sat there for a while with no clue what was going on, and then I saw the cameraman gesticulating at me. I had no idea what he wanted until I heard him say something like, 'You're on. Say something.' I hadn't heard a thing. I didn't know if the people in the UK were still talking, or what they'd said to me if they weren't. I think I mumbled some thanks, but it was a shambles, and I looked like a sleepy idiot.

After the US tour we went to Europe, where, bizarrely, I was accused of being a Hitler fan after a show in Germany. Apparently, one of my little jerky arm movements had been interpreted as an attempt to recreate the Nazi salute. It was nothing of the kind, and it was a ridiculous thing to say, but it summed up what to me seemed to be an almost desperate need to find fault with anything I did. The support band for three of the German shows was Simple Minds, so that was a good line-up. The tour just seemed beset by problems both big and small. I think it was in Belgium where one of the crew fell from the rigging when the set was being built and landed on his back across a flight case. He ended up in hospital. I can't say I enjoyed that first European tour too much.

We then went to Japan, which was a fascinating place, and somewhere I enjoyed very much. I was struck by the culture and so impressed by the people. Plus, they had the most organised fans in the world. Girls would be waiting in your room, having somehow got a key after finding out which one was yours. As each song finished, there would be brief applause and then absolute quiet as they waited for you to speak. As I didn't speak between songs, it created some awkward moments while I tried to hurry the band into the next song to avoid the quiet.

New Zealand was next, and it was a very different experience. Within minutes of arriving at the hotel, someone tried to start a fight with Ced because, according to the man, he was 'black'. We went out to a club, band and crew, and were chased out by a gang of skinheads. I also saw my first serious anti-Gary Numan demonstrations. People outside the venues with 'Gary Numan Go Home' written on a banner, and other things even less polite. They were handing out leaflets supposedly decoding what they read as anti-religious lyrics. The power went off during one show after someone set off the fire alarm. One of the road crew, who was surprisingly adept at balancing things on his nose, came out and kept everyone entertained until the power came back on. I've been back several times since, for tours and a holiday, and really enjoyed it, but that first visit was horrendous.

In Australia, things were much better, and the tour was hectic and exciting. There was no anti-Numan movement like we'd seen in New Zealand, and I was even presented with a gold disc for *Replicas* sales in Australia. However, our first show in Australia had way too much drama. Paul Gardiner, who had never really been totally happy that Ced, Chris and Rrussell had joined, and would sometimes get drunk and tell them, decided to try tequila before the show. Not getting the swift effect he was looking for, he drank more – a great deal more. As we walked out on to the stage to start the first song of our first-ever Australian show, it appeared that every drop of it hit him at once. I was already strolling down the middle of the stage to the front when I heard the most awful clanging noises coming from Paul's rig. The next thing I see is Paul running past me, with bass attached, randomly hitting notes as he goes, none of them the right ones. He was clearly on his way to running off the stage and into the crowd itself. Drunk as a skunk. I watched in horror, only to see his bass cable reach its limit which, luckily, stopped Paul in his tracks and seemed to ricochet him backwards. He hurtled back up the stage, arms flailing, into his gear, which he knocked over. The last thing I saw was an arm coming out from behind the curtain, grabbing him by the neck and hauling him off stage. That was my dad. On with the show. We didn't see Paul again until later that night in the hotel.

At another show, Paul complained of aches in his legs, so he decided to put Deep Heat cream all over them just before we went on. When the show started and the heat of the lights hit him, it all went horribly wrong. 'My legs are on fire,' he shouted and then started to open the waistband of his trousers and pour cold beer down them. It seemed to help, but we now had beer all over the stage and the electrical gear.

While we were touring Australia, Beggars released the first single from *Telekon*, 'We Are Glass', although the song wasn't actually included on the album itself. I'd filmed a video before going out on tour that, at one point, showed me smashing TVs with a sledgehammer. In Britain, *Top of the Pops* refused to show the video, as they said it was promoting violence. I thought that was a little over the top, but as I wasn't in the country the video was all we had. That ban definitely hurt the single.

In Sydney, I was asked to join a group photo with Bob Geldof, Michael Parkinson and the actor Warren Mitchell. I heard Mitchell ask Parkinson who I was and the rather dismissive reply: 'Just another pop star.' I gathered I was unlikely to be a guest on Parkinson's chat show any time soon. It gave me an inkling as to how transient being a 'pop star' could be – how very much here today, gone tomorrow it all was, unless you were careful. I'd already read numerous articles that said I'd be gone within two years. It had been one year since 'Are "Friends" Electric?' already, so if they were right, I didn't have long left. I thought they were wrong, but I was already beginning to think about what drastic action I might need to take to save my sanity and make sure I stayed around for longer. After we played three nights in Sydney's Capitol Theatre, we came back to the UK, and I returned to the studio to finish recording *Telekon*.

The next single, 'I Die: You Die', also not included on the album, was released on 30 August, and *Telekon* came out a few days later on 5 September. It was my fourth album in less than two years, and I'd played fifty-three concerts around the world in just eight months. *Telekon* was different to anything I'd done before. Whereas before I'd sung about machines and my thoughts about the future, I now wrote about the overwhelming assault of pressure and emotions that came with success. Songs like 'We Are Glass' and 'Remind Me to Smile' were about fans and the strange and sometimes difficult relationship with them that now seemed to be a part of life. 'Sleep by Windows' was another. In 'I Die: You Die', I wrote about my deeply problematic relationship with the UK music press. It so often sounds ridiculous to say anything negative about something that you'd wanted all your life, something that so many people dream of for themselves. It seems ungrateful and petty, whinging at its worst by a pampered child. I totally understand that. But all that dreaming and desire is done largely in ignorance. In truth, you have no idea what's involved, what your life will be like. Becoming famous was absolutely nothing like I expected, and *Telekon* is an uncomfortable journey through that shock realisation. I was still young and inexperienced, childish almost. I can say, without question, the Asperger's part of me has never been so raw and challenged as it was then. I felt everything slipping away. Control, sanity, the ability to live the life I wanted. Of the life I'd actually dreamed of, this certainly wasn't it. I wanted to write better songs, I wanted to learn studio craft, to be better at what I did. Although the constant criticism and vitriol from press and strangers alike didn't bother me too much on the surface, it niggled away underneath. It chipped inexorably away at my confidence until there was little left. I became increasingly embarrassed by what I saw as my lack of ability. More than that, I wanted to have real friendships, to not be followed, to not be pushed about at a petrol station by idiots, to not have my car scratched or the tyres let down every time I parked it, to not be threatened. I wanted to be able to have a girlfriend who didn't sell her story to the papers. I just wanted to run away. In fact, it began to feel like I had to. If I was going to survive the madness I had to get away from it.

As *Telekon* came out, I launched into another, even bigger, UK tour to promote it. This tour would be twenty shows, including four nights at Hammersmith Odeon, and the stage set was even bigger than *The Touring Principle* show. This time we had three radio-controlled robots: two small, square-shaped versions and one tall one, with a full-size mannequin inside that we lit up called Big Al. Unfortunately, BIg Al was top heavy, and after nearly toppling over a few times had to be retired. But as spectacular as the *Teletour* stage set was, I'd already decided that it would be my last tour. In my panic, in my desperation, I'd come to the conclusion that it was touring that was to blame for pretty much all of my problems. Touring took me away from home, away from calm, from the studio. It took away the time I needed to develop as a songwriter, to have real relationships. Touring put me in the spotlight, which I absolutely did not want to be in any more. It exposed me to the world and gave people the opportunity to throw daggers which, despite my Asperger's and my emotional 'boxes', were wounding me. I felt as if I was bleeding slowly to death. Now, when I look back, I marvel at my weakness. At how something that now seems so easily managed was so difficult for me. But I've been doing it for over forty-two years now. You learn a great deal in that time, about so many things. What I do know is that, weak or not, my decision to run away was the best thing I could have done. Without a shadow of doubt, it saved me from spiralling into oblivion, like so many have done before and since. The way I went about it, however, was probably the biggest mistake of my career. A good decision poorly executed.

Telekon went straight to number 1, my third number 1 album in a row. But I was very aware that, even though it seemed to be continuing the phenomenal success of the previous year, *Telekon* had actually sold a lot fewer. About half of what *The Pleasure Principle* had sold, in fact. It was a loud warning that perhaps things were already beginning to slide. At the time, it just reinforced my thinking that I needed to stop touring and concentrate on my songwriting. I was very happy with *Telekon*, and it remains one of my favourite albums, especially from the early years, but I thought I could do much better. The lower sales seemed to be saying the same thing.

Around that time, I heard the legendary singer Robert Palmer was playing two of my songs in his live set. I was blown away by that – someone of that stature actually playing my songs live. It was a huge boost to my confidence and self-esteem after the year-long battering I'd taken from the press and others. I went to see him play at Hammersmith Odeon, and we met up after the show. He invited me to visit him at his place in Nassau in the Bahamas, so after the UK tour ended Paul and I flew out to meet him. We played him *Telekon*, and he immediately connected with a song on it called 'I Dream of Wires'. Over the next couple of days, we worked in the studio directly opposite his house and helped him record a fantastic cover version of the song. I was very proud. He also said he had a couple of songs he'd been working on that he couldn't finish and asked if I wanted to have a try. I was set up in the house next door with a small cassette player and an acoustic guitar and finished them. They were called 'Style Kills' and 'Found You Now'. 'I Dream of Wires' and 'Found You Now' were released on Palmer's *Clues* album, released that same year. 'Style Kills' was used as the B-side for his single 'Johnny and Mary', and I believe both 'Found You Now' and 'Style Kills' were on the B-side of his 'Some Guys Have All the Luck' single.

After our stopover in the Bahamas, Paul and I continued on to North America for our second, and much longer, North American tour, starting on 14 October, in Toronto once again, only this time at the vast Maple Leaf Gardens arena. I decided to sneak out to watch the support band's set but quickly got recognised and had to make a run for it. Unfortunately, I'd forgotten my Access All Areas pass and when I got to the backstage exit the security wouldn't let me through. I couldn't think what to say and, as people were running towards me, all I could think to do was point at the stage, which I obviously wasn't on, and say 'I'm him'. That meant nothing to security of course, understandably, and it wasn't until the fans arrived and started to leap all over me that he realised who I was and let me through.

In New Jersey, at that time at least, a strong union existed for stage crew and I was nearly beaten up by one of the house crew for moving my own keyboard. They took it very seriously. At another gig two unions got into a dispute over one of our props. On the *Teletour* I had a small car, essentially a wheelchair with a sci-fi-looking aluminium frame on top. During 'Down in The Park' I would sit in the car, drive it around the stage, singing the song with a radio mic. The house crew couldn't decide if it was electrics, which one union took care of, or part of the stage set, which another union took care of, so they couldn't decide who was allowed to lift it onto the stage. Eventually, they shared the job. At one point they even said I couldn't drive it myself as it was a union job. They suggested that the electrics man drove it during the song and I would sit on his lap, something clearly impossible given the size of the car. We had to buy them off so that I could drive my own car, during my own song, in my own show.

Paul continued where he'd left off and accidentally created some of the best moments of the tour. He always carried a fair amount of medication for a variety of ills, mostly imagined, I think. At one of our day stops he ran out of something or other and, either drunk or sleepy, rang down to reception. In his broad but slow English accent, he tried to explain that he needed more pills. The receptionist totally misunderstood and called the paramedics, thinking he'd taken an overdose. The first we all knew of it was when a helicopter hammered overhead, hovering just above Paul's room. Then the paramedic turned up and headed straight for Paul's door. The first Paul knew of it was when, wondering what all the noise and fuss was, he opened his door to see a fireman with an axe just about to smash his door in. Paul simply said, 'No, mate, you've got it all wrong. I need some more,' and held up his empty bottle. I miss him.

That US *Teletour* was done very much against the wishes of the US label Atco. I discovered later that Atco felt there was still a great deal of work to be done with *The Pleasure Principle* and wanted to continue with that. They did not want a new album at that point, and they certainly didn't want a new US tour to promote it when they were still promoting the last album. They would have much preferred to hold off on the release of *Telekon* and toured *The Pleasure Principle* again in the USA. I know I was pushing to get *Telekon* out, so part of the fault may have been mine, but I was definitely unaware of exactly what the Americans were saying and their depth of feeling about it. I got caught up between the desires of the UK company to get another big-selling album, so their yearly figures would look good, and the USA trying to stop them so that it didn't kill what they were doing with *The Pleasure Principle*. Atco clearly knew what they were doing, and we should have let them finish their campaign. By going out too soon with *Telekon*, we seriously undermined their efforts, and I'm sure it created a lot of ill feeling. Given that situation now I'd definitely side with the US point of view. Back then I was all for pushing forward and releasing more new music, and WEA had their own reasons for encouraging me to do just that. Atco therefore pulled back considerably on their promotional efforts for *Telekon*, which really hurt the album in the USA. Added to that, I'd started to say very publicly that this was my last tour and I was getting out of touring for good. So, the promoter also got upset. Why put in a lot of effort on someone who's loudly shooting himself in the foot and won't be coming back to build on all the effort people were putting into the tour. I was making major mistakes, again and again. The tours were losing vast amounts of money, even though we were selling out huge arenas at times, thanks to the size and complexity of the spectacular stage sets. The set designs were entirely down to me, so every penny lost was my fault. My dad was trying to rein me in constantly now with dire warnings of how much money we were haemorrhaging, but I was having none of it. In my blinkered mind, I still believed the shows had to be spectacular to earn fan loyalty. The fact that *Telekon* had sold half the copies of *The Pleasure Principle*, so fan loyalty clearly wasn't being secured with these mega shows, didn't seem to register. The North American *Teletour* venues were massive. Things seemed more successful than ever. Each night I would walk out on stage and everything felt good. I was unaware of the war raging between the UK and US labels and I was also unaware of the damage I was doing by announcing I was going to stop.

We had the usual dramas, of course, that seem to be part and parcel of touring. We were thrown out of the hotel in LA because someone pushed Chris into the swimming pool with his clothes on. I honestly couldn't see why it was a problem, but the hotel manager became very upset and threw out the entire party. Band, crew, guests, all of us. It was all very unnecessary, because we were checking out anyway. I was actually at the check-out desk when I saw Chris go in.

Back in England we released a song called 'This Wreckage' as the third and final single from *Telekon*. It was another mistake. 'This Wreckage' was not the best song for a single. There were a number of other songs that would have been far more suitable, but I was trying to make another statement and show another side to the album. They should have stopped me choosing the singles – my judgement was clearly not the best. 'This Wreckage' barely scraped into the Top 20.

My final TV appearance of 1980 was to film my slot for the very popular *Kenny Everett Christmas Show*, where I'd be performing 'I Die: You Die'. It was a great slot to get and would be seen by a massive audience. It really was a major opportunity. The show's director was a man called David Mallet, who also directed many of David Bowie's promo videos at that time. After recording my bit for the Kenney Everett show, David Mallet told me that Bowie would be there next Thursday to film his part for the show and that I could come down and watch. I couldn't believe my luck. I would be in the same room as Bowie, watching him close-up. I never thought something that cool would happen to me, but come the Thursday I turned up at the TV studios, with Rrussell Bell as my guest. There was a small side room off the main studio, and I stood at the back, behind a fair number of people, including Bob Geldof, Paula Yates and others. I couldn't see well, but for the next few minutes I did catch a few glimpses of Bowie over Bob Geldof's shoulder. Pretty soon everything stopped, and it was clear there was a problem. I had no idea the problem was me. David Mallet took me to one side and said that Bowie had seen me and didn't want me there, and I had to leave. So, with that, Rrussell and I found ourselves ejected from the TV building, looking for a taxi to take us home. I was so, so disappointed. Here was a man that I'd idolised for years, bought every album, been to see in concert, bought every book about him, read every article, posters on my bedroom wall. It seemed a petty, totally unnecessary and humiliating thing to do. He was a world-class living legend, and I was a new upstart at best, and yet he felt the need to embarrass me and have me removed. My respect vanished in that moment, but my understanding grew, so I genuinely didn't feel bitter or angry. I actually felt a little sad, because he was just like the rest of us after all. Unsure, insecure, nervous, human. It was the last thing I'd expected. A few days later, I found out I'd been kicked off the TV show as well, and that did make me a little angry.

Not too long after that I found myself in New York on a promotional trip for the *Telekon* album. While there I was invited to a Broadway theatre by the US label to watch Bowie perform as *The Elephant Man*. When we arrived I was slightly embarrassed to find our seats were just a few rows from the front, and right in the middle. There was no way he wouldn't see me, or so I believed. Bowie's film acting prior to that show had seemed to generate a fair amount of ridicule in the press and so I wasn't expecting much. To be honest, still smarting a little from the recent studio eviction and Kenny Everett TV show removal, I was almost looking forward to him being terrible. He really wasn't though. In fact I thought he was amazing, and I left the theatre highly impressed. I was so blown away by it I happily said goodbye to the label people and headed off into the New York night, lost in my thoughts of the show and, without giving it too much thought, confident I knew the way back to my hotel. Confidence entirely misplaced as it turned out. My Asperger's doesn't really allow me to call for taxis so I thought I'd walk it. I was positive the hotel was close so finding it wouldn't be a problem. Unfortunately I somehow got lost and, feeling horribly conspicuous in full Gary Numan make up, found myself wondering around several dark alleyways, totally lost. I couldn't figure out how I could have gone from the bright lights and bustle of Broadway to the quiet, dirty, empty (hopefully) little streets I was now nervously walking along. I expected to be attacked and murdered at any second but eventually, and with great relief, once again found the bright lights and soon after, the sanctuary of the hotel.

I'd had to put my flying lessons on hold for over a year, as I'd been recording and touring constantly. With a small break now, though, I was able to finish all the written exams and flying tests and received my Private Pilot's Licence on 1 December 1980. A little while later, I bought my first aeroplane, a Cessna 182. I would often drive to the airfield late at night and just sit in it. It was hard to believe I actually had my own plane. Flying, always a huge interest, now became vitally important to me and often helped to balance the ups and downs of the music business. I enjoyed the fact that flying had standards that when reached couldn't be taken away. Your ability was not set at the whim of a journalist's comment or opinion; it was a measurable fact. It boosted my self-worth when, at times, it felt like it was being sucked away by the music business. It was going to get a lot worse yet.

I'd got to know the band Japan a little during the year. Their publicist had brought them along to a few of the *Teletour* gigs, and in turn I'd become quite a fan of their music. Towards the end of 1980, their bass player Mick Karn came to the studio and played fretless bass on some of the new songs I was working on. Rob Dean their guitarist played on one or two as well. At some point, and I can't remember which one of them made it, I was invited to join them as a guest on their next Japanese tour, which was soon to start. It was a fairly loose arrangement, but I flew out to Tokyo and waited. They were supposed to call me when they arrived for us all to meet up. I didn't hear anything, and I was soon on a wild goose chase to catch up with them. It was only when I watched their show from the side of the stage that night that it finally dawned on me that my guest spot wasn't going to happen. When it was over, they came off, walked straight past me and headed off into the night. Maybe I had it wrong and hadn't really been invited, or maybe they'd gone off the idea of me guesting with them and no one had the courage to tell me. But either way I had got all the way to Japan and was following them around all day like a brainless puppy yet no one said anything. I was disappointed.

So, I found myself back in Tokyo looking for something to do. I saw a poster that said Queen were playing at the huge Budokan arena in Tokyo that night, so I bought a ticket and went to see the show. I got there very early, found my seat, sat down and waited for the show to start. As more and more people came in, I began to feel what seemed to be a wave of excitement rippling through the crowd. Something was going on, so I stood up to see if I could make out what it was. It was only then I noticed that everyone was staring at me. I was the cause of the commotion. Almost immediately security arrived and escorted me backstage. I'd met Roger Taylor, Queen's drummer, once before on a radio show, but that was my only connection. Many years before, one of the first bands I'd ever been to see had been Queen when they played at the Rainbow in London, the same venue I'd seen Silverhead and Nazareth play. I went to many shows at the Rainbow, but what set the Queen show apart was the way they treated the fans. Usually after a show we'd all crowd around the stage door waiting for the band to come out. They would always hurtle out of the door, into a waiting limo and speed off. Not Queen. They invited everyone in, talked to us all and signed autographs. In fact, they signed the £5 note I needed to buy my train ticket home, so sadly I had to spend it only a few minutes after they'd signed it. It was a powerful lesson in how to look after your fans and one I've never forgotten.

At the Budokan, I explained what had happened with Japan and why I was there, and they took me under their wing. Queen were playing to more people at that one show than Japan were on their entire tour. They were immensely popular, and yet they couldn't have been nicer or more welcoming. After the show, they took me along to their aftershow party, which was at a sushi restaurant. At one point, as we sat cross-legged on the floor and the food was being served, Freddie Mercury noticed I wasn't eating, so I explained that I didn't like sushi. I quickly added that I was just very happy to be there, very grateful to them for inviting me and not eating really wasn't a problem. I was hanging out with Queen after all. Freddie was an amazing character. Overflowing with anecdotes and charm, he was funny and entertaining, truly larger than life. A short while later, I saw his limo return to the restaurant, and the driver walk in with a

McDonald's bag. Freddie had arranged for him to go and get me some McDonald's to eat. I liked him, and without doubt he is one of the greatest showmen we've ever had.

During the evening, I told them I'd been to see them many times before, including when they'd supported Mott the Hopple at the Hammersmith Odeon, and the time they'd signed my £5 note. I asked them why I'd never seen them guest on other people's albums and, surprisingly, they said it was because they were never asked. So, I asked them. When we got back to England, Roger Taylor came over to the studio and did some amazing drumming on a few tracks. John Deacon came and hung out for a while as well. One evening I said to Roger I had to leave to go and watch my brother John play with his band Accent at a small pub called The Airman. John was the drummer in the band. Roger said he'd come along, so later that evening we both walked into the pub and watched the band play. I'd just had three number 1 albums in a row so was extremely well known, and Roger was in a truly legendary, enormously successful band. The two of us walking through the door together caused quite a stir, to be honest. Roger was fantastic. He had a good chat with John and the band, made some encouraging comments about John's drumming, and then we left.

The other cool thing with Roger happened one night when we drove down to the local chip shop. He had a beautiful Aston Martin at the time. We pulled up directly in front of the shop, and as we walked in I noticed a man being refused entry to the nightclub next door. I knew the man. He was an old schoolmate, although we'd fallen out years before. I'd found him fumbling around on top of my former girlfriend, who until that moment I was still very much infatuated with, in a quiet corner of a car park. So, as he was being refused entry to some shitty little club, I was walking by, hugely famous and successful, with Roger Taylor from Queen. I fully accept how sad, pathetic and small-minded I was to feel a glowing wave of satisfaction because of that. But I did. I didn't say a word to him, just the slightest nod of recognition, but it made my day. A very quiet but supremely satisfying moment of revenge.

Chapter Eight

1981

By now I'd earned a small fortune. Millions. I'd never had money before, and as my dad had always looked after the family's affairs I knew nothing about it. In many ways, I was almost entirely unaware of its value. I'd done only a handful of small jobs since leaving school and then become famous and now wealthy. I was like a small child when it came to money. I'd bought a few toys, the plane for one, but mostly I'd been spending vast amounts on touring – losing vast amounts, I should say. The one sensible thing I did buy was my first house. It was on the Wentworth Golf Course estate in Virginia Water, Surrey, one of those areas we'd driven through when I was a kid looking at all the rich people's houses. Now I had one of my own. To begin with, I lived there with Garry Robson. I had one of the rooms upstairs and he had another. The house had no furniture and no carpet for a time. For quite a long time. The floor in my room, which I'd set up like a bedsit, was partially covered in flattened boxes. It also had a bed, a TV, a video player, a kettle and a deep-fat fryer. Everything I needed. In the corner was a built-in wardrobe and a phone and a clock beside the bed. For some reason I had no real interest in making it a comfortable home. I believed the house had a presence – I do of most houses, actually – and I felt strongly that my house didn't really want me moving around it after 10 p.m. After ten it felt different, like it wanted the place to itself. So, I would always make sure I was in my room by ten, and I wouldn't come out again until the morning. Garry Robson had a steady girlfriend, so I was often alone in the house. It didn't feel haunted, but it had something. It felt mischievous rather than spiteful, but I absolutely took notice of the feelings I got from it.

On one occasion, Garry came home from work with a sample disc of a new kind of drum machine. We'd barely got to the top of the stairs when we heard a young girl's voice call out gently, 'Gary.' I assumed it was a fan snuck over the gate somehow and ran back down the stairs. We'd left the front door open, but there was no one there. I looked outside, assumed she'd run off and went back up to listen to the drum demo. Again, 'Gary' came drifting up. This time I was a little annoyed, and a few seconds later I was back at the door, but still no sign of the whispering girl. Garry shot off in one direction, and I went the other, making our way around the outside of the house. We met at the back, no sign of her, ran back around to the front, still no sign. We searched everywhere, but there was no girl. It was odd. I couldn't see any way that she could have hidden or run out of view in just a few seconds. When we got back upstairs, we heard her once again, but this time we stayed right where we were. I don't believe there was a girl, and I didn't want to find out what was calling my name.

Another time, Garry was about to leave and saw the door latch turn itself to open the door. Up to then, all of the eerie things that had happened to me had been when I was with Garry, including seeing the man in the Underground at Piccadilly Circus. I'd thought that it took the two of us together for things to happen, but that turned out not to be true. After he moved out, things carried on happening. I came home from the studio late one night and the house was completely dark. I would always leave lights on, but I convinced myself I simply must have forgotten. The next day, when I left, I made sure I turned everything on. The house should have been lit up like a fairground when I got back that night. To my horror, as I drove up the short lane to my house after the session, it was once again completely dark. One night I was in bed watching TV when the light turned itself on and then back off again. I was terrified but didn't dare leave my room until the morning. I decided I wasn't going to go back and moved back in with my parents briefly. I thought my dad would make fun of me for being scared of my own house, but he was surprisingly understanding. I stayed a few days and then went back, in the daytime, to pick up a few things, and it felt completely different, just the way it used to. Even better, actually. I moved back in and lived there for several more years after that, and nothing strange ever happened again. I even bought some furniture and carpets.

After I'd made my decision to quit touring, I decided that my final show would be the most spectacular of all. We ended up booking not one but three nights at London's Wembley Arena, on 26, 27 and 28 April 1981. I wanted to say goodbye and thank you to the fans with the biggest show they'd ever seen. I was absolutely genuine about my decision to stop touring. I really did believe that it was the root of all my problems, and I still believe that getting out of it was a wise decision. But what I should have done was just backed away. Given it some time, done some growing up, waited to see how I felt in another year or two having not toured for a while. Making a big announcement that I was going to retire was stupid and child-ish. But I was still so young, and the overwhelming effects of a rapid onslaught of newfound fame were still raw and painful. I clearly needed a break, some time to truly absorb what had happened and to adjust to a very different life. So, a good deci-sion in so many ways, but done with a loud, damaging fanfare of an announcement it just didn't need. By saying I was retiring from touring, and so in many ways appearing to turn my back on everyone that had helped me get to the top, the fans espe-cially, I shot my career in both feet, and it would take nearly four decades to truly recover. Announcing my retirement from touring was a catastrophic mistake.

But life was weird and getting weirder all the time. I was receiving all kinds of threats, including death threats. One letter I received came with a live rifle bullet and a message that said, bizarrely, 'I was going to kill you at Wembley, but I was enjoy-ing myself so much I didn't bother.' My dad moved his car one day to find a petrol bomb underneath it. My mum was put under police protection for a while after they became aware of a plot to kidnap her, in exchange for a large ransom presumably. People threatened to beat me up, burn down my house, kill the dog, hurt my girlfriend. My brother was bullied so much we had to take him out of school. It's no wonder that I wanted to get away from all of that.

The three Wembley shows were indeed spectacular. I'm told it included the largest moving structure ever seen on a stage in the UK at that time. The set included a colossal, motorised semicircle of flashing lights that went from one side of the arena to the other. It had lifts coming up from below, multilevel stages, movement artists, a giant film screen and more. I used parts of the *Touring Principle* set, the *Teletour* set and then a vast range of new pieces all at the same time. It was magnificent, even if I say so myself. We added a number of sub-bass speakers to a large chamber under the floor of the venue so that every time the big synths came in the floor would shake. You literally felt the music as much as heard it. All three shows quickly sold out.

From the stage, the place looked vast. I looked out at a sea of faces disappearing into the distance and up into the heavens. Each night we played non-stop for two and a quarter hours, having rehearsed the music alone for two months beforehand. The light show we rehearsed at one of the big film stages at Shepperton, and we had to hire extra generators to supply the amount of electrical power the show needed.

The shows were emotional. In many ways, they were everything that was good about being a pop star. The adulation, the hysteria, the excitement. It was a truly incredible experience. I sang the words to 'Please Push No More', a song I'd written about leaving it all behind and why, long before I'd said I was even thinking about it. Even as I sang it, I realised I wasn't sure. When it was all over, the gear all packed and the trucks driven away, I walked back out on to the stage. I sat down and looked out at the vast empty arena, and I thought to myself, 'What have you done?'

It had all happened so quickly. It had been just a little over three years since that first single had come out, and it was already all over. Although I fully intended to throw myself into studio work and continue to make albums, something vital had gone. I've described what becoming famous was like for me many times over the years, in many ways. But imagine you're standing on the platform of a train station. You have your expected journey somewhat planned out. You think you know where you're going, roughly how you're going to get there and what to expect when you arrive. Then a shiny express train comes thundering through the station. It's not stopping and moving so fast it's a blur, but you put out your hand and make a grab for it. Miraculously, you manage to hang on, so you hurtle away from everything you've ever known in the blink of an eye. It's a fast, furious, dangerous ride, and, try as you might, you feel as though you are losing your grip almost immediately. It's not the journey you expected – it's frightening and loud, strange and uncomfortable. On this train you have absolutely no idea where you're going. You can see inside but through windows that seem to distort everything you see. You can't get in, though. Inside the distorted shapes look glamorous, luxurious, and the people seem serenely self-assured. They seem confident, successful, quite at home, as though they belong. You try as hard as you can, but, sooner rather than later, you lose your grip and fall heavily onto the ground. Dirty, torn and battered you stand up and watch the train disappear into the distance. It's dark, you have no idea where you are or which way to turn. A fog closes in and you lose sight of the tracks. You lose all sense of direction, so you begin to walk, somewhat aimlessly, slowly away. You are totally lost. That was how I felt the day after Wembley, and the next day and the day after that. In many ways, I remained lost for the next twelve years.

I was soon back in the studio putting the finishing touches to the next album, *Dance*. I also wrote two songs with Paul Gardiner called 'Stormtrooper in Drag' and 'Night Talk'. Paul's drug problem, which for a long time had been nothing to worry about, was now growing into something completely different. I discovered he was on heroin and had been for a while. Working with him was becoming increasingly problematic. He came to the studio one day, and, while he was playing, keeled forward and hit his head on the end of the console. He hit it so hard I thought he'd knocked himself out, but he was sleeping, or some drugged version of it. He was wedged in so tight we couldn't move him. Hours later he suddenly woke up and carried on playing as though he'd never stopped, even though there was no music playing. It was the strangest thing, and very worrying.

It was during the *Dance* sessions that I saw something else very strange. It was the early hours of the morning, and I was on my way home from the studio with my new girlfriend at the time. Things were very quiet, and we seemed to be the only car on the road. As our small road crossed over a motorway, I saw what I can only describe as a huge light coming out of the clouds, shaped like an upside-down pyramid, with the pointy end just touching the surface of the road. The cloud was low, and the light seemed to be coming through it from above. It was a perfect square shape, like the base of a pyramid, but only the edges. I stopped the car, got out, expecting to hear the noise of a helicopter, but there was nothing. No noise at all. I found that very unnerving and was about to get back into the car and drive off when the light vanished. But we'd watched it for a while, both before we stopped and after. It was definitely there, but I have no idea what it could have been.

In June, I went on a course to learn how to fly multi-engine aeroplanes, for what's known as a Group B rating, and passed on 3 July. I got the Group B in the minimum number of hours possible, so I was quite proud. A few days later, I bought another aeroplane. This one was a twin-engine eight-seater called a Piper Navajo. I had it painted in Telekon colours, all black but with some red lines down the side and up the tail. It even had the Numan face logo on the tail that Garry Robson had created way back when. I loved it. I thought it looked very striking. I even started a small air-taxi company called Numanair and had the plane re-registered as G-NMAN. I did harbour ambitions to see it develop into something bigger, but as a business it didn't really work out.

I bought more toys: a Ferrari 512 Boxer, a V8-engine speedboat, even a hovercraft. I went out in the boat with Rrussell once and nearly killed myself. I had no idea how to drive them properly. I thought you just went as fast as you could and hung on. At one point, I let Rrussell drive it and went forward to take some photos out of a hatch. We hit a particularly nasty wave, which nearly threw me out and over the side. It was only my ankles getting caught in the hatch that saved me. We put a crack in the hull and had to head back before it sank. Another time, I took the hovercraft to a beach and was giving a boy a ride when his dog mistook the tremendous noise of the machine as danger, thought the boy was being hurt and attacked us. I couldn't stop, and we hovered straight over him. I remember seeing the dog pop up the other side, completely unharmed, and run off. I was once pulled over in the Ferrari and clocked by the police at an average speed of 94 mph. I was lucky to keep my licence, because I was doing well over 150 at times. It was about 3 a.m., and the motorway was very quiet, but it was pretty reckless.

Because of the Ferrari I had a fairly heated discussion with Rick Parfitt from Status Quo about cars one evening, in particular the merits of Ferraris verses Porsches. We'd spent the day at Roger Taylor's house, the Queen drummer, and as we were leaving and walking to our cars the conversation turned to the pros and cons of each. Rick was particularly impressed by the huge wing on the back of his Porsche. Now, as luck would have it, I'd watched a documentary that very morning on that exact feature. It turned out that the wing's primary reason was not for grip, or handling improvements at all – it was for fuel consumption. When I pointed that out to him, that it was an economy measure, he was less than happy. So much so in fact that I thought for a minute he might punch me. Being green hadn't really become a thing back then.

At the end of July, I started a helicopter pilot's course. I found that it came naturally, and I went solo pretty quickly. In fact, apart from one other, I went solo quicker than any other student the club had ever had, or so I was told. I was extremely proud of that as well. I got my licence just three weeks later. The initial licence only allowed me to fly piston-engine helicopters, so I immediately did another course to convert onto the jet-engine Jetranger helicopter. I flew the Jetranger to an animal park in Southam, where we filmed the video for the next single, 'She Got Claws'. On the way back the next morning I became a little unsure of where I was so hovered next to a train station so I could read the name of the station. I knew where I was then.

The 'Claws' single came out at the end of August and reached number 6 in the charts. This was the first time I'd let people see the new style, something quite different to the black-clad images I'd had before, although not a million miles away from the grey-suited figure on *The Pleasure Principle* sleeve. This one was far more like the ghost I'd seen on the underground, but with make-up, scratches down my face and a gold-and-pearl brooch (that I'd bought for my Nan in Tokyo and borrowed back). I'd actually used him even before *The Pleasure Principle*. I put the grey man standing against the wall of the park as I was looking out of the window on the *Replicas* cover. Very weirdly that man isn't always there any more. I've signed lots of *Replicas* sleeves in recent years where you can barely see him, if at all, and others where he's clearly visible. I think it depends on when or where the sleeve was manufactured. Perhaps the original artwork is fading and the grey man is becoming harder to see. Strange that a picture of the ghost I saw is fading away. When my mum saw the grey man on *Replicas*, she found it quite unnerving. She told me she had seen him before in a recurring dream she'd had as a child.

The *Dance* album entered the charts at number 3 in September 1981. It was a very different animal to the things I'd done before, and I loved it. I thought I'd successfully changed shape and gone in a new direction, musically and visually. I had a new image, based on the underground ghost, and a definite change of style musically. I remember Martin Mills from Beggars Banquet sitting down and listening through it with me. At the end he said, 'I can't really hear a single.' I knew from that, and the conversation that followed, that he didn't think it was the album I should have made. I still love that album, but the sales made it clear the fans were not so keen. *Dance* sold 60,000 albums in the UK, less than half of what *Telekon* had done and far less than a quarter of the sales of *The Pleasure Principle* and *Replicas*. Where *Telekon* had been angry and full of paranoia, *Dance* was sad and haunting. In many ways, it was an open door into the way I was feeling at the time. Martin Mills was right: if I wanted to build momentum after *Telekon*, and especially after Wembley, *Dance* was definitely the wrong album. But as a songwriter, what can you do? You write songs based on how you feel, about your experiences, your fears, your hopes. Not every album is going to be the same or look at things the same way. That's arguably what makes an artist interesting, but I understand why it can also mean the end of them.

Around this time, I was blackmailed by a woman I'd been seeing. She wrote a particularly unpleasant article about what it was like to be with me, offered it to the papers and then said if I gave her more money, she wouldn't have it published. It was then that I realised why she'd been so difficult to be with. Why she was so loving one minute and so horrible the next, pushing my buttons at every turn to make me as erratic and volatile as possible. Luckily, someone at the label knew something about her brother, and it all just quietly went away. I was told, in no uncertain terms, not to ask any questions, just be glad it was over. It was a sobering learning experience. I'd become nothing more than an opportunity for some people, an unsavoury short cut to a bundle of cash. It was hurtful and demoralising and did nothing for my faith in the goodness of people. For a long time after that, I treated everyone with a great deal of suspicion.

My old band were keen to stay together after Wembley and formed a new band called Dramatis. I visited them in the studio while they were recording their debut album, and they played me a track called 'Love Needs No Disguise', a song about our time together. It was great, and they asked if I wanted to sing the vocal, which I was happy to do. We made a video for it, and it was released on 5 December on the Beggars label. It reached number 33 in the chart, which wasn't too bad. The album it came from, *For Future Reference*, came out soon after. I would have been more helpful in promoting it if I could, but I had a major project of my own under way at the time . . .

Nine

1981

I had always wanted to have an adventure. A real, tell the story to your grandchildren by the fireside type of adventure. Something that would test me in ways nothing else could. My entire life I had been protected. I went from being the son in a loving, caring family to a pop star. I hadn't done anything that required real courage. Even my success felt tarnished and diminished by the constant ridicule in the press. Despite everything I'd achieved in the charts, I didn't feel I'd done anything for my dad to be truly proud of, and that meant everything to me. I saw my dad as a 'man's man', and I felt I hadn't done anything 'manly'. I didn't drink, didn't fight, didn't seem to do many of the things other young men did. I had very little pride in my musical achievements – after all, all I'd really done was strut around on stage in make-up and a leather jumpsuit. I saw myself as lucky, not talented. I must point out this was nothing to do with anything my dad had ever said to me – far from it. This was all in my own head. But those long-felt but unspoken insecurities ran very deep. I decided I was going to fly around the world in a light aeroplane.

I'd seen a documentary on TV about a lady who had flown from England to Australia in a light aircraft. The man who had arranged that flight for her was the famous balloonist Julian

Knott, so I got in touch with him and asked if he would help with my trip. We met a few times, talked about what was required and he agreed to take on the planning for me. Initially I was going to make the trip with my former flying instructor Tim Steggles but it became obvious after a while that Tim wouldn't be able to spare the time to come with me.

A few weeks later, I struck up a conversation with a well-known air-display pilot called Bob Thompson in the Blackbushe-airfield restaurant and told him what I was planning to do. He listened for a while and then told me bluntly that, if we didn't already have the plane and all the visas and clearances in place, it wasn't going to happen. I assured him that Julian was on top of everything and had done this sort of thing before. Bob was right though. When I questioned Julian about progress, he admitted that he hadn't done anything. He hadn't thought I'd intended to go through with it. There was no aeroplane waiting to be adapted for the long distances, no airspace clearances and permissions in place, no ongoing maintenance arranged around the world, no hotels booked, nothing. I got back in touch with Bob Thompson and told him the terrible news. He just said, 'We'll do it.' I learned that he owned an airfreight company, so he and his team got to work arranging the visas and clearances at short notice. He was also ex-Royal Air Force, a jet pilot, a helicopter pilot, a leading aerobatic air-display pilot and he had years of valuable aviation experience. Bob would be the pilot who accompanied me around the world, and he agreed a rather lucrative deal with my dad. Because we were so close to the time we'd planned to leave, and needed to avoid the worst of the weather, everything was done in quite a rush. We had no time now to drum up any meaningful sponsorship, but I was absolutely committed to going ahead. If we couldn't get sponsorship, I'd pay for everything myself. It would end up costing me more than £180,000. I had only got my pilot's licence a year before, and even though I'd since qualified in multi-engine planes and helicopters, I still only had relatively few hours logged. In no way did I have the experience needed to be in charge of a flight so daring. Bob would be in charge, and in the time it took us to fly around the world I would learn more about flying than most private pilots would learn in a lifetime.

Bob and his team found a suitable plane, a Cessna 210 Centurion, a high-wing, six-seater, single-engine aeroplane. It was turbocharged, had de-icing, a retractable undercarriage, an oxygen system, good range capability, and excellent navigation and radio equipment. We would need more than that, though. For the sort of trip we were planning, we'd also need specialist gear. The rear four seats were removed and the space filled with extra fuel tanks. We also had extra-long-range fuel tanks fitted in the wings. To enable us to carry all that extra weight in fuel, we'd need to get rid of as many unnecessary items as possible to keep the weight down. So, we stripped out everything we could. Even the carpet was removed.

We planned to fly eastabout, so across Europe, into the Middle East, Asia and across the Pacific to North America. From there we'd route across the North Atlantic and back to the UK. It all sounded straightforward enough. We would wear parachutes at all times and use oxygen masks whenever we were above 10,000 feet. We also had an RAF-supplied life vest each that contained a variety of useful equipment, including a locator beacon, flares and shark repellent. We also had a life raft. Sorting out the red tape was harder than expected, and a number of dubious officials in some of the embassies only became helpful when sums of money were exchanged. I was actually shocked by that. It seemed the sort of thing you only saw in spy movies, and I had no idea that to travel in some parts of the world it was quite normal, although still highly illegal. Bob said we should also wear gold epaulets and masquerade as commercial pilots wherever possible, as it could make things easier for us in some countries.

We set off from Heathrow Airport on 18 September 1981. The plane actually let us down for the first time that morning as it was positioned into Heathrow. The undercarriage doors on the front wheel well closed before the nose wheel had retracted, which definitely wasn't supposed to happen. That bent a few things and so had to be fixed before we could leave. There was a lot more of that to come, unfortunately. The flights across Europe were long, and the small space, plus all the extra gear we were carrying (and wearing) made it cramped and uncomfortable. When we got to Switzerland, I looked down at the savage beauty of the mountains rising up towards us. It was frighteningly beautiful; I knew that, if we had any problems, we would have little chance of surviving a crash. I listened intently to the engine for hour after hour as the jagged peaks slipped slowly by below us. As we made our way towards the Greek islands, the sea crossings became longer and the focus of my nervousness switched from crashing into mountains to crashing into the sea. In a high-wing aeroplane like the Centurion, should you be forced to land on water, you have to wait for the cabin to fill up with water before you can open the doors. Until then the pressure of the water outside forcing the doors closed is too strong. It was not something I was keen to experience. When you are cruising along on long flights the autopilot is flying the plane so you have lots of idle time to sit back and worry. Which I did. A lot. After the first day or two you also run out of things to talk about beyond the immediate job in hand, so Bob and I soon had oceans of silence between us for much of the time.

We needed to fly as high as possible as the thinner air of high altitudes meant that the engine burnt less fuel. The higher you flew, the further you could go. From Athens we crossed the Mediterranean into Syria. The Syrian authorities were most adamant that they wanted us to fly at 21,000 feet. We were so heavy, and it was so hot, that we just couldn't keep the plane up there. We tried again and again but each time it would slow down and begin to sink. The best we could do was 19,000 feet. The Syrians were becoming increasingly angry and we were concerned that they might send the military up. With our parachutes, oxygen masks, military-spec life vests and fuel tanks filling the cabin, we did not look like a typical light aircraft. For a while it was a serious concern, especially when we lost radio contact with Syrian Air Traffic. Luckily an airliner flying way above us heard what was going on and relayed messages for us and we continued across the desert to the United Arab Emirates. I soon came to understand the difference between sitting at home by the fire talking keenly about having an adventure and actually having one. Real adventures are dangerous and scary, and you can actually die in any number of horrible ways; every day seemed to find a new way of scaring me shitless.

After reaching India, we planned to cross the Indian Ocean to Thailand under a major airway. That way we'd be able to stay in touch with the airliners high above us should anything go wrong. Still only halfway to our turning point, we flew into the most intense rainstorm I'd ever seen. A monsoon. I could barely see beyond the windscreen and couldn't even make out the tips of our short wings. Eventually, we flew out the other side and things seemed OK. We reached our turning point under the airway, turned right and headed out to sea on our way to Thailand. I'd read a lot about this particular ocean, and its shark-infested waters, and I'd been dreading this leg of the trip. Everything went well for about half an hour or so, but then the engine gave the tiniest cough. The calm 'What was that?' that came out of my mouth was a remarkable display of the finest acting. Inside I was screaming, FUCK, FUCK, FUCKITY FUCK!!!!! Then it got very much worse, very quickly. The lovely smooth, steady rumbling of the engine began to sound more like a bucket of bolts being tossed around. It sounded decidedly unhealthy, we were seventy miles out over a shark-infested ocean and it was the only engine we had. We figured that water from the monsoon had worked its way into the electrics and killed half of the ignition system. Luckily, plane engines are designed with two ignition systems, for safety, and can fly reasonably well with just one, but you need to get it down as soon as possible. We felt especially vulnerable, as there was no way of knowing if the other system would succumb to water damage as well. Within seconds, I had the dinghy clipped to my harness, straps were checked and I got as ready as I could for whatever was coming next.

We declared an emergency and slowly made our way back to India, across seventy miles of ocean, the engine spluttering every second of the way. With strong headwinds against us, it seemed to take for ever, and it was a most nerve-racking experience. The nearest available runway was at a semi-military airfield, a place called Visakhapatnam. As we came over the airfield, Bob calculated that we were still too heavy to land, but with the engine now running so badly we had no choice but to try it. The landing could have been a bit softer, to be honest, but the plane was undamaged, and we were both relieved to get out and set foot on dry land once again.

We waited for a long time, but no customs or immigration officials turned up, so the airport manager said we could go into town and find somewhere to stay. We needed to sort out repairs for one thing, so we might be stuck there for a while. After the taxi driver diverted to a fuel pump and insisted we pay to fill up his tank (which was a can under his seat), we eventually arrived at what was once perhaps, in its heyday, a horrible hotel. Now it could only be described as a shithole. It was, and I was soon to find out why, otherwise occupied by Russian families. My room had a very friendly lizard living in what I assumed to be the bathroom. Eating would be a problem, for me at least. The only thing vaguely edible for my limited diet were chips. The only drink was a Russian version of Coca-Cola, which tasted nothing like Coca-Cola, but I'd been told to avoid the water at all costs.

Customs and immigration officials eventually turned up and took us back to the airfield. They were very unhappy that we'd left before they'd arrived. We told them the airport manager had given us permission, so they began arguing with him about the rules and who had the right to do this and that. It was eventually decided that the immigration rule book was two years newer – 1949 compared to 1947, I think – so the authority was theirs. The airport manager was reprimanded and dismissed from his post, which seemed harsh. When I suggested that this was a strange way to resolve a dispute, I was blamed because I was English, and the English had given them the rules in the first place. I didn't really know how to answer that. It's funny now, but they were very aggressive, very shouty and in your face. Guns were conspicuously held at the ready, and it was all very intimidating. Our passports were taken away, and we were asked again and again why we were there. When I explained that I was a British pop star and I was flying around the world for an adventure, they asked to see my press cuttings, as though I took them with me everywhere I went.

They asked us why we had camera equipment. I explained we were making a documentary film about the trip when we returned to the UK. They ignored that and asked if we'd been photographing the Russian submarine base. What? 'What Russian submarine base?' I asked. 'The one twenty miles north of here,' he answered, which hardly made it seem like a closely guarded secret. It was all so incredibly mad, like a Keystone Cops film but for real. I was wearing two watches, one for local time and one for UTC (Coordinated Universal Time), which we used for flight planning. They thought that was suspicious. As if I'd fly all the way to India to smuggle a watch and spy on the Russians while I was at it. A cheap watch at that. It had cost me £2.99 from a Texaco garage. We hadn't seen any Russian base – presumably we'd been in the monsoon when we'd flown over it – and air traffic had cleared us to fly the route we'd taken. None of it made sense. We were 'unofficially' arrested, though, and taken back to the 'hotel'. We were allowed downstairs to eat, but we were not, under any circumstances, to leave. They told us that if we didn't cooperate, they'd take us to Customs House. They made it sound like the prison in the movie *Papillon*. I had no desire to be botty ravaged, so I was instantly the shining star of cooperation. When it had all begun, I must confess I was very English. I had a passport that effectively said that the full might of the British Empire would come crashing down on anyone interfering with one of her Majesty's subjects while overseas, and I actually believed it. I found out that was less than true when I was allowed to call the British Consulate in Delhi and spoke to a Mrs Fitzgerald. I explained the situation but instead of sending out the British Army to rescue me she said, 'You're too far away. I can't help you,' and put the phone down. For some reason, the call had routed via an exchange in St Paul's in London. Before I put the phone down, the operator at St Paul's quickly came on the line and asked me if there was anyone else I needed to speak to. That lady saved the day. She was able to put me through to my dad, who called the newspapers, who published the story, which forced the Foreign Office to get involved and things started to happen.

Before we were allowed to leave the Indian officials had one last go at proving we were spies. They asked if we'd taken photographs of the military plane parked not far from mine at the airport. The plane in question was a Britton Norman Islander, built on the Isle of Wight. I explained that I'd once been on a tour of the factory and watched them being built. More than that, Bob used to be a test pilot for the company and had almost certainly flown the very aeroplane they were pointing at and accusing us of spying on.

They gave up and the next day we were allowed to fly out on an internal Indian airline to Calcutta, leaving our damaged Cessna behind for now. Before our departure, they handed back our passports and asked if we'd be happy to write to their superiors, telling them what a good job they'd done. I lied and assured them we'd do exactly that. Sadly, they'd exposed and ruined every bit of film we'd taken of the trip so far, but they did give me back one unused roll of cine film. As we taxied out, I managed to sneak some footage of a soldier guarding my Cessna from my window seat.

We stopped off at a place called Hyderabad where I survived possibly the worst landing I've ever experienced that couldn't technically be classed as a crash. From there we continued to Calcutta where we were met by two men, a journalist and photographer from the *Daily Star* newspaper who were supposedly 'rescuing' us from our captors. At one point the *Daily Star* men said it was possible to go and say hello to Mother Teresa. We took a cab a short distance, got out and knocked on a plain door set within a long wall. A nun came to the door and I said, 'Could we see Mother Teresa, please?' Off she went and shortly after that Mother Teresa herself came to the door, said hello, shook our hands and drifted back inside. It was absolutely surreal.

I saw things in India I had never seen before. A level of poverty I was truly shocked by and totally unprepared for. Outside the hotel I got talking to a boy who explained that the old ladies begging with children hired the children from younger women. They made more money if they had a baby. He even said that some of them deliberately crippled themselves for the same reason. I could barely believe it. He was nineteen, seemed very together, and he explained how hard it was to escape the poverty you were born into. He told me that if he was ever able to save enough money to buy a rickshaw, he could earn enough to give his family a decent life, so I bought him one the next morning before we left. I have often wondered if his story was true. I hope so, and I hope the rickshaw brought him the life he expected.

We flew back to England on a British Airways 747, and I was invited to sit in the cockpit for much of the flight and talk about my recent experiences with the crew. I felt very guilty. I was changed by what I'd seen in India. I had no idea everyday life could be so brutal and unforgiving for so many people. My ignorance of the harsh realities of the world was shameful, but I was learning. When we arrived back, the press were very interested but some suggested it had all been a publicity stunt. I was very disappointed with that. This was a real adventure, with real dangers. I thought it would have earned me at least some respect, but it didn't seem like it had. I told them we were going back out as soon as possible.

The Cessna was fixed, and Bob flew it back to the UK with the engineer. While that was happening, I was overseeing the conversion of my Piper Navajo. By now it was October and the expected weather meant that we would need to fly westabout instead. We needed to get across the Atlantic before the really bad winter weather set in. The Navajo had two engines rather than the single of the Cessna, which, on the surface, seemed like a safer option. The truth is, though, for many of the flights the Navajo would have been too heavy to fly on just one engine should the other one fail, and you had twice as many parts so twice as much chance of one failing. It was swings and round-abouts, really. The cabin had all the passenger seats removed and two huge fuel tanks fitted. With another four tanks in the wings, the range of the plane was enormous, but it felt very much like a heavy, cumbersome, flying bomb to me. For it to fly with all that weight, everything had to run perfectly, especially in the early stages of the flight, and most especially during take-off.

On 25 October 1981 we set off on our second attempt. Filled to the brim with fuel, we climbed slowly away and headed north. I especially hated the take-offs, anxiously listening to every beat of the engines, knowing that the slightest hiccup would likely mean the end of it all, and us.

We stopped off in Iceland on our way across the North Atlantic and were driven out to see a local landmark by someone from the Icelandic record label. We never made it. Out in the wilderness somewhere our label friend got hopelessly lost. We ended up on a tiny road going who knows where, and then the car slid off the road into deep snow. We were not only lost, but stuck. I was amazed when he told us he had no shovels, no blankets, no equipment of any kind. I'd assumed that Icelandic people would carry all that sort of thing as a matter of routine. It's a harsh climate. We took it in turns using the car jack to try and dig out the wheels, although Bob and I seemed to do the most work. It was getting us nowhere, though, but fortunately, after several hours, another car came by and was able to pull us back onto the road. The driver said we were lucky, not many people used that road any more. It wasn't long before things were going wrong again, this time after we'd reached Greenland, a staggeringly beautiful but ferociously hostile place – an epic wilderness of ice, jagged mountains and unbelievable cold. We stayed overnight at a military base near Sondrestrom, where the next morning we found a small but worrying oil leak in the right engine. An engineer came out and tightened up a few things, and we took off once again. An hour later the leak started again, so, with oil pouring back along the side of the cowling, we turned and flew back to Sondrestrom. I must confess I was pretty uncomfortable flying over such hostile terrain with a poorly engine. The engineer came out for another look, did some more work and sent us on our way once again. It lasted longer this time, but after another two and a half hours or so the engine started leaking again. It was dark by now, and as I looked out of the window (the engine was just a few feet away, on my side) I could see flashes of flame as the oil, and whatever else might be leaking by now, touched the turbocharger shroud, which glowed red-hot and ignited. It was disconcerting to say the least. We decided to divert to a place called Frobisher Bay on Baffin Island, not too far from the Arctic Circle. I shared my time looking between the small fiery explosions going on beside me and the sinister dark of the bitterly cold sea below. In the moonlight, the icebergs seemed to have an eerie glow that faded away under the water. I found that somewhat unnerving.

We were in a difficult situation. We couldn't tell how much oil the engine was losing, but it looked bad. The flare-ups in the engine bay were constant and alarming. If it lost too much oil, the engine could seize and the propeller blades jam facing the airflow, creating a huge amount of drag that would likely make it impossible to stay airborne on the remaining engine. We could shut the engine down ahead of that and feather the propeller so the blades were side on to the airflow. In that configuration the plane would normally be able to struggle on with just the one engine still working. But we were so heavy that seemed very unlikely. Our only workable option at that point was just to keep going, watch the gauges for any signs that the engine was about to quit and be ready.

Happy baby. 1958. *(Author's collection)*

Two years old perhaps, with my favourite toy truck. 1960. *(Author's collection)*

It would appear that I was moody from the beginning. Weymouth. 1961. *(Author's collection)*

With my brother John and our 100cc go-kart. 1972. *(Author's collection)*

(above) 16 years old. 1974. *(Author's collection)*

(right) On my way to see Bowie at Wembley Arena. 1976. *(Author's collection)*

My first car, a Morris Marina Estate. 1976. *(Author's collection)*

Rehearsing for another terrifying, tiny gig. This was taken long before I found a way to deal with the nerves. 1977. *(Author's collection)*

A very early Tubeway Army gig. 1977.
(Author's collection)

In my bedroom, soon after 'That's Too Bad' was released. 1978. *(Author's collection)*

Just another
pop star. Sydney,
Australia. 1980.
*(Ultracolour Photography.
Darlinghurst. Australia)*

Rock City Studios,
Shepperton.
Recording the
Telekon album. 1980.
(Author's collection)

Telekon tour. 1980. *(Author's collection)*

Getting ready to fly around the world. Take 2. 1981. *(Glenn Rankine)*

Building the enormous Wembley set for rehearsals in the Shepperton film studio complex. 1981. *(Author's collection)*

Flying the Jetranger helicopter. Blackbushe. 1981. *(Author's collection)*

Glad to be alive. Plane crash. 29 January 1982.
(Author's collection)

The long climb back begins. *I, Assassin* tour.
USA. 1982. *(Author's collection)*

Fans surround the
aeroplane as I arrive
back in the UK
after my year out.
1983. *(Author's collection)*

Getting ready to fly in the T33 for the 'Warriors' promo video. I had no idea the ejector seats didn't work. 1984.
(Author's collection)

Gemma getting my autograph, many, many years before we got together. 1985.
(Author's collection)

Air display pilot. 1988.
(Author's collection)

(above) Flying the mighty Yak 11. 1992.
(John Dibbs/Author's collection)

(right) Upside down in my beloved Harvard. Alongside me in the other aircraft is my team-mate Norman Lees. Norman was tragically killed in a Spitfire accident sometime later. 1992. *(John Dibbs)*

With Tim Dorney (Republica), Saffron and Steve Malins. Over the years Saffron has helped me in so many ways and I am hugely grateful. Steve Malins has done so much to help my career over the years that it's hard to know where to start. I very much doubt I would still have a career without him. 1996. *(Gemma Webb/Author's collection)*

Having made that decision, we began to count down the miles to Frobisher. Then we had a second problem. The cabin heater failed and the temperature inside rapidly dropped to minus 58 degrees Celsius. With the autopilot looking after the flying, and already wearing survival suits, we wrapped ourselves in any extra layers we could find, including somehow sliding into sleeping bags, but the cold was horrendous. It was almost impossible to function, to even adjust a radio setting or tweak the autopilot. The plane just kept on going and it began to feel like my best friend. I talked to it regularly. Offered it sympathy for what it was going through, and encouragement to keep going: 'Not far now.' It was keeping us alive, and I was so incredibly grateful. As we approached Frobisher, there was a howling crosswind and swirling snow flurries making vision difficult, and the aeroplane was kicking and bucking around like an untamed horse, but Bob took the landing and, as usual, did a great job.

The engine was not looking good. Bolts holding one of the cylinders had sheared or twisted and you could move it up and down by hand. No wonder it was leaking. We were very lucky it had kept going for as long as it did. I flew out to Los Angeles where I met my dad who had flown in with the spare parts we needed. We both flew back to Frobisher and Dad decided to join our adventure for a while. I have to say, the people in Frobisher were hardy, tough individuals, but they couldn't have been kinder or more helpful. Thanks to them we were soon on our way again, Dad sitting on the fuel tanks in the cabin as we had no seat for him.

We then meandered across North America. For me it was not only a big adventure, I was also trying to promote the *Dance* album. As I wasn't touring, I thought my trip would be a good way to generate interest for the album, and that it might encourage people to see me in a new light. After all, what other pop star had ever flown his own light aircraft around the world, across deserts, mountains and oceans, to promote an album.

It would be a lie if I said Bob and I got on well throughout the trip. It seemed to me that, at times at least, he was fed up with the amount of media attention that I was getting at certain stops. He was very much the man in charge of the trip and had planned it meticulously. But that's what I'd paid him handsomely for, so it was swings and roundabouts to me. Bob was a fantastic pilot, and the trip would have failed many times if not for his skill and knowledge, but I wanted people to know that I wasn't just a passenger. Although Bob handled all the more demanding legs, I was doing much of the flying myself, and we were both facing exactly the same dangers. I knew that I was a relative newcomer to flying and had much to learn, but I felt that Bob often gave advice more to put me down than to be helpful. Looking back, though, it could simply be that I took it badly, as our relationship clearly struggled at times. There was a lot of stress, a lot of fear at times, and we were sat side by side in a tiny space dealing with those situations, day after day after day. It's not surprising, I guess, that we grated on each other at times.

In San Francisco, we had to instal several more fuel tanks to give us the range to cross the mighty Pacific Ocean. We now had so many tanks in the cabin that the only way to get from the door at the rear to the cockpit at the front was to squeeze along a very small gap on the right-hand side of the plane. It was so tight that we had a cable put in that we used to pull ourselves along, one at a time, lying on our sides. It took a minute or two to slowly inch our way along when the plane was parked on the ground. God knows how we would ever get out if we had an emergency and had to escape in a hurry. Fuel tanks were even added to the nose locker, to every nook and cranny we could find. We even had thirty gallons in cans stacked at the back so we could top up the cabin tanks if necessary. The Navajo would now be 27 per cent over its maximum design weight at take-off, and all of it highly inflammable aviation fuel. That would not have been acceptable to the British authorities, but I've always assumed that they were aware, and once we'd left Britain turned a blind eye. Without that extra fuel we'd never get across the Pacific.

We took off for Honolulu in Hawaii at night to make sure we arrived in the daytime. My mum, dad and brother John were there to see us off, and my mum often remarked afterwards how the sound of the engines fading slowly away sounded small and lonely, and how the ocean looked vast and menacing. It looked pretty menacing from where I was as well. At one point, we both fell asleep, and when we woke up realised the plane had flown for a good hundred miles with neither of us watching it. We were almost exactly halfway to Hawaii, flying just above the clouds at 12,000 feet, when both engines stopped. No spluttering, no cough, they just stopped. One second I'd been dreamily looking up at the beautiful starlit night sky, thinking about how small and insignificant we were in our small machine, the next I was laser-focused on this new drama. We'd flown roughly 1,200 miles and had about the same still to go, and there was absolutely nothing but deep ocean the entire way.

We tried different fuel tanks, turned on pumps, pushed and pulled anything and everything we could think of, but nothing worked. The aeroplane sank down into the clouds below us and almost immediately we were enveloped in utter darkness. So far from land, with no ambient light of any kind and with the starlight now lost above, the only light came from our flashing beacon outside and the glow of the dials. I'd never known such impenetrable dark. The aeroplane was still controllable, but it was going down, and there was nothing we could do to stop it. My two biggest fears are deep water, especially at night, and sharks, so this was my worst nightmare come to life. The eerie quiet as the plane descended, with just the noise of the air going by and the whirring gyros in the cockpit, was unsettling. Bob said later he'd expected me to panic, but it was quite the opposite. I was strangely calm. I accepted immediately the dire reality of the situation, and my mind, instead of crumbling, began to work through my options. Our rate of descent meant we had about fifteen minutes or so before we hit the sea, so we had plenty of time to think about what waited for us. That we were going to crash into the middle of the Pacific, at night, seemed absolutely certain, so I started to plan how best to prepare for it. To have even the slightest chance of surviving a water landing we would need to see it coming. But the landing light was on the nosewheel, and we couldn't extend that, as landing on water with the wheels down wouldn't work. So, surviving the crash seemed highly unlikely. If by some miracle we did, we would need to get out quickly before it sank. The chances of even one of us crawling along that tiny gap to the rear door before it disappeared beneath the waves was remote; the chances of both of us doing so seemed impossible. I reasoned that if I survived the crash and managed to get to the door first, before the plane sank, I would almost certainly be hurt and bleeding. Getting the dinghy inflated quickly would be vital. Bobbing around in the ocean in my life jacket, in the dark, waiting for the sharks, was too horrific to contemplate.

We said very little. Bob whistled a tune I didn't recognise; I hummed quietly to myself. The altimeter wound itself inexorably downwards, and there was nothing more to do but wait for the end to come. As we passed 2,000 feet, I estimated we had about two and a half minutes at most left in the air. I accepted that this was probably the end and yet still clung to the tiniest thread of hope that somehow I'd get through it.

I was peering forward, trying to catch a glimpse of the waves when, without the slightest hiccup, both engines roared back into life. For some reason I no longer remember, Bob had decided not to feather them, so the props carried on spinning all the way down. He also left the electrics and fuel on, so they simply restarted by themselves. Up came the nose, and the Navajo climbed back into the sky once again. A few minutes later, we broke through the cloud, drifted back up to 12,000 feet and carried on. The relief was immense, and I was euphoric, but thirty minutes later it happened again.

The second time was worse. Before I'd just accepted it and made myself busy, thinking through my options, which kept my fears at bay. The second time I found it harder to accept, and my nerves were raw and edgy as we plummeted down once again. I felt more scared and less prepared, but there was nothing to do but wait. For the second time, as we got close to the waves the engines roared into life. This time, though, as we climbed back up, Bob figured out what was happening. We had a small, unheated pipe for the nose tanks feeding airflow into them to create pressure, and that pipe was freezing over as we skimmed through the top of the cloud layer at 12,000 feet. This was causing a lock that prevented the fuel from flowing. As we descended into warmer air, the ice slowly melted, and the fuel was able to flow again. We were just incredibly lucky that it melted before we hit the sea. We continued at a lower, warmer altitude, below the cloud, and seven hours later landed in Hawaii.

Each day we flew, with only occasional breaks when the plane needed to be serviced. We would often spend fifteen hours at a time in the tiny cockpit, over thousands of miles of ocean. Through the Marshall Islands, Guam and on to Japan. The problems kept on coming, and so did the lucky escapes. Waiting to take off from Tokyo, we had a problem with our clearance and had to return to the parking area where we discovered that an oil filter had been incorrectly fitted by local maintenance. If we'd taken off then we'd have gone down for sure. We flew south past the Philippines, who wouldn't let us land, and into Papua New Guinea, and then on to Brisbane, Australia, where we got into some serious trouble. Nothing mechanical, we inadvertently broke a rule about being sprayed with bug killer before opening the door. As we taxied in, having just flown from London to Australia, quite an epic moment I thought, I opened the top half of the rear door and filmed us motoring slowly past the terminal. That was a big mistake. Apparently we were supposed to wait in the plane whilst the bug spray was handed to us through a small window at the front. Only after we'd sprayed the inside of the plane could we open a door and get out. Neither of us had any idea that such a rule existed. We were marched off and had to endure a very worrying few hours while our fate was decided. It really did seem to be a big deal. All the media interviews I had waiting were abandoned. The authorities all but ransacked the aeroplane, even going up behind the control panels and moving wires this way and that, looking for what I have no idea. As we still had half the world to travel I was very concerned about what damage they might be doing to the equipment. It seemed massively over the top but there was nothing we could do other than sit quietly and wait. Eventually we were told that we could go on our way once we'd each written a letter apologising for rule breaking. I hadn't expected a ticker-tape parade, but I did think making it all the way to Australia was quite a feat. I expected at least a friendly conversation about it.

We flew on the next day, taking a clockwise route that would eventually bring us all the way around South Australia, up the West Coast to Port Headland. On the way I had to go to the back to be sick. I actually fell headfirst into our little portable toilet and then found I was paralysed and couldn't get out. A doctor in Perth came out to the aeroplane, gave me some Valium and said it was an anxiety attack brought on by a childhood memory, which made absolutely no sense to me whatsoever. I think I just hyperventilated.

As we were leaving Port Headland for Indonesia the left engine cut out as we turned on to the runway. Bob suspected it was just the heat of the day, restarted it and we took off. I found that pretty unnerving, though, as we then had to cross the Timor Sea, which I'd been told was the most shark-infested sea in the world.

Arriving in Jakarta, air traffic navigated us towards the wrong airport initially, and straight towards a huge lightning storm, as terrifying as it was impressive from the air. When we did land the authorities were unfriendly and aggressive and I took a general dislike to the place. From there we flew to Singapore, where I had to judge a Gary Numan lookalike competition where no one looked like me at all. Then it was on to Bangkok where I gave a press conference in full make-up, gangster-style, and then on to Calcutta.

After my last experience in India I wasn't looking forward to returning one bit. As soon as we arrived a rickety old fuel truck came up, put the nozzle into our left-wing tank and began to pump aviation fuel. The operator put too much pressure through the hose, the nozzle flew off the end and the hose then started snaking around through the air, spewing out gallons of highly flammable fuel all over the hot engines, and me. Apart from that, though, this visit to India was much better. The next day we flew to Karachi, Pakistan. It was during our approach to Karachi that the problem in the right engine reappeared, oil once again streaming down the side of the cowling. Just as before, bolts had sheared and twisted and so I took the first available commercial plane back to England, drove to the airfield where I met my dad and picked up some spares. We then drove back to Heathrow, got on the same jet and flew back to Pakistan. I'd been in England just a few hours. It took a couple of days to fix but as soon as it was done Dad flew back to the UK and Bob and I took the Navajo to Dubai where the starter motor on the left engine failed. We got it bodged enough to get out of Dubai and into Rhodes in the Greek islands where the starter failed completely. I called my dad less than three hours after he'd arrived back in England. He drove down to the airfield yet again, picked up a new starter and flew out once more to save the day. When he arrived he looked absolutely shattered. We decided that as we were nearly home he should stay with us for the last few legs back to England.

We flew to Rome, refuelled and took off again. The French air traffic controllers, unsurprisingly, were on strike, so we had to route around France rather than over it, which added a lot of time to the final leg. At 9 p.m. on Christmas Eve 1981, after more close scrapes and brushes with the authorities along the way, we landed back at Heathrow, and our adventure was over. No press, no interest, no welcome, just an unfriendly customs man who kept us there until gone midnight. Merry Christmas. To add insult to injury, Kodak lost the forty rolls of film I'd taken in to be developed. We ended up with virtually no record of the trip whatsoever. It was bitterly disappointing but at the time I was just glad to be back. The next night we had our usual family Christmas gathering of aunts, uncles, grandparents and cousins, and it was the most surreal feeling. For the last few months, I'd spent almost every day anxious, strapped into a machine high over oceans, deserts and mountains, often battling through bad weather or nursing some mechanical problem. Now, I was sat by a cosy fire with family, and I found it extremely hard to adjust. Being home felt unreal.

For a while I was changed. It's not every day you think you're going to crash into the ocean and be eaten by sharks, or you skirt the tail of a hurricane in an overloaded and wallowing aeroplane. Eventually, though, you slide back into the familiar. Problems that seemed inconsequential in the air become part of your everyday life again. It did change the way I felt about myself, though, which was very important to me. I was scared constantly, so I'm certainly no hero, but I didn't give up. I learned that courage comes in many forms, and I had done more than enough to now feel at ease with myself. Without Bob, the trip would never have happened, so the credit for its ultimate success is his entirely. I was a part of it, though. I was there for every second, lived through every terrifying moment. I think I grew up more in those few months than I had in the previous twenty-three years. It gave me pride in myself, sadly lacking before, and of course it gave me a wealth of new experiences and emotions to draw on as a songwriter.

Chapter Ten

1982

Just a few weeks later, on 29 January, I was flying back from Cannes with a friend, my old flying instructor, in charge. Despite my round-the-world-flight exploits, I still liked to fly with experienced people for longer trips, as I learned so much from them. Back in the Cessna Centurion once again, now fully repaired, I'd been to the Midem music festival in the south of France. I was in the front with my former instructor, and my dad and our friend Bill Fowler from WEA, the record label, were in the second row.

As we flew back across France, a small problem that had become apparent on the way out, and which my instructor said he would arrange to have fixed and didn't, began to get worse. I was beginning to doubt his judgement, and I decided to change course slightly. As we crossed the French coast and headed out over the Channel, instead of flying directly towards our destination, which would have meant a long stint over the sea, I decided to go the shortest way across and so spend the smallest amount of time over the water as possible. This caused something of an argument, but it was my aeroplane. I'd had a growing feeling of unease as the flight had progressed, and the arguments he was making made little sense to me. If we lost the engine and came down in the sea, we would have been lucky to get all four of us out before it sank, and luckier still to survive in the bitterly cold sea for more than a few minutes.

I made the right decision. Just a few minutes after we crossed the English coast and were once again over land, the engine quit. At that point, I have to say, he was flying and did an amazing job of finding a field to put down in. Unfortunately, the problem with the plane meant we had no electrics so couldn't lower the flaps to help slow us down, or the wheels to land on. I leant down and frantically hand-pumped the wheels down as he guided us towards the field, and as I felt the lock clunk into place I looked over my shoulder and saw a tree go by the window above us. I sat up just as we made contact with the ground. The aeroplane hit hard and took off again, so fast were we going, and floated for quite some way before touching down again. It was clear we weren't going to stop before we ran out of field in the direction we were heading. Without a word between us we both simultaneously pushed on the right rudder and tried to turn the plane across the field. If we had made that turn, I'm positive we could have stopped it in time. Sadly, the left undercarriage leg collapsed, the plane went down on to its belly and from then on we were just along for the ride.

Like before, when I was going down over the Pacific in the Navajo, I seemed to become disconnected. As the high embankment at the end of the field came towards us, and it was clear that we were going to drill straight into it at some speed, I was completely calm and strangely inquisitive about what was going to happen. I remember seeing blades of grass go by in the slowest of slow motion. I saw dust particles floating gently through the air. I remember wondering where the pain would come first. I thought to myself, it will be my feet, and I instinctively pulled them back from the rudder pedals, as though that would somehow help. I was actually fascinated by the experience, as though it was happening to someone else. It was the strangest feeling. The only time I can remember real fear was when I noticed a small house on the other side of the embankment. The thought that we might smash through their house and hurt innocent people was truly horrific. That brought the reality of the situation crashing back.

As we reached the embankment, we both pulled back on the control column in a last desperate attempt to minimise the impact, and it worked. Instead of ploughing straight into the embankment, the plane hit it and ricocheted steeply upwards. The right wing sliced into a telegraph pole, which swung the plane ninety degrees to the right and killed all the speed. It then fell ten feet or so into the middle of a small road that made its way past the field. I shouted to everyone to run for it. I ran, my friend ran, my dad ran, and then I noticed that Bill hadn't run. He was still sitting in the plane. I ran back to get him, and he seemed pretty dazed. Bill was quite a big man, so it was with some difficulty that I was able to help him out.

A lady tried to drive under the wing to get by. When I said not to as it might explode, she grumbled about needing to get home to cook her husband's dinner, turned around and drove off. It was as though planes crashed in front of her all the time, a daily nuisance. She didn't even ask if we were OK. The next person I met asked for my autograph! The emergency services arrived and so did customs. I had to officially reimport the aeroplane back into the UK while it was still a wreck in the road. A news crew turned up and, still in a state of shock, I was driven away to a local TV station. Within an hour of the accident, I was talking about it on live TV. I have no idea what I said, but I doubt it made much sense. I have a feeling I was chatting away like an excited child on speed. After the accident, I slept for about sixteen hours a day for at least a week.

The press were kind initially but from the very beginning got it all wrong. They said I was flying for a start, which I wasn't, and that we'd skilfully avoided a school, which was a complete lie. Then it became nasty. They said we'd landed on a motorway, narrowly avoiding two petrol tankers, and it got progressively more stupid from then on. They made a mockery of me. They said I was dangerous and should have my pilot's licence taken away. My flying skills became the butt of every joke on TV, radio and in the press. Even the aviation community got in on it. I had to suffer behind-my-back sniggers, sarcasm, ridicule and finger pointing every time I flew anywhere, and it went on for years. I explained a thousand times that I wasn't the pilot, and it wasn't his fault anyway. The plane had a design flaw in the fuel routing, something that would eventually end up in a huge court case in the USA when someone crashed and died because of it. No one cared. Blaming me provided a much better headline, so it stuck. It took away so much of what I thought I'd achieved by flying around the world.

I had my first hair transplant in January '82. My hair had been getting thinner for a while, and I wanted to do something about it. I had no intention of keeping it a secret. I'd seen too many people get ridiculed for things like that by trying to keep it under wraps, so I decided I'd just own up to it straight away and take what came. I certainly saw no shame in it, but I also saw no point in making a big deal of it either. The company that did it asked if they could use me in their advertising afterwards, which was OK with me. The operations are harsh, and a little gory in the detail, but they seem to work well enough. I've had four now in total, but the last was many years ago. I was working on the next album, *I, Assassin*, when I had it done the first time. I remember going back to the studio and my face was so swollen that Pino Palladino, the bass player on *I, Assassin*, went out to the office and asked who I was and why I was in the studio.

Pino was, and still is, an extraordinary player with a unique style. After listening to him play on some of the *I, Assassin* songs, I decided to make the bass a lead melody instrument instead of just underpinning the grooves, which is the way it is usually employed. It gave the album a very different sound and feel to anything I'd done before, and I was massively proud of it. By mid '82, it had already been two years since I'd decided to retire from touring. Although I'd played Wembley in '81, the reasons for it, the thinking behind that decision, were now two years old. In that time, I'd flown around the world and been in a plane crash. I was a very different person to the battered and shell-shocked man of 1980, and the idea of touring again started to make sense. I'd had the break I needed. I'd begun to put some of the pieces into place, to understand how it all worked. I still had a huge amount to learn and to experience, of course, but I felt I was now better equipped to deal with it.

For the album sleeve, I returned once again to the ghost I'd seen on the Underground. This time I dressed as an alternate version of him, standing outside on the street under a lamp post. It was in a photographer's studio, actually, but looked pretty real, the long grey coat, grey suit, hat, all reminiscent of what I'd seen going on the Piccadilly Circus escalator.

Lyrically, *I, Assassin* also moved on a little from the previous albums. The paranoia was largely gone, and I found, at times, a lighter way of seeing things. I felt more prepared for what was to come, more complete as a person. I'd had so many major experiences in the previous year or so, and I'd also been arrested twice. On 9 March, the day after my twenty-fourth birthday, I appeared in Uxbridge Magistrates Court charged with carrying an offensive weapon. The previous summer I'd been having a bad day. I'd been forced off the road in my car by an idiot, and I'd had skinheads give me a hard time at the airfield, where I thought I was going to get beaten up again. Later that day, a group of lads in several cars tried to box me in and make me stop, which was quite scary. It was just a day filled with nonsense like that, and I decided to give up on it, go a to a roadside burger van I knew and then go home. My girlfriend Michelle and I went to this particular van often, and had got to know the people who owned it. I had a small rounders bat in the car and took it with me for no reason other than wanting something to fiddle with while I waited. You could often wait quite some time.

We'd been there a while when a group of lads came along, one with a big stick, and a passing police car pulled over to talk to them. The lady officer got out, talked to them briefly and allowed them to move on. She then pulled away, drove past the van and parked in the lay-by in front of my car. I watched her get out and walk back to the van, assuming she also wanted a burger, but then she pointed at me and beckoned me over. I thought nothing of it other than it was a slightly rude way to ask for an autograph, which is what I thought she wanted. But she then started to ask me about my little rounders bat. Why was I carrying a weapon? A weapon? I told a small lie that I'd been playing with a ball and lost it, so she asked me to go and find it. It all seemed so unnecessary, and, coming at the end of what had been a horrible day, I was finding it hard not to get annoyed. I said no to the search, and she said she didn't like my attitude. I pointed out that the Ferrari we were standing next to, with the GN4 licence plate, was mine, and did she honestly think I was going to mug my friends' hamburger van and run off unnoticed with his takings in a Ferrari? She said, 'If you don't calm down, I'll arrest you.' Now, I was agitated but certainly not shouting or being aggressive in anyway, so I didn't need to calm down. It was an odd thing to say in a situation that was still relatively composed, so I said, 'Do it then,' or something like that, and she did. I was arrested. I wasn't allowed to drive my car to the police station, so I had to wait for another police car to take us. I told them not to move the Ferrari, I'd get someone out to move it for me, but they did anyway. It took them thirty minutes to drive it the two miles, so they clearly went for a joyride.

At the station, they took my fingerprints, I had my mugshots taken and I signed autographs for what seemed like everyone in the building. It was dark by now, and my girlfriend, still dressed in skimpy summer clothes, asked to use the phone, but they wouldn't let her. She was made to go outside in an area she didn't know, a young girl on her own, dressed as she was, to find a phone box to call my dad and let him know to come and pick us up. Of all the unfortunate and unnecessary things they did, I thought that was the worst.

On the day of my first scheduled court appearance, my lawyer called and said he'd applied for a postponement and told me not to go. I went to the studio instead and carried on with the *I, Assassin* sessions. Apparently, though, the postponement wasn't granted, and I should have been there. My lawyer explained to the court that the fault was his, but the prosecution still said I had 'shown a cavalier attitude towards British justice' and another warrant was put out for my arrest. I had to drive from the studio to the same police station, where, standing in the car park, I was officially arrested once again, this time for absconding from bail.

When the court case did happen, I was very nervous, but I was genuinely shocked when the policewoman who'd arrested me stood up and lied a number of times. According to her, I'd said, 'Go on copper, nick me if you dare,' when she'd advised me she was thinking about arresting me, which was a total lie. She said I was hiding the bat up my sleeve in a suspicious manner, even though I was wearing a short-sleeved T-shirt on the day, which made that impossible. She even got the colour of my car wrong. Another policeman stood up and denied that anyone at the station knew who I was and that no one there had asked for my autograph. They also denied they hadn't let my girlfriend make a phone call. Another officer claimed that he'd been at the burger van the week before buying a hot dog, and it was waist-high in nettles, so I couldn't have been playing with a ball. It wasn't, and the van didn't sell hot dogs, so that was all a lie as well. What really surprised me is that three police officers all stood up and lied but hadn't got their stories together. Their lies contradicted not just my account, but each others'. I just couldn't understand why they would do it. Why would you go to all the trouble of going to court to lie about somebody who genuinely hadn't done anything wrong? It rocked my faith in the honesty and integrity of the police. I'd been a huge supporter of them and had always trusted the honesty of their accounts when I'd read about various incidents in the news, naively perhaps, but I had. I have no doubt their contradictory lies actually helped me, and the case against me was dismissed. I was advised to pay my own costs as a gesture of goodwill, but mainly to avoid getting picked on by the police in the future. That came as a shock as well.

The 'Music for Chameleons' single, the first from *I, Assassin*, came out a few days before my court appearance on 6 March. We were able to get two *Top of the Pops* appearances for it, which helped it get into the UK Top 20. One of the reasons I'd been so nervous about the court case going against me was that I was soon to leave for America and being found guilty of an offensive-weapon charge, even a small bat, would have made that impossible. Those police lies could have had a disastrous impact on my life and career. I needed to go to America, as I'd planned to start touring again to support the *I, Assassin* album, but only to play one modest-sized tour in the USA. Not only that, I had a hefty tax bill to pay, and I'd run out of money, so I needed to leave the UK and stay out for a year.

I left for America in April. When we arrived at Heathrow, we were mobbed by fans and the police had to hide us in a storeroom in the terminal. It was chaotic but actually very exciting. I hadn't expected anything like that, and it was a fantastic send-off. I moved to Los Angeles for a while and, still with my girlfriend Michelle, settled into an apartment on Horn Avenue, just off Sunset Boulevard. I bought a Jeep and a gun (I thought everyone in California had a gun, not true at all), and spent a lot of time at theme parks, Magic Mountain especially. To avoid getting into trouble with US tax officials, I also had to move to Vancouver for about six weeks. Back in the USA once again, I had to fly to New York to film a slot for *Top of the Pops* for the latest single 'We Take Mystery (to Bed)'. The band and I sat in the back of an open-top Chevrolet and were filmed driving around the streets of New York. We saw a lady get mugged as we were driving along. A man grabbed her necklace and ran off into the throng of people. It was over in seconds.

While I was away in New York filming the *Top Of The Pops* film for 'We Take Mystery' I offered my Horn Avenue apartment to another man working for a different British TV company. They were due to film with me when I got back to Los Angeles and he was there early to do some location research. He arrived at the airport, took a cab straight to the apartment, dropped his bags and went out to the nearest bar to get a drink. Apparently he'd barely had a sip when someone walked into the bar, approached a man sitting at a table in the corner, pulled out a gun, shot the poor man in the face, and walked calmly out again.

I had a few of my own much smaller adventures while I was there. I came out to our Jeep one morning to find the rear speakers had been stolen, although the nuts, bolts and clipped wires had been left all very neatly arranged. I was actually grateful they hadn't done any damage. I also felt lucky in that the man who parked his car in the next bay to mine had been help up at gunpoint as he got out of his car only a few days before

The new band arrived in LA a few weeks before the *I Assassin* North American tour was due to start and I'd rented a beautiful house high up in the Hollywood Hills for them to stay in. They each had their own room, it had a swimming pool and amazing views of the Hollywood area. We only rehearsed for a few hours a day as I had so many other things to do to promote the tour and album so they had plenty of free time every day. I'd even bought a big car for them to use as they had so much down time. All I asked was that they paid for any fuel they used, which would have been about $1 a gallon at that time, shared amongst five of them, so roughly 20 cents each. That, apparently, was asking too much and they staged a revolt. So the free car, three hours work a day, wages, per diems and a beautiful house with a pool high up in the hills wasn't enough. I was so angry I could have fired them all right then and there but, with the tour only a week or so away, I had no choice but to swallow it. It would be the one and only time that line up would ever tour with me though.

Another time I was driving down from the band house late at night, heading back to my apartment, when a woman came running out of a house and waved me down. She was shouting that her friend was inside and the men in there wouldn't let her leave. Unbelievably she seemed to expect me to go in and sort it out somehow. I suspected the men inside were more likely refusing to pay the ladies for their services and I certainly wasn't going to butt into that. I called the police instead.

A few days before the tour was due to start I got a knock on the door of the apartment one evening to hear news that one of the other residents had lost her pet snake on the ventilation system. A large boa constrictor apparently. I never did see the snake but knowing it was loose in the building made it difficult to sleep at night. I did my best to stay awake for the next few days, sitting in an armchair and staring at the ventilation grill in our room, until it was found. I was terrified.

I viewed the *I, Assassin* North American tour as a kind of test. If it went well, and more importantly if I enjoyed it, it would open the door to touring again on a more regular basis. If not, well then I'd go back to the original plan of staying away from touring. It did go well. The attendance numbers were down compared to what I'd done before in North America, but even that didn't bother me. I felt more confident, more capable of handling crowds, large or small, a little more at ease. I just felt very different to the way I had before, and it was fun. We still had our share of incidents, though. To keep costs down we'd decided to use two RVs (camper vans) instead of a tour bus. In the early stages of the tour, the band RV caught fire and, thanks to the fire extinguisher I'd packed, to much ridicule from the band, and my dad being incredibly brave, we managed to save it. But it wasn't going any further, so we eventually had to abandon that idea and go with a tour bus after all. We had to evacuate another hotel when the fire alarm went off. At one stage, Chris Slade, the drummer on the tour, got a bit drunk and played things I didn't want. When I spoke to him about it afterwards, he pushed me all the way down the bus into my dad, who pushed him all the way back again. It was just like being back at school. The last show was in Chicago, and the next morning we came down to the hotel reception, expecting to find our transport to the airport waiting for us. Instead, we discovered that the tour manager and his girlfriend had run off with all the money. So, we had no money and no tickets. We did have one credit card between us, which was enough to save the day.

Despite all the mayhem, I'd really enjoyed the tour. I began to see touring as an essential experience, something to look forward to. After the tour, I returned to Jersey in the Channel Islands, where I would stay for the remainder of my tax exile year out. I flew from New York to Paris. It was a very cool moment for me to look out of the window as we pulled on to the stand and see my own aeroplane, the black Navajo, parked right next to us, with Michelle waiting. I got off the 747, collected my case, walked across to my own plane and flew to Jersey. I'd never felt so flash. On the flight from New York I'd sat close to the Reverend Jesse Jackson – we were both back in economy – and he asked if I'd seen the light. I eventually convinced him that I was not to be saved. After Los Angeles and the tour, Jersey seemed quite dull at first, but I grew quite fond of it after a while. I spent much of my time taking different flying courses and got my night rating, IMC rating and an aerobatic certificate. I also learned how to fly tailwheel aeroplanes, a technique quite different to the nosewheel planes I was used to. I had the Ferrari brought over for a while but the island had a maximum speed limit of 40 mph which meant the car rarely got out of first gear. It was vandalised as well so I sent it back. I kept the Navajo there though and would give rides to my new Jersey friends. I wrote most of the next album, *Warriors*, while I was there. One of the songs, 'My Centurion', came from my experiences leading up to the plane crash. It talked about that sixth sense you sometimes have in a machine when you feel something's wrong long before it happens.

After a while, Michelle got bored and, the day after my twenty-fifth birthday, went back to England. I thought that was pretty shitty. Before she left, we were staying in a couple of rented rooms that were part of a larger house, and it was there I did the bulk of the writing. The lady who ran it was odd, in a number of ways, and would let her children come into our section to look at us, occasionally at the most inappropriate times. She eventually saw my synth set-up, which was actually very modest, and claimed I was using too much electricity and threw us out, so I moved into a hotel near the airport.

Not long after Michelle left and went back to England I called her up for a chat and the phone was answered by her sister, who assumed was a different man. It was at that moment I realised that Michelle had moved on in more ways than one, and we were over. I was surprised, and yet not in a way. A week or so later some of the band came over and we went out a few times. It was good to have some company for a while. I also met a girl that I started to hang out with for the weeks that I had left in Jersey. One day we arrived back at the hotel to find a gaggle of Radio One DJ's in the foyer, one of them being Jimmy Saville. Apparently there was a Radio One roadshow that weekend on the island. This was long before the truth about Saville was discovered and made public. All I knew then was he had a very creepy interest in the girl I was with and came across as seriously slimy.

I also remember that hotel having the most determined housekeepers. Day after day, despite putting a Do Not Disturb sign on my door, they would just walk into the room and start cleaning it. Even if I was still in bed sleeping. They didn't seem to care at all. On one occasion, after getting back late the night before and hoping for a lie in, I actually barricaded the door with suitcases and a chair. Even that didn't stop them. I was woken up by the sound of the door being repeatedly banged into. I sat up, bleary eyed and disheveled, and watched the suitcases and chair being pushed back as each bang on the door opened it a little further. Having made enough space in she came, ignored me completely, plugged in her vacuum cleaner and got to work. It was as though I was invisible.

After *I, Assassin*, I had a pretty difficult time with WEA, who I now talked to more than Beggars Banquet regarding releases and marketing strategy. Although it had two Top 20 singles with 'Music for Chameleons' and 'White Boys and Heroes', and a Top 10 with 'We Take Mystery (to Bed)', the album hadn't done too well, and they were not happy. They insisted that I start using a producer on the next album to add a more commercial element to the music, but I was far from keen. Working with producers meant debate and compromise, and I didn't like either of those. I'd had a meeting with them after *Dance* came out in '81, and they'd said to me then they were content with the sales I was achieving. Not in a way that said they were happy, more in a way that said they weren't going to invest in promoting me any more. They felt the albums could sell those numbers without them doing much. I was very upset with that attitude, and I'd hoped that *I, Assassin* would do better and give them a reason to get behind me and start to push again. Unfortunately, *I, Assassin* sold about one third of what *Dance* had done, so it really was a disaster. My sales were now pitiful compared to what I'd been doing in 1979. It made it impossible for me to argue too forcefully about their producer suggestion.

WEA had their own problems. They had changed managing director several times in the months prior to my stay in Jersey, and senior people in various departments seemed to come in and out of the company like the wind. But then Mike Heap arrived as the new MD. I had a good history with Mike. He'd been at WEA when Beggars first became a part of it, and he said all the things I'd hoped to hear. He recognised that I'd been treated badly and that my recent albums had not been promoted properly. He then promised me a virtually unlimited budget to promote *Warriors*. I couldn't have wished for more. I agreed to use a producer and asked an old hero of mine, Bill Nelson, if he would be willing to get involved. Mike even said WEA would cover the cost. Bill, one of the best guitar players I'd ever heard, and a great producer, flew out to Jersey to meet me. His band Be Bop Deluxe were one of my favourites, and I was a huge fan. He seemed easy to get along with, so it was all agreed. Bill would produce the album, WEA would pull out all the stops and push it hard all over the world, and my career would get back on track. A few weeks later, Mike Heap seemed no longer to be in charge. The new team that came in didn't care for me at all, and every promise Mike had made was withdrawn. The album would have minimal promotion, at best, and they couldn't seem to care less if I was even on the label. If anything, it felt like they wanted me gone. It was a pretty devastating turn of events.

Chapter Eleven

1983

Considerably disillusioned, I flew the Navajo back to England in May and had the most amazing welcome from the fans. As we flew over Blackbushe Airport and prepared to land, I could see what looked like thousands of people lining the fence. I thought I might have arrived during an event and asked air traffic what was going on. They came back with, 'You've got quite a welcoming committee down here.' I honestly couldn't believe it. It was just an incredible thing to see and so unexpected. As we taxied in many of the fans climbed the fences and started to run towards the plane, which still had both engines running. I quickly shut them down before anyone got hurt and climbed out. It was the best homecoming I could have wished for. With all the other troubles and disappointments going on, that welcome picked me up and gave me a confidence boost I was badly in need of.

I started working on *Warriors* straight away. Some time before, I'd bought shares in Rock City Studios in Shepperton, and by now pretty much owned all of it, so we recorded the album there. Having not been too keen on using a producer to start with, I was now very much looking forward to working with Bill Nelson. Unfortunately, things started to go wrong almost from day one. We were clearly very different people, and our opinions on almost every topic seemed at opposite ends of the spectrum. Our attitudes to life, music, why we did what we did, just about everything seemed to be at odds with one another. I found him a tad pretentious and somewhat pompous, and he found me shallow, and lots more besides probably. I will admit I did begin to play up to it more than a little. I said things that were deliberately shallow that I knew would irritate him. When we talked about why we were in the business, I said for me it was to sleep with as many women as possible. It wasn't, but, as I suspected, it really annoyed him. I used to find discussing inspiration, the feelings from where songs come from, slightly embarrassing. Less so now, but back then it felt incredibly pretentious, so I would hide under a blustering display of blokeishness. At one point, we were talking about creativity, and he said something to the effect that all artistic people have their creativity beamed into them from 'across the cosmos' and we channel it into art for the good of the people. That was pretty much it for me. I just didn't think that way at all, although when I consider it now, it is a lovely idea. Despite doubting we'd ever have become close friends, I very much regret not trying to find a way to build a better relationship with Bill. The twenty-five-year-old me was very different to the person I am today.

When the album was finished, I didn't like Bill's mixes. I thought they were bass light and 'tinny' sounding. I had them redone, so Bill had his name removed from the credits. He did some incredible work on that album that I don't think I fully appreciated until long after it was finished. Relationship issues aside, it was an honour and a privilege to be in the studio and listen to him play.

Back in '83, I was desperate to make my albums more music-ally proficient, so I brought in amazing musicians to make up for what I saw as my lack of ability. Although I'd sold millions of albums and had won many awards, I felt like a fraud, embar-rassed by and undeserving of my success. So, as well as Bill Nelson, the album featured a line-up of extraordinary musi-cians. Pino Palladino, who'd played bass on *I, Assassin*, was supposed to play on *Warriors* but got a gig elsewhere just before the sessions started and pulled out. Pino recommended his bass tutor, a man called Joe Hubbard. Joe was another phenomenal bass player but would soon cause me no end of trouble. Dick Morrisey, who had played saxophone on the *Bladerunner* soundtrack, came in several times and did some extraordinary work. Tessa Niles, an incredible singer, featured on vocals. The album was just overflowing with superb musicianship. I have never thought of myself as a good player of anything. I can play guitar a bit, I can play keyboards a bit, a few other things even less, but I'm not particularly good at any musical instrument. I now wanted my albums to be faultless as far as the musicianship was concerned, and, from my perspective, that meant they needed less of me. I saw it as a way of deflating much of the scathing media criticism I expected with each new album.

I play well enough to be able to write songs, and I'm OK with that, but I know I will never be a great player. I think in truth a small part of me is just too lazy to devote the time required to become a really good musician. But a much bigger part of me has always been genuinely frightened to learn. I have no idea what small gift I was born with that enables me to write the songs I write, but I've always been terrified of doing anything that might change it. I write in what I see as a stumbling, faltering kind of moving experiment. I know nothing about musical scales or what notes work with what others. I just play and experiment until things sound right, and that stumbling method has worked wonders for me. So I've always worried that if I became more proficient, if I knew what should and shouldn't work, my writing would become predictable, that it would follow the rules. In many ways, it goes all the way back to that day in college when I was told that what my music sounded like didn't matter. If I learn the rules, I could lose whatever little spark of magic or uniqueness I seem to have. I didn't realise it at the time, but I was beginning to walk a path that would see me increasingly bury, hide and sometimes even erase my own performances on my albums.

The image on the new album sleeve was based on the early Mad Max films. It never really worked quite the way I'd hoped in photos or video, but it worked well enough on stage with the full broken-down-city set all around it. I'd found a man in Wales who could make one-off leather clothes, so I flew the band there in the Navajo to have him measure us all up. Each band member designed the look they wanted, and I had the clothes made up for the tour.

For the video for the first single, the album title track 'Warriors', I hired a T33 Shooting Star, a Korean War-era jet fighter. I met the pilot Dizzy Addicott, strapped in and off we went. I found out later that my video was the jet's first flight after being rebuilt in something of a hurry. The parachute hadn't been packed, and the seat harness was twisted and would have done more harm than good if we'd been forced to land somewhere. At one point, a fuel warning light came on, and we had to scamper off to get some fuel before getting airborne once again. I loved every second of it, happy in my ignorance. Dizzy was an amazing pilot and a truly larger-than-life character. A Second World War fighter pilot, and then a test pilot after the war, he was now a display pilot on the British airshow scene. He drank, smoked and womanised, and he was already way beyond retirement age. He stayed at my house for a while and tried to get off with my girlfriend. I loved him, though. He taught me more about aeroplanes and flying than anyone I've ever met, and he was endlessly entertaining. It was thanks to Dizzy, and a friend of his called Peter Hoare, that I would soon become involved in air-display flying myself. I was regularly invited to co-pilot Peter's DC-3, a big twin-engine transport plane from WW2, at various airshows. Dizzy said to me during one of our many discussions in the DC-3 that if I really wanted to learn how to fly an aeroplane, I should get myself a Second World War trainer called a Harvard. He said, 'If you can learn to fly that well, you can fly anything.'

My love of airshows has been with me since I was a small boy. Mum and Dad would take me every year, and I loved the noise and excitement. The daring skill of the pilots was always so impressive and seemed unobtainable. As unlikely to happen as becoming a pop star. So, I started looking for a Harvard. If I was ever going to be an air-display pilot, I'd obviously need to master flying one of them.

The 'Warriors' single fell foul of a new, and very brief, rule about what was acceptable for the UK singles chart. The single reached number 20, so we released a picture-disc version. Nothing unusual about that – bands did it all the time. The picture disc would generate new interest and new sales, and would help keep the single moving up the chart, hopefully giving it another shot at getting airplay, which I found difficult to get. For whatever reason, that week the company compiling the chart decided that picture discs were not acceptable and my picture-disc sales were excluded from the count. The single had originally risen up the chart quite nicely but, with those sales excluded, it actually dropped back a few places, and it killed it completely. The very next week picture discs were reinstated, but for me the damage was done, and it was a horrible blow. The 'Warriors' single felt very much as though I was pulling myself back into the mainstream again, but that bit of bad luck really hurt. The album reached number 12 in the UK album chart, and I was left to wonder what could have been but for that chart decision. It seemed like bad luck was the only luck coming my way at that time.

There were other signs that I was far from over. I did a record signing in the Oxford Street HMV store to promote *Warriors*, and 3,000 people turned up. It actually stopped traffic for a while. That was a huge boost after all the disappointments. The *Warriors* tour would be my first UK tour since *Telekon* in 1980, and my first UK shows at all since Wembley in '81. It doesn't seem too long a gap now, but it felt like a lifetime back then. I wanted to make a statement with the tour. I wanted to show that I had a new confidence with touring and that I was glad to be back. We would promote the tour ourselves, something we'd never done before, which was quite a challenge. We booked forty shows to run over an eight-week period – a truly massive tour for the UK.

Although I knew money was not so plentiful, and I had to be more cautious with the stage design, I really didn't do a very good job. The set was big, really big. It was all custom built and enormously expensive. It required a large crew, lots of trucks, all the things that took money that the tour wasn't going to pay back. I justified it all by claiming that the tour had to be big, had to be spectacular, if it was going to re-establish me in the UK. I said that ultimately it would all be worthwhile and the money we lost would eventually come back in better album sales in the future, and more profitable tours. But first we had to get back the fans I'd lost by doing my Wembley retirement. My dad, who had the horrendous job of trying to control my overly optimistic spending, never really saw it my way. Just the cladding of the set cost £50,000, so I can only imagine how frustrated he must have been with me. But we did it my way, and I couldn't have been more wrong.

The tour was pretty successful. Although some shows were less well attended than I'd have liked, most of it sold well. The set itself was built to look like a ruined city from an apocalyptic future, and it looked great. Once again, the keyboards were high up in the taller buildings left and right of the stage, and the drums were at the top of a lower tower in the middle. It was a very effective, striking set and perfectly suited our image. I was very proud of it, but it really was horrendously expensive to build and to move around each day.

Chris Payne, Ced Sharpley and Rrussell Bell rejoined the band for the *Warriors* tour. My brother John took over second keyboard duties, plus some sax, and Joe Hubbard played bass. The first day of rehearsals was a disaster. The lighting designer, the man who would, with me, program every light for every song, fell sick. Luckily, I knew a fair bit about the lighting console, and I was able to program the entire show myself. Each day I'd work on more songs expecting him to arrive, and each day he'd call in sick. It wasn't just programming the lights, of course – he needed to be there to learn the songs and what I wanted from the lights for the entire two-hour show. He needed to rehearse as much as the band, more so in many ways. Each day lost meant less time to get the show as slick as it needed to be. I was there until well into the early hours every day, and it was exhausting. As this was my 'comeback' tour, the pressure was already horrendous, but the lighting situation was adding to it enormously. I was told with just a few rehearsal days still to go that the lighting designer wouldn't be coming back. It was all shaping up to be a total catastrophe when James Dann stepped in as the replacement and took it on. In just two days, he had to learn every song, every lighting cue I'd programmed, and how the show went together technically. It was a huge task, and he did an amazing job. With James on board, we had a tour, but it was a very shaky and unnerving way to start.

Joe Hubbard had irritated me during rehearsals. Most days we were only playing about three hours a day, as I needed the rest of the time to work on the lights, and yet on one day when we played longer he complained about being overworked, which, given the situation I was in, didn't go down well with me. During the tour, his complaints about things from the size of the sandwiches to the sound of his bass became a constant pain in my arse. When the tour was over, I was glad to see him gone.

Compared to the strain of rehearsals, the tour itself felt easy. It took the first few weeks to get used to, but then it seemed to become a way of life, and I honestly felt I could have gone on for ever. I felt more confident on stage and very much at ease with the touring lifestyle. Little dramas still happened, many of them self-inflicted, but I was able to deal with them with a hint of maturity that had previously been lacking. It was all so much more comfortable than before. The break from touring really had done me the world of good. In other ways, the tour brought out the worst in me. I slept with as many women as I could, barely asking for a name. We had a variety of competitions running, such as who could sleep with the most in twenty-four hours, the most at the same time, lots of school-boy stuff like that. It all seemed harmless fun, but it showed a horrendous lack of respect. I did meet one very pretty girl, Tracey Adam, who was having none of it. She got her autograph and, much to my disappointment, went home. I would see her again, though, and she would become a part of my life for the next nine years.

We treated hotels like playgrounds – firework fights in the corridors, parties all through the night. We were banned from more than one. Nothing to be proud of looking back, but it seemed like we were having the best time back then. In London, Paul Gardiner joined us on stage. He didn't play, just walked on and waved to the crowd, who went absolutely berserk. They loved seeing him again, and I know their reaction meant the world to him. Sadly, that would be one of the last times I saw him alive.

I played to more than 80,000 people on the *Warriors* tour, more than I'd ever done before, and it made quite a difference to the album. WEA really did do very little to help it, so the number 12 chart position was very much down to the success of the tour. Once again, WEA stated that they were satisfied with the sales, about 50,000 for *Warriors*, but I wasn't happy with that. I wanted to at least get back to the 300,000 I had been selling in 1979, and although that was a big task, it certainly wasn't going to happen with a label that was happy to do nothing and accept sales of 50,000.

An exciting opportunity to step away from all the stresses of music came when I was invited to be part of the crew on an offshore powerboat for a race near Poole, Dorset, on the south coast of England. The race was to raise money for Cancer Research and, once again, it was thanks to Queen drummer Roger Taylor who, when the crewman intending to take part had to pull out, put my name forward. In all honesty I had absolutely nothing to do other than hang on. I think the rules stipulated a crew of three but the driver, Tony Fletcher, didn't really need anyone else. It was an amazing experience though. I've always loved boats and have always been impressed by offshore powerboats in particular. It was hard going though. It seemed to me that with every other wave the boat would get airborne and I'd find myself floating in the air, only staying with the boat at all thanks to my vice like grip on two handles behind the front seats, that Roger and the driver were more comfortably and securely sat in. Roger had warned me beforehand that I needed to keep my legs bent at all times or they might break with the force of the boat hitting the waves. Once we were up and running at speed I had no doubts that such a thing was not only possible, but likely. My legs stayed bent. Some of the impacts were brutal though and more than once I found myself splattered onto the floor of the boat. I loved every minute of it.

We released a second single from the album called 'Sister Surprise', but WEA did almost nothing for it – no video, virtually no promotion at all. I did do one *Top of the Pops*, but without even a small campaign to back it up it really is like pouring a glass of water into an ocean and expecting to see the sea level rise. I talked it over with my dad, and we both felt that we'd gone as far as we could go with WEA/Beggars, so we left the label. Even that came with the sting of bad luck. As we left, yet another MD arrived, with yet another new team, and they turned WEA's fortunes around. It would soon be a major force in the business again, but too late for me.

Once we were no longer under contract with Beggars Banquet, we talked to several other labels. No one was willing to sign me without wanting to listen to new music first. That's not unreasonable, even for an established artist, but it bothered me. I took it as a sign that they needed to be persuaded, and that didn't make me feel that I would have their wholehearted backing. I'd just been through a situation that made one thing very clear: being with a big label that wasn't truly behind what you were doing was almost as bad as having no label at all. It was that thinking that led me to start my own label, Numa Records.

Like the Wembley decision to step out of the limelight of touring and catch my breath, starting Numa was another good idea in principle but badly executed. Instead of just devoting all my resources to making Numa a vehicle for my career going forward, which would have been the smart thing to do, I decided to sign other bands and tried to make it into a real label. It was the worst thing I could have done. Money, or the lack of it, was very much an issue by now, but I insisted that all the bands were treated the same as me. If they couldn't have a video, I wouldn't have a video, and so on. When I should have been focusing all my attention and what limited money I had into rebuilding my own career, I diluted it amongst a roster of different artists. I tried to create my own start-up version of

Beggars Banquet, and I really wanted to do what I could to help new bands, so I signed Hohokam, Grey Parade, Steve Braun, Larry Loeber and Caroline Munroe. My idea was that Numa would be their first step. We would try our best to get their career under way and then allow them to move on when a bigger, better-funded label showed interest in them. I wanted Numa to be the label that found the artists that had been overlooked and deserved a chance. I was advised again and again that I was going about it the wrong way, that I should concentrate on me first. I just didn't listen, and, once again, I was completely wrong.

Chapter Twelve

1984

1984 had the most awful start. Paul Gardiner was found dead on a park bench on 4 February. He'd committed suicide with a deliberate overdose of heroin. I knew Paul had troubles, and had for some time, but he'd only spoken to my mum a day or two earlier, and he'd arranged to come in for a visit a few days later. He seemed reasonably together, and we were all hopeful that he was getting through it. There was no indication at all that he was suicidal, quite the opposite. I'd talked to Paul many times about him rejoining the band as soon as he sorted himself out, told him that his place would always be waiting for him. Part of the reason for bringing him on stage in London during the tour had been to try and give him a sense of what was waiting for him, how much people cared for him.

I don't think the reality of him being gone touched me fully until I saw his coffin being carried in for the funeral, but it hit hard then, the sad waste of it. Paul had been such a good friend, and a staunch ally, through the most tumultuous days of my life. He was easy-going, kind, just a lovely person to be around. We'd gone from nothing to number 1 together, and now, so soon after, he was gone. Before he died, he'd been working at my Rock City Studios, recording two songs: a cover of the Velvet Underground's 'Venus in Furs' and a new song he'd written called 'No Sense'. The band and I finished them for him and, as a tribute to Paul, made 'Venus in Furs' the first release on Numa Records.

My money situation was going from bad to worse. I sold the Ferrari to start with, but the shedding of toys didn't end there. I'd bought my brother an aeroplane called a Tiger Moth, a beautiful old open cockpit biplane which he absolutely loved, but we had to sell that as well. I felt terrible doing that, but then I had to sell the Navajo. I watched it fly away for the last time. It was heading back to the USA to its new owner, and I thought about all the times it had pulled me through difficult moments. It felt like I was betraying a family member. I did hang on to some of the money, though, and bought another plane, a Harvard, the type Dizzy Addicott had recommended. The one I bought had been used by the Royal Air Force during the war. It had a 600-horsepower radial engine, a 40-feet wingspan and looked every bit as intimidating as the reputation that came with it. I would eventually spend about a thousand hours flying the Harvard and flew it in airshows all over Europe for more than ten years. I became proficient in low-level aerobatics and close-formation flying. I was even an Air Display Pilot Evaluator for a few years and as such was tasked with making sure that incoming display pilots had the required training and skills so would be less likely to kill themselves, or anybody else.

To begin with I was rather scared of the Harvard. I'd heard no end of horror stories about how difficult and dangerous it was. One man said it was the only plane he ever flew that felt like it was trying to kill him when he pushed it back into the hangar. Luckily, I had two great pilots, Peter Hoare and Dizzy, to teach me. Dizzy especially spent a lot of time flying in the

Harvard with me, teaching me as much as I could absorb each time we went up, until eventually I began to tune my senses into what the aeroplane was saying. I became increasingly at home in it, until flying it became as natural as getting out of bed. I became familiar with every noise it made, every feeling it gave, every shudder and cough. I felt absolutely at one with it and would often talk to it as we flew along. I got used to the feeling of blood draining from my head with the G force from the manoeuvres. I got used to being just a few feet off the ground, being upside down, feeling the aeroplane kicking and shaking underneath me. I grew to love it very quickly, and what it could do, and what it taught me to do. I would always give it a friendly pat and a hello when I walked up to it, and say thanks and goodbye when I left. I treated it much the same as a beloved pet, and felt a similar bond.

I flew the Harvard solo for the first time on 8 March 1984, my twenty-sixth birthday. But even as I made my early baby steps towards becoming an air-display pilot, the dangerous nature of display flying became apparent. Through Dizzy and Peter, and my short time flying the DC-3 at displays, I'd got to know a few of the display pilots. I was shocked at how many died. These were highly skilled and experienced people, far better than I could ever hope to be, and yet just a tiny mistake was all it took. I saw for myself the incredibly unforgiving nature of display flying, and it was sobering. There is so little margin for error – even the smallest mistake is likely to be punished by a fiery crash. I remember clearly the first time I saw a man die, the first of so many, sadly. I'd been talking to him not thirty minutes before. It was such a different world to music, where the worst that could happen was a bad-selling album or tripping on stage and getting embarrassed. Display flying was the most exciting thing I'd ever done.

On June 22 I was invited, along with a plane full of other celebs, to fly on the Virgin Atlantic inaugural flight from London to New York. A shiny Boeing 747 sat sparkling on the tarmac, Sir Richard Branson was in full PR mode and it was all very exciting. At one point during the flight Steve Strange came and sat next to me and asked if we were friends yet. No, not as far as I was concerned, and so he wandered off again. When the plane landed in New York everyone gathered their things and made their way through the terminal and all headed off to their hotels and some huge celebratory party in the city put on by Virgin. I, however, hadn't gone on the trip for the party – I just wanted to fly on the jet. As they all made their way to the waiting limos I went back into the terminal and waited to get back on the plane and fly back to London.

While all this was going on, I was also recording my next album, *Berserker*. I'd been a big fan of the Fred Saberhagen Berserker books and also read up on the Viking berserkers of old. They weren't connected, but I loved both, and I just loved the word. Many of the fears I'd experienced through my flying adventures, old and new, found their way into the album. The songs talk of a waiting, unseen threat. Something cold, coming ever closer. That faint but undeniable awareness of a danger lurking, growing more dangerous by the minute. Songs like 'Cold Warning' and 'My Dying Machine'. The album has no central character or theme as such, but I was writing about things dreadful and unstoppable. Things of immense power. The songs were full of my own experiences but all wrapped inside vague suggestions of half-guessed-at menace. The only real exception to that was a song called 'A Child with the Ghost' that I wrote for Paul Gardiner.

The idea for the *Berserker* image came from a photograph I'd seen of a woman painted to look like marble. Perhaps because of the Viking berserker connection, I also felt the sleeve should be as cold and stark as possible. I dyed my hair blue, painted my face white, blue make-up, blue lips, white clothes. It was, by far, the most striking image I'd come up with at that point, and I thought it suited the music perfectly. A German music magazine used the sleeve image on a front cover and won an award for best cover of the year.

I was very happy with the album, both musically and visually. On *Berserker* I'd started to work with a new synth called the PPG Wave. The PPG was owned by two men, Mike Smith and Ian Herron, who would do battle with it each day to try and get the best out of it. It was a computer-based synth and behaved more like a difficult child than a piece of technology. On a good day, though, it was highly impressive. The PPG was the heart and soul of *Berserker*. I was able to use sound in ways that hadn't really been available before. One of the most used sounds, for example, was of a chair leg being dragged. It often adapted sounds without you asking it to and either ruined what you had or created something new and unique. We sometimes used bizarre noises instead of drums or anything conventional. Every day in the studio was a walk into the unexpected. It was also my introduction to the world of sampling, and we spent much of our time walking around Shepperton Studios recording anything we could hit, scrape or drag. We became obsessed with trying to find the most unusual sounds and then manipulating them into something we could use musically. It felt very inventive, and it was great fun.

Berserker was released on 9 November and was the first album on Numa Records. I was very excited by what might lie ahead for the label, and I had such high hopes for the album. We'd employed a man to look after the day-to-day running of the label, and he made a major mistake as soon as we launched the album. I understood why. The 'Berserker' single had been released a few weeks earlier and went into the chart at number 36. We were lucky enough to get a *Top of the Pops* slot, which moved it up the chart a few places. Things were looking quite optimistic. Although we'd always struggled to get decent radio play, we felt confident that would pick up with a chart single and a good *Top of the Pops* performance. The radio play would make a huge difference, and the single's further rise up the chart seemed all but guaranteed. Not only that, the pre-orders for the album had also been strong. We felt very confident, and with some justification. Our label manager decided that we would need a large number of records manufactured, single and album, to meet the expected high demand, so they were ordered. We pressed many thousands. Many, many thousands. But, disappointingly, the radio stations ignored the record completely. It was as though the Top 40 only had thirty-nine singles in it. For us working our very first release as a label, it was a crushing moment. Not only was the single – a chart single no less – entirely ignored by radio, which itself heralded major problems for the future, but we'd pressed a huge amount of stock, at considerable expense, that we were now unlikely ever to be able to sell. It was the worst possible result. We lost so much money on that first release it pretty much ruined us at the first hurdle.

I also lost a lot of sleep. To realise that my radio problem was now so bad that even a chart single wouldn't generate so much as a single play was hard to deal with. It would be all but impossible to compete when other chart acts were being played seven or eight times a day on every station across the country. I'd never had good radio play, but I'd always been able to rely on a few here and there. This almost total blank for 'Berserker' signalled a new, and perhaps insurmountable, barrier. For the first time ever, I began to wonder if my career was salvageable.

For the first few years of my career, everything I'd done had worked out beautifully, and I genuinely believed that I had a natural instinct for decision making. I trusted it completely. But as things started to go wrong, it took me far too long to grasp the fact that I had very little instinct at all – I'd just been incredibly lucky. I was getting some things right still, but I was also making far too many mistakes. Eventually, even I began to lose faith in my decisions.

In late November of 1984 we started a nineteen-date tour of the UK to promote *Berserker*. This time Andy Coughlan was on bass and Karen Taylor joined the band on backing vocals. The rest of the band members – Chris Payne, Ced Sharpley, Rrussell Bell and John Webb – were the same as the *Warriors* tour. I was more aware than ever of the need to cut back on the budget for the *Berserker* tour, and I did try. I used the square lighting panels from the *Teletour* to construct a curved row of tall columns around the back of the stage and panels from the first *Touring Principle* tour for the keyboard risers. The end result looked pretty good, still had the size and a fair degree of spectacle, but it was clearly a step back from what I'd done before. I was certainly aware of that. Despite the obvious cost saving, it still cost more to play the tour than the tour made. It seemed that every time I cut back, my career slid even further. My dad summed it up perfectly when he said to me, 'We're always one step behind the problem.' As much as I was slowly beginning to grasp the seriousness of our money troubles, I was still doing too little to help. I was still of the opinion that the fans would only come back if the shows, as in stage sets and lighting, were as impressive as they could possibly be, even though it clearly didn't seem to be making much difference. The way I saw it, without help from radio, and with no money to make decent promo videos or buy any advertising, playing live was the only avenue we had, so the shows had to be dazzling. If I'm honest, it was also about saving face. I was desperate to still make it look as though we were doing well, even though it was becoming increasingly obvious we were not. All anyone had to do was look at the dwindling crowd sizes.

After the *Berserker* tour, my relationship with Tracey Adam developed to the point that she moved in with me in my house in Virginia Water. Unfortunately, I was not the easiest person to live with. In fact, I was pretty horrible at times. Way too many times. I was often stressed, anxious, immature, self-righteous, impatient, argumentative, rude and arrogant. Just the worst partner. Our relationship got off to a shaky start soon after she moved in and became ever more confrontational. It went from bad to worse to unbearable, and although we stayed together for nine years, we really shouldn't have. I don't know how she stood it for so long. It often seems to be the way that you can't fix yourself within a relationship, and yet you can when it's over. After I split with Tracey, I was able to really look at the way I'd been and recognise so many of my faults. I vowed to become a better person in my future relationships, which, as it turned out, would only be one.

Beggars Banquet had been going through their archives and had found a whole bunch of unreleased recordings of my punk songs that I could barely remember even doing. They were all gathered together, and an album called *The Plan* was released at the end of '84. I was very surprised to see the album chart in the UK Top 30.

A few months after *Berserker*, I was visiting our offices at Rock City Studios when I was asked if I wanted to sing a guest vocal. Bill Sharpe, from the band Shakatak, was working on a solo album and had a song called 'Change Your Mind'. The studio engineer for Bill's session was Nick Smith, who had also engineered a few of my albums, and they both felt my voice would suit it. It went surprisingly well, and I had the vocal done in just a couple of takes. 'Change Your Mind' was released on the Polydor label in February '85 and was immediately play-listed by Radio 1, which I definitely hadn't expected. Thanks to Polydor and a decent budget we filmed a great video for it, got a spot on *Top of the Pops* and the single reached number 17 in the charts. The press were very interested in this strange collaboration, as our musical styles were vastly different. It was also a new experience for me to be a singer on someone else's music. I wasn't looking for that as a way forward, so I had no intention of making it a new career direction, but I enjoyed the experience. I really liked Bill, and although it wasn't my type of music, I certainly kept the door open for more collaborations in the future.

Chapter Thirteen

1985

Owning Rock City Studios made a lot of sense to begin with. Rock City had two twenty-four-track recording studios, offices, storerooms, a games area and a small café. It was ideal for what we had planned. It wasn't just the Numa bands that used it, either – it was still run as a commercial studio. Sting would use it whenever he was filming at the Shepperton film studios, and Cliff Richard used it, as well as many others. Unfortunately, the owners of Shepperton decided that they only wanted businesses directly connected to movies on site, so it was made increasingly difficult for us to stay there. My dad wanted out fairly quickly, but I was keen to hang on. Having Rock City was an essential part of Numa Records being able to operate as a label. Without it we would never be able to afford to record the bands.

My brother John also released a single on Numa called 'The Experiment of Love'. John had put up with a lot by being my brother. Constantly bullied after my initial success, my parents eventually had to take him out of school, and he finished, like me, with no qualifications whatsoever. For a while after leaving school, the things John were interested in were all the things I'd already done, music and flying in particular. I think he struggled to find his own way for a while, and yet never did he have a bad word to say. When he joined the band, he was a fantastic addition, rarely putting a note wrong night after night. Eventually, though, he decided that he would pursue a career in aviation, and through dogged determination and a lot of effort became an airliner captain. In fact, he became a fleet manager and trained new captains. He also became an air-display pilot and flew with me in the Harvard Formation Team for a number of years. Afterwards, he flew for other historic collections and displayed some of the rarest aeroplanes in the world. He even became qualified as a steam-train driver at one point. John took early retirement a few years ago and now lives with his new wife Becky in Whitby. He's built a home studio and is recording new music under the name Donovan Silver. I couldn't be more proud of him.

However, I found some of the other acts we'd signed to Numa difficult to deal with. Some had an arrogance that I couldn't understand. It was as if signing to my tiny little label somehow made them see themselves as rock stars. It was both unexpected and disappointing, and I began to wonder why I was bothering. My decision to share whatever money Numa had equally between the artists, including me, meant that I was hobbling my own career to try and help them. I would have been OK with that if I felt that it was appreciated, but for some of them it didn't feel like that at all. Quite the opposite at times.

On 27 April I released a double live album and single from the *Berserker* tour called 'White Noise'. It crept into the Top 30, along with a four-track live EP taken from it that peaked at number 26. Strangely, 'White Noise' made number 2 in the Belgian chart, which came as a very welcome surprise. By now I was also hard at work on my next album, *The Fury*. On this album, Mike Smith and Ian Herron joined me once again, and they'd also be co-producers. I had intended working with a producer called Colin Thurston, but after contributing to just one track he was called away to work on the new Human League album.

With each new album, my optimism for what might happen seemed to be renewed. Musically, they continued to evolve. Each one had a distinctly different sound to the one before, and I think that helped fuel my optimism. I wasn't churning out more of the same – each album was a step forward, and with that came the chance that they would be viewed afresh, by radio especially. The first single from *The Fury* was called 'Your Fascination' and, despite a decent video, received no airplay at all. Peaking at 46, it didn't even make the Top 40. The next single, 'Call Out the Dogs', only reached number 49. The third single, 'Miracles', did about the same. None of them got any radio play, and my fears of being forgotten were borne out. Even worse, I wasn't even getting into the Top 40 now, and so any slight pressure that some stations might have felt to play the records had vanished. Things were worse than ever.

The album did a little better than the singles, reaching number 24, but things were definitely not going in the right direction, and my fall from glory seemed to be nigh-on unstoppable. It was all very disappointing to say the least. But it was so much more than that. For several years, I'd been confident that fighting my way back up was just a matter of time. Not if but when. I'd come back to touring full time in '83 with a clear plan. I'd concentrate solely on the UK to start with, get the home market safely on the right track, and then I'd start to move out globally and bring everything back up to the same level. But here I was after three more albums and things were still very much going downhill. I was running out of ideas. I was so confident that each of those three albums, *Warriors*, *Berserker* and *The Fury*, were more than good enough to rekindle the interest of the lost fans and to build new ones. But they hadn't, and I continued to slide further away from sight. I was becoming increasingly irrelevant. I was also sliding into debt. We had no money to promote the album or the singles, so we had no way of fighting back against the lack of radio play and media indifference. I began to feel a little desperate, but I had no idea how much further I still had to fall.

I toured *The Fury*, around the UK once again, in September of '85. As before, I used parts of old stage sets to try to build a new design but on an even tighter budget. This time I used all the square panels from the *Teletour* and built a wall of them, eight feet high and forty feet wide across the stage. The musicians would stand on top of that and I would roam the stage alone. I also had three long motorised columns that would lower down from the roof to form high towers. It even had a hydraulic lift that carried the band up onto the wall. Although the singles hadn't fared too well, and the album sales had been a little disappointing, the tour went surprisingly well. It still lost money, of course – I was still one step behind the problem – but I was happy with my performance on stage. Each time I went out on tour, I seemed to gain another layer of confidence, and I was feeling more at home on stage than ever.

In 1985, my display flying began to gather momentum. I joined the Harvard Formation Team, and I began to add an aerobatic element to the team's display. My formation-flying skills were improving dramatically, and I soon found myself a regular display pilot. It was hard. My pilot reputation was in tatters after the press handling of the Centurion accident, and it felt like I was constantly under suspicion. Nonetheless, display flying became my new obsession. It was an entirely different challenge, and one that I revelled in. In the music business, things were going ever downwards, and my self-esteem was being sucked away. But with the flying, I was slowly becoming accepted into a very different world, and I was getting better all the time. In the flying world, my self-esteem was building. The one helped offset the other. I feel strongly that I was able to deal with the problems I was having with my music career precisely because my successes in flying were balancing me out. It gave me something totally absorbing to escape to and so provided the respite I needed. I genuinely believe that without air-display flying, the new challenges, the new friendships, the new successes, I would likely have crumbled under the weight of trying to save my music career. It was often said by people around me in the music world that I was neglecting my career, but the opposite was true. I was saving it. It was just hard for them to understand that I was saving it by doing something else completely. I wasn't even fully aware of it myself at the time. I just knew that one was making me utterly miserable, and the other was the most enjoyable and rewarding thing I'd ever done. Display flying had certainly become my main interest.

I didn't abandon music, not at all. Throughout the latter months of 1985 and into '86, I worked on the next album, *Strange Charm*. In April '86, we released the first single from it, 'This Is Love', a fairly dark ballad with an achingly beautiful sax solo played by Dick Morrissey. It reached number 28 in the charts, the best anything had done for quite some time, and my battered hopes were raised briefly once again. One day I got a call saying to turn on the radio – Radio 1 were actually playing the song. It was so unusual, and I was so happy. I turned on the radio and listened to the end. I could hardly believe it. Maybe now my radio problem was finally over, and, just in the nick of time, I would finally start to claw my way back. But then it all came crashing down. After the song was over Steve Wright, the DJ, apologised to his listeners, saying the song was utterly depressing and that he'd been forced to play it. If Radio 1 hadn't already done enough to virtually ruin my career by ignoring me, they were now rubbishing my music to an audience of millions. I wished they'd carried on ignoring me. It was horribly embarrassing and extremely damaging. It really did hit me hard. One moment it felt as though we had turned an important corner, and the next things were far worse than ever. What tiny fragment of confidence I'd hung on to vanished in that moment, and I was more lost than I'd ever been.

One of the things I've always noticed is that no matter how much success you have, no matter how legendary you're considered to be, you are always inundated with advice from people who have never done it themselves. Everyone seems to see themselves as an expert, to know what you should be doing, what you did wrong, what you should write next, what clothes you should wear and a thousand other things. You should do this, do that, work with Tom, Dick and Harriet, make a dance track, do something else, anything else. I was always able to ignore them totally, confident that I knew what I was doing. As my career began to struggle, maintaining that confidence had become harder, but I still avoided advice like the plague. After 'This Is Love', I was bewildered and lost all faith in my ability to make the right decisions. So, I started to listen to advice, and that was arguably the biggest mistake I've ever made.

I put out another single in June called 'I Can't Stop' and made a cheap, terrible video for it. We were now very much in debt and so did a deal with a local video company to make videos for us for £5,000 each, which was pitiful. We somehow managed to get a slot on *Top of the Pops*, and the single staggered up to number 27. With both singles we'd got back into the Top 40 at least, which was something, but the lack of radio play was just crippling. It was so frustrating to see singles get into the chart, see all the other new entries get added to radio playlists all over the country and continue to rise, but my singles be ignored and slide back down again. We spent what little we had on radio pluggers to try and help our situation with airplay, but it was all for nothing. At one point our plugger was told not to go into the building if he was plugging Gary Numan. They weren't even prepared to listen to it.

The radio situation was so desperate that my dad arranged for a meeting with the senior producer at Radio 1. During that meeting, my dad was told that the problem was all my songs sounded like 'Are "Friends" Electric?'. That meeting was cut short for some reason, so they picked up the discussion the following week. At that second meeting, my dad was told by the same producer that if I wrote songs like 'Are "Friends" Electric?' again, they would definitely play them. When it was pointed out that he'd said exactly the opposite the week before, he flatly denied it, and we were no closer to finding out what the real problem was.

So glaringly obvious was this deliberate policy of blanking my records, even when they were in the chart, the fans decided to take action themselves. They organised a day of protest outside Broadcasting House, the then home of Radio 1, in London. A large number of people turned up, but it made no difference. In fact, it made things worse. Radio 1 thought that I'd organised it, and they seemed to dig their heels in even further. I thought it was a lovely thing for the fans to do, and I very much appreciated their effort. I'd always said that the fan–artist relationship was a very even thing. I make the albums, fans buy them, neither of us owes the other anything. I felt differently after that day of protest though. What they'd done was tried hard to make a difference, not for themselves but for me. I was enormously touched by that, and so grateful. I felt like I really owed them.

Things elsewhere were worse than ever. The studio sessions for *Strange Charm* were noticeably different. I was bad-tempered and anxious throughout. Disagreements about what was best for a track are not uncommon when you're working on creative projects, but they are usually good-natured. On *Strange Charm*, the stress and the disappointment of the way things were unfolding around me really began to have a negative effect. I was constantly stressed, unhappy with many of the things I was writing, unhappy with everything. With *Strange Charm* I seemed to run out of ideas, and the album only had eight songs. I was relying too much on the PPG to save the daily dramas and took out my frustrations when it didn't on Mike and Ian. It was an unhappy album. It also performed really badly, barely scraping into the Top 60. It actually sold similar numbers to *The Fury* and *Berserker* over time, but with very little promotion, no radio play and particularly no tour to support it in that first week of release, the sales were too low in any given week to make much impression on the chart. I don't remember now why I decided not to tour *Strange Charm*. Perhaps because the tours always lost money, and we had no more to lose; perhaps I knew the album wasn't what it should have been. As for the album itself, I realised that only the hardcore Numan fans would even know it was out, because it just wasn't mentioned anywhere.

Chapter Fourteen

1987

N uma Records was clearly not going to work out. If we were going to have any chance of doing better, with so many things against us, it was becoming increasingly clear that I would need the muscle, and the money, of a major label, or at least a better-funded label than Numa. While we were starting to look around to see what interest there might be, I had an offer from a new label called GFM to sing a guest vocal on a song called 'Radio Heart' by the band of the same name. It was a good offer, and the money felt like a lifeline to a drowning man. Unfortunately, it wasn't really my thing at all, lightweight pop music, and it was my dad who eventually persuaded me to say yes. He knew how vital that money was to us, and it bought us valuable time. The song picked up a healthy amount of radio play, becoming a Top 40 single when it was released in the spring of '87. I didn't, however, feel it did anything for my situation. It wasn't my song, and it wasn't a style of music I would ever want to write myself – I was just a paid singer. If anything, it just showed that to get on the radio I would effectively have to stop being me. I recorded two more singles with Radio Heart, 'London Times' and 'All Across the Nation', that year. Neither of them did as well as the first. I didn't really want to be involved at all, and I was very unhappy. I said no to doing an album with them, and I began to argue a lot with my dad. He was taking all the pressure of trying to keep us going financially, and he was having a nightmare time. We were building up huge debts, and here was I saying no to something that could really help. I was made to feel as though I was letting the family down by not being willing to swallow my pride and just do the album. It wasn't pride, though. I felt strongly, very strongly, that if I was ever going to find a way back, I would destroy what small amount of credibility I had left by continuing with something like Radio Heart. I felt that it was likely to lose what few fans I had left. More than that, though, I just didn't enjoy it. The whole point of being in music was to make music you loved, music you felt passionate about. Radio Heart was the absolute opposite of that. I might have been a little lost as far as my own direction and creativity were concerned at that time, but I still knew I wasn't ready to sell my soul completely.

I came pretty close. In September '87, Beggars Banquet released what they called the E-Reg model of 'Cars', a remix by Zeus B. Held. It had 'Are "Friends" Electric?' on the B-side. I didn't know it was being planned, so it was a surprise to see it released, and even more so to see it reach number 16 in the singles chart. I even agreed to go on *Top of the Pops* and perform it, but a feeling of it doing more long-term harm than good, for a temporary flash of recognition, sat hauntingly on my shoulders. Beggars released a double album of old material called *Exhibition*, and I decided to tour that album, as I had no new material of my own ready. It was not the best way forward. A back-catalogue chart single and then touring an album of back-catalogue material – it reeked of aimless despondency. It was all rather sad.

The tour stage show was another attempt to do almost as much but with a lot less. We used architectural light tubes, multi-stage levels and moving stairways. We even had a man-sized pod that descended from the roof. Many of my bigger ideas had to be left out of the design, as we just didn't have the budget. The best we were hoping for with the tour was to break even financially but sell a few more albums because of it. A year later, I would release a live album, still on Numa, called *Ghost*, from the *Exhibition* tour.

The first man I saw killed at an air display was at an airshow near Coventry that same year, in the summer of '87. Something went wrong and the aeroplane hit the ground. I heard that strangely dulled 'crump' sound and then watched the sickening sight of a column of smoke rising slowly into the air. We were walking towards our aircraft to get ready for our own display when it happened. I found it very shocking, and I sat under my plane and, to my surprise, cried. I hadn't expected it would be quite so emotionally overwhelming. It clearly wasn't for every-body, as someone from the crowd shouted out and asked for my autograph as I sat there. One of my team-mates, an RAF pilot, came over and asked, 'First time you've seen that?' I just nodded. 'You'll get used to it,' he said. I didn't think that could possibly be true, but he was right. There would be so many more. Four members of my own team would be killed in differ-ent accidents in the coming years.

It certainly didn't shake my love of display flying. In many ways, it was the way I expected to go, sooner or later. In me it seemed to bring out a curious mix of extreme confidence on the one hand and an acceptance of the inevitable on the other.

I love the honesty of machinery, of aeroplanes especially. I have always felt far more comfortable with machines than with people. If a machine lets you down, you can be sure it didn't do it on purpose, and it usually gives you some warning if you're listening carefully enough. There is no malice or spiteful intent, and you can't always say that about people. With a machine, you don't have to constantly try and figure out what's really meant. There's no need for reading between the lines. I just don't have the skills for dealing with the subtleties of people.

One of the more memorable moments of recognition about my Asperger's came during a conversation I was having with my dad about my Harvard team-mates. He asked me what one of them did for a living, and I didn't know. I'd been in the team over two years, and he couldn't quite believe that I didn't know something that basic. 'How can you not know?' he said. 'I've never asked,' I replied. He looked at me a bit sideways and said, 'Why not?' To me it was all very obvious why not. 'Well, if he'd wanted me to know what he did for a living, he would have told me, and he didn't. So if I'd asked, I'd be prying, and that would be rude.' My dad just laughed. 'That's not being rude, that's conversation,' he said. 'You asking him questions shows you're interested, and that's a good thing.' That was a very important lesson for me, and I've remembered it to this day. When I meet people, I should ask what they do for a living. Social interaction is really not my thing.

I can't remember exactly when I came up with this, but at some point I discovered that eye contact is important, even though I have no natural feel for it. I don't know when to look into someone's eyes or when it's OK to look away. I read something about it once, and I eventually came up with a system. I will look into someone's eyes for no less than two seconds and no more than five. It used to be three seconds, but I've adapted it over time. My theory is anything less than two seconds doesn't show enough interest; anything over five is too intense and can seem a bit creepy. So, whenever I'm talking to someone, I'm always counting and adjusting my eyes according to the count. Plus, I have to remember to ask what they do for a living. I find having a conversation with anyone I don't know really well, and sometimes even people I do know well, to be extremely stressful – a bit like riding a bike before you've mastered it. I feel like I could fall off at any second and make a fool of myself.

Chapter Fifteen

1988–1989

I'd recorded a second single with Bill Sharpe called 'No More Lies', which was released on 30 January 1988. It got to number 34, but that was not what Polydor had hoped for. When they failed to generate any radio interest, they pulled back considerably on the promo effort, and the single disappeared fairly quickly. It was during a TV slot for 'No More Lies' that I found myself on a show with Bros, very much the favourites of the moment, and Sinéad O'Connor. That was probably the lowest point for me so far. I felt horribly out of date and totally irrelevant. It wasn't my music I was performing, and I didn't want to be doing it. I looked awful, and I felt like a sad remnant from the past. I had never been so miserable, and I was utterly ashamed of myself. I think that TV show, although it was far from the end of my decline, really brought home to me not just how far my career had fallen, but how absolutely devoid of new ideas I was. I was hopelessly out of touch, and I had no answers whatsoever.

I had other problems as well. As I began to plan the next studio album, it dawned on me that I had become totally dependent on the WaveTeam and their PPG system. Having used them for several albums, I'd allowed myself to become very out of touch with the latest technologies. I'd used samples but didn't really know how sampling worked. I'd used sequencing but, again, didn't really know how sequencers worked, and so on. Synths had moved on, but those advances had escaped me. My reliance on the PPG, and my reliance on Mike and Ian operating it, had rendered me a technical dimwit. It amazed me how quickly I'd lost touch. It seemed like only yesterday that I was on top of everything and now just a review of a new synth read like a foreign language. We were soon to move away from Rock City as well, so studio time would have to be rented in the future, and that would be expensive. I certainly wouldn't have the luxury of being able to write the album in the studio. I would need to be much better prepared in advance, and for that I'd need to bring myself up to speed with all the latest equipment and techniques. I'd also need new gear so that I could pre-record at home before even booking a studio. But we had no money.

To make matters worse, I was presented with another tax bill for £200,000, and I had absolutely nothing to pay it with. In fact, I was about £200,000 in debt so worse than nothing. We put the Wentworth house up for sale and were lucky enough to sell it just before the housing market crashed. That paid the tax bill and a few other pressing debts, but the overall problem of being broke remained. We had to borrow more and more, and I invented ever more lies to cover up my embarrassment and to try to convince people we were still doing well financially. I was worried that if people knew, it would send yet another powerful signal that my career was all but finished.

We eventually borrowed enough money to buy some new equipment, and I set to work learning as much as I could. I started very small, very simple, and then, as I began to understand and get to grips with the concepts, I moved up to more complex gear. Slowly but surely I began to get on top of it all once again. Just doing that felt good. It felt as if I was taking back the controls of my career once again, after having drifted. My intention was to set myself up as a small and efficient one-man cottage industry. That would take a lot longer than I anticipated, and not before I took another diversion.

During this period of reacquainting myself with the current technology, we were approached by Miles Copeland, the former manager of The Police. Miles was a rich and influential man and wielded considerable weight in the music business. As an ally he could be extremely helpful. Although we were close to signing an agreement to distribute Numa albums in the USA, it wasn't a great deal. But, to us at the time, it was better than no deal at all. Miles then made us an incredible offer for me to sign with him instead that was worth £1 million over the following five years. It was a dream come true, a lifeline to a drowning man just as he was about to slip under the waves for the last time. I thought that we were not only saved from career oblivion, but soon I'd be big news in the UK and the USA, if not the entire world. Miles had two labels, Illegal and IRS. Although they weren't major labels, they were well funded and had knowledgeable teams running them. They could certainly do a much better job than we'd been doing. I would be the most expensive artist they'd signed, a label priority, and they promised me great things.

The optimism of the IRS deal made me choose a new house that was a little more expensive than I'd originally planned. I took out a worryingly large mortgage and, confident that Miles

Copeland was taking me back to the top, moved in. The new house was in Essex, on top of a hill, had a few acres of land, more than enough rooms and was very pretty. With no neighbours anywhere close, or even in view, I could make as much noise as I liked making music.

By the time I signed with Illegal, I'd already recorded most of the next album, which I was going to call *Cold Metal Rhythm*, before we left Rock City, and although I was working with The Waveteam again, I was producing this one myself. I went to a studio called Black Barn to finish it, and it was here that Miles came to listen. He was upset that one track, 'Devious', had lost the 'magic' that the demo had. Generally, he seemed happy with it, which was just as well, as changing things at that late stage would have been quite expensive.

IRS expected things to go well from the start, but I don't think they truly grasped how deep the radio resistance to me actually was. When the first single 'New Anger' was chosen, by the label not me, I remember a somewhat overweight senior figure at the label dancing around his office. It was a little embarrassing, but I was impressed with his enthusiasm. He was full of praise and talked about what a huge hit it was going to be. It felt great to be listening to that kind of positivity at last. When it only reached number 46 in the chart, he was a very different man. He said I'd chosen the wrong single, even though I hadn't chosen it, and that he was never keen on that song at all. He flatly denied, to my face, that he'd chosen 'New Anger'. It was pathetic, and my heart sank. This was the worst kind of record-company bullshit, and these were the people I'd thought were going to make a difference. They then said that the word 'cold' had negative connotations and would need to be removed. So, the album was titled

Metal Rhythm. It seemed a petty, inconsequential change, but I was keen to be as agreeable as possible and so made very little fuss.

I played an eighteen-date UK tour, including three nights at the London Astoria. To try and keep tour costs down, we set up a gruelling schedule, with just one day off: eleven shows, day off, seven more shows. I don't know how we survived. Even with that rather extreme cost-cutting measure, I was still spending too much on the design, and so yet again the tour lost money. Not the huge amounts we had in the past but still too much when you're trying to get out of debt. I tried everything I could think of to make the shows as big as possible but without spending silly money, but I think anyone taking any notice could see that they were getting less impressive each time.

In the USA, they changed the album title to *New Anger*, changed the sleeve, and not for the better, and messed around with the tracks, which was really quite upsetting. They added some songs from *Berserker*, which made absolutely no sense at all to me, because the two albums had entirely different sounds and were years apart. I was horrified by what they were doing. In the UK, the album barely scraped into the Top 50, as did the next single, 'America'. It was all very disappointing.

Miles came up with a number of strange ideas. I was desperate to tour in North America again with *Metal Rhythm*, but I needed him to back the tour financially. He suggested that to reduce costs I use a girl band to support me on the tour that would also be my band for my set. This was a band that he managed, so I could see the sense of it from his point of view, but it made no sense to me. For one thing, I would need to rehearse with them for weeks, which would cost more than flying my own band over. More importantly, there wasn't enough of them to play all the parts needed for my music, and they couldn't play all the instruments I needed. It was just a mad idea. He also wanted me to record a cover version, because, as he said, 'Everyone's having hits with covers.' I couldn't imagine anything worse. I'm a songwriter first and foremost, and I'd already sold myself down by doing collaborations my heart wasn't into, for money. Doing a cover version was just a horrible idea. Worse, he wanted me to do a version of a really old song called 'Sixteen Tons of Number 9 Coal' or a '60s song called 'My Baby Just Wrote Me a Letter'. He kept saying 'Just do it the Numan way'. I was fucking horrified and didn't know what to do. Eventually, although I hated the idea, I suggested a compromise. What if I was to record a Prince cover? He grudgingly went for that, so I recorded two Prince cover versions, '1999' and 'U Got the Look'. Miles thought they sounded too much like the originals, so neither one ever came out as a single. '1999' ended up as a B-side of something I no longer remember, and the other one later got used on what I firmly believe is the worst album I ever made, but I'll get to that.

After the third single with Bill Sharpe came out, it was decided that we would record an album. I like Bill very much, he's a great player and songwriter, but, if I'm honest, it isn't really my sort of music, and I wasn't overly keen to do the album. My dad, as my manager still, was pushing me to do it, saying it would be 'a second string to my bow'. I wasn't sure I wanted a second string, though. I was still concerned that by doing these collaborations, no matter how well written and slickly produced they were, I would alienate the fans who were still with me and lose even more. Coming at a time when IRS seemed to want to change everything about me, and were forcing me to do things I hated doing, recording another collaboration album of music miles away from my own felt wrong. But we did it anyway. With my career still spiralling downwards, I'd become far less certain of my arguments and more easily persuaded.

The album was called *Automatic* and was released with little fanfare by Polydor in June 1989, only reaching number 59 in the chart. My creative contribution to it was essentially limited to the lyrics and vocals. Bill did everything else, along with Nick Smith. They put together a well-crafted album, but, in truth, I was little more than a guest vocalist. As for any meaningful campaign to help it, Polydor really did just throw it at the wall to see if it stuck, and it didn't.

To make my next album, *Outland*, and the albums that would come after that, I knew I needed a small studio of my own, at home ideally. So, I started to put together my own twenty-four-track home studio in the new Essex house. When I say studio, I pretty much mean a sound desk, recorder and some speakers. It really was just put together in a room next to the kitchen. No acoustic treatment, no design at all, just squeezed into what space I had with a view over the field. I had to take out another loan to buy the equipment, which, given our poor credit, was not easy. The IRS advances were good, and very helpful, but so far not enough to get us out of the deep hole we were now in. I did have some things I'd held on to when we sold Rock City, so with the loan finally secured, I ended up with a very modest but reasonably good-quality home set-up. I wired it myself, and for the next few months sat with a pile of manuals and figured out how everything worked. To me, the choice I had was very simple. I either got completely on top of operating every aspect of my own studio, or I would have to stop making albums. Going to commercial studios was no longer possible, as we simply couldn't afford it. Having my own meant that I could continue to make albums for many years to come. To begin with, though, I found it quite difficult. I was now not only writing and producing everything, but I was also the sound engineer and doing my own maintenance. In many ways, the constant studying reminded me of being back at school, except that this time I was happy to work as hard as I could. By now, a part of me had begun to feel almost as though it was me against the world, and that actually helped my attitude considerably. I enjoyed that feeling of having my back against the wall. The new set-up was beginning to feel like the cottage-industry idea I'd been looking for. I still had IRS to deal with, though.

I flew to the USA to do some promotional work for the *Metal Rhythm/New Anger* album. It was a good trip overall, and I did a fair amount of press, but some things were a bit awkward. At one point, I was put in a room and given a list of phone numbers to call. These were record-store managers across the USA, and I was expected to call them, talk up the album and make a more personal connection. It was about as far from what an Asperger's person was built for as you could get. To make it worse, not many of them knew I was calling and were busy, and several of them barely knew who I was. It was embarrassing, humiliating and pointless.

Later that year, in October, I released a live album on IRS called *The Skin Mechanic*. I'd recorded the music the year before during the *Metal Rhythm* tour. I toured *The Skin Mechanic*, which was unusual, as you wouldn't usually tour to support a live album, playing fourteen shows around the UK. During that tour, I had a peculiar thing happen one night as I was partying in a hotel. I ended up with my body entirely locked, wrapped around a toilet while I was being sick. Eventually I had to be picked up, still shaped like a toilet hugger, and laid on the bed while a doctor injected me with something to relax the muscles. I'd pulled all the muscles in my neck, and my feet and hands were blue. The next morning the band went ahead to the next venue, and I followed later in a car. Three hours before it was due to start, I still couldn't stand up, but in the end I was somehow able to play the show.

Chapter Sixteen

1990–1991

After the tour, I got straight on with the album. Ian Herron was running his own studio by this time, so it was just Mike Smith and me. The only major problem occurred when a lightning strike hit close to the house. Somehow it found its way into the studio and did a huge amount of damage. Tapes were scorched and several pieces of equipment burnt out, including the main console, which had to be replaced. Despite these setbacks, *Outland* was finally finished in early autumn, and Miles Copeland and Steve the label MD came to the house to listen. It was a very stressful hour, as so much was riding on their reaction. They'd already taken up the second option of our deal, which meant another big and badly needed advance. But after so many strange suggestions and flip-flopping opinions, I was nervous about what plans they had in mind. All I wanted to hear was that they liked the album and would release it as it was.

Their reaction was exactly what I'd hoped it would be. They said it was brilliant, exactly what they were hoping for. They congratulated me and Mike, said lots of lovely things about what they were going to do to promote it, and left. We were all completely over the moon – for about a week, when we had a phone call saying it wasn't what they wanted after all and they needed some changes. They wanted to change the word 'infected' to 'affected' in one song. I couldn't understand how that would make any difference at all. I had to get the girl singer to come back, remix the entire track and then rent for the second time the special equipment we'd used to compile it. Redoing that one word cost me several thousand pounds. I sent them version two, and they were very happy, for about two weeks. Then they asked for some more minor changes. I did them and sent version three. Then they asked for some more, so I tweaked it yet again and sent version four. Finally, they were happy for long enough to see it released. I'd been working on it so long by then I was sick of listening to it.

The year had an awful surprise in store for us. My mum was told she had breast cancer. She took it all in her stride, as though it was a minor, temporary nuisance. She had an operation to remove part of one breast fairly soon, and I remember going to visit her in the hospital after it was done. She did her best to be upbeat and bright, but it was plain to see it was an ordeal. The doctor who took care of all her cancer treatments turned out to be a big Gary Numan fan. I hoped it would help get her that extra ounce of attention. Eventually, she would have both breasts removed, and it would become a lifelong battle.

I was finding it harder and harder to deal with Miles Copeland's suggestions about what I should be doing to make my music more successful. I began to feel as if I'd been signed not for what I did, but as something to be moulded into what Miles thought I should be. He thought I should get a dance remix of an *Outland* song called 'My World Storm', so he sent over a couple of men for me to work with. They spent the first twenty minutes or so telling me how I'd messed up my entire career, which I listened to very patiently. Then they began working on the song, leaping around, pushing faders and pressing buttons, all the time praising each other with words like 'wicked' and 'crucial'. I took it for as long as I could before leaning forward to tell them the panel they were using wasn't turned on and all their crucial twiddling was doing fuck all. I ended up calling them the Bollocks Brothers, and that was the end of that remix.

I think many of the ideas that Miles came up with would have worked well for someone else. He was genuinely creative and always looking for ways to adapt what you were doing to try to reach a bigger audience. In many respects, he is exactly what so many artists need. It's just that I cared more about the music I made than I did simply reaching a bigger audience. I wanted success, obviously, but by doing something I cared about, not by doing anything just to bring in new fans. The most important thing for me was that I needed to enjoy what I was doing – I needed to be proud of it. Unfortunately, because I resisted and argued against so many of his ideas, Miles came to think of me as uncooperative.

Outland was released in March '91, reached number 39 and sold more than 30,000 copies in the UK, which wasn't too bad at all. I was actually quite pleased with that. IRS only released one single from it, though, a song called 'Heart', mainly because they were still upset that I hadn't wanted to go down the dance-remix route, I think. I'm not sure that releasing another single would have helped much. *Outland* was also released in the USA, but I suspect IRS had already decided not to bother by then, as they did almost nothing to promote it. I did one interview with a US journalist who wasn't even aware I had a new album out, which pretty much said it all.

The fourteen-date *Outland* tour started that same month with a slightly changed band line-up. My brother John was still there, as was Cedric on drums, but Mike Smith on keyboards, Keith Beauvais, a new guitar player who had played on both *Metal Rhythm* and *Outland*, and backing singer Jackie Rawe joined.

Mike Smith and I worked on another project during the year. I was asked to write the music for a low-budget horror film called *The Unborn*. Rodman Flender, the film's director, was a fan of an old instrumental song of mine called 'Asylum' which he thought had the right vibe for his film. I'd wanted to get involved in film music for some time and so this seemed like a gentle, low-pressure introduction into that world. Mike and I wrote well over one hundred pieces of music for the film, initially without even having a script. We just wrote lots of things that we felt could work for a horror film. Eventually we got a rough cut of the film, which really helped, and then Rodman came over and helped shape the final score. I very much enjoyed working on it. I thought IRS would be keen to release the soundtrack, but, surprisingly, they weren't the slightest bit interested. I eventually released it myself as a side project instrumental album with Mike called *Human*.

In the summer, I started to hear rumours that IRS were dropping lots of bands from the label. An old support band I'd worked with called Yen were dropped, and there were rumblings that IRS was being sold to EMI. This was very worrying. The next advance due to us was the one that would finally clear our debts and put our heads above water after years of struggling. We got in touch with IRS and eventually received a letter from them saying that, yes, EMI were buying into them but that I was 'a key ingredient and featured prominently in their future'. That came as a massive relief. Unfortunately, two weeks later, we got another letter saying I was out. No reason, no deal, no apology and no money. It was a bitter disappointment.

Numa Records was relaunched straight away. The difference this time was that I would be the only artist on the roster. We quickly released a new single, 'Emotion', and on 14 September went back out on tour again. I cheekily called it a European tour, but it only had one show in Belgium – the rest were all in the UK. Still, that was my first European show since 1980. In truth, the *Emotion* tour came way too soon after the *Outland* tour, so I decided to try something different: I played some smaller venues. I thought they would be easier to fill, for one thing, and they wouldn't need such a big, expensive light show. In the club venues, the fans could also get up closer. I hoped that a club-like vibe would create an even closer relationship between us. It was great fun, and despite being dropped by IRS, I was able to forget my troubles for a while. When it was over, though, I had some serious thinking to do.

Chapter Seventeen

1992

Losing the IRS advance plunged us back into real money trouble. The bank threatened to repossess my house, so we put it up for sale. At one point, we even discussed adapting my mum and dad's garage and moving in there. The only thing that saved the house was that no one came close to offering enough money for it. The very best offer we had for it was way below the mortgage I owed. I think some of the people who came to view it had a sense that we were in trouble and made ridiculously low offers, expecting us to grovel for their breadcrumbs, I suppose. Everything went up for sale, including the aeroplane, but even if we managed to sell it all, it wouldn't be enough to get us out of trouble. So, we decided to make drastic changes to the way we ran things. Tracey was a qualified graphic designer, so she took over the artwork duties. The home studio was already in place, so we begged and borrowed and lied our way along and managed to survive from one day to the next. We cut back on absolutely anything and everything that wasn't absolutely essential. And I came up with as many ideas as I could, beyond just making albums, that could help generate income. We started to operate three telephone lines that fans could ring and listen to different things. One was for information, one for new music and the third for competitions, where the prize would be a day out for groups of fans doing various fun things with me. Things like paintball, karting, flying, Laser Quest, anything we could think of that allowed me to mix and have a closer relationship with the fans. That close relationship was so important. I felt incredibly grateful to each and every one of them for staying with me through all the ups and downs, and still being there to support me. I really enjoyed those fan days. Eventually, I think I become too familiar, and they began to do more harm than good, so I wound them down.

I felt enormous pressure to make the next album as good as it could possibly be – it was as though our future depended on it more than ever before – but things went badly from the very beginning. I was so desperate for every song, every note, to be special, I would listen back at the end of each day and erase everything I'd done. Nothing seemed good enough, and day by day my confidence crumbled a little more. To begin with, I was writing furiously, coming up with a torrent of ideas, but none that I thought were as good as they could be. That pace slowed to a crawl, and each day became a demoralising disappointment. I went for months and didn't keep a single thing, not one second of recorded music. In a way, I almost hoped the album would find its own way, and I'd hear something while I was playing or going through sounds that would ignite a spark and I'd be up and running. But nothing came. I had no idea how I wanted the album to sound. No idea what I wanted to write about. I was hopelessly and completely lost, and everything just stopped. When I needed to be at my very best, I found I was completely empty. I'd read about writer's block, but this was the first time it had touched me, and it couldn't have come at a worse time. The pressure just ramped up until I could barely function.

My relationship with Tracey had been struggling for a long time, but I think the stress of trying to make that album, and the serious financial problems we were in, just added so much extra weight that it started to buckle. We'd nearly split up a number of times already, but the arguments were getting more frequent, and more ugly.

I'd planned to do another tour in March '92 to support the new album, but it wasn't close to being finished. I released a compilation album of Numa songs called *Isolate* and toured that instead, and it was every bit as desperate as it felt. Keith Beauvais couldn't do the tour, so he recommended a friend of his called Kipper, a larger-than-life character and a great guitar player. Suzie Webb (no relation) also joined on backing vocals. I released another single, 'The Skin Game', but it sold badly and *Isolate*, unsurprisingly, did no better.

During the tour, I often spoke to Kipper about my struggles with the new album, and he offered to help. As soon as the tour was over, he worked on four songs, and I went to his place with Tracey to listen. They were better than anything I'd come up with, but I knew it wasn't the direction I was looking for. But what could I do? I had gone for months and not written anything I thought worth keeping, so I talked myself into using Kipper for the entire album, which I'd decided to call *Machine + Soul*. He was very good, and as a piece of music there's nothing wrong with it, but as a Gary Numan album it's the worst thing I've ever done. It had nothing 'Gary Numan' about it, absolutely nothing. I was so lost for ideas I even put one of the Prince covers I'd done on it. I tried and tried to convince myself that it was the right album, but I knew it wasn't. It was all I had, so I released the worst album I've ever made when I needed to have made the best. I don't think I have ever felt more ashamed and hopeless. The sleeve was shit as well. I hadn't just lost my way musically – I'd lost it in every way. I was the lowest I'd ever been.

It sold really badly, which came as no surprise. *Machine + Soul* sold barely half of what the IRS albums had done. For a moment, I wondered where all the fans had gone, and then I looked at the album sleeve and it all made sense. The next single, also called 'Machine + Soul', didn't even make the Top 70. I honestly thought it was all over, and I thought I deserved it.

Tracey and I were also over, although we hadn't quite acknowledged it. In June, we decided to make a documentary about my new flying team, The Radial Pair. Tracey had ambitions to become a film-maker, so it would be good experience for her, and the documentary would be useful for me. The Radial Pair team was put together by me and my Harvard teammate Norman Lees. We flew a two-ship formation aerobatic routine, and the documentary was an attempt to make a cool film to show what we could do and to raise our profile so we'd get more airshow work. It was a strange feeling knowing that I was flying around in my own aeroplane while I had crippling debts. But airshows paid, and through them, and some other paying flights, the Harvard earned enough money to pay for itself. At that time, I still got a lot of media attention from flying and virtually none from music, so it was also keeping me in the public eye. Tracey did a great job on the film, and I released *The Radial Pair* video, with a backing track of my own music, later in 1992. We argued constantly during the making of it, though, another sign that we were at the end of our relationship. Tracey became friendly with the cameraman – they clearly took a shine to one another – and I had met someone called Gemma O'Neill. For both Tracey and me, it was the time to call it a day and move on.

Gemma had been a fan for years, and I'd often noticed her in the crowd whenever I toured. She stood out. Sometimes I'd see her after the show, but only ever to sign an autograph and then she'd leave. She didn't hang around, didn't party back at the hotels. She was strikingly good-looking, and long before I got to know her I would find the crew peeking out at her from behind the stage curtain. On the *Emotion* tour I didn't see her around until one of the very last shows. I played a song each night called 'Time to Die', which is about the final thoughts of someone dying, and that night during the song Gemma left. The tour manager, Andy Keightley, noticed she was crying as she walked out and ran after her, found out why and invited her back after the show to meet me, hoping it would help cheer her up a little. I assumed she was there for an autograph, but I happened to say I hadn't seen her on that tour, which was unusual. That was the most I'd ever said to her up to then, I think. She told me that her mum was in hospital with cancer, with not long left to live, and she was only there that night because her dad had pushed her to go. So, we had our first proper conversation. We sat and chatted in a quiet corner for a long time and then, as always, she left. She was remarkable, and I thought about her often after that. Many months later, I heard that her mum had died, so I called and asked how she was. At first, she didn't believe it was me and thought it was a cruel joke. She asked me questions to prove who I was, but she'd only read about me in magazines, and some of the answers I gave didn't tie up with what she thought. It took me some time to convince her who I was. I think she put the phone down at least once before she was convinced. I had a long drive up to Shropshire for a radio interview the following week, and I invited her along. During the journey, I gave her all my best stories, but she knew them already. After a while, I stopped trying to be entertaining and we just talked, and as we talked I began to realise just how extraordinary she was.

I have met so many incredible people over the years – the beautiful, the gifted, the rich, the successful, the glamorous – but I'd never met anyone like her. I never will. Even amongst such glittering company, she stood out in every way. I was damaged. My relationship with Tracey, the slow-motion destruction of my self-esteem, my failing career, my enormous debts, had all taken their toll. I couldn't bring myself to commit to another relationship. I'd spent nine years with Tracey, and it had come to nothing. I was thirty-four now, and I didn't want to make that mistake again, or any mistakes again if I could help it. I was very honest about it. I told Gemma that I would see other people and that it was OK if she wanted to as well. I honestly believed that it was foolish to meet someone and without really knowing them at all commit yourself to an exclusive relationship with them almost immediately. After Tracey, I thought it made more sense to see different people casually and naturally discover the person you were most suited to. It was only then that making a commitment made any sense and the relationship had any real chance of surviving. It wasn't an open relationship with Gemma – it was not committing to any. Gemma was in a strange place herself in some ways. Her mum had just died, and all the things that would normally be unacceptable in a relationship now seemed less important, so she decided to go with it, until such a time as she found it too painful. I am very aware of how it sounds, but it really was the right thing to do, and the strength and longevity of our relationship I think proves that. We continued in that non-committed way for about a year, maybe fifteen months, and in that time it became clear to me that I actually had no interest in being with anyone else . . . ever. Twenty-eight years later and nothing has changed. She is everything that I am not, everything I need to be complete. Even now, after all the years we've been together, I still miss her when she's out, even when she goes to the shops. She was once asked during a careers talk at school what sort of job she wanted when she left. She replied, 'I won't need a job. I'm going to marry Gary Numan.'

Chapter Eighteen

1993

In August 1993, a new dance-remix version of 'Cars' was released by Beggars Banquet. It was not something I wanted to get involved in, for all the same reasons as before. In many ways my career from '79 onwards had been overshadowed by the huge success of 'Are "Friends" Electric?' and 'Cars', so to keep being associated with those same songs just added to the public feeling that they were the only things of worth I'd done. It cemented me to the past, and it destroyed any chance of my rebuilding some credibility. But with no current success and no money, I was once again persuaded, or badgered, into getting involved. It didn't do that well, which I was strangely grateful for, so my soul-selling weakness went largely unnoticed.

I had a clash with the UK's Civil Aviation Authority (CAA) in September. Norman and I were flying at a small airshow in the West Country. The weather was horrendous, low cloud and rain with a strong wind blowing towards the crowd. The pilots decided to fly anyway and just do what they could. We didn't want to disappoint the spectators who had braved the weather, nor did we want to let down the organiser who had put so much work in. Norman Lees and I were flying our two-ship Radial Pair display which would normally be a fully aerobatic routine. In that weather though all we could do was fly around close together, staying under the cloud, and at least let people see these lovely old aeroplanes in the air. Norman was asked if he could give commentary during the display that would be relayed to the public through the PA system. This was cleared with the CAA representative there. It had been obvious for some time that this particular CAA man did not like me. I have no idea why, perhaps he disapproved of people from my profession getting involved in display flying. A surprising number of people did to begin with, but it got better over time. At one point during the display, as we were flying towards the crowd, I gave Norman the command to change position and so move his plane behind mine. Unfortunately, he was commentating at that moment and missed the call. So, as I looked to begin a tight turn to the right, I saw Norman was still sitting on my right wing, making the move impossible. I had a choice; I could turn anyway and hope Norman didn't hit me, or I could turn gently, climbing as I did so, and risk no more than flying over the crowd slightly. I chose the latter. Flying over the crowd was strictly forbidden but, given the situation, it was by far the safer thing to do given that Norman was in the wrong place. When we landed the CAA man loudly and publicly banned me. The other pilots immediately objected to his decision, knowing only too well the circumstances, and the ban was lifted within minutes. But the damage was done. The next day it was all over the press with headlines like 'Flop of The Props', and I was made to look like a reckless idiot all over again. Sometime later I quietly received a letter of apology from the CAA but it wasn't sent to the press and did nothing to repair my reputation as a pilot. I was bitterly upset by the whole affair.

Our financial woes took another dive soon after that. My dad had a conversation with someone we owed money to. It wasn't a lot, and this man was actually a friend, someone who had worked as part of our road crew and earned a lot of money from us over the years. It was explained to him that we were struggling financially but we would get his money to him as soon as possible. He shook hands, was sympathetic, said he understood and left. That evening his partner rang up and said if we didn't pay him in full, immediately, they would force us into bankruptcy. It was a nightmare. It felt as if our fragile house of cards was about to come tumbling down around us. I don't know what my dad did to get us out of that, but he did, and we survived another day. I think that was the worst moment. My big fear had always been that our appalling situation would become public. Not just because of the humiliation – it would also take away any chance of us being able to borrow money in the future. It could easily be the thing that ended it all. No new albums, no more touring, nothing. I was worried about everything, of course, but I was especially worried about my dad. He bore the full weight of trying to find a way through these seemingly endless problems, and I, more often than not, made things worse. I knew he wasn't sleeping, and he was often difficult to be around – just a very different person to the dad I'd known. It was horrendously stressful for him, and for my mum, and I could see no way out of it other than making more albums and trying to become ever more efficient as a business. I felt totally responsible for the mess we were in, and I knew that it was entirely down to me to get us out of it. My dad had the task of keeping us afloat in this stormy sea, but a real rescue would have to come from me, and that seemed more unlikely by the day.

I bought desktop-publishing software and taught myself how to create album covers, T-shirts, posters, fan-club magazines, even backstage passes. With Tracey now gone, we would have had to pay someone to create artwork for us, money we didn't have. Learning graphic design meant that I could do everything instead. For a long time, after my mortgage was paid each month, I was only allowed £600 to live on per month. When Gemma met me, she would buy all the food and house supplies. My sofa had broken all its springs, and I'd put a piece of wood under the cushions to stop you sinking to the floor when you sat on it. My TV was a small fifteen-inch portable placed on a kitchen stool. I used to pretend that I was eccentric and liked things that way. It made me laugh when Gemma was accused by some of the fans of being a gold digger. If they'd only known. I had absolutely nothing but debts and worries, and there didn't seem to be much chance of things ever getting better. She came along when I was about as down as I've ever been.

Gemma also made a very big decision that I was largely unaware of during that first year. She'd been offered a placement at the University of California to take a foundation course in criminal psychology, and she would work as a nanny for a family while she was there. It was all agreed – everything was in place. It was a dream come true for her, but then she started to see me, and I was not committing. So, she had to decide whether to move to California and pursue her dreams or stay in the UK and take a chance on me. It really was a very hard decision, and I was not a good bet, to be honest. I'd done little to make her feel secure in our relationship, and yet she saw, I think, a growing bond between us. She chose me, and my life was changed for the better in more ways than I could ever count.

In October of '93, we toured the UK yet again with the *Dream Corrosion* tour. I've read things I've written about the tour previously, where I say I loved doing it, but I find that hard to believe. When I look back on that tour now, I can clearly remember feeling utterly dejected at how poor the attendance was at some of those gigs, and yet I also remember having a fantastic time. The crowds seemed more enthusiastic than ever, and I was more comfortable on stage than I'd ever been. I was at rock bottom financially, and I'd just released my worst-ever album. I was playing some songs that I didn't really like, I didn't like the way I looked or the clothes I wore, and I had little confidence in what the future held. I should have been a broken shell, and yet I was having a good time. It's often said that touring is like living in a bubble, a world within a world, a life within a life, and I think perhaps that's the reason. On tour, all other problems are outside. Touring has its stresses and strains, obviously, and they can be considerable, but they are different. It really helps to take a break from pressure, even if you're just replacing it with pressure of another kind.

When the tour was over, Gemma officially moved in, and our non-commital relationship was over. Almost immediately, I was asked to support OMD on their latest arena tour. I jumped at the chance. For me, it was back into another tour bubble, and I could push back having to readjust to the worries of normal life – even more so on that tour, as none of the concerns that often come with touring were mine. Not my show, not my lights, not my crowd, not my worry. The last time I'd toured with OMD had been in '79 when they'd supported me. Some people thought I'd feel awkward about that change of roles, but

I honestly wasn't bothered at all. I was just glad to be out on the road again having fun.

Soon after the OMD tour, I flew to Bergamo in Italy to shoot a video for my final involvement with the Radio Heart team. The song was called 'Like a Refugee', and we were to shoot a promo video for it with a remarkable marching band called Da Da Dang. They dressed like robots and marched through the streets of Italy in costumes that glowed in the dark. It really was quite spectacular. The song didn't get anywhere, and Radio 1, as usual, didn't play it, although they did make me 'God of the Day', which was about as bizarre as singing with Da Da Dang.

Chapter Nineteen

1994

I started work on the follow-up album to *Machine + Soul* with Kipper, but straight away it didn't really work. I still had no idea what I was doing or what I wanted, but I knew another album like *Machine + Soul* wasn't it. I was so unsure about my future I'd even started to think about what sort of normal job I'd need to get and how I would deal with the inevitable ridicule. By now I was well over £600,000 in debt, and there didn't seem to be any way in the world I was ever going to get out of that. Getting another record deal seemed all but impossible. I'd fallen too far for any label to be interested, and creatively I was still nowhere. I seemed to be heading towards a very different life, one where I would likely be in debt for ever. I hadn't given up hope by any means, but the awful reality of how precarious my position had become had never felt closer.

I talked about my long fall from grace with Gemma, and why it had happened, so many times, but I didn't like what she had to say. She tried to explain to me that I might not be the best guitar player, or keyboard player, but I played a certain way and my fans liked it. I might not be the best singer, but my voice was unique. I tried to explain that by taking me out of the albums I'd made them better musically. She answered by saying I'd taken out the only thing the fans wanted in them: me. We argued and argued, for month after month. For a long time, I didn't accept what she was saying at all, but she was extraordinarily patient and chipped away, little by little, until I began to see my situation through her eyes, and presumably through the eyes of so many other fans as well.

She was also introducing me to music I hadn't heard before. For several years, I'd all but cut myself off from music. I was still making my own albums and touring, but I'd pretty much stopped listening to music for pleasure. I've mentioned already that one of the problems with losing your confidence is that you start to listen to bad advice, and the moment you do that you lose your way. You lose sight of what you like, what you want to do, you become confused and uncertain. I'd been listening to things because I'd been told I should write stuff like this band or that singer – that it would get me back into the chart. It was terrible advice, and I should never have listened, but I did. When Gemma arrived and began her slow rebuilding of my confidence, I was still completely lost. She introduced me to a whole world of music that I'd missed completely. Every day she would play things, and I'd run in and ask who it was, what it was called. It was all incredibly inspiring, and it rekindled my feelings about music, my love for it. It actually made me realise that I hadn't enjoyed being involved in music for years. Now, suddenly, it was like being a teenager again. I remembered why I'd wanted to be a musician in the first place, and it was exciting. It felt as if I hadn't been truly excited by it for years.

I went back to the new album and started from scratch. I would once again do everything myself – even more than before, in fact. I'd write it, produce it, engineer it and record it in my own studio. I'd design the sleeve – I'd even do the artwork. The album was to be called *Sacrifice*, and I would let it be whatever I wanted it to be. There was no outside advice now, no record company, so no record-company pressure or bullying. I was my own man again, and I would do exactly what I wanted to do. I had no one to please but myself and virtually nothing to lose. The only thing that mattered was that I genuinely loved what I did. I became so obsessed with this newfound independence of thought that I vowed that if I was working on a song and I started to consider whether it might sound good on the radio, I would erase it immediately, and I did, more than once. I was absolutely determined never to lose my way again, never to become corrupted by thoughts of commercialism, the business of making music. I would only write songs that I truly loved, and never for any purpose beyond that simple desire. My music would become *pure* again, untainted and unchanged by schemes and strategies. I still wanted to be successful, but I wanted to achieve it with music I was proud of, music that was written for the love of it, not part of some devious plan to write something that might somehow attach itself to whatever bandwagon was passing.

With *Sacrifice*, I abandoned all thoughts of future chart success. I simply made making music a hobby again. I had no idea if the album would even be released, but it felt good. It felt as though a huge weight had lifted off my shoulders, a weight that had crushed my creativity. Ideas began to flow faster than ever. I discovered I had things I wanted to write about beyond the one-dimensional career grumblings of the last few albums. I started to write a book (one of many I have yet to finish) called *Pray, the Final Treachery of God*, about a space between life and death, where some people, in the moment of passing, get a glimpse of heaven and realise it's not what they'd been led to believe, but something dark and seething with malice. In that moment, and in their horror, they open a door into a space in between. A place where even God, in all his fury, can't reach them. But something can. Something far more terrible even than the God they hide from, and it's coming. *Pray* was a story to exercise the mind, to allow me to get ideas out in a different way to writing songs. Nonetheless, many of those ideas found their way onto the album.

I have no religious beliefs whatsoever. I find the very idea of God to be so ridiculous as to be laughable. Or it would be laughable if it wasn't so dangerous. People seem capable of taking almost any part of any religious book and finding a way of adapting those words to justify doing great evil. It has been a lifelong source of incredulity to me that people can truly believe that by doing something horrific they will somehow be welcomed by their God. If your religion really wants you to do something horrendous, maybe you should find a different religion. It baffles me. Even at a much lower level you see cruel things done to the innocent by supposedly devout people on a daily basis, convinced of their own moral superiority. The hypocrisy of it all is staggering. The stupidity of it even more so.

Those thoughts about religion are woven throughout *Sacrifice*, but it has more than that. It looks at many things, mostly disturbing, that had affected my life in the years leading up to that point. Frightening dreams, the feeling of things waiting for you, of being alone. It was darker and heavier than anything I'd done before. Even the sleeve was black. For the first time in a very long time, I felt that I really knew what I was doing. I thought back to my machine analogy, where all the pieces needed to be turning smoothly together for the machine to work properly. With *Sacrifice*, it felt as if they were doing exactly that. The only thing I got wrong, and it was a big thing unfortunately, was the mastering. With money being such an issue at the time, I decided I'd master the album myself rather than use a professional engineer. We just couldn't afford to pay for that last and vital stage of the recording. I really did think I could do it, but I made a complete mess of it. The album has a lack of clarity that lets it down badly.

Sacrifice was released on 24 October 1994, and although the singles from it didn't fare well, the album did much better, eventually selling far more than *Machine + Soul*. Strangely, whereas *Machine + Soul* had reached number 42 in the chart, *Sacrifice* only made it to 94, my worst album-chart position ever. The thing about *Sacrifice*, was that it started to bring fans back from the cold. For most fans, it seemed to be a welcome return to form, and the response to the album was better than anything I'd had for years. My fan-club membership soared. *Sacrifice* sold slowly but steadily as word of it spread, and it felt very much as though we'd turned a corner. I was confident about my writing again, happy with the way I looked, happy to be making albums. It was all so different.

A month later, in November, I toured the UK once again. This tour was a little different in that I decided to play only cities where I'd done particularly well before. This meant just ten shows, but we achieved better attendance at each and lower costs overall. It worked well, and for the first time ever, I actually made money from a tour. I was still light years away from the heights of '79, but, at long last, we were heading gently in the right direction.

Another encouraging development in '94 was that other artists started to cover my songs. Smashing Pumpkins did a version of 'M.E.', and Beck did 'Cars' when he played London. To have other people cover your songs, especially artists who themselves are great songwriters, is such an honour. Chart success is a great thing, no doubt about it, but you are always aware, at least I am, that luck and the hard work of others plays a huge part in that success. But to have your song covered by someone else? Luck plays no part in that. It's only about the song, and it's a direct reflection of your standing as a songwriter. As such, I have always felt more pride when a high-calibre artist covers one of my songs than I ever have from being in the charts.

During the rehearsals for the *Sacrifice* tour, Kipper had turned up on a cool-looking motorbike. I'd not had any interest in bikes at any point in my life, but now they suddenly seemed like the best thing ever. I became obsessed and bought every magazine I could find. I made my own little booklet of every bike I liked the look of. After the tour, my brother John, who had also decided to get into bikes, rang me up and said he'd found the exact bike I'd been hoping to get, a Yamaha Virago 535. I bought it and it was delivered a few days later. I didn't even have a licence to ride, so I just parked the bike in the garage and stared at it. A week after the tour, I had my first lesson, and a week after that I had my bike licence. I loved riding, and for a while I went everywhere on it. I fell off it once and I got knocked off once; the former was my fault and the latter most definitely wasn't.

Chapter Twenty

1995

The first song I wrote in 1995 was called 'Absolution', and it was released as a single in late March. 'Absolution' looks at the dangers of blind faith. The blind faith of love, but especially that found in religion. I'd bought a new synth and wrote the song as a useful way of learning what it could do. It took about six or seven hours to go from writing the first note to having a finished track, with lyrics and vocal, mixed and ready for release. It followed the same style as *Sacrifice* in that it used heavy synth drones over massive drum loops, but it was even heavier, more powerful and anthemic. As far as chart success and radio play went nothing had changed and the single was ignored. I expected that. I hadn't even tried to get plays for 'Absolution', so it wasn't a disappointment. It did occur to me that I was now selling four times as many albums as singles. Singles were usually used as a promotional tool to sell albums, so, for me at least, what was the point in singles? I decided to stop putting out singles for a while.

After the success of *Sacrifice* I was nervous that I wouldn't be able to do anything better. *Sacrifice* to me felt as though I'd stumbled back onto the railway tracks I'd been travelling all those years ago when I was on the outside of the train. I'd fallen off, picked myself up and walked away into the fog. Meeting

Gemma was like finding a light in the fog that guided me back to those tracks, and I found my way again. But it was different this time. The only way I can think to explain it is that my newfound direction, my rekindled love of making music, fantastic as it was, seemed precarious. As though the tracks were clear under my feet but almost buried just a few yards ahead. I could see the way they were headed, but I wasn't sure I'd know that I'd be able to stay on them if they turned. It felt all too easy to get lost again. The ups and downs, the disappointments, the press, everything that had happened, had made me unsure of myself. A quiet anxiousness about everything I did had now replaced the supreme confidence I'd had when I first grabbed on to that train and went for the ride of my life. I was either damaged or wiser. Perhaps a bit of both.

Although I was happy with 'Absolution' that fear of not being able to make a better album than *Sacrifice* gnawed at me, and I found reason after reason to delay making a serious start on the next one, *Exile*. I did write a few songs, and *Exile* was definitely a work in progress, but I would find the slightest excuse not to work on it. For the first time, it seemed like a huge challenge, not so much for the work involved but for the mental strain I now felt. Where before I had launched into a new album mostly with enthusiasm, it now felt like a long, steep and arduous climb towards a distant point obscured by clouds. A journey filled with danger where you could stumble and fall at any moment. It was all in my head. Every day working on it was like a roller-coaster of emotions. I began to dread spending time in the studio, because a day when few ideas came was almost impossible to deal with. I talked to myself constantly to try and overcome the terror that I felt when something didn't quite work out. Every idea that didn't measure up felt like I was dragged a little closer to the edge of a deep chasm, one that I wouldn't escape from. It was horrible for the most part, and yet, when an idea suddenly made sense and a song came together, the feeling of elation was so strong it balanced out all those days of anxiety. I thought I was just scared of losing that fingertip hold on a better future, but *Exile* was just the beginning of those sorts of feelings. They've never gone away. Each album since has been more difficult than the one before.

Good things were happening. I started to hear about more bands recording cover versions of my music or playing my songs live. Every week it seemed another cover version was being talked about. I could also see a shift in the way my name was being mentioned in the media. It was subtle to begin with but unmistakable. Whereas before any reference had been scornful and dismissive, now I was mentioned in more glowing terms, as an innovator or a pioneer. My earlier albums were now talked about as being inspirational and groundbreaking. Even *Sacrifice* had had some good reviews. I could pretty much count my good reviews before *Sacrifice* on one finger. It all felt slightly unreal.

It was in 1995 that I began to look at the internet as a possible new tool. I'd read so much about its potential, so I went online and made it my mission to understand how it might be useful for my career. It looked as if it could be the answer to a range of problems that had hampered us as a small, independent label, and I saw huge opportunities. Simply trying to let fans know what you were doing had always been problematic. Letting people know about a new album or a tour, for example, usually required expensive advertising. The internet seemed to offer a way that would essentially allow me to speak to fans directly. The cost of a web designer seemed excessive, so I printed out pages and pages of instructions on how to programme HTML code and set about building my own website. In the November, I launched *NuWorld*.

NuWorld quickly became my main outlet for information. In just a few minutes, I could post updates that every fan could see instantly. I could promote my own albums, tours, merchandise, anything I wanted. In so many ways, the internet was a complete game changer for the music business – not all of it for the better, but nonetheless it put a considerable amount of control back into the hands of the artists. It made it possible for bands to go their own way to a degree that hadn't really been possible before. A powerful label is still a mighty force to be reckoned with, but the internet made it possible for smaller fish not only to survive, but to thrive, opening up a whole new world of possibilities for me. I wasn't against the idea of signing to a label again, but it no longer seemed as vital as it had.

In October '95, I heard that Carling were going to use 'Cars' for a new advertising campaign for their Premier lager. The advert ran for eight months on TV and was also in the cinema for quite some time. Beggars re-released it as a single, and in March '96 it became a Top 20 single in the UK once again. I was even asked to do a *Top of the Pops* performance for it, which was nice to do, but I did feel a bit awkward. I didn't really want to go on national TV doing that same old song, but with everything else going well, it seemed like it might actually be helpful this time. Polygram then licensed a bunch of my older songs from Beggars and released a TV-advertised album called *Premier Hits*, which got to number 21 in the album chart. As much as possible, I wanted to use the new interest to push my new music, not the older stuff, and it was difficult trying to navigate a way through. For example, I turned down an offer to appear on the *Big Breakfast*, a very high-profile TV show at that time, because they wanted me to sing a duet of 'Are "Friends" Electric?' with the presenter. The show had an audience of millions, but, desperate as I was for the exposure, I thought that would be a mistake. I was asked to appear on another TV show called the *White Room*, a very hip and influential show. Bands performed three songs and the show would use two of them. I was told to play 'Cars' and 'Are "Friends" Electric?', and I could choose the third. I said no initially, because I suspected they would only use the two older songs, but I had a phone call with the director who promised me they would use the new song and one of the old ones. I said yes based on that promise, but it seemed that the director wasn't able to keep his word. Sure enough, they used 'Cars' and 'Are "Friends" Electric?', so it looked like I was trotting out the same old past glories. I was furious when I saw what they'd done.

I did manage to get some exposure for the new material, and it really helped. I performed on the Bob Mills *In Bed With Medinner* TV programme and played 'Scar' from *Sacrifice*. Even then, though they made me play my two most famous songs, it was worth it just to let people hear something new. However, it did feel very much as though I was trying to run with weights tied to both legs, and the weights were those two old songs. No matter how hard I tried to keep moving forward, those two songs seemed to drag me back. On the rare occasions I was interviewed on the radio, they would play 'Cars' when it started and 'Are "Friends" Electric?' when it finished, usually not even playing the new stuff I'd gone there to talk about. It seems strange but I started to resent my own successful past. Those two songs seemed to have created a silver cloud that cast a shadow I was finding impossible to escape from. It was incredibly frustrating, but things were still very much better than they'd been. Most importantly, I now had music that I was passionate about, music that I felt was worth fighting for.

Chapter Twenty-one

1996

The modest but encouraging success of *Sacrifice* definitely generated a new wave of interest in me. Many fans that had long deserted the sinking ship of my career now came back by the thousands. But if I was going to make the most of that new interest and seize this unexpected opportunity, I would need a better label than my own Numa Records. I decided to take advantage of the *Premier Hits* album that Beggars were involved in and tour it. But instead of playing all old songs, I used it as a vehicle to play newer material. While I was doing that, my dad was looking around to see if another record deal was possible.

The *Premier* tour, as it was called, was very important to me. I took the opportunity to include four of the new songs from the unfinished *Exile* album in the set. As such, it became the first step in letting fans hear where I was going musically and would serve as a good comparison to some of the older songs that made up the *Premier* set list. Along with the lighting designer Andy Keightley, and the moving light programmer John Barnes, I spent long nights working on the show. I'd be there all day working on the music with the band and then all through the night working on the lights. We barely slept more than a few hours each night. All three of us were determined to make the show as spectacular as we could. We were still tweaking it right up to the moment the doors were opened for the first show in Folkestone. I also had a new look for the tour. One that moved me away from the leather-clad style of old into a more filmic, Gothic vibe. I was now thirty-eight years old, and I wanted something that recognised that. I also thought it suited the new *Exile* songs perfectly. Meeting the fans after the shows confirmed much of what I'd thought when *Sacrifice* was released. I spoke to fan after fan who said they were the first shows they'd been to for years, and not all of the people I met were old fans returned. I noticed many younger people turning up.

I also met Steve Malins on the tour. Steve was a music journalist but, unusually, was a fan too. He'd written the sleeve notes for the *Premier Hits* album and brought Stephen Merrit from the Magnetic Fields to the show in London. Steve was aware of the subtle change in my standing and was keen to help. He told me how difficult it had been to be a Gary Numan supporter as a UK music journalist and how deep the hostility towards me had been. He explained that when a Gary Numan album arrived at their office it would be given to someone known to dislike me to guarantee a bad review. Same thing for the shows. There was a deliberate and sustained effort to do as much damage as possible to my career. It came as no great surprise, but even I was unaware of just how much had been stacked against me. But he also saw signs that it was changing, that a new generation of people were coming in to music journalism that did not hold that same negative bias. He thought it was important I started to become more accessible.

Gemma's help extended beyond advice on how I looked at my music. She also pushed me to get out and rejoin the world at large. I was extremely reclusive when we met. If I wasn't touring or flying at airshows, I tended not to go out much at all. I certainly didn't go to see bands any more. Gemma agreed with Steve and thought it would help if I did, but I found it very difficult. I'd frequently cause arguments before we left so I wouldn't have to go. It was an ordeal for me, and I was very awkward. The Asperger's part of me reared up and fought back. I blamed her for bullying me and did my best to make her feel bad about even suggesting it. But, again, with great patience, and with Steve pushing me just as much, she put up with all my nonsense, and we did start to go out more. It made quite a difference. For one thing, I was no longer enclosed in my own little bubble. I was meeting people, being forced to engage for much of the time, but meeting people nonetheless. I got to hang out with other bands, and I was amazed to find out how many of them saw me as some legendary pioneer. I hadn't expected that at all. I also started to meet music journalists, some of whom, if they'd thought about me at all, had low opinions based on things they'd read in the past, but in truth I was nothing like that. During my trips out with Gemma, I had many casual conversations with the press backstage at gigs, and I firmly believe that it helped build a better relationship with them. By now, many of the people who had written about me so negatively before had gone, and the new generation of music journos that Steve had mentioned were in place. They seemed less hostile. In fact, they seemed to see me in a very different light altogether. It all made me feel better about myself. I was amazed, actually. For years, I'd thought of myself as something of a laughing stock in the music business. My long decline had been very visible, and when added to the press vitriol of the early years I assumed that my credibility was absolutely zero. It may well have been for much of the time, but now it didn't seem to be that way at all.

In June, my grandfather died, and a kinder, more gentle man I will never meet. His name was Frederick James Lidyard, but everyone called him Jim. My brother John and I called him Poppa, actually, because he didn't want to be called Grandad. He served in the Second World War, although exactly what he did was never clear, and he only talked about the war once in my entire lifetime. He was about to leave my parents' house when he told a quick story, and that seemed to open a floodgate. For the next few hours I just sat and listened to the most extraordinary tales. Every story, even the most disturbing, was told with a good dose of British humour, but the things he had seen were unthinkable, truly horrific, and yet I never once saw him angry or impatient. I loved him very much.

In August, I played at the V96 festival. I'd never even been to a festival before, so it was daunting to walk out in front of 35,000 people who had probably come to see someone else. I have to say I felt considerable pressure from some quarters to play a set of old songs, but I saw it as a chance to show people something different, something new. Without radio play, and with TV really only offering me slots to play old stuff, playing new songs in front of a huge crowd seemed to be one of the only ways I was ever going to get them heard. It went well.

I then spent a week during the summer working as an instructor at a rather unique pilot-training school. The idea of the school was to take people already qualified as air-display pilots and teach them the more demanding skills of formation flying, aerobatics and ultimately formation aerobatics. It required considerable skill, and I was proud to be one of only two civilians in the line-up of fourteen instructors – the other twelve were all current or ex-military. As an instructor, you need to let the student make mistakes so they can learn from them, but only up to a point and you need to be very clear where that point is so you can step in and avoid disaster. Quite often I found myself in an aeroplane where the pilot seemed intent on destroying the plane and both of us in it. It was very demanding but great fun. One week was enough, though.

In the twelve months leading up to that week-long stint, another four of my friends had been killed in crashes. One of them had been a member of the Harvard Formation Team, another my former aerobatic instructor Hoof Proudfoot, whom I was very fond of. When I'd first met Gemma, I'd shown her around the house in Essex. I had no photos of me as a musician on the wall, but I had several of me with my air-display pilot friends. She mentioned afterwards that I hadn't shown her one photograph where all the people in it were still alive. In every single photo, at least one person pictured had died in an accident, sometimes more than one. It hadn't dawned on me, but she was right. It didn't have much effect on me at the time. Air-display pilots died all the time. It was a known danger that we all faced and accepted because we loved flying old military planes close to each other, upside down and close to the ground. It was the most exciting and challenging thing you could do. But after Hoof died, I noticed a change in Gemma. She became truly aware, I think, of how dangerous it was, and her tacit support for me flying off at the weekends disappeared. She wanted me to stop. In a way it came at the right time. Much as I still loved the flying, things had changed. The Harvard team was no more, and The Radial Pair team seemed to get booked less and less. When I did turn up, so many of the pilots I'd known had died I often didn't know many people there. It had turned from something exciting and rewarding into something depressing and lonely. I didn't want Gemma sitting at home worrying, and I wasn't getting the satisfaction from it I used to, so I decided to pull out of display flying.

Gemma and I had been riding around Essex on the motorbike whenever we had the chance that summer and autumn. To give ourselves somewhere to go, we would pick churches, ideally in a quaint village, and ride out to see them. Neither of us can remember exactly how it came about, but during one of those trips we started to talk about what sort of church we would want to get married in. It wasn't a strange conversation – it seemed a perfectly natural thing to talk about – but I hadn't proposed. It wasn't the romantic dropping-to-one-knee-with-a-sparkling-ring experience I'd thought it would be. It just drifted into our day as easily as choosing where to stop for lunch. Just the same, it was hugely important. Gemma did insist that I propose properly at some point, so I planned to ask her on 13 December, her mum's birthday. I messed it up slightly when I got the time wrong and asked her just before midnight on 12 December. I even went down on one knee, and although she'd chosen it, I had a ring for her by then.

Chapter Twenty-two

1997

As 1997 got under way, there was an interesting development with the *Sacrifice* album in the USA. I did an artwork
collaboration with an American comic company, who released
the album in February under the name *Dawn*. Dawn was a
successful female comic character created by an artist called Joey
Linsner. The music was all *Sacrifice*, but the artwork was essentially all Joey. It was a cool collaboration, and it meant that
Sacrifice finally had a release in the USA. This was an important
step for me. With things beginning to improve in the UK, I was
already beginning to look overseas again. If I could re-establish
myself in the UK, perhaps I could do it elsewhere.

Steve Malins called me one evening and told me about a
project he'd been working on with Beggars Banquet. He called
it *Random*. It would be a double CD, and it would have twenty-
six different bands covering my songs – some new and rising,
others well established. It was amazing news. It was such an
honour, and Beggars were fully behind it. Steve explained that
in his work as a journalist interviewing numerous bands he'd
noticed how many times I'd been mentioned as an influence, so
he started to ask them if they would be interested in recording
a cover version for a tribute album. He then persuaded Beggars
to get involved and front the money for the recordings, and it

all came together. As I remember our conversations at the time, Steve felt that it would bring me greater credibility once it became known that so many bands saw me as influential and were prepared to take part in the *Random* project. It was the single most important thing to happen throughout that entire period, arguably one of the most important of my career.

The finished album was fantastic, and I was incredibly grateful to the artists that took part (Jesus Jones, Damon Albarn and Pop Will Eat Itself to name a few), and to Steve for making it happen. It was released in June and seemed to do exactly what we'd hoped. It brought me recognition as an influential songwriter, and it did seem to change attitudes towards me. Another wave of interest came flooding in. I was asked to present awards at various events, and I became as close to fashionable as I'd ever been. *Random* sold well, especially for a covers album, and I noticed that the reviews were mostly very positive and complimentary. Not just about the bands' cover versions but the songs themselves. It actually made me nervous. It was such a novel thing to read articles about me that were complimentary I couldn't believe it would last. Every time I picked up a newspaper or a magazine that I was in I expected it to have gone back to the spitefulness of the old days. I said so to Steve: 'It can't last. It's just a matter of time before it all changes again.' But he thought differently. He thought things had changed. Not just for the moment, but for good.

Becoming aware of just how much new interest there was wasn't the total confidence boost you might expect. I'd become so used to putting out albums that were ignored, except by my own small following, I suddenly felt very vulnerable. I was already dealing with demons of my own trying to make *Exile*.

Now it seemed that people were waiting for it, with high expectations. There was a long list of people, way more than the twenty-six on *Random*, who were talking about me as being important to them and the music they made, and what they became. High-profile people like Trent Reznor and Billy Corgan to name just two. Now I had a newfound reputation that I had to live up to, and I found the pressure of that to be considerable. I was referred to as a pioneer, as ground-breaking and influential. It was lovely to hear, of course, and lovely to read, but it didn't fill me with confidence. It terrified me. Coming back into the light meant that I now had to deliver. I had to make an album that deserved this newfound reputation, something worthy of the high praise I'd been receiving. It wasn't just me writing for the faithful any more. It made working on *Exile* even harder.

Another small blip in our finances meant that I'd had to sell much of my studio equipment. To keep recording I'd bought two Akai MG1214 machines. They were glorified porta-studios in many ways, each capable of recording up to twelve tracks. By slaving (combining) the two together, I was able to create a rather bodged twenty-four-track system, but it was far from ideal. I never dreamt that I'd be making an album using porta-studios, but it worked surprisingly well considering. I was actually rather proud to have made such a good-sounding album on such basic equipment.

Exile was eventually finished in June, and despite all my worries I was happy with the end result. Like *Sacrifice*, it was mostly a one-man effort, in that I produced it, engineered it, wrote the songs and played almost everything. It took a different slant on the religious theme. With *Exile*, I took the point of view of what if I was wrong? What if God did exist? This time it was more about what if there really was a God that allowed the horrors of the world to take place day in day out? That would be truly terrifying. Every song was connected to the central idea that God and the Devil are one and the same, and that Heaven and Hell are the same place. It's our perspective that makes it one or the other.

In August, I was offered a new record deal by a company called Eagle Records, which you would think I'd be over the moon about. When it first arrived I was not in the best of spirits, and I actually turned it down. In the months leading up to this, I'd sent out letters and copies of *Exile* to about twenty-five UK labels (although not to Eagle), and several more in the USA, looking for a new record deal. Every one of them had come back with either a blunt no or they'd ignored my letter completely. That disappointing lack of interest, and the poor manner in which it was done, made me very angry. But it also fired up a fierce determination in me to prove them wrong. So, in the afterglow of the rejection, I'd decided to keep Numa Records going after all and do whatever I could to make *Exile* a success and turn Numa into a decent independent label. It was with that mindset that I received the Eagle offer, and I just wasn't interested to begin with. That first offer was already far better than anything I'd been looking for, but I'd just lost all willingness to battle with record labels. To my amazement, Eagle came back with an even better offer, and that's when I started to look more closely and realised how good it actually was. It wasn't just good money – they said they were happy to release the album as it was, with no alterations whatsoever. They were also keen to release it in territories outside the UK, which would make *Exile* my first truly international release since leaving IRS in 1991. I realised I was being pretty stupid and agreed to sign.

August was special for another reason. On 28 August, I married Gemma at Leez Priory in Essex. The months leading up to it, once the album was finished, were very hectic. We were both fully involved in the planning and went to countless wedding fairs, deciding on everything from the venue to flowers, food, clothes, fireworks, carriages and what seemed like a never-ending list of things to sort out. We loved every minute of it. We'd decided not to have a religious ceremony but still wanted the feel of one. Gemma was a non-practising Catholic, and I had no time for religion whatsoever, so Leez Priory seemed an ideal choice. A stunning Tudor mansion with a long history, set in forty acres of beautiful grounds, it also had a tower, where we would get married. It had all the feel and ambience of a traditional religious wedding without any of the references. The tower room was small, up a tight winding staircase, and it didn't have a long aisle. So I arranged for the guests to form an aisle across the grass from the mansion to the tower, and I waited for Gemma there. It was everything I'd dreamed it would be.

During the ceremony, she forgot my name, and hers, but I couldn't have wished for a more perfect day. A harpist in the corner of the tower room played a song of mine called 'You Walk in My Soul' as we entered, a line from which I also had engraved in Gemma's ring that simply said 'Until God takes me away'. It may seem a strange thing for an atheist to have put on a wedding ring, but it was simply a poetic way of saying 'for as long as I live'. Gemma knew exactly what it meant. *Hello!*

magazine covered the wedding, and during the interview they mentioned something they called the *Hello!* curse. Apparently, many of the marriages the magazine covers usually fail within three years. I have no idea how true that was, but we've been married twenty-three years now, so I think we're good.

My brother John was my best man, and he gave a very moving speech. One slight hiccup was when they played the music we'd chosen for our first dance. Neither of us had the slightest intention of dancing, but we'd chosen a song for the occasion anyway called 'Closer' by Nine Inch Nails. I hadn't really thought it through properly, because the lyric in the chorus is 'I want to fuck you like an animal'. My nan was not best pleased. After the wedding, we invited all our closest friends back to our hotel room and partied all night. We didn't even get to sleep in our own bed, but it was a night to remember just the same.

A few months before the wedding, Gemma and I decided we would start trying for our first child. We figured that she wouldn't really be showing much by late August so would still look slim and lovely in her wedding dress. I honestly thought I'd pop it in and that would be that. I'd been brought up to believe that girls got pregnant if you even looked at them with a suggestive expression, so I had no idea that it wasn't always easy. But it wasn't. The wedding came and went and still no baby, but we kept trying.

Eagle released *Exile* in October, and, initially at least, I was disappointed with the sales. I'd hoped that, with Eagle behind it, it would at least make the Top 40, but it peaked at 48. As time went by, it just carried on selling. Much like *Sacrifice*, it sold steadily over time rather than having a huge surge in the first week. So, while the chart position was not what I'd hoped for, the sales were very much better, and they showed a significant improvement over *Sacrifice*. The reviews were also good for the most part, which was quite a relief. I was still expecting my newfound favour to quickly disappear. The fans seemed to love it, and the feedback was overwhelmingly positive. My recovery was still going in the right direction.

The PR push for *Exile* was impressive, and I did far more quality press, radio and TV than I'd done for a very long time. One of the more interesting was when I did a joint interview with Mark E. Smith from The Fall. He was an extraordinary character and, much to my surprise, had many flattering things to say about me. The odd thing was he kept repeating them . . . a lot. After quite some time of listening to exactly the same comments, nice as they were, I was running out of ways to respond. He seemed to be bothered by that, and it all started to tilt a little towards the aggressive. I pretended I needed a trip to the bathroom, got around the corner and literally ran away.

I also had a chance to do a joint interview with Afrika Bambaataa for a feature in a magazine called *Hip Hop Connection*. He was a fascinating man and told me things about my influence on hip hop and electro that came as a complete surprise. Apparently, some of the songs from *The Pleasure Principle* album, songs like 'Cars' and 'Metal', had been important in the development of early hip hop, and 'Films', another song from the same album, was one of the most-sampled beats. I was absolutely blown away when I found out about that.

I was asked to do a live TV session for VH-1 and was allowed to play songs of my choice. No more demands for 'Cars' and 'Are "Friends" Electric?'. That alone spoke volumes to me as to how things were changing. I had a slightly new band line up for VH-1: Richard Beasley on drums, David Brooks on keyboards, Ade Orange on keyboards and occasional bass, and the newest member Steve Harris on guitar. Steve felt like the missing link in the band. An excellent guitar player and an absolute force of nature on stage, he made a significant contribution to the visual impact of what I was trying to do.

The *Exile* tour was so much better. The new image worked well, the fan reaction was amazing, and the music was heavier, more aggressive. I played a lot of material from *Exile* and *Sacrifice*, and when I did play older songs I'd reworked them to give them a much heavier feel. I was even signed up during the tour by a major concert agency, which played well for my ambitions to start touring overseas again. The best moment of all was at the final show in London. I'd never known a crowd reaction like it. It was exhilarating. Every song we played was greeted with a deafening roar. It was the most exciting show I'd ever done, and when we came out for the encore there was a full ten minutes of screaming and chanting before I could even hear myself speak over the PA to say thank you. It was very special and incredibly emotional. They lifted me to a height I'd not known before, and the gratitude I felt was overwhelming. I wrote about it in my book *Praying to the Aliens*, every word of which I still stand by:

These people had been with me through thick and thin. They had been solid in their support no matter what the press had said and no matter how wayward my own songwriting had sometimes been. When they saw me falter and lose faith they hung on to it for me. They fought on my behalf when

I hadn't the heart or the willingness to do so for myself. Now, it seemed, they sensed that it was all turning around, that it had all been worthwhile. I stood there and soaked up the energy as if I were a dead man being raised. It was a truly awe-inspiring moment for me.

A few days later, Gemma and I finally went on our honeymoon. A hurricane changed our plans quite late in the day and so we eventually found ourselves on the Caribbean island of St Lucia. It had its moments. One day I decide to try my hand at wind surfing. I was surprised when the instructor just pushed me out and then shouted at me from the beach to stand up. I fell off straight away and he shouted at me to stand up again. This went on for quite some time and with each fall my little wind surfer drifted further out to sea. After a while I'd drifted so far out I could no longer hear Mr Shouty, not that it made much difference, and I was so exhausted I could only lie on the board and wait for my strength to come back. It was then I noticed that the tide was about to take me past the last headland before the open sea itself. I'm a terrible swimmer but I decided that staying on the board and drifting out to sea would be suicide so my only chance was to try and swim for the headland. When I say I'm a terrible swimmer I really do mean it. Even in a pool I can't go more than twenty yards, but I didn't think I had any choice but to try. I was extremely scared, of drowning, of deep water, of being carried out to sea before I could reach the rocks. I took one last despairing look at the distant shore and, much to my relief, saw a small sailboat heading my way. As it got closer I noticed it was my shouting instructor. I could have fucking died if he'd left it a few seconds later. To make matters worse he proceeded to slag me off all the way back to shore by saying I wasn't manly enough. If I could only have strapped him into the back of my plane and rolled him around the sky for a few minutes I'd have seen how manly he was. Near drowning aside, 1997 had been an amazing year.

Chapter Twenty-three

1998

Eagle continued to work on securing licensing deals and releases for *Exile* around the world. As 1998 unfolded, they were able to get the album released in the USA, Canada, South America, Japan, Malaysia, Australia and most of Europe. For so long, with very few exceptions, I'd only released in the UK, so it felt good to now see the album coming out in different parts of the world.

Things were getting busier everywhere. I recorded a guest vocal for a Magnetic Fields track and flew to Vancouver to record a guest vocal for a cover version of 'Cars' that the band Fear Factory were working on. My song 'Dark' from *Exile* appeared on the soundtrack album to the film *Dark City*. It also appeared on the soundtrack for the *Tomb Raider 2* video game. On 9 March, Beggars released *Random (02)*, another tribute album, but this time of dance remixes of my songs. I found the promotional work on that quite difficult. I'm not a fan of dance music but I was genuinely flattered that so many artists from the dance world had contributed. It seemed rude not to speak about it in glowing terms, so I did my best to be positive. The truth was it just isn't my kind of music, and I really didn't know much about the people on it.

In March, just a few days after my fortieth birthday, I set off on my first European tour since 1980. With no touring for

eighteen years and very few albums released there, I wasn't
expecting many people to turn up. I approached it very much
as if I was a new band starting out. The venues were small, and
I had no idea if anyone would know about me or if those who
did would be willing to come to a show. My other worry was
that if they did come, what would they expect? The last time
I'd played in Europe the music had been very different, and I'd
been a completely different kind of performer. The rather static,
nervous, wooden man of old was long gone – now I barely
stood still for a second. The music was a much heavier form of
electronic and far more aggressive than anything they'd seen me
do before. To have stood there like an icy-cold android just
wouldn't have worked. In any case, I'd moved on from that.
Now I felt the music and just went with it. I didn't plan or
rehearse any moves, no beat-by-beat choreography in front of
the mirror like I had for *The Old Grey Whistle Test* TV show a
lifetime ago. Now I just walked onto the stage, felt the music
and let it happen. I had no idea what they'd make of it.

When I first made it in 1979, one of the many criticisms that
came my way was that I hadn't paid my dues, and by that they
meant I hadn't slogged around shitty clubs for years before I was
successful. I never did understand why that was seen as a necessary rite of passage, but I was certainly doing it now, so the tour
was an interesting experience. I would watch each night as the
show progressed. It was easy to see the disappointment on the
faces of some of the old-school electro people at first. It was not
entirely what they'd come to see. Every night, I'd watch that
disappointment change to appreciation, and it was very satisfying. More than that, however, I saw fans who were younger,
who clearly didn't know the words to 'Cars' or 'Are "Friends"

Electric?' but seemed to know every song we played from *Sacrifice* and *Exile*. That was particularly encouraging.

The strangest show was Berlin, our fourth gig of the tour. When the house lights go down at the start of a show you usually hear a cheer from the audience, but there was nothing. The intro tape started, nothing. The band walked on, still nothing. I walked on and was greeted by absolute silence. I don't remember hearing a single clap, cheer or whistle. It wasn't as if we were being ignored – there wasn't even any conversation burbling amongst them. They were just still, silent and staring, and it was most unsettling – it made me really angry. I whispered to Steve, 'Let's make it harder than ever,' so we launched into a blistering set. Steve was a maniac, sweat dripping, and I was matching him drop for drop. We leaned off the stage and got into as many faces as we could reach. We played as though we were the most confident, arrogant band in the world, in front of the best audience possible. As each song thundered out, they slowly started to get into it, and we began to hear noise and see arms up in the air. By halfway through, the place was alive and screaming. We played two encores that night and left thinking we'd won a stunning victory, but it was the strangest start to a show I've ever known.

I came back from that tour feeling I'd achieved something important. The attendance had been surprisingly good for one thing, and I felt I'd reintroduced myself, and the new music, quite successfully. I'd also done a reasonable amount of press during the tour, and it had all been positive. Most of all, I came back feeling that I had come of age as a performer. I had a confidence now that just hadn't been there before to the same degree. I also had a band around me that could not only play well but were as committed to it as much as I was, and they'd become my closest friends. We got together regularly and had some of the best parties I've ever been a part of. It was such a strong feeling of closeness and comradeship, and it made touring a real pleasure. I felt ready for anything.

A week after we got back to the UK, Eagle released the 'Dominion Day' single from *Exile*. They'd put up money for me to make a decent promo video for it, and I did as much promotional work as I could to support the single. Unfortunately, a distribution problem meant that the singles didn't all make it to the stores for the first week; in fact, they dribbled out over three weeks. This destroyed any possibility of a chart position in the UK, which was a shame. It did get to number 5 in the German alternative chart, probably due to the impact of the Euro tour, and it also gave a noticeable boost to the sales of *Exile*. It was the first time I'd seen a single actually help an album for years.

A few weeks later, at the end of April, we left for the North American *Exile* tour. *Exile* had been licensed by Eagle to a label called Cleopatra in the USA, and they'd released the album in February, so the timing was good. It had been sixteen years since I'd toured America and I felt much the same about that tour as I had about the European prior to the first show. I doubted many people would remember anything about me, but I was wrong again. Not entirely, to be honest – the places we were playing were small and sweaty for the most part, but people came. In the USA, though, and the two shows we played in Canada, they seemed just as ready for the new stuff as they were for the old – more so, in fact. They were much younger and going for it from the first song. The majority of people coming to the shows seemed to be too young to even remember 'Cars'. I couldn't understand how they knew about me at all. I'd released nothing in North America for so long – there'd been no tours, just nothing at all, and yet here they were. I was very aware of how much smaller it was, of course. When I'd toured the USA and Canada before in 1980, I'd been playing arenas in many cities. Now I was doing clubs. But the way I looked at it, I was glad to be doing it at all. It had been such a difficult journey since the heights of 1979, I was genuinely grateful to still be in a position where touring around the world was possible, and genuinely grateful that people still wanted to come out to see me play. It was quite humbling. It had been twenty years since 'Are "Friends" Electric?' went to number 1, and I really had thought it was all over at times. But I'd battled on as best I knew how, and now here I was in the USA again. I was finally stepping out on the long road back. I was brimming with optimism. Over the next fifteen years, I would learn just how long that road actually was.

The tour was twenty-four shows long, with plenty of nights back to back, so it was hard. But as it progressed, we found various groups of fans would turn up night after night, and we became quite close to some of them. It made it feel like a travelling circus, and the atmosphere for most of it was exciting and fun, like a really good party that just rolls on from one night to the next but for a month. I loved it. In Baton Rouge, I met Trent Reznor from Nine Inch Nails, who told me he used to listen to *Telekon* every day when he was working on the classic *Downward Spiral* album, Clint Mansell, who had once been in Pop Will Eat Itself and who is now a celebrated film composer, and legendary music producer Alan Moulder all for the first time. Trent was recording his double-album masterpiece *The Fragile* at the time, and he brought me a copy of an amazing cover version of my song 'Metal' that he'd done.

Every night, things happened that were remarkable for one reason or another, but in Jacksonville, Florida, we had one of the worst crowds I've ever known. The promoter of that show had billed me as some kind of British dance-music legend, and the people who turned up seemed to be expecting exactly that: dance music. We were a terrible disappointment to them. It was the only show on the tour when it seemed no Gary Numan fans turned up. None at all. Most of the crowd played pool while we were on, and I think those who did watch only did so because they couldn't get on the pool tables or slot machines. During the set, a sewage pipe running across the ceiling started to leak and dripped actual shit onto the sound desk. It was a horrible ninety minutes, and as soon as the main set was over we all made a run for it. But outside things were even worse. The bus was about 100 yards away from the stage door, and as we ran towards it we heard a loud bang. A girl ran past screaming that someone had just tried to shoot her in the head. I couldn't get on the bus quickly enough, and I was glad when not long after we rolled out of Jacksonville.

Many of the shows had sold out, including the bigger ones like The Fillmore in San Francisco. When we arrived in Los Angeles, the label's PR rep said that Brian Warner had been in touch and wanted to sing 'Down in the Park' with me. I had no idea who Brian Warner was and was pretty dismissive of the idea until she explained that it was Marilyn Manson. I'd met Manson before at a Beck show in London. He'd even done a cover version of 'Down in the Park', but I didn't know his real name was Brian. He didn't look like a Brian. Whatever, he was obviously welcome. That night Wayne Hussey from The Mission joined us on stage as well. When Manson came out for 'Down in the Park', I expected the crowd to go truly ballistic, but it was actually quite a mixed reaction. Some people loved that he was there, of course, but others didn't seem pleased to see him at all. I have no idea why. I thought he was great. He was making his *Mechanical Animals* album at the time, and I was a big fan.

One of the things that had been so different about this tour, and the European tour before it, was that I'd taken no production at all. The gigs were so small for the most part that it would have been pointless. Doing those tours taught me that I didn't need lights. With a great band around me, and the confidence I now had in myself on stage, they weren't necessary. That isn't to say they aren't a good thing to have, they most certainly are, but I learned that you can still put on a good show without them. On those tours nobody seemed to care. We often had little space to move around, so all you had was the music and the way you presented it. No lights to hide behind, no huge stage sets to keep the audience entertained should you not be good enough. In a way, it was a coming of age for me.

A flurry of reissues of old albums was released by Beggars Banquet and Eagle throughout 1998, including an Extended version of *Exile* that had longer versions of every song. Something like fifteen Numan albums came out that year. I was able to upgrade my studio and bought a new digital RADAR (audio recorder) system by Otari. I was also able to move the studio out of the house and into a building outside. My dad came over and for several weeks we refurbished a rather dilapidated old shed in the garden. By we I actually mean my dad, but I was an enthusiastic assistant. By the end of it I had a really good studio. A room away from the distractions of the house, lovely though they were, and just a really nice place to spend time and work on music. I was very happy with it.

In the summer, I was asked to do a cameo in a comedy film that Martin Clunes was making called *Hunting Venus*. I was told that Simon Le Bon, Tony Hadley and The Human League were going to be in it as well. I've never really had any desire to be an actor, but at times, especially when my music career was going badly, it seemed like it might be a sensible thing to try and get into. I took a few acting lessons once when another film I was asked to be in looked like it might happen. It didn't, but I paid for a course of ten lessons and stopped after just four, I think. It's not for me. I can barely remember my own lyrics let alone pages of dialogue. Anyway, playing myself with just a couple of lines in *Hunting Venus* seemed like it wouldn't be too challenging, and I was a big fan of Martin Clunes, so I said yes. It was as nerve-racking as I'd feared, even though I had almost nothing to say, but I did enjoy it. With that done, I started to write songs for my next album, *Pure*.

Chapter Twenty-four

1999

In 1999, another barrage of old albums and best-of compilations was released. If anything, there were more than the
year before. I guessed it was a result of things now going
better. Beggars had a fair amount of albums that they perhaps
saw an opportunity to rework. Most of the re-releases seemed
to be coming from Eagle. Eagle had signed me for a three-
album deal, with an increasingly lucrative advance for each of
the three albums. *Exile* had been the first, and they'd exercised
their option on the second, so that would be *Pure*, whenever
it was finished. Part of the deal was that Eagle also acquired
the rights to my entire Numa Records catalogue. As they
pushed out re-release after re-release, I began to wonder if
perhaps that was the main reason they'd signed me. After all,
if you could lift a flagging career even a little, that artist's back
catalogue became much more valuable. Beggars definitely
seemed to be doing the same thing with their Numan back
catalogue. It's not a bad thing to do, and I wasn't speaking out
against it, but it did make me start to wonder if Eagle's commitment to me was less for the new music and more to acquire
the back catalogue. A bit of both, most likely, but as the year
unfolded I began to wonder if their option for the third album,
with the most financially rewarding advance for me, might be

less certain than I'd previously thought. Time would tell, and much would depend on *Pure*. I still had a long way to go with that one.

It was noticeable that I was not spending as much time in the studio as I used to. That feeling of climbing a mountain with each new album, the fear that ideas wouldn't come, was growing all the time. Starting a new album, I knew what was coming, the emotional strain of it all, and I wanted to avoid it whenever possible. I still wanted to make albums, still wanted to write songs, and I needed to be in the studio to do that. But making albums now felt like a very different animal. I was no longer single or in a bad relationship. I had somebody I really wanted to be with twenty-four hours a day. Perhaps that had something to do with it, but I think really it was just the fear of failing, of running out of ideas. Losing all the ground I'd made up. Progress on *Pure* was slow. Very slow.

In March, *Hunting Venus* was released. It was fun to be a part of a very different world briefly, but the fuss around the film was soon over, so I turned my thoughts back to music. I'd come home after the North American *Exile* tour with the seeds of a new idea about playing live in the UK. Rather than going out on long, expensive tours with big light-show productions that rarely made any money, I would try something different. I wanted shows to become important events for fans. Some of the thinking actually came from a conversation with a fan I'd had the year before. My experience of touring with no production in Europe and North America had added even more fuel to the idea. The fan I'd spoken to had mentioned that he hadn't come to see a show on a recent tour because, as I 'toured all the time', he'd decided to save his money and catch the next one instead. It made me think that maybe I toured too often – maybe I was simply too available. Coming to a Gary Numan show wasn't special – it was run of the mill. I decided I wouldn't tour the UK that year or the next. What I would do is play a handful of one-off shows (or 'weekenders', as they were often known) around the country. I wanted to take away that certainty that it didn't matter if you missed this or that tour because I'd be back next year. I wanted to be less predictable and encourage fans to see me when they could, because you never knew when I'd be back. The first was in Nottingham in April, at the Rock City venue.

In May, Gemma and I were flown back to Vancouver by Fear Factory. Their cover of 'Cars' had come together well, and they were going to release it as the fourth single from their *Obsolete* album. To that end, they decided to make a promo video and wanted me to be in it. I had a great time working on the video and became friends with the band, Burton C. Bell especially. 'Cars' didn't appear on the original album but was added as a bonus track to a digipak version released on 23 March. It was noted in the press at the time that it was only when 'Cars' was added that the album gained significant mainstream exposure. It was eventually certified gold in Australia and the USA. Fear Factory very kindly presented me with a gold disc for it as well, which still hangs proudly in my house.

Another one-off show followed when I played at The Forum in London. I was sure that, at least for now, it was the right thing to do. The one-off shows were sold out, the crowds were loud and enthusiastic, and I was able to go home with some money to help our recovery. In August, we were asked to play the Eurorock festival in Belgium, and it was a great trip. I was still relatively inexperienced playing festivals, but the confidence I'd built up in recent tours helped enormously. During the day, I'd walked past some of Echo and the Bunnymen as they sat outside their bus. I didn't know their names, so I just said 'Hello, Bunnies', and they blanked me completely. That evening we played our set, and it couldn't have gone better. The crowd loved us, and as we walked off the stage we could hear them chanting for more. It was a supremely satisfying moment, but it seemed to annoy the Bunnies even more, as they were the headlining band and next to go on. Someone came running up to me as I was walking back to the dressing room and said that the Bunnies singer, Ian McCullough, had broken or lost his set of in-ears, the small headphone speakers that fit into the ear for us to hear the music. I lent him mine and an hour later wished I hadn't. He wasn't happy with the crowd for some reason, took my in-ears out and threw then on the floor, breaking them. At £700 a set, I thought that was a tad ungrateful, and he didn't pay me for them. I met Ian when he came to a Manchester gig years later and he apologised. He was actually very funny, but he still didn't give me my £700 back.

At some point that summer, Gemma and I came to the obvious conclusion that something was amiss as far as us making babies was concerned. We'd been trying for two years and nothing had happened. We decided to see a doctor and started a series of tests. It was slow progress. The NHS is a fantastic idea, often ruined by government penny-pinching. We would wait months to get an appointment to see a specialist, months more for the test he or she recommended, months more for the result. It was frustrating in the extreme. I had three tests to see if my sperm was up to the job. Test one came back great, test two came back as rubbish and test three said they were average – I can't remember the exact words used, but that sums it up – so they weren't entirely conclusive. One thing they wanted to try, and I apologise for the graphic nature of this account, was to look at the sperm when it was in Gemma. Apparently, we would need to do the dirty deed and get to the hospital within thirty minutes or else it would be too late. But the hospital was a twenty-five-minute drive away and the department was a five-minute walk from the car park. So, I would start the car and park it by the front door of the house, leaving both car doors open. Gemma would be waiting inside the front door, braced for impact. I would rush in, do what was needed, and then it would be a high-speed drive to the hospital, try to find a parking space near enough and then a run to the room we needed to be in. It wasn't exactly romantic, and we usually giggled the entire way there. If we were lucky, the medical staff were ready and waiting, took a sample and my job was done. It was at one of those sessions that they made a discovery that seemed to be the answer. Gemma's body was supposed, at the right time, to become a welcoming haven for my little swimming chaps, but it wasn't. It was 'hostile', apparently. They let me look through the microscope, and I could see my chaps struggling. Some of them had two heads, which couldn't have been Gemma's fault. All in all, it was pretty upsetting, and I actually felt a genuine pang of sadness to see them in distress.

Towards the end of our time with the NHS, we were called in by our doctor. As we walked in to his office, he slapped a file down onto his desk and said, 'Congratulations, you're pregnant.' It didn't feel quite right, as we hadn't had any tests recently. Gemma looked over at the file and noticed it didn't have her name on it. He had the wrong file, and she wasn't pregnant. We decided we'd gone as far as we could with the NHS. Our only serious option seemed to be IVF. That was hugely expensive, so we put the idea on the shelf for the time being.

Around that time, Fear Factory had a show at Brixton Academy. Their *Obsolete* album had done very well, and their tour had sold out. Brixton was the jewel in the crown of the tour, and they asked me if I'd like to come on stage and sing 'Cars' with them. It was an honour, of course, but I was very nervous, and Gemma had to work hard to convince me to do it. I just couldn't believe that a Fear Factory crowd would want me there. I turned up in the afternoon, did the soundcheck with the band and then hung around backstage for hours until it was time to do the song. I was so nervous. When Burton introduced me and I walked out, I was honestly expecting a barrage of beer cups and boos, but it was amazing. I did the song, the crowd were fantastic and I walked off feeling pretty good about myself.

In September, EMI re-released *Metal Rhythm*. If you remember, when I was signed to IRS they were bought out by EMI and I was dumped. So, EMI clearly didn't want me on their label, but now they were releasing my IRS albums. I found that quite offensive on the one hand, yet strangely satisfying on the other. Then Eagle released a best-of album called *New Dreams for Old*, which was a peculiar mix of things, some recent, some old, some seemingly borrowed from EMI. To be fair, as I was slow coming up with a new album, they probably had little choice but to lash the thing together and do the best they could.

I worked on *Pure* throughout the year but not as intently as I should have. I was slowly building up a collection of songs. They were all still very much at the rough demo stage, and I seemed to go on and off them as often as the wind changed direction. I just wasn't confident about what I was doing. I'd been happy with the production I'd done on *Exile*, but I wondered if maybe this next one needed some outside input.

Chapter Twenty-five

2000

Gemma decided she was going to do a skydive for charity, so on a cold winter morning we found ourselves somewhere in the north of England at a small airfield. I was very impressed with her determination. She went through all the briefings and listened to the instructions, but I was pretty sure she wouldn't take much of it in. She's not the best at giving anything her undivided attention. She was going to do a tandem jump and would be strapped to an instructor who would actually be in charge, so I don't suppose it made too much difference, unless something went wrong. She wore a very large and loose-fitting polo-neck sweater, and as soon as they jumped from the plane it shot up over her mouth so she couldn't breathe, and the first few seconds were all a bit of a panic. Once she'd managed to remove the jumper from her mouth and breathe again, she apparently had a good time. I was very relieved to see her land safely.

I have to say that Gemma has a daredevil streak in her that far exceeds mine. She will go on the most horrific bungee jumps, rides, swings, anything at all. Things that I can barely even look at. Once in Auckland, New Zealand, she had a go at leaping off the tallest building in the city on a wire. I couldn't even walk out onto the platform to wave her off. When she landed they said she could have another go for free, but only if she went off backwards, so she did. In Las Vegas, she went on everything that was either ridiculously high or hanging off the side of a skyscraper. I can't do any of it. I can fly planes upside down all day long, but I can't even drive along mountain roads, as vertigo kicks in so badly I have absolutely no control over my muscles. It feels like I'm being electrocuted. Why it doesn't happen in a plane I have no idea.

The most incredible bit of news arrived at the very start of the year. We received a message saying that General Motors were putting together a TV ad that would be screened during half-time of the Superbowl, and they wanted to use 'Cars' for the music. That was amazing enough, as the exposure for a Superbowl ad was simply enormous. But the amount they were offering to pay was just jaw-dropping. I'd seen very little success with my music being used in films and adverts, what's known as synchron-isation rights, even during the heights of '79 and '80. It had been a constant disappointment over the years, because I knew it could sometimes be good money, but I was staggered when my dad said how much they were paying to use 'Cars' for that one ad. It wasn't even 'Cars' – it was some actors singing the lyrics over a cover version of the music. I was going to earn a small fortune for doing absolutely nothing, apart from writing the song in the first place, I suppose, and the advert would be seen by millions of people the world over. It was an incredible moment. In one stroke, half our money problems went away. In truth, it would be well over a year before the money arrived, but just knowing it was in the pipeline made a huge difference to how we felt.

Quite unexpectedly, and not connected to the Superbowl ad, I was presented with a prestigious BMI award for 'Cars'. If I remember the wording correctly, it was 'in recognition of great national popularity as measured by broadcast performances', or something like that. I was very proud to receive it. At that point I'd received very few awards, so it came as a very welcome surprise.

Things were also taking shape with *Pure*. I'd got to know Rob Holliday, who was not only the guitar player in Curve but also in a band I loved called Sulpher. Rob worked with a man called Monti, the Curve and Sulpher drummer. I'm not sure exactly how it came about, but I remember talking to Rob about the worries I had with *Pure* and what I could do with it to move it on from *Exile*. At some point, it was suggested that Rob and Monti get involved and try producing one of the songs. I didn't know what would come of it, but I knew I was a fan of what they did, so there was a chance it might be pretty good. I sent them the title track and waited anxiously. It was more than good – it was brilliant. I remember when they sent that first song back and I listened to it in the studio for the first time. It blew me away. Gemma was out somewhere, but I called her up and asked her to come straight home to hear it. It was everything I'd hoped it would be and more. After that, I sent every song I had to them, and over the next few months the album came together. The relationship wasn't without its problems. Rob is still a good friend, but back then I found him sensitive in the extreme, and Monti I found quite difficult in other ways. The work they did on *Pure* was just phenomenal, so it was worth every headache. Rob and Gemma became great friends, and she did a lot to smooth out the ripples when things got heated.

As our attempts to have a baby had gone nowhere, Gemma and I visited a place called Bourn Hall, near Cambridge. Bourn

Hall was – and still is, I believe – one of the leading clinics for IVF treatment – the first in the world, actually. We had a series of meetings and tests and felt comfortable with the staff and confident that IVF was our best chance to have a baby. We were incredibly lucky to begin with. Seven weeks after the eggs were implanted we went back for a scan to see if there was a heartbeat, and there was. Gemma was pregnant on our first attempt. It's hard to describe that feeling. You've wanted this baby for so long, been through so much to get to this point, and here you are looking at a screen, watching a little dot flashing, listening to its tiny heart beating so fast, and that's the sound of your baby. The first sound you ever hear. It's such a remarkable moment, so unbelievably emotional. It's the best day you've ever had.

The next few weeks were wonderful. All we could talk about was the baby. Mum and Dad were over the moon, Gemma's dad, all our friends and family. It was just the happiest time, and we made a thousand and one plans for all the things we were going to do. Three weeks after the heartbeat scan, we went to Harley Street in London for an ultrasound check-up. We were very excited. We wanted to get photographs printed and have a video of the scan so we could show everyone. I'd read a great deal about what they would be looking for during the scan, and I was fully confident, eager to see the results. Gemma lay on the bed, the lady operator put my video cassette into the machine and started to record, and the scan began. We both asked lots of questions as the strange images drifted across the screen. From where I was sitting, I could see another screen where the operator was entering the various measurements she was taking as the scan progressed. It came to the Nuchal Translucency measurement, one that I knew was especially important, as it would detect any chromosomal abnormalities. I watched her enter the numbers and, to my horror, I saw the reading shoot way outside of the green range. I knew straight away that wasn't good at all. Then I saw her reach down and stop the video, and my world just collapsed. Even now, writing about it all these years later, it makes me cry. Poor Gemma was still smiling at the screen she could see, totally unaware of what was to come, and I couldn't do anything to soften the blow. It was just a horrible truth that we would have to face. The scan was stopped, and the lady very kindly explained what it meant. I can't remember too much about what came next, but I think Gemma had a fairly unpleasant test called an amniocentesis. We had to wait for an hour or two for the result, so we walked to Regent's Park and talked. We'd always been absolutely sure about what we would and wouldn't accept in terms of abnormalities, but all of that went straight out of the window. None of that mattered now. But the most overwhelming sadness wasn't for us, it was for the baby.

When we went back, we were told it was Turner syndrome. I'd never heard of it, but apparently it only affected girls, so we knew the baby was a girl. We'd already decided that if we had a girl we would call her Elfin, so now we weren't talking about 'a baby', we were talking about Elfin. They gave us as much information as we could absorb, but they said we should go home and learn all we could over the next few days. Rather chillingly, they said that it was highly unlikely she would survive the pregnancy. We spent the next few weeks gathering every bit of information we could find.

I think it was two weeks later I was standing in our field, on a rabbit mound, having my photograph taken for the *Pure* album sleeve, when Gemma started to bleed. She was rushed to the hospital, but that was it. Elfin hadn't made it. Every time I look at that sleeve, I remember that moment as though it happened just a minute ago. It's an experience I wouldn't wish on anyone. We were absolutely heartbroken. I wrote two more songs for *Pure*, 'Little Invitro' and 'A Prayer for the Unborn', both looking at what happened in different ways. To this day, when I sing 'A Prayer for the Unborn' I have to be very careful not to think about what happened. I just try to sing the words and not think of the meaning, but it's hard, and when I do think back it's almost impossible to get through. It's been my favourite song from the day I wrote it. In fact, Andy Gray did a remix of it which made it even better. Not to play it almost feels like an insult to Elfin.

Pure was scheduled to be released in October, so, once the sleeve designs were done, Gemma and I flew to Florida for a holiday. The thing we had as a couple that helped after we lost Elfin was that we'd never looked at having a baby as serving a purpose, to fix a struggling relationship, for example. We didn't 'need' to have a baby – we just wanted one, very much. We had a great life together, and if it turned out that a baby just wasn't to be, we would continue with that great life, happy with one another. So, as upsetting as it was, it caused no division between us. Quite the opposite. If anything, sharing that tragedy brought us even closer together.

In Florida, we made ourselves as busy as we could to keep our minds occupied. Jet-skis, theme parks, air-boat rides, just constantly out and about, doing as much as possible. It was difficult at times. The sadness would come to each of us in waves and at different times. As one of us was thinking of something else, the other would think of Elfin and get upset, so it was always there. But we did our best to support each other and, as I say, kept busy. We also talked about trying IVF again, and by the time we flew back to England, we'd decided we'd go back to Bourn Hall as soon as possible.

Eagle Records released *Pure* on 9 October 2000. The fans loved it, the reviews were overwhelmingly positive, and I was greatly relieved. By the time the album was finished, I'd grown to feel very positive about it. My uncertainties during the making of it had evaporated, and I thought it was the perfect follow-up to *Exile*. It was harder, even more aggressive, more anthemic – it was exactly what I thought it should be for that time. It more than consolidated the new direction I'd taken with *Sacrifice* and developed with *Exile*. *Pure* made it very clear that I'd found the path I wanted to be on. Chart-wise the album didn't do anything spectacular – it only reached number 58 in the UK – but once again sold steadily over time and would eventually outsell *Exile*. That had been a deliberate strategy. I'd been looking at the way I toured a new album to see if I could find a way to extend the time it sold for. Usually an album makes most of its sales in the first few weeks. A tour soon after the album came out could extend that a little, but then it would usually settle back to a trickle. With *Pure* I wanted to try something different. So, I played one major show in London on 20 October at Brixton Academy, but that was it for the UK for now. The idea was to come back early in 2001 and tour the UK then, hopefully generating another wave of press and reigniting interest in the album and a second wave of sales. I was far more interested in selling as many albums as possible than I was trying for a high chart position by putting all the effort into that first week of sales. The way I feel about this has changed many times over the years. At that time I was of the opinion that chart positions didn't mean much. A chart position was an ego massage for the artist and something to brag about for a label. What really mattered was selling as many albums as I could, because that paid the bills. I didn't need my ego massaged – after all, I'd been number 1 three times before – but I definitely needed to pay a lot of bills.

I was given a great opportunity when I was asked to appear as one of four guests on *The Jo Whiley Show*, a TV programme in which you would chat and discuss various new releases. Unfortunately, it didn't give the result I was hoping for. As the show progressed and we made our comments, my favourite track was a collaboration single called 'Carmen Queasy' by Skin from Skunk Anansie and Maxim from The Prodigy.

A few days later, I read in the press that Jo Whiley was accusing me, or all but accusing me, of being a racist. The article claimed that when I'd voiced my opinion about the current state of hip hop, the studio had gone quiet and an awkward silence followed, or some shit like that. It was 100 per cent untrue, and I was about as angry as I've ever been. I wrote my version of events, which was also printed in the same publication, highlighting that my favourite song of the show was performed by two people of colour. Regardless of that, how can simply not liking hip hop make you a racist? You absolutely cannot make accusations like that. It's incredibly irresponsible and dangerous.

Not too long after the Jo Whiley debacle, we lost another baby. This time was less traumatic but still very upsetting. We'd had another IVF attempt at the end of September, just before *Pure* was released. Everything looked good to begin with – a positive pregnancy test and other encouraging physical signs – but then things started to go wrong. We were told that it was ectopic and couldn't survive. Gemma had to go to hospital to have it removed so was unable to travel to Germany with us for the start of the European tour. For me and Gemma it was a sad start to the tour, but, arguably, being on the road was the best thing for us. Touring is a hectic business, and we could be busy together.

The tour wasn't huge, just ten shows, but we visited Germany, Switzerland, Austria, Denmark and Belgium, and it went reasonably well. Europe was still just ticking along as far as I was concerned. The *Pure* tour was only my second since 1980, so I knew it would take some time to rebuild a sizeable following there. I just had to keep at it. I hadn't had the huge success there that I'd had in the UK back in the day. In the UK I was trying to do two things: bring back the people I'd lost since Wembley in '81 and attract a new generation of fans. In Europe, I felt like the original fans were probably already back – there was just a lot fewer of them to win back compared to the UK, so it was more about finding a way of reaching new people. The tour was another step towards that goal, and it felt good to be out on the road making an effort. The support act was a great German industrial band called Dkay.com, who we all loved. Every night was an experience with them, and it made the tour a real pleasure.

We'd been using the same bus company for a while and the bus was way past its prime. So was the driver, to be honest, who, despite his age, was also a big fan of the ladies, if not in person than via poor-quality video. The bus arrived in Copenhagen and we all decided to go for a walk, leaving the driver to 'get some sleep'. We'd only gone a few yards when Gemma decided to go back and get another jacket. She entered the lounge to find the driver with his trousers around his ankles and his knob in his hand watching porn. True story. We hadn't been gone more than a minute. He didn't even seem to be embarrassed. All he said was, 'It would have to be a woman', as though me walking in and seeing that would have somehow been all right.

The same driver also fancied himself as a bit of a chess master. Before one of the German shows I mentioned to him that Gemma had been school chess champion, which is true, and he found that impossible to believe. He challenged her to a match, and she beat him easily, which obviously messed with his ego considerably. He said she'd been lucky, challenged her to a rematch, and she beat him again, and again, and I think once more before he accepted it wasn't luck. He never asked her for another game on the whole tour.

In December Gemma and I made a last-minute decision to visit Jersey. I'd only been back once since I'd lived there briefly in '82/'83, and that was in '84 when I'd been co-pilot on the DC-3. It was the fortieth anniversary of the D-Day invasion and we were to lead an RAF Hercules aircraft that would drop paratroopers over a field near a famous bridge, as in the movie *A Bridge Too Far*. In that field was a gathering of important people, including Prince Charles. It was quite an honour to be flying the same type of plane that had dropped the paratroopers at that same spot during the war. It went well, we arrived on time, the parachutists all landed in the field and I'm sure it was all very emotional down on the ground. On our way back to Jersey however, where the planes taking part in this celebratory flypast were based out of, we had some trouble. The right engine, the one next to me yet again, began to run quite badly. A series of loud bangs could be heard coming out of it, and little shoots of fire could be seen. It was still running, though, and no fluids were leaking that we could see. Shortly after the second bang the owner of the plane burst into the cockpit and shouted 'do something!' Neither the pilot nor I were quite sure what he thought we could do beyond what we were already doing. Anyway, we throttled it back a little and about twenty minutes later landed safely back at Jersey airport where it was discovered that a plug was missing. That definitely shouldn't have happened but it was soon replaced and we flew back to England the next day.

Anyway, now I was going back to Jersey, and Gemma and I found ourselves on a ferry out of Southampton heading for the island on a bitterly cold December day. Outside was freezing, with snow whipping past the railings. The sea was very rough and the ship was pitching and rolling badly. It was really quite unpleasant. Eventually someone started to be sick, and then everyone started being sick, and it was horrendous. I didn't feel too bad to begin with but the noise and smell of a shipload of people throwing up was too much for me. I wrapped myself up as much as I could and went outside. I got as close to the middle of the deck as possible, where the pitching would be the least unsettling, and looked out to sea. I'd been told that if you fix your eyes at some point in the distance it helps stabilise your inner ear canal and so helps prevent sea-sickness. I was out there for about seven hours in total I think. I nearly froze to death but I wasn't sick.

Chapter Twenty-six

2001

In February, I had a most enjoyable experience at the BBC Studios in Maida Vale recording another John Peel session for Radio 1. A small crowd was allowed in to watch, and we were given ample time to work with the BBC engineers to get the set-up and sound exactly as we wanted it. It was one of the best-sounding radio sessions I've ever done, and it was especially good to be back on a John Peel show. John had been the first person to ever play my music on the radio in 1978, and he was also the person who gave me my first ever radio session, and the second actually. I owed him a lot.

About a week before the UK and Ireland *Pure* tour was due to start, Eagle released a special box set 'Tour Edition' of the album. Unfortunately it was only released in the UK, which was disappointing, but it had all the songs from the original release, plus a second CD with an extra seven tracks. These were mostly live versions of *Pure* songs and a couple of older tracks, but also two *Pure* remixes by Andy Gray, one called 'Listen to My Voice' and the other 'A Prayer for the Unborn'. I'd got to know Andy through Saffron from the band Republica when I'd worked with them on their cover of 'Are "Friends" Electric?' for *Random* in 1997. He's been a good friend ever since, and he's done so many incredible remixes of my songs over the years, but his version of 'A Prayer for the Unborn' was just extra special.

We got the tour under way on 13 February, the day before my mum's birthday. Again, it wasn't that long, just ten shows, but for the first time I played in Belfast and Dublin. I was still trying to play UK cities I thought we would do well in, and the Dublin and Belfast shows were more of an unknown quantity. I was glad to finally be there and the shows were great. Both Gemma's parents were born in Ireland, her dad in Dublin and mum in Cavan, and while we were in Dublin to play the show, I finally got to meet some of her Irish relations, and so began my love for Ireland.

From Dublin onwards, we played seven shows without a break. Where the music had evolved and become heavier and more aggressive, so had the way we performed. The shows were harder now, more physically demanding, and playing seven back to back was exhausting. If I was feeling it, then so were the others. Richie on drums most certainly was, but so too were the crew, who work hardest of all. I really didn't have too much choice. Days off were a luxury I still couldn't afford. Too many could mean the difference between going home with a small profit or going home with yet another loss, especially when the tour income is still modest, which it definitely was back then. It costs thousands every day to have people out on the road. The bus alone can be £1,500 and upwards per day! Add wages for band and crew, food, hotels and so on, and you begin to see the problem. You pay that whether you have a show or not. The tour schedules were hard on everyone, band and crew alike, but they were absolutely necessary. In the USA it was even harder.

I'd been asked earlier in the year if I wanted to host my own TV show on the Men and Motors channel. I was a little wary, as I associated Men and Motors with soft porn as much as I did with cars. However, I had a meeting with the very enthusiastic team from the channel and decided I'd go for it. It would only be a handful of programmes, all with me doing something fun in different types of vehicles, and no naked boobs anywhere. They also said they'd pay me quite well, so that clinched it. I was still somewhat reluctant to turn down well-paid opportunities unless I thought they were career damaging. It was a lot of fun working on the series. I got to drive all kinds of cool vehicles, from super cars to racing cars to mud karts, and it put me on the TV regularly for a while. I found out I was no good at rally driving but pretty decent at finding a good line through a fast corner in a single seater. I enjoyed every minute of it. I found out recently that all my Men and Motors programmes are now on a Men and Motors YouTube channel.

The US leg of the *Pure* tour kicked off in Washington DC on 17 April, and the next day we were in New York. We'd started our third attempt at IVF not long before leaving for the USA, when two more eggs had been implanted at Bourn Hall. It seemed to be going better, but sadly Gemma lost the baby as we arrived in New York. Playing a show that night was hard, and I was worried about the toll these disappointments were taking on Gemma. We talked about it a lot. A man feels a great deal of hurt when these things happen, but it surely can't compare with that of the woman, and I was only too aware of how much harder it was for her physically. The process isn't easy, for many reasons, and when you add the emotional toll to that it could easily become too much. I made it clear that the second she wanted to stop, we would stop. She'd have absolutely no argument or problem with me. But she didn't want to – she wanted to try again as soon as we got back to the UK.

Despite yet another sad beginning, I loved that tour. We played at The Paradise club in Boston, a great venue but one where you're not allowed to use a smoke machine on stage, so the lights don't really work. It's the smoke hitting the lights that allows you to see the beams. I think it's a local rule after a smoke machine caused a fire many years before. Up into Canada and a show in Montreal, where the lady at the front desk of the venue refused to speak to us in English when we asked where the dressing rooms were. Fair enough I suppose, but she could have pointed. On to Toronto, always a favourite. Back into the States and Royal Oak, north of Detroit, which looked eerily deserted as we drove in. On to Cleveland, Cincinnati, Chicago and Minneapolis. Then to Boulder, where Gemma and I went for a walk in the woods, and I convinced myself we were being stalked by a bear. We weren't. Then to San Francisco, always an amazing city to drive into from any direction, for another show at the legendary Fillmore. For some reason there's nearly always a fight during a Numan show at The Fillmore, and that show was no exception. Then Los Angeles, always a pleasure. After LA, a short trip down to San Diego, another one of my favourites, and then back to Anaheim, which to me is just another part of Los Angeles, for the final show at the Anaheim House of Blues, which is actually in downtown Disney, or was back then. Every night of the tour was fun, every day a different adventure. I loved being with the band. Literally everyone we met loved Gemma – it was all good. After that final show we went back to Wayne Hussey's place for an end-of-tour party, which was nothing short of epic. Someone there had more piercings in her private parts than I thought was humanly possible. Gemma and I had decided to stay for a while longer, but the rest of the band and crew had to somehow drag themselves to the airport for the flight home later that morning. We said goodbye and left them to it.

There was one encounter during the tour though that was upsetting. I've said many times how important fans are to me, how they have lifted me up again and again when things haven't been going too well, how grateful I am for that support. And yet, within that, there will always be those that take that to a much darker level. People that seem to flick from adoration to hatred so very quickly. On the tour I did the usual thing, stood at the front of the bus after the show and signed autographs for anyone that cared to wait. It usually took a couple of hours or so and was a good chance for me to meet fans and share some time with them. At one of these sessions, one of the last people in the queue gave me a letter and asked me to read it later, when I was finished with the signing. I did exactly that, but what I read was horrendous. He'd written, 'I'm glad your baby died'. He went on to say that maybe now I'd spend more time in the studio and speed up the rate at which I was releasing music. It was then, and still is, the most heartless thing I've ever read.

In June, Basement Jaxx released a single called 'Where's Your Head At'. The song was built around the main synth line from 'M.E' on *The Pleasure Principle*, and it also used a sample from another song of mine called 'This Wreckage' from *Telekon*. There was some toing and froing about how best to pay me for using those samples, especially as the 'M.E' riff was so integral to the song, and it was decided I would get a co-writing credit and a share of the publishing revenue. I was happy with that. The single did incredibly well all over the world. 'Where's Your Head At' reached number 9 in the UK and was used widely on adverts and elsewhere. It made a very serious contribution to my financial recovery, which was close to being complete. All we needed now was the third Eagle advance and we'd be good. It was almost too good to be true. It had taken nearly ten years to recover from the crushing debts of the *Machine + Soul* era, but we were so close. Unfortunately, there would be one more setback to deal with, and it was a big one, but it would come much later in the year.

Before that new challenge, though, I was pleased to hear from my booking agent that he'd been able to get five festival appearances for me that summer. I've always found it hard to get on the bill at festivals. I have no idea why. I've never had a bad reaction at a festival – usually they go very well, and yet I struggle to get booked. I've done a lot over the years, but it's all been by doing one or two here and there. In July of 2001, we took a tour bus out to Sweden and played at the Arvika festival, where unfortunately I probably had one of my least enthusiastic receptions. It was polite, no cans flew at my head, but I can't honestly say it was anything more than that. In August, we played at the Eurorock festival in Belgium again, and then at Reading and Leeds in England. I was nervous about those two. I remembered reading a review many years before where the John Foxx-fronted Ultravox had played at Reading and had been bombarded with beer cans and mud. I expected something similar. Even more worrying was the fact that I was playing on the dance stage. I couldn't think of a place less appropriate, and I was convinced it was going to be a disaster. I was completely wrong, and I was greatly relieved.

More compilations and reissues were released, which I was far from happy about. From what I could make out, Eagle were now licensing out songs from my back catalogue to other labels who were then putting out their own Numan compilation albums. It seemed ridiculous to me. There were so many Gary Numan albums coming out, all regurgitating a variable mix of old and not so old songs, that is was becoming stupidly messy. I found myself meeting fans and signing albums I didn't even know existed. Having so much Numan material coming onto the market felt cheap and grabby. It looked to me as if it had been recognised that a significant number of my fans were keen to collect anything that had my name on it. These compilations were put out simply to cash in on that, and not by me, I hasten to add – I very rarely see any income from these types of releases. I thought they were clear attempts to rip off the fans, because they offered nothing new. Same old songs, same old rehashed pictures, just relying on the fact that they would be able to sell enough to make some money. The quality didn't seem to matter, and the fact that fans already had all of the songs didn't matter, but I was powerless to stop it. I no longer owned the rights to my Numa back catalogue – Eagle did.

I was asked in the summer to present an award at the Kerrang! Awards in London. I think it was to give an award to Feeder as Best Live Act, but I'm not sure. At the aftershow party, some-one came up behind Gemma, pulled her head back and put a Vicodin pill in her mouth. Luckily, Burton C. Bell from Fear Factory saw it happen and managed to rescue her, but it was a seriously stupid thing to do. Gemma had started another round of IVF treatment and was self-injecting each day as part of that. Taking a narcotic had the potential to cause all kinds of problems. Then, as we were leaving, we received a panicked phone call from another friend who had left the party earlier with her boyfriend. He'd also won an award that day. Apparently, he'd got drunk and turned nasty, pinned her to the bed and put a knife to her throat, frightening the life out of her. While he slept, she called us, so we went straight round and picked her up. It was a mad day.

In September, we got on another tour bus and drove to Germany to appear at M'era Luna, a big festival in a country I really wanted to do well in. I was very confident that we'd have a good set. Marilyn Manson was on the bill, plus another couple of bands who had covered my songs, so I expected the crowd to be receptive to what we were doing. Unfortunately, it didn't go quite as well as I'd hoped. I went out expecting a good reaction from the start, but it was lukewarm at best. Slightly disappointed with that, I nonetheless went for it with all the energy in me, and so did the band, and we were good. It just didn't seem to be what the crowd wanted. The reception barely lifted above tepid, and the scattered applause at the end had stopped before we'd even got off the stage. It was quite a letdown. To make a bad day worse, Steve Harris somehow managed to hit his head on the only sharp corner in the bus and had to go to hospital for stitches before we left on the long drive back to England. That appearance at M'era Luna seemed like a lot of effort for essentially nothing.

We did one more show in 2001, at the Shepherd's Bush Empire in west London towards the end of September. After the disappointment of M'era Luna a few weeks before, it felt good to be in front of a partisan crowd once again. It was a great way to end the run of *Pure* shows, but it was also the last I'd play as an artist signed to Eagle Records. We'd learned that the label had looked at the results of the two studio albums they'd sold and decided not to exercise their option for a third, at least not under the deal we'd agreed. The news came as quite a shock. I had no idea they'd been thinking along those lines. They said I was still unrecouped and paying me the advance we'd agreed for a third album would obviously make that position worse. They were willing to take a third album but for a greatly reduced advance. I thought very hard about it but ultimately decided not to accept their reduced offer. I completely understood the thinking behind what they were saying, although I didn't agree with it, but it didn't exactly fill me with confidence about their belief in me and their commitment to whatever album I would have delivered next.

When a label advances you money ahead of an album, they will then take that back from the artist's royalties from sales – that's perfectly normal. So, quite often the only money you ever see as an artist is the advance, unless things go particularly well. But the label are also earning their own considerably larger share beyond the artist's small percentage. So, we believed Eagle were actually well in profit overall, but it's difficult to know for sure. I slightly resented their stance, which seemed to be that they'd lost money on me and I was therefore a disappointment, which I just didn't think was true. They also had a set formula for how they promoted albums, at that time anyway. They advertised in the same magazines and outlets regardless of what album or artist they were promoting, and that hadn't really worked for me. Our argument had been, for *Pure* especially, that Numan fans are unlikely to be reading the majority of outlets they advertised in – heavy-metal magazines, for example – so it was money wasted. Surely, we said, it would be better to spend that money in places we knew Numan fans went to for their music information. This argument fell on deaf ears. They had a fixed process for promoting their albums, and if it didn't work, it was presumed you were the problem, not the process. We'd also noticed a certain amount of belt tightening from Eagle during the *Pure* campaign. I had to pay for the promo video made for the song 'Rip', for example, as they wouldn't fund it from the album budget, but I hadn't seen that as a sign they were having second thoughts about keeping me. I probably should have. I suppose, from their point of view, they now had the two studio albums and my entire Numa back catalogue. They could keep licensing songs to every shitty little label that wanted to put out their own Numan compilation for years to come, and it wouldn't cost them anything going forward. I felt at the time as though I'd been tricked into something and then, when it suited them, encouraged to move on and leave them to exploit my catalogue in any way they liked. I'm not so sure now – perhaps they genuinely didn't see any merit in our argument and thought of me as being too big a risk to continue with. What I do know is the next year another four compilation albums of Numan music would be released, all full of songs licensed by Eagle. Eventually, the catalogue would revert back to me, but not for several years.

The Superbowl money had finally arrived, but losing that next Eagle advance was still quite a blow. It was a sizeable sum, and the one we were really looking forward to, the one that would finally see our financial recovery complete. That was the one that would have lifted us out of debt for the first time in about fifteen years. But these things happen. It certainly wasn't the first time we'd been let down and disappointed, so we just got our heads down and thought about what we could do. Then Steve Malins got in touch with some interesting news. He'd become general manager of a small independent label called Artful and thought it might be worth me talking to them. He explained that Sulpher had already signed to them and had released their album *Spray* earlier that year. That sounded good to me. Here was a label that was comfortable putting out the type of music I was making, and they were tied to Universal so had access to considerable funding.

Chapter Twenty-seven

2002

The loss of the Eagle advance money meant we needed to do something quickly to try and fill the gap. Much as I hated the constant flow of compilation albums seeping into the market, I couldn't think of anything else to do in the short term but make one of our own. Around this time, Richard X did a mash-up of 'Are "Friends" Electric?' and another called 'Freak Like Me' by Adina Howard, under the name Girls On Top. His version was called 'We Don't Give a Damn About Our Friends', and it was all over the radio. Steve Malins then called me and suggested the idea of making our own compilation that spotlighted my career from '78 to the present day, nearly twenty-five years' worth of music.

Universal invested a considerable amount of money in the project. We started to put together what we hoped would be the Rolls-Royce of Numan compilation albums, called *Exposure*, and by 10 January had the desired track list complete. Every song was carefully selected to give the most accurate snapshot of my career so far. I added a new song as well as two new versions of songs from the first *Tubeway Army* album to try and give it some added value and interest to the fans. The truth is it cost a small fortune to license the tracks from Beggars Banquet and elsewhere, and putting out a compilation album was not exactly what I'd hoped to be doing as 2002 got under way. But I'd had a very good few years, and there was definitely a feeling that we were on the verge of a breakthrough moment. In hindsight, it was probably more about consolidating and rebuilding than it was a breakthrough. Not a false dawn exactly – more maintaining a slow upward climb.

I got involved in a collaboration project with Junkie XL around that same time. It came about through Republica's Saffron once again. Saffron had been a friend of ours ever since we'd got to know her during the making of *Random*, and she was the one who had convinced me to switch from using huge side-fill and floor-wedge onstage monitors to an in-ear system. That was one of the best bits of advice I've ever had. The volume of the speakers on stage needed to be so high to be heard over the sound of the amps and drums it was all but impossible to hear your voice clearly, if at all. As a result, you needed to sing as loudly as possible to have any chance of that cutting through the rest of the noise. That meant two things: first, you weren't really singing the songs the way you'd recorded them; and second, you'd usually destroy your voice after about two shows. It happened to me every tour, and it was a nightmare. On one tour, I was sent to a doctor in London, as I had a big show that night, and my voice had disappeared completely. He inserted wet cotton wool dipped in cocaine up my nose to deaden it before inserting a camera that then travelled all the way down to my vocal chords. They were inflamed and rubbing together so not able to make any noise. He sent me off to a chemist, where a concoction was prepared, along with a strange device that I had to build that would spray just the right amount of this evil liquid into my throat. This liquid would lubricate the vocal chords, enabling me to make at least a small amount of noise I would hesitantly refer to as singing. Anyway, that happened all the time until I switched to in-ears. The difference was immediate. On stage, I could hear everything clearly, I could sing the songs the way they were mean to be sung and I have never had any voice problems since. Not due to straining it through over-singing anyway.

Saffron introduced me to Junkie XL, aka Tom Holkenborg, and Gemma and I went over to Amsterdam to meet him. He was such a cool man. Easy to be with, interesting, knowledgeable. I have nothing but respect and good memories after hanging out with Tom. I eventually did a vocal on a song of his called 'Angels', which he put on an album called *Radio JXL: A Broadcast from the Computer Hell Cabin*, released in 2003.

In April '02, the royalties from the Basement Jaxx 'Where's Your Head At' single started to arrive, and it was only then I realised just how successful it had been. It was a very welcome surprise, and it finally signalled the end of our money troubles. It had not only sold very well in numerous countries, it had also generated a great deal of synch income, so losing the Eagle advance was no longer such a problem. Although it didn't win, 'Where's Your Head At' was nominated for Best Dance Track at the Ivor Novello Awards later in the year.

I played another two one-off shows in April 2002, one at the Manchester Academy and the other at the Shepherd's Bush Empire in London. The one-off show/weekender idea was really turning out to be a good one. Their success, and the greatly reduced cost of doing them, was adding to the strength and sustainability of our recovery. What made an even greater difference was what happened next.

In early 2002, I received a request asking me to approve a new version of the Richard X 'We Don't Give a Damn About Our

Friends' track for commercial release. It would be called 'Freak Like Me' and would be a single by The Sugababes, who had resung the Adina Howard vocal. It would, however, still use 'Are "Friends" Electric?' as the music under the vocal, and I was to be given a 50 per cent songwriter share. It was released on 22 April and went to number 1 on 4 May. I was actually swimming at a villa in Mexico when I got a call from Steve Malins saying it had gone to number 1. It would go on to sell more than 330,000 copies in the UK alone. I would love to say I was ecstatic at the news, but that wouldn't be entirely true. I was happy, I really was, but I have a tendency to take good news and immediately look at what's likely to come next. I said something along the lines of, 'Well, it can only go down from there,' and went back to the pool. Gemma was so angry with me for not being more upbeat and nicer to Steve for letting me know. In many ways, this was the sort of success we'd been looking for for years, and I was very glass half empty about the news. I have no idea why I often react in that way to good news. I find it hard to just accept it and live in the moment. Perhaps it's the end result of so many disappointments. I wish I knew.

Exposure was released on 1 June. Universal had done a good job with the marketing spend for it, and it was actually added to the music racks in Asda and Woolworths, which is not something I'd seen for a very long time. *Exposure* was released on our own Jagged Halo label but as an imprint of Artful Records. It seemed popular with the fans and reached number 44 in the UK chart, which was a real surprise. It also got some great reviews. *The Times* gave it a four out of five and said it was 'a timely reminder of Numan's achievements', and it received a four-star review in *Kerrang!* magazine and another in *Rock*

Sound. I hadn't expected that yet another Gary Numan compilation album would have got anywhere near the chart or get good reviews in the rock press. It was all very encouraging. We'd tried hard to make it a good compilation, so it was nice to see people recognised that.

I decided to try my chances on releasing a single again to see if it might help keep, or even build, interest in *Exposure*. I'd chosen a song called 'Rip' and been lucky enough to make a really good video for it, thanks to a friend of Steve Harris who directed and edited it for me. Although I'd paid for it to be made, we'd actually filmed it while I was still at Eagle. Unfortunately they'd done nothing with it, but we were able to go back to them and do a deal that allowed us to use it to promote the single. At that time, *Kerrang!* also had a TV channel, and they ran a regular Top 10 video chart that fans could call in and vote for. Before the single was officially released, the video went to number 1 for two weeks. I found myself in the incredible position of having The Sugababes at number 1 in the national UK chart for 'Freak Like Me' and a number 1 in the *Kerrang!* rock chart with 'Rip'. It was quite a special moment, but I don't think my number 1 was entirely welcome at *Kerrang!*, to be honest. One of their journalists wrote a scathing review of the single and referred to me as an old man trying to look young again in my leather coat, which seemed a bit harsh and not entirely relevant to a music review. There was nothing they could do about it. 'Rip' was eventually officially released on 1 July, and to help it as much as possible I did record-store signings in Birmingham, Manchester, Leeds, Glasgow and Edinburgh, as well as all the press and radio interviews we could get. The success of 'Freak Like Me' had made media opportunities a little easier to get, and Steve Malins, who had also been doing my PR for some time, took full advantage of it. Incredibly, 'Rip' got to number 29 in the national chart. I was very proud of that. On one of the press days in London, I went on the Underground to get to an interview location. It was the first time I'd been on the Tube since the late '70s.

As well as 'Rip', I'd now made three albums that were far heavier than anything I'd done prior to 1994. The music was not radio friendly, a million miles away from pop, and yet even without radio play it was finding its way into the chart. It was good to have some success again but especially because it was very much on my own terms.

In other areas, though, things weren't quite so successful. It would be true to say that my dad was not Gemma's biggest fan, not then anyway. I always breathed a sigh of relief when a visit was over and it hadn't turned into something unpleasant. It was never big rows, just an uncomfortable feeling of waiting for something bigger to happen. A comment here, a rolled eye there, a hint of sarcasm. It created tension that was difficult for me. I loved my parents, I owed them so much, but I loved Gemma, and I couldn't see that she ever did anything to deserve the thinly veiled hostility that came her way. It was disappointing and seemed totally unnecessary. I remember when I went to see my mum and dad to tell them we were getting married. That turned into a huge row with my dad, so it wasn't the happy moment I'd hoped for. I know Gemma put up with a lot of things that she'd normally have jumped all over somebody for, and I was grateful to her for that, but she shouldn't have had to. It didn't create a chasm between my parents and me, but I didn't see as much of them as I used to. I noticed after a while that they didn't really visit unless there was a specific reason. I missed them, so I started to invent things – say I needed help with the garden or clearing out a shed. It seemed the only way I'd get to see them socially, my dad especially. I thought about it a lot and decided that we should have a joint hobby, something we both loved that we could do together, so I convinced him that we should buy a boat. We both loved being out on the water, and it would give us some quality father-and-son time, not just music-business conversations. I also hoped I'd eventually be able to get to the bottom of his problem with Gemma.

Money was better – not amazingly so, but definitely better – so we bought a second-hand twin-engine fast cruiser called a Falcon 27. We moved it to a marina not too far from Portsmouth, renamed it *Halo*, and spent many happy hours that summer rushing up and down off the Sussex and Hampshire coast. Gemma loved it too on those days when my dad wasn't around. I took it very seriously, obviously, and signed us up for a variety of courses. We did our Day Skipper course, diesel engines, radar, VHF and others. Much of it seemed not too dissimilar to things I'd learned for flying, the navigation especially, and I threw myself into studying everything I could about boats and boating. Gemma said I was obsessed again, which was almost certainly true.

In August, I was again asked to present an award at the annual Kerrang! Awards, this time to Rammstein for Best Live Act. I loved Rammstein, having spent a particularly fun evening with them once. Going to awards ceremonies was good for me. Although I was presenting awards rather than receiving any, I met a lot of people that in my more reclusive days I would never have got to meet. I was able to talk to people who had done cover versions of my songs and say thank you. At those

Kerrang! Awards, for example, I met Dave Grohl, whose Foo Fighters had done a version of 'Down in the Park'. I was constantly flattered by how many artists and musicians would talk to me about my influence on them and the music they made. It made me feel differently about myself. Not in such a way that I suddenly thought I was God's gift to music, but it did make me feel good about myself.

Andy Gray and I were asked to demonstrate how to write and record a song in a day for a British music magazine. The idea was that the journalist and photographer would meet with me at Andy's studio and chart our progress throughout the day. I hadn't co-written too many songs before that – I generally prefer to write my own stuff alone – and I'd never written a song side by side with someone before. But Andy is great to work with, and it didn't seem too weird or uncomfortable. I played some ideas on a guitar, Andy had some of his own, and we started to put together a song that we would eventually call 'Ancients'. In truth, it wasn't really done in a day. A version that the magazine could use was, but over the next few weeks several more parts were added to it, including a contribution from an orchestra in Europe that Andy was working with on a film score he was recording. It was decided that we would add the song to a new double album of remixes called *Hybrid* that we were planning to release in 2003.

I was also asked to record a guest vocal for a song by Rico called 'Crazier'. Rico was another Artful signing and just a lovely man. When I first heard it I thought it was a great song, and I really liked Rico, so I had no hesitation in saying yes. It came out really well, and I loved it. Artful suggested putting it out as a Rico versus Gary Numan joint single, so we also added it to the track listing for *Hybrid*, which would be released first.

In September, the Falcon was lifted out of the water and put into storage for the coming winter, and I went back out on the road for a three-date mini tour to promote *Exposure*. We played in Glasgow, Liverpool and London on consecutive nights, but that was the total push on *Exposure* as far as live shows were concerned. The shows were getting good reviews. Just like the singles and albums, my live shows had been universally panned when I first started touring, so to see some good live reviews was a treat for me. After the London show at the Hackney Ocean, *Kerrang!* magazine wrote: 'This evening he matches, if not surpasses, his first glory days' and gave it four stars. It was notable that we were now getting positive comments across a wide range of press, including the metal magazines.

That year's Q Awards in October saw Sugababes winning the Best Single award for 'Freak Like Me'. I was asked to present them with their award, which I was more than happy to do. The success of 'Freak Like Me' had meant a lot to me. It had been twenty-three years since 'Are "Friends" Electric?' had gone to number 1, and to see it there again, albeit merged with a different vocal, made me feel rather proud. I lost count of how many people came up to me that afternoon and commented how fresh it still sounded, how it could have been written yesterday. It did sound good, and the fact that it really hadn't seemed to date at all gave me a new appreciation for it, for what I'd done. Like 'Cars', I'd often written off 'Are "Friends" Electric?' as being one of the things that had made it difficult for me to progress, but I shouldn't have. 'Are "Friends" Electric?' was now considered a classic, and I'd written it, and I should have been very, very proud of that.

After the *Exposure* mini tour Gemma and I went to Ireland, with Richie and Steff once again, and hired a boat. We spent the next two weeks motoring up and down the River Shannon and around the many lakes. Although I love boats I am not the calmest of captains and I think I added a level of anxiety to parts of the trip that made it a less than tranquil holiday for the others. Too worried about making mistakes and looking stupid in front of people perhaps? Part of my obsessive need to do things properly? A bit of both probably, but it doesn't make me the easiest person to be around. These days we make sure that we don't have holidays where I have any responsibility. I think I might be just too tightly wound up. The Irish holiday was still enjoyable though. We ran aground once. Gemma got attacked by a swan. One evening we moored up and walked along a long, dark lane to a restaurant where we were told that a man had been murdered in the exact spot we'd parked our boat and now haunted the dockside. That was a difficult walk back in the pitch-black.

It had been a good year on almost every level, except for perhaps the most important one of all. We had two more tries at IVF and neither worked. I worried even more about Gemma and the strain it was putting on her. One of the attempts had seen a heartbeat, which filled us with hope, but it was gone at the next check. It was just one heartbreaking disappointment after another. For much of the time during these attempts, she was self-injecting a drug that would help to thicken her womb lining, and the procedure to implant the eggs, and all the tests leading up to it, were not exactly pleasant. To go through all that again and again, only to fail, takes a great deal out of you emotionally. We once more talked about whether she really wanted to keep trying, but she said she did.

Chapter Twenty-eight

2003

I n January, Dad and I decided to buy a new boat. We sold the Falcon, and I sold one of my cars, and we bought a beautiful trawler-style boat called *Suncrab*. I absolutely loved it. At thirty-four feet, it was a little bigger than the Falcon, with cabins front and back – it looked like a miniature ship to me. It had lovely wood carvings on the interior doors, two bathrooms, a little kitchen. It was light years away from the multimillion-pound gin palaces you see Hollywood superstars relaxing on, but for me and my dad our little boat was perfect.

Later that month, Gemma and I went back to Bourn Hall for another attempt at IVF. The procedure for getting sperm to egg was not usually the most romantic. On this latest attempt, we were ushered into a private room, told where the porn mags and videos were kept, and left to it. They seemed to think it a little strange that Gemma was with me, as men usually went in there alone, which I couldn't quite understand at all. I'd been given two cups in which to place my man's business. The first bit was supposed to be directed into the cup on the left, the rest into the cup on the right. The staff had made great efforts to stress the importance of absolute cleanliness. To that end, there was a strange-shaped sink in the room that actually had a small cutout into which you could dangle your bits to make sure they were efficiently cleaned. It gave us the giggles, but I dangled and washed as thoroughly as possible. Gemma had put on her PVC nurse's outfit, and we did our best to make it a two-person effort. After all, as far as we were concerned, making a baby should come from a moment of togetherness, not a lonely man having a fiddle, and this was the best we could do.

The first problem with the scrupulous cleanliness request was lipstick. That definitely shouldn't have been where it ended up, but no way was I going back to the ballbag sink to clean it off. Come the moment, so to speak, I put the left cup in position and missed completely. I quickly changed aim and successfully hit the second cup with the rest, but fuck me, the first bit was all over the carpet. It was funny as fuck, but really not. What to do? We were on a very specific schedule, and if it went wrong that day, we'd have to start a completely new cycle. Neither of us wanted that, so I made a decision and scooped up as much as I could from the carpet, handed it in and said nothing. We drove home wondering if we'd made a terrible mistake, or if we'd end up with a baby with red, bristly hair.

We assumed they would check it carefully with a microscope and most likely identify all sorts of hideous contamination, and we'd have to go through it all again, but no one said a thing, so neither did we. It all proceeded normally. Actually, this time they wanted to try something slightly different. They suspected that despite the injections during previous attempts, Gemma's womb lining just wasn't getting as thick as it ideally needed to be, and the eggs were not latching onto it properly. They decided to delay the next implantation a little until the egg had reached the blastocyst stage. It was hoped that the egg at that stage might have a better chance of attaching to the womb. So, in late January, as Gemma lay on the bed waiting, they took the most incredible photo of a fertilised egg, microscopically small, before they implanted it and gave the photo to us. It looked like a tiny planet bubbling, and it will always be one of the most amazing photos I've ever seen. A photo of a human being when it was only a few cells. All we could do now was go on as normal and hope for the best.

In January 2003, Eagle released a live album called *Scarred*, taken from my Brixton Academy show in October 2000 when we'd launched *Pure*. The sleeve notes were written by Fear Factory vocalist Burton C. Bell. I had no problem with *Scarred*, and it made sense for Eagle to release it. I was less happy about another wave of Eagle-licensed compilations and reissues that came out as the year progressed. There were eight in total, four studio compilations and four old live albums, as well as *Scarred*. It really was ridiculous.

Hybrid came out on 10 February, twenty-five years to the day after 'That's Too Bad' had been released and started everything for me. I loved *Hybrid*. It had contributions from Sulpher, Andy Gray, Curve, legendary producers Alan Moulder and Flood, and more, and I thought every one of them had created an exceptional new version of my original. I even added a new version of 'M.E.', plus the new songs 'Ancients', that I'd done with Andy Gray, and 'Crazier', that I'd worked on with Rico. The feedback was fantastic, from the fans and the media. The *Independent* newspaper put a picture of me on the cover and wrote: 'The one and future king of electropop is finally cool again.' It felt like that to me as well. I'm not too keen on elec-tropop as a description of my music, actually, but I certainly felt I was considered cool again, or at least inching my way towards it. Attitudes towards me were clearly changing. *Hybrid* had other good reviews as well. *Mojo* magazine wrote: '*Hybrid* reveals the dark soul of a true pioneer' and gave it four stars.

I was still locked into my weekender idea, so we only played two shows to support the initial release, 8 February in Bristol and 9 February in London. A few weeks later, we flew to Cologne, Germany, to record a live TV session for a show called *Music Planet*. The Devils, the side project of Nick Rhodes and Stephen Duffy, were on the same show. We were allowed to play nine songs, and I wanted to make a strong statement about who I was and what I was now doing in 2002. So, of the nine songs we played, only one was old. Everything else was either new or very recent. It was just too good an opportunity to waste, and I wanted to ram home that I wasn't just 'Cars' and 'Are "Friends" Electric?' I had no opposition at all from the show. The only old song I played was 'Down in the Park', and I only did that to make the connection with anyone watching that it was my song, not Marilyn Manson's. We did a hugely updated and heavier version of it as well.

In April, we were back in Germany, this time in Berlin with Rico to film the promo video for 'Crazier'. It was filmed partly in the 'Vinzenz' house, an old building with an amazing spiral staircase and seemingly hundreds of rooms. We then went to a cellar crammed full with strip lights, followed by an old deserted swimming pool. It was an exhausting shoot. By the time we finished, I'd been awake and working for more than twenty-four hours.

The video was also to be incorporated into a film and used to help promote it. If I remember correctly, the director of the film also directed the video. When it came time for the edit, the end product was way too much of the film and not enough of me and Rico or the band. Steve had endless phone calls with the director and eventually, frame by frame, we were able to get the video we wanted. It took until late May before it was finally approved, but it was worth all the effort. The 'Crazier' promo was particularly good.

Our latest IVF experience had been going well. Extremely well, in fact. Both the implanted eggs that had gone in in January had developed into embryos with heartbeats. One of them was small and didn't seem to be growing at the expected rate. We had more checks over the next few days, and at first nothing changed very much. The heartbeat was still there, but it was still too small. We were advised it was unlikely that embryo would make it. Then, against expectations, it started to grow more rapidly, and for a few days things seemed more positive. Unfortunately, on our next visit, there was no heartbeat at all, and the little one had died.

Sad as that was, our main concern at that point was the condition of the remaining embryo. Was that one OK? Things looked good, so we got on with our lives, following every instruction to make sure the baby had the best chance. A few days later, sometime in May I think, we were upstairs waiting for a new car for Gemma to arrive. Just as it turned into the drive, Gemma cried out and I saw blood. The next few minutes were a mad panic of apologising to the car-delivery man and driving off to the hospital as fast as possible. We called Bourn Hall, and they said they strongly suspected that it was the dead embryo being let go, but all we could think of was that it was the good one and Gemma was miscarrying again. As soon as we rushed into the hospital, they had a machine ready and started to scan for signs of life. Almost immediately we saw a mad little heartbeat flashing away, and a wave of overwhelming emotion hit us both. The sense of relief and happiness is just impossible to put into words, and then it was immediately followed by guilt that we were happy – the bleeding was the final stage of the other embryo dying. It was a strangely difficult moment emotionally, and it brought home the precarious nature of carrying a baby for nine months.

Losing one of the embryos made the rest of the pregnancy a very worrying time. Although Gemma had surprisingly few problems – no sickness, for example – every ache, every twinge, we thought could be a sign that something was wrong. We regularly returned to the clinic in Harley Street, where we'd had the terrible news about Elfin. We went there every month for scans. We didn't really need to, but it was always comforting to see the baby alive and well. We recorded every session on video and made them take dozens of photos. By the time Gemma was seven months, I had hours and hours of grainy black-and-white footage of this vaguely baby-shaped lump twitching and moving around. We knew it was a girl quite early on, which helped with the naming dilemma. We saw her having hiccups, sucking her thumb, burping, even dreaming, I think. It was our favourite half-hour of the month. When we got home, we'd put the video in the machine and spend hours watching it all over again.

The thing I did notice during the pregnancy was that Gemma didn't get any of the bizarre cravings for food that I'd heard so much about. Instead, she had geographical cravings. For as long as I'd known her, she'd talked about wanting to live in America, in Los Angeles especially. As her pregnancy progressed, she became increasingly sensitive to all things American. If a TV show came on and an American police siren was heard, she'd burst into tears. Anything at all that even reminded her of America was enough to get her started.

In early July, 'Crazier' was released and, thanks to the keen voting of the fans, once again went straight into the *Kerrang!* video chart at number 1. I think that was just too much for them, as it was the last time any of my singles were allowed to be voted for. It also reached number 13 in the UK chart, my highest position since 'We Take Mystery (to Bed)' in 1982. We were even invited to appear on *Top of the Pops*, the first time Rico had done it, and we were both interviewed by *The Times* during the afternoon. It was mentioned in the article that I was now 'dripping in cred'. It was all very exciting and added yet more momentum to all the good things that had happened the year before. It didn't hurt the sales of *Hybrid* either.

An unexpected wave of new interest came when the posthumously published journal of Nirvana singer Kurt Cobain came out. In it he wrote that my song 'It Must Have Been Years' from *Replicas* was one of the songs he was listening to when he wrote the classic *Nevermind*. That seemed to push my credibility up another level.

As the 'Crazier' effort ended, Gemma and I flew out to Cyprus for another holiday. Gemma was very pregnant by now, so it was a gentler two weeks of sunbathing and swimming pool rather than the rushing around doing as much as possible that she usually insisted upon. Gemma is a terrible person to go on holiday with if you just want to relax, which I do. She organises a hectic schedule of activities from the moment you arrive and is unhappy if any one of them doesn't happen. Holidays with her are harder than working, by far. It's common to be up at 6 a.m., rushing off to do something or other. She'll squeeze so many things into a day you can barely find the energy to climb into bed at the end of it. She's like that every day, and she's annoyed if you don't think it's fun.

In August, Artful released the *Hybrid: Special Edition* version of the album. This included all the music on the original album but also contained much more, including several remixes, as well as the 'Dominion Day', 'Rip' and 'Crazier' videos, plus four of the songs from the *Music Planet* TV show filmed in Cologne. We were even able to add the Fear Factory video for 'Cars'. It was a great package.

I managed to get another couple of collaborations completed during the year. One was a guest vocal for a cover of 'Metal' by Afrika Bambaataa, the other was a vocal and co-write (I did the lyric) for a song called 'Pray for You' by Plump DJs.

I'd planned to play two more UK shows in September to support the special edition of *Hybrid*, one in Manchester on 20 September and the other in London the following night. The baby wasn't due for another five weeks, so we had no worries about Gemma coming along. We'd been rehearsing all that week, and the 19th would be the last day of practice, so it was important. I'd already planned to have video director Paul Green and his crew come to Manchester to film the show for a live video I'd planned called *Hope Bleeds*. But very early that morning, Gemma's waters broke, and chaos reigned. It was five and a half weeks too soon for one thing, and that was a big worry for us. We grabbed our prepared bag, rang the doctor (who said not to worry, five and a half weeks was unlikely to be a problem) and headed off to the hospital. I think we were there and Gemma in bed by about 6 a.m. It was all so hectic and panicked until we got to the hospital, and then nothing much really happened. My mum and dad arrived soon after, and Mum set to helping as much as possible. Dad kept out of the way for the most part but was never far. They were both as excited and anxious as I was, I think. The hospital staff checked on Gemma regularly, but it all seemed to be going very, very slowly. The baby seemed fine and not under any duress. She just didn't seem to be in any hurry to come out.

We'd had no arguments about who would choose the name. It seemed to me that after all Gemma had gone through, and what she would most likely go through during the birth, the very least I could do was give her a free choice with the name. I didn't feel I had any right to make any demands whatsoever, to be honest. So, we agreed that Gemma would choose the first name, and I would choose the middle name. Actually, we'd already decided to give her Elfin as her middle name. Gemma said she needed to see her first before she could name her but changed her mind. So, long before her waters broke, she had already named the baby Raven. Raven Elfin Webb.

As the morning wore on, still nothing much was happening. Gemma, in her first-child naivety, had decided not to have any drugs for the birth. She wanted to feel the full experience. Back at the house, the band had turned up and were getting on with rehearsals as best they could. But I still hadn't decided what the final set list would be, and I needed to sort out some of the equipment. The doctor said, as so little was happening, I had lots of time, and it would be OK to nip home quickly and sort out the rehearsals, so I did. As I walked into the rehearsal room, and got hugged and back slapped by everyone, my phone went. I was told the baby was coming and to get back as quickly as possible. I sped back as fast as I could. Too fast it seemed. As I got close to the hospital, I was pulled over by the police and given a ticket for speeding. I apologised, accepted the need for a ticket with no argument, but asked if it could be done quickly as the baby was coming any minute. I shouldn't have said that. It seemed to give the policeman all the incentive he needed to write me a ticket in super slow motion.

My ticket in my pocket, and safe-driving lecture still droning in my ears, I parked the car and ran to Gemma's room, desperately hoping I hadn't missed the birth. I was shouted at by several nurses to stop running, which I understood but ignored completely, and burst into the room at about 3 p.m. I was in time, but only just. By now, the pain Gemma was going through with each contraction was excruciating, and she was bitterly regretting her no drug decision. She'd changed her mind while I was out, when the contractions had started to come faster and more viciously, but by the time she said anything it was already too late. All she could do now was grin and bear it. And all I could do was hold her hand and hope she didn't crush it. The baby was coming, and it wasn't going back. It seemed such a traumatic thing for Gemma, and I felt totally helpless. Pushing, waiting, pushing, screaming, crushing, and on and on. After a lot more pushing and hand crushing, I heard the nurse say the baby was crowning and had a look. Sure enough, I could see the tiniest part of her head, and it was amazing. I don't want to give the impression that I was calm and collected through all this, by the way. I absolutely was not. I was in what I can only describe as a quiet, dreamy state of shell shock. It was all so incredibly loud and dramatic. Nothing I had ever experienced, and I'd experienced a lot, had prepared me for the birth of my first child. It was frightening and exhilarating and overwhelming and absolutely beautiful.

At 3.20 p.m. exactly, Raven came out, and she was perfect. A little small, of course, but intact and very much alive. I had asked to be the one to cut the cord once she was born. It was important to me that I separated her from the womb. I don't really know why, but I cut it, and she was her own person, living off her own body. It was the most amazing moment of my life, only equalled by the birth of two more babies, but I'll get to that. She was checked over, cleaned and brought back to us. I felt like I'd been to war and back, and I hadn't done anything. What Gemma must have felt like I can barely imagine.

After the birth I held her and just stared for the most part. My mum was there, my dad came in, everyone was happy. Gemma was exhausted. I swear I was so overwhelmed by the experience that if the doctor had told me to open the window and jump out, I would have done it without question. But then things took a slightly worrying turn. Raven was OK, but Gemma wasn't. The placenta that should have followed soon after the birth hadn't. An urgent call went out to a surgeon who was driving home, and she immediately turned around and raced back to the hospital. Not long after giving birth, Gemma was having emergency surgery to remove the placenta and other bits that needed to come out. It was one last piece of drama before it was all over.

I stayed for as long as I could, but eventually I had to leave – the bus was coming to the house that night to take us to Manchester for the show the next day. It was the most surreal drive home from the hospital. The band were there when I got back. I packed, trying hard not to forget anything important, got on the bus and went to sleep. I think I was the happiest I'd ever been, but it was a strange thing having to leave for a show when your newborn child and wife were elsewhere. I couldn't wait to get back to see them both.

By the time we arrived in Manchester, the news was already out. I'd probably mentioned it on the website – I can't remember. I was still in a daze, but I remember feeling like I'd grown up another level. As though being a father somehow made me more complete as a human being. I'd had a similar feeling when I'd got married, actually. Getting married, having a child: these were things that mature people did. It took you beyond being a young man still finding your way. These were real, lifetime commitments, and they had a sense of gravitas that made me feel different. Better.

The Manchester show was just an incredible experience. When I walked on stage, it had only been one day since Raven had been born, and I was still completely buzzing with the experience. The crowd genuinely seemed to be sharing it with me. I saw lots of congratulations signs being held up, and some-one near the front was waving a baby-grow in the air – it was all so very touching. At one point I spoke to them and said, 'I'm a fucking dad,' and the place absolutely erupted. I'm not sure why I swore – wish I hadn't – but I was still floating in a hazy bubble, I think. The night became a celebration, and it was magnificent. It was the only place I wanted to be if I couldn't be with Raven and Gemma. The next night we were in London, and it was much the same. The crowd were amazing, more messages, more baby clothes, just the most incredible atmos-phere, and such an outpouring of support and affection it brought a tear to my eye. It meant the world to me.

With all the shows for 2003 complete, I went home and started learning how to be a dad. I loved almost every part of it, and I was totally hands-on. We split nappy duties, burping, feeding, everything. I didn't see it as a mother's responsibility only – I saw it very much as something we should both be a part of, sharing the effort and the difficulties, learning together. Despite trying really hard, and buying every gadget we could find that might help, Gemma wasn't able to breastfeed as successfully as we'd hoped. So, we had to turn to formula, which meant we could share the feeding through the night. I actually used to look forward to waking up at 4 a.m. and watching *Rolie Polie Olie* on the TV while Raven drank her milk. Gemma usually woke up as well, so we started to have a cup of tea and Rich Tea biscuits every night until we put on so much weight we had to stop the biscuits part.

I decided that I would do very little work for the next two years. I just wanted to be a dad, and I didn't want to miss anything. Not the first step, the first word, the first smile. I wanted to be there for everything. I did write one new song, called *Jagged*, that I sent to Steve Malins in early December. A few days after that, Gemma and I had our first trip out without Raven when we attended the London premiere of *Return of the King*, the third instalment of the *Lord of the Rings* movie trilogy. It was a special night for me, as *The Lord of The Rings* has always been a favourite book of mine. I first read it when I was very young, and I read it at least once every year until I was well into my twenties. At the premiere, I was able to meet members of Tolkien's family, and I was blown away to meet Sir Richard Taylor, the founder of Weta Workshop, which created so much of what you see in the films. Sir Richard told me that my albums had often been playing when the team were working on their creations for *Lord of the Rings*. I can't tell you how proud I was to hear that.

Chapter Twenty-nine

2004

For the next few months, I did virtually nothing but dad stuff. I did write another new song that I sent to Steve Malins in February called 'Does God Bleed', which would eventually be called 'Halo'. Apart from that, we went out a lot, enjoying having a baby, enjoying buying all the equipment. Raven's pushchair was more like a Batmobile, it had so much equipment and supplies loaded into it. Everything became a mission. Just getting out of the car took a substantial amount of time. We visited everyone we could think of, which was probably the last thing they wanted. I don't think anyone finds babies interesting apart from the parents and, in shorter bursts, the grandparents perhaps. We were aware of that and did our best to hold back on the coochie-coo nonsense around our friends. My mum did send me a picture of the first potty poo Raven did at her house, and I was actually pleased to get it. The things you find cute and interesting can get pretty weird.

Outside of baby stuff, though, it was a quiet start to the year. I played a three-show weekender in March, with shows in Nottingham, Cardiff and London, to celebrate the twenty-fifth anniversary year of my first chart success. At the London show, I was supported by The Killers, who didn't do too badly after that. I have a history of taking on support bands who often go on to greatness, which I've always been rather proud of.

Eagle released another live album called *Live at Shepherds Bush* that I'd recorded at an *Exile* show in 1997. Annoyingly, they continued to license out songs from my catalogue for low-budget Numan compilation albums, and another three came out throughout the year. Beggars Banquet kept up with their re-releasing schedule of old albums and put out four in Japan. I actually had no problem with what Beggars were doing. Re-releasing old albums around the world on new formats or with added songs, or simply just keeping them alive, was a very different thing to rehashing disjointed career compilations with no thought or care to the songs included. I thought what Eagle were doing cheapened me, not so with Beggars.

By the time June came along, and disappointed by a lack of transparency in Artful, shall we say, we'd decided to move on. My problems with Artful had nothing to do with Steve Malins or any of the people who worked there – far from it. The problem was that both my dad and I found the man who owned the label increasingly difficult to deal with. We had misgivings about him and didn't want to continue with the label. We were in a slightly precarious position. Although I'd decided not to work while Raven was very young, I had still written a number of songs for the next album, an album that Artful was supposed to release. We had an agreement in place, in fact. From our point of view, so many promises had been broken, so many lesser agreements not honoured, we felt fully entitled to tear up that contract and keep the album for ourselves. So that's what we did. My dad wrote to Artful on 8 June letting them know that we wouldn't be releasing any new material through them, including the new album, and the next day Steve Malins resigned from Artful as well. A week later, I announced it on my website and told the fans I was once again setting up a label of my own, called Mortal Records.

I wrote another song for the new album, 'Haunted', but progress overall was still painfully slow, which was entirely my fault. The previous album, *Pure*, had received some of the best reviews I'd ever had, certainly far more good ones than bad, so I found myself in a position I was completely unaccustomed to. It was such a nice feeling to read positive views in the press, I didn't want it to end. I was so sure that with the next album it would all just go back to what it had been before that a part of me didn't want to make another album and see it disappear. So, I just drifted for a while – for quite a while, actually. Far too long.

In July, we flew to Borneo for two weeks. Raven was only nine months, so it was quite a daunting trip – people with babies on aeroplanes are usually about as popular as a shark in a swimming pool. But she wasn't too bad, and after three flights we arrived. Borneo was very cool. Gemma, as expected, had each day's mission worked out but, luckily for me, she was severely limited by having Raven with us. The holiday had been built around a partial boat charter, so several of the days were spent boating. It was fun to arrive at the harbour and step aboard a big, sleek powerboat and have the captain say, 'Where do you want to go?' I had no idea what there was to see, so we let him take charge, and it was fantastic. We would travel for an hour or so and then an island would appear. Our boat would curve into a secluded bay where we were the only people. Anchor up, swim, walk on the beach, eat. Get back on the boat, go somewhere else. It was all so easy and yet so exotic. In fact, the boating part of it was so good we added some extra charters to what we'd planned. We had a floating device with a canopy that meant we could take Raven in the water without fear of her drowning or getting burnt. We were a bit worried about sharks, but the captain assured us they didn't come in to where we were; it was either too cold or too warm. Too something, anyway. I don't think I swam once without feeling a little uneasy.

We also took a trip to see some orang-utans in the wild. I happened to notice that I had a photo of Raven where she looked remarkably like an orang-utan and laughed about it with Gemma, which seemed to offend the woman standing behind me. That night we stayed in a one-room lodge in the forest. Gemma went for a night jungle walk with a guide but I had no interest in that. I'm not a big fan of snakes and I'd already seen one during the day. Apparently they came out at night so that definitely wasn't for me. To make it worse there was a list of rules and warnings on the door. One of them said if you see a snake crossing your path don't antagonise it. What idiot antagonises a snake? It put the fear in me, though, just reading that one might 'cross my path'. I noticed the door to the lodge had a small gap under it, surely big enough for a snake, so I blocked that with towels, picked up Raven and sat on the bed until Gemma came back. While we were in Borneo Raven took her first steps, which ticked off one of the things on my dad list.

Back in Essex we bought a cheap overground swimming pool. It was a failure, to be honest – always cold and very ugly, stuck out in the field as it was. When I was young my dad had built an assortment of things, furniture, shelves, cupboards, useful stuff like that. He was quite the dab hand at carpentry. I thought it was time I gave it a try so I set to making an elevated deck next to the pool, partly to try and hide it as much as anything. It took me the entire month of August. I had no idea what I was doing – I certainly didn't inherit my dad's carpentry skills – but as usual I became quite obsessed. By the end of August, I'd made a very decent deck, if I say so myself. It was the first thing like that I'd ever made, and I was ridiculously proud of it.

I tried a few different things with the production on the *Jagged* album, as it was now called, as I'd put a few songs together by now. I gave Andy Gray a couple to work on, and a couple more to Rob and Monti. Nothing was quite right, although, to be fair, they did do plenty of good things to the tracks. The problem was that I was looking for a direction and still hadn't found it, so I wasn't able to give them the clear guidance they needed. I went back to writing more demos and waited to see what would come.

I played just two more shows that year, in September, one in Birmingham and yet another at the Shepherd's Bush Empire in London. I'd almost lost count of how many shows I'd played at the Empire, but it felt like I was always there, and that was becoming a little frustrating. I liked it as a gig – it was just about big enough to feel like it was big enough, if you know what I mean – but I seemed to be stuck at that level. As well as everything seemed to be going, I measured my position not so much by album sales, or even chart position, but by the size of the venues I could play. By now I'd done the Empire about nine or ten times. Apart from one brief moment at Brixton Academy in 2000, which didn't sell out, I'd been playing at the Empire, or other London venues of similar size, for nearly ten years. I saw moving up from the Empire as an important next step, but it would be another nine years before I would be able to take it. What I really wanted to do was get back to Wembley Arena, but that seemed a million miles away in 2004. The Wembley shows in '81 had been the trigger for my long, painful career decline. Pretty much from the moment I walked off that Wembley stage for the last time, getting back there became my biggest desire, my biggest challenge. Getting out of the Empire was a small step up; getting back to Wembley Arena was everything, the jewel in the crown of my slow climb back to relevance. I knew I had a very, very long way to go, and at forty-six years of age, it felt to me as if time was beginning to turn against me. Yes, I was climbing back up – it just wasn't anywhere near quick enough.

In October, Gemma and I were invited to be guests at the launch of the UK Music Hall of Fame. I wasn't being inducted – I would just be one of the many celebs in the audience, but it was at least nice to be one of them. The entry to these events is hideously embarrassing. You're picked up and driven to the venue, where you join a queue of cars some distance away. Someone comes to the window, checks who's in the car and speaks into a radio. At the appropriate time, your car is allowed to move forward to the drop-off point, and you get out to a barrage of cameras. You then walk the red carpet, where photographers shout at you to look this way and that. It feels very much like being a lesser prize on a game-show conveyor belt. If someone more famous turns up, you're abandoned, or if you turn up and the person ahead is less famous than you, they abandon them. It all feels coldly brutal, and I genuinely don't like it, but it's all part and parcel of going to those events.

We took our seats, and I looked around as casually as I could to see who was there; it was jaw-dropping. You could literally start at the As and slowly work your way to Z and a celebrity fitting the letter was there. We were sat one row behind The Rolling Stones and one row in front of someone else equally huge, although I forget who it was. Lots of people made speeches, some more pretentious than others. When Madonna took the stage, Gemma could no longer restrain herself and shouted out, 'I love you!' to which Madonna politely said, 'Thank you.' As far as Gemma was concerned, that was a conversation with Madonna, and she's stuck to that view ever since.

Chapter Thirty

2005

In early February Gemma and I had a most unexpected surprise. After Raven was born, we'd gone back to sex with the same mindset we'd had before: we couldn't have children naturally, so there was no need to be careful. But it seemed things had changed. Gemma took a test and, unbelievably, it was positive. We traced back to when it was likely to have happened – one of our band-and-gang gatherings – and were horrified. Without saying too much, we were both somewhat the worse for wear that night. We made a frantic but brutally honest call to our doctor, who assured us there was nothing to worry about. With that settled, we were able to fully enjoy the news, and it was amazing. During our time at Bourn Hall, it had been mentioned that it wasn't uncommon for couples who couldn't have children to get pregnant naturally after IVF. It was as if the IVF process taught the body what it needed to know or gave the works a kick-start, so to speak. We just hadn't expected it to happen to us. It was the best accident we'd ever had.

One of the regular friends at our band gatherings was Ade Fenton. I hadn't always liked him if I'm honest – I used to think he was too up himself – but once I got to know him better I discovered he was nothing like I thought, and we became the best of friends. He'd become quite a successful techno DJ by the time I started writing *Jagged* and had released a number of things in his own right, on his own label. At our gatherings, he would often put on his techno tracks for us to check out, and I hated them all. Techno just wasn't my thing, and I made no secret of it. But then he started to bring along other music he'd written and produced, what he called 'real' music, and it was much more to my liking. I took a lot more interest in it, and I noticed over a few months how much better he was getting at production. It was very impressive. I can't remember now whether he suggested it or the idea was mine, but in March I asked if he'd like to produce one of my new songs as a tryout. I gave him the audio for a song called 'Scanner' and waited a few weeks to see what he did with it. What he did was brilliant – I could hardly believe it.

Over the next few months I was writing far more. My worries about losing my newfound press approval had been overtaken by the fact that I hadn't put out any new studio music for nearly five years. I needed to stop drifting and get on with it. Whatever the reviews were going to be for *Jagged*, it had to be done, and I reminded myself that pretty much every negative thing they could say had already been said. I actually felt as if the praise for *Pure* had made me soft and vulnerable, which was absolutely not the way I needed to be. Survival in the music business requires extraordinary resilience. You have to be emotionally armoured to withstand the slings and arrows that are fired at you, and I couldn't afford to get soft and hang on the praise of others. I remembered what I needed to be.

I gave Ade Fenton two more songs, just to make sure his work on 'Scanner' hadn't been a fluke. They came back and were equally brilliant. He seemed to know exactly what I was trying to achieve with all three of them and had the skill to develop those rough ideas of mine into something better. The new direction I was looking for opened up like a door onto a vast new landscape, so I decided to take a gamble and asked Ade to produce the entire album. It was to be the start of a long and successful partnership. The only problem was it was now August, we'd pretty much have to undo everything I'd done so far and rebuild it, and the album had to be finished by December.

I said in an interview at the time, 'The whole process with Ade was excellent. He is such a good person to work with that even on the rare occasions when I thought a track had gone in the wrong direction, he'd say, "Fair enough, we'll have another go." With Ade it was just easy, there was no attitude, no ego problems.'

Gemma took Raven for a photo-shoot with a child modelling company. It was an interesting experience. Raven was not the most communicative of children much of the time. She was different. Much of the way she was we put down to her possibly inheriting some Asperger's traits from me. Her reactions were often the opposite of what we expected, if she reacted at all. We would take her somewhere, give her something, do exactly what she'd said she wanted to do and get nothing. It was frustrating and quite upsetting at times. I wanted her to be happy, to love life, but she often seemed reluctant to take part in things. So, I expected nothing except a blank refusal to participate in the photo session, but, surprisingly, she was unusually friendly and charming. She was signed up, and soon after we had our first audition, for Pampers nappies, I think. It did not go well.

Raven refused to do what little was asked of her. She wouldn't smile, wouldn't stand, wouldn't sit, wouldn't do anything. She went to one more audition after that, which was even worse, so we gave up.

For some time, the future of our house and land in Essex had been in some doubt. Stansted Airport was looking to double in size and, unfortunately, our house was very much inside the expansion area, so it became worthless. A house in imminent danger of being bulldozed and the land taken from you tends to affect its value. After some time, and a great deal of local opposition, the British Airports Authority set up a process whereby a fair value for the house and land could be reached, and they would buy it from us. They would also pay our removal costs and stamp duty for the new house. It was actually quite a good deal, but, in truth, we were being bribed to leave. They also said that when their expansion plans were given official approval, we would get a further 10 per cent of the agreed value as a bonus. Bribe or not, we decided to accept and move on.

Gemma and I began our search for a new house. I've read that buying a house is one of the three most stressful things people face in their lifetime. I don't understand that at all. Throughout the summer we spent a great deal of time visiting house after house in East Sussex, and we loved every single minute of it. We looked high and low, and eventually found the most perfect place in a tiny village called Waldron. It was the prettiest house, set in seven and a half acres of land. It had a babbling stream running from one end of the land to the other, a wood, a meadow and three little bridges that crossed the stream – it was as perfect an English picture as we could have hoped for. All we had to do now was sort out the price.

There had been one minor incident when we went to view Weavers for the first time. We'd pulled up at a busy roundabout with one car in front waiting for a gap. After a frustrating wait the car in front started to pull away; I looked to see what else was coming and saw the gap was even longer than usual. Unfortunately the driver in front decided she'd wait for them to build some traffic lights and, even though there was enough space for us both to get out, decided to stop. I was still looking to the right, thinking she'd be long gone, and crashed into her. Definitely my fault, regardless of her change of heart. I jumped out and apologised profusely, but she was not happy. She was even less happy when she wrote her address down and I burst out laughing. She lived in a village called Upper Dicker. Who wouldn't have laughed at that?

While the estate agents and legal people sorted out the house purchase, I secretly arranged to take Gemma on a trip for our wedding anniversary. It was our eighth anniversary, so not a particularly important one in the scheme of things, but I wanted to do something special to mark it. I'm not usually any good at things like that. It's rare for me to organise surprises – I'm even terrible at buying birthday and Christmas cards – but on this occasion I did OK. I arranged for a long weekend in Venice. We flew to the airport and picked up a water taxi that took us to our hotel, and it was all incredibly beautiful and romantic until we got to our room, which was like a big two-storey box with no windows. We decided to say no thanks to that and looked for somewhere else and ended up in the presidential suite of another hotel nearby, overlooking the lagoon. It was ridiculously over the top, but it was amazing. While we were there, the estate agent called and wanted to negotiate the price of the house in Sussex. My Asperger's makes me reluctant to speak on the phone, and Gemma has dyscalculia (dyslexic with numbers), so what followed was the maddest of calls, with Gemma trying to relay numbers to me, badly, and me making counter offers, which she was repeating incorrectly – it was all a bit chaotic. Eventually it was all agreed, and we left Venice the next day the happy owners of a new house in the country. It was a very lovely weekend.

We flew back to the UK and flew straight back out to the south of France for another boating holiday. This time we would cruise the Canal du Midi in the south of France. The brochure had made it sound like a holiday to die for, but it was terrible. Trying to find somewhere to moor the boat was a daily battle that we usually lost. It wasn't scenic, it stank, large sections of the canal were full of dead fish and very few people we met were friendly. It was the least enjoyable holiday I'd ever been on. Raven got very sick at one point, and towards the end Gemma bent down to pick up her up and realised she was now so pregnant she couldn't do it. From that moment on, Raven became the child from hell. She bit, pinched and scratched her way through life for a while after that.

We hadn't been home too long when I noticed quite a change in Gemma. I couldn't be sure if it was because Raven had become more difficult, or something else had changed, but she started to get very down. It wasn't all at once, but a slow fall into unhappiness. Her bubbly nature wasn't quite as bubbly, and she was a little quick to anger, easily upset. She wasn't herself.

Late on 17 October, our daughter Persia started to come. The doctor was waiting when we arrived at the Portland

Hospital, and this time Gemma had no hesitation in asking for an epidural, or anything at all that would make it as painless as possible. We were told that there was a better but more expensive drug that would take away all pain but still allowed the mother to push when needed. It also helped to reduce the likelihood of forceps or ventouse being required should the baby need help. We had friends whose baby had been severely damaged by forceps during birth and we wanted to avoid that possibility. So, expensive epidural it was. It was great, actually. During the birth, Gemma would be chatting away, the doctor would say push, and she'd push and then go back to chatting. It was so different to Raven's birth. Gemma asked me to film it, so I set my camera up, left it to run and just enjoyed the experience of watching Persia come into the world early on the 18th, on time, a normal weight, free of all drama. I thought she looked like the actor Ray Winstone when she came out. I cut the cord again, and we settled down to stare at her for the rest of the day. Mum and Dad came to visit with Raven, who couldn't have been lovelier to Persia, and it was a very happy time. For some reason we'd always called Raven 'P', and for equally inexplicable reasons we nicknamed Persia 'Podster', or 'Pod' for short. Unfortunately, I lost the memory card that the film of the birth was saved on, and I've never been able to find it.

We didn't move into the new house straight away. We wanted to get Persia home and settled for a few weeks before we went through the chaos of moving house. I needed pictures for the *Jagged* sleeve, and I thought the trees at the new house, called 'Weavers Cottage', would be a perfect backdrop. In early December, we set off for Weavers to meet up with photographer Steve Gullick. We nearly didn't make it. I filled the car with fuel on the way but put diesel in it by mistake, and we broke down. We arrived hours late but luckily Steve had used the time to recce the land and found a few suitable places. The *Pure* sleeve had been shot outside at the Essex house, and now *Jagged* in the garden at Weavers. It worked, though, and I suppose it saved on renting a studio.

With *Jagged* complete, we started to talk to labels to see what sort of distribution deal we could get for it. I had no interest in signing with a label as an artist any more, but I did need distribution for my label, and we eventually signed a deal with a company called Cooking Vinyl.

We almost got through the rest of the year without any more drama, but not quite. On New Year's Eve, I was waiting downstairs for Gemma, as we were going out to a firework display. I heard her coming down the stairs, then a thud, then she screamed. I ran to the bottom of stairs to find her hugging Persia, who was wrapped in about a dozen layers of clothes so thick she was in a rigid starfish shape. Gemma was beside herself, crying and making little sense. It turned out she'd tripped as she came down the stairs, about five or so steps from the bottom, and Persia had flown out of her arms and landed face down on the floor. Gemma thought she was dead because she wasn't crying. I picked her up, and she looked OK. Smiling, happy, not bothered at all. I think she had so many clothes on, and the carpet she landed on was so thick, that she just bounced and escaped without so much as a scrape. But, better safe than sorry, we drove straight to the nearest A&E to get her checked out. They wanted to keep her overnight to be sure, so that's where we all spent New Year's Eve, curled up in plastic chairs next to Persia. She was perfectly fine.

Chapter Thirty-one

2006

In January, we moved into Weavers. We had various bits of work done to it, small structural changes here and there, new paint everywhere, and we were very happy. The land, even in the dead of winter, was a joy to walk around. If you wanted your kids to believe in magic and fairies, and I did, it was the ideal spot. Every inch of it was like something out of *Lord of the Rings*. But Gemma wasn't entirely OK. Once the initial glow of being in such a beautiful place had begun to fade a little, the change I'd seen in her before started to reappear. It was slow to begin with. Some days seemed normal, others not so much, but there was a clear trend downwards. At first, it was easy to put it down to having two young children, but it seemed more than that. She started to dread opening the bedroom door and starting her day. She became less sociable, more argumentative, more erratic. We went to the doctors a couple of times, but saw men, and they didn't help. They put it down to fatigue, stress, lack of sleep, things like that, so we carried on and tried our best to deal with it.

We decided that it might be good for Raven if she was able to socialise with other children more. When I was little, I lived in a street with lots of other kids, and every day was spent playing with other people. It's nice having a bigger house with no

One of the best days
ever. 28 August 1997.
(Author's collection)

With Dave Grohl, Kerrang
Awards. 2002. *(Author's collection)*

Saying goodbye to Mum and Dad (and Uncle Jess) at Heathrow airport before moving to California. Such mixed emotions. Excitement to be starting a new life but sadness to be moving so far from them. 2012. *(Author's collection)*

Splinter. This is when the long, slow climb back to the top began to feel real. 2013. *(LaRoache Brothers)*

Some people seem to take awards rather casually. They mean a great deal to me, probably because I don't get that many. 2015. *(Dave Dupuis/Author's collection)*

I genuinely believe that somewhere in the world there exists a perfect partner for all of us. This is mine. Yosemite, California. 2016. *(Author's collection)*

My brother John. Air display pilot, airline pilot, musician; he can even drive steam trains. Love him to bits. 2016. *(Gemma Webb/Author's collection)*

The Ivor Novello award. The programme said, 'This Ivor Novello Award honours an exceptional songwriter who has inspired the creative talents of others.' Rather proud of that. 2017. *(Richard Young/Shutterstock)*

(above) An important part of the success of the *Savage* album, in my opinion, was the visual style. That was all Gemma. She found the clothes and put it all together on the day. 2017. *(Author's collection)*

(left) Working with Persia on the 'My Name Is Ruin' video shoot. 2017. *(Micah Smith/Author's collection)*

Gemma had just told me *Savage* was number 2 in the UK album chart. I'm crying like a baby. Totally didn't expect to have such an emotional reaction. Decades of hope and effort were rewarded in that moment and it was a bit overwhelming. 2017. *(Gemma Webb/Author's collection)*

With Ade Fenton in the BMG offices on *Savage* chart day, and I'm still emotional. I cannot say enough about Ade's contribution to the album (and all the others he's worked on with me). Exceptional. 2017. *(Gemma Webb/Author's collection)*

Mum and Dad. I owe them so much it could never be repaid. I wouldn't have had a career without them. Eternally grateful. 2017. *(Author's collection)*

Easter Island. The photographer mixed mud and sea water together and painted Gemma from head to toe. I'm semi-photobombing her shoot to be honest. 2018. *(Author's collection)*

There is an immediate shift when you have a wife and children. Life is no longer all about you and what you want; it's only about what you can do for them. 2017. *(Gemma Webb/Author's collection)*

The Royal Albert Hall. A dream come true. 2018. *(Author's collection)*

On stage with Persia at the Royal Albert Hall. One of the proudest moments of my life. 2018. *(Anne-Marie Forker)*

Arriving at the Nordoff Robbins O2 Silver Clef award ceremony where I received the Icon Award. 2019. *(Author's collection)*

With Trent Reznor
and his very lovely
wife Mariqueen.
Trent has lent a
helping hand to
me many times,
in many ways.
I admire him
enormously. 2019.
(Author's collection)

The *(R)evolution* tour. 2019.
(Joori Peeters)

One of my favourite photos of the two of us. Gemma is as vital a part of my life as the air I breathe. She is unique in every way, a truly special person. Not a day goes by that I'm not aware of how incredibly lucky I am. 2019. *(Author's collection)*

A hint of what's to come. 2020. *(Gemma Webb)*

neighbours, but it takes away that street socialising that is arguably an important experience for kids. So, Gemma got on the phone to the lady in charge of our local Montessori playgroup, Little Haymakers, to try to get Raven accepted. Earlier that day, I'd had a run-in with another driver and shouted out, 'Fuck me, mate, move over.' Raven had heard and obviously kept it at the ready. As Gemma was speaking to Little Haymakers, Raven, sitting beside her with Persia, leaned over and said perfectly clearly, 'Fuck me, baby sister, move over.' Luckily, they still let her in.

In March, I released *Jagged* through Cooking Vinyl. The reviews were not what I'd feared. In fact, they were every bit as good as they'd been for *Pure*, if not better. It had taken me five years to put *Jagged* together, a time span fuelled in no small part by my fears of what was to come when it was released, and I couldn't have been more wrong. The album had taken a turn lyrically from the *Sacrifice*, *Exile* and *Pure* albums I'd made previously. With *Jagged*, I wanted to move away from my thoughts on faith and religion, but I had little else that fired me up. So, I looked at my past, and in particular the less savoury side of it. I wrote about the things I'd done, the people I'd met, the things I was ashamed of, and some that I wasn't ashamed of but probably should have been. It was like a catalogue of guilt. One of the best press comments I read about *Jagged* was that it 'was so pulverisingly powerful that listening to it on headphones was not unlike putting one's head into a machine that compressed cars into metre-square cuboids'. Which was exactly what I was trying to do.

A few days before the album was released, we played a single show at The Forum in London to launch it. For the main set, we would only play songs from *Jagged*. I didn't see that as being a brave move when I came up with the idea, but the fact that everyone else did seemed to unsettle me a bit. Ideally, I'd have put *Jagged* out a week or so before the show so that fans could get familiar with it, but it didn't quite work out. A small delay here, a small problem there, and it's easy for an album to slide back a week or two from the desired release date. The album coming out after the show did make me worry a little, but the songs sounded immense in a live setting, and I was proud of what we'd made.

Gemma's day-to-day mood was getting worse. She seemed to be permanently down and unhappy, so we went back to the doctors and saw a visiting locum, a woman this time. She knew straight away what the problem was: postnatal depression. Gemma was immediately put onto antidepressants, and two weeks later she started to become the person I knew again. It was an amazing transformation. A few weeks more and she was happy, bubbly, singing her mad songs to the animals, full of life once again.

I released two DVD/CDs in April called *Fragment 1/04* and *Fragment 2/04*. *1/04* was filmed and recorded at my Birmingham Academy show in 2004; *2/04* was filmed at Shepherd's Bush the same year. My idea was to start releasing *Fragment* DVD/CDs regularly. They were not the expensive, multi-camera, slickly produced shoots we'd normally release. The *Fragment* series was intentionally rougher, more basic. I wanted to make live films that were grittier, that felt as if you were at the show, jostling at the front, rather than watching a highly polished version of it. I still think it's a good idea, but unfortunately those were the only two of that nature I put out. I'm not sure why. I think I just forgot I'd had the idea in the first place.

The full UK *Jagged* tour got under way on 19 April at the Birmingham Academy. We played fourteen shows on that tour, had a few days back at home and then drove to Amsterdam to start the European leg. We then played nine shows in a row, no days off, and had one rest day before playing at the Rock Affligem festival in Belgium. During the nine-day run, we played a few shows in Italy, which did not go well. At one of them, I think we had about fifty people, maybe less. At another, half the crowd was behind a glass window in a separate room, and no one seemed to like us that much. I'd looked forward to my first shows in Italy, so it was a big disappointment. The rest of the tour wasn't much better. In Germany, where the previous shows had done well, we now found ourselves being moved to smaller venues. I couldn't understand what was happening. The albums were getting great reviews, and things seemed to be very much on the up. I'd hoped that this tour would see us selling out everywhere and perhaps being bumped up to bigger venues, but the opposite was happening. That European tour was totally demoralising, and it would be another eight years before I felt confident enough to try touring there again.

Having not included London on the main UK tour in May, I'd put on a one-off show at the Hammersmith Palais in June. It was a phenomenal night and did a lot to restore my flagging post-Europe morale. I had the night recorded and filmed but never did get around to finishing it off. I still have the tapes somewhere. A rare festival appearance at a very muddy GuilFest later that month was the last UK show before we left for North America once again for the next leg of the *Jagged* tour.

The only single to be taken from *Jagged* was called 'In a Dark Place', which I released on Mortal in July. I'd actually written parts of it for a collaboration between Chris Vrenna, who had played with Nine Inch Nails back in the day, and Paul Raven from Killing Joke. It took me so long to work on the demo they sent me that by the time I actually did something and sent it back, they'd completely forgotten about the idea and moved on. Either that or they didn't like it, because I never heard a thing from them. I made a video for 'In a Dark Place' on the land at Weavers with Paul Green and the band. My big mistake was having a party the night before. Everyone who was going to be in the video was there, plus an assortment of other friends, and it was another epic. It was a sorry-looking bunch of spanglers who answered the door to Paul and his crew the next morning. I think he did an amazing job of getting everyone to stand up for the next few hours while he wheeled around us with his cameras. It was not my most professional moment, to be honest.

The day Gemma and I left for the US tour, a small mistake would lead to another big change in our lives. After accidentally getting pregnant with Persia, Gemma had acquired a gadget that said when it was safe to have sex, when it was doubtful and when you absolutely shouldn't. It gave you the information via a green, amber or red light. The night before had been a steady green, but I was too tired. The next morning, I wasn't, so, still believing we were in a green period, we did the deed before getting up to leave for the airport. To my horror, Gemma came out of the bathroom with the machine glowing bright red. Even so, I wasn't too worried, as I still clung to the feeling that, despite Persia coming along, we were not good at making babies naturally. We packed, drove to Heathrow and boarded the plane to Detroit, where the tour was due to start the next day, and I really didn't think any more about it for a while.

For the next three weeks we moved across America, playing most nights, until we arrived in Anaheim, Los Angeles, on 20 August for a show at the House of Blues in downtown Disney. I was in the dressing room, with about ten minutes to go, when Gemma came in and told me she was pregnant. It was totally unexpected and with the show about to start, I just couldn't quite process the news. I remember initially feeling frightened more than excited. It was different to how we'd reacted to the first two. We played three more shows on that tour, flew back to the UK and played a couple more, but when we finally got home, we talked about nothing else for several days.

My fear was very real. Having lost the first baby so tragically, and then several more after that, I was aware of how easy it was for things to go wrong – how delicate a process it could be. To have had so many problems and disappointments and then find ourselves with two perfectly healthy children seemed almost like a miracle. The chances of having yet another perfectly healthy baby seemed, to me anyway, unlikely, as though we might be pushing our luck. My fear was that should anything be wrong with it, a third baby would have a devastating impact on Raven and Persia and the life I thought we owed to them. I wasn't sure I wanted to take that risk by having a third, and yet I couldn't imagine not taking it. I was absolutely torn, and it was one of the most horrible few days I've ever had to deal with. Gemma definitely leant more towards just going for it and hoping for the best. We didn't argue about it at all, not once, but we went round and round and round for days, and I have to confess, I was beginning to lean the other way. I really wasn't sure we should take the risk. I woke up early one morning, 22 September, if memory serves, and while Gemma still slept went down to the kitchen. Our baby folders were on the table, three large volumes that included vast amounts of information on everything to do with babies you could possibly think of. At that point, Gemma was at eight weeks, so I turned Volume one to the eight-week section, and there was a photo of an embryo. It was a tiny but almost fully formed little baby, and it broke my heart, and my decision was made. We would have three. I ran back upstairs, couldn't speak, cried, showed her the picture, mumbled something about choosing names and that was that. I almost made the worst decision of my life (although I doubt Gemma would ever have agreed) but instead made the best. Echo Moon was on her way.

I was asked to take part in a reality-TV show called *The Race* in November. It was to be two teams, one of men, one of women, and would be a battle of the sexes. We'd be based at the legendary Silverstone circuit, and each day we would be taught how to drive a particular type of racing car, with a race at the end of the day. I believe the idea was to decide once and for all whether men or women were the better drivers. Each team had five celebrities in it, and each team would be captained by a Formula One racing driver. Eddie Irvine led the men's team, David Coulthard the women's.

Initially, we were supposed to sleep on a tour bus, one for the men, one for the women, but that lasted just one night. After that they brought in mobile homes, and I was allowed to have my caravan delivered, which gave me some badly needed privacy each night. The cars were covered in cameras, and a team of instructors took care of us and showed us the techniques and skills required. It was brilliant, and I was in my element. From the outset, though, the men's team was faster, and the gap between the two soon became so great that as a competition it lost all meaning. That's not a reflection on women drivers at all – I just think that, by chance, they'd picked a couple of people in the men's team who were quite good. That would be me and Brian Johnson from AC/DC, who I happened to get on really well with. The TV peeps employed a series of dubious moves to make it look as if it was closer than it was. One thing they tried was during one of my races. We were driving huge monster trucks that you steered not only with the steering wheel but with a switch that turned the rear wheels independently. They were also designed to hit ramps and get airborne, and they were hugely powerful. The blue one was fast, the red one less so, so the blue one was given to my competitor and the red one to me. We launched down the first straight, took off over a jump, and made the 180-degree turn, and, I'll admit, at that halfway point she was slightly ahead. But she then hit the next jump awkwardly and rolled the thing upside down. I got airborne, didn't crash and crossed the finish line. That evening during the live TV part of it, where we sat in a makeshift studio with an audience, a graphic quickly flashed up on the screen with a red line drawn arbitrarily across it that they claimed was the finishing line, which it was nowhere near, giving the victory to the crashed truck. I was furious, for about thirty seconds, at what was blatant cheating. But then I remembered it was just TV, and it didn't really matter and sat down slightly embarrassed. I did ask them to put the graphic up again, but they refused, knowing it showed anything but the true finishing line.

The big finale was a longer race in single-seater racing cars. We'd been told that we had to make a compulsory pit stop during the race. We'd come in, wait for ten seconds and then be sent off again to finish the race. We were also told that the red traffic light at the pit-lane exit was not to be ignored under any circumstances. So, come the race, I found myself out in the lead, and Brian Johnson was second, but quite some way behind me. I realised I could make my pit stop and still get out in front of him. It all went well until I got to the pit exit, where I saw the red exit light blazing away. I waited, and I waited, and I waited. Finally, I ignored it and just exited the pits, but I'd been there a long time. Brian had taken the lead and was some way ahead. It was a great race, and we crossed the line just feet apart, but Brian won. I thoroughly enjoyed it, but I was a little disappointed. Brian had been great fun and a really good, fast competitor throughout the week. So, Brian got a cup for the victory, and I got a cup for the overall championship. It was one of the best things I've ever done.

Although *Jagged* had been released in March, I hadn't written a single song for the rest of the year. I think with Persia coming along, and then moving house, releasing the album and then so much touring, I just hadn't really been home enough to think about it. Plus, with all the drama with Echo and *The Race*, I'd had a very busy year doing other things, and I had one more thing to do before the year was out. I'd decided to do a short four-date tour on which I would only play songs from my 1980 *Telekon* album sessions. I'd been thinking about it for a while. As a rule, I hate nostalgia – I have a real problem with looking back. I'm always keen to move forward, to not dwell on the past and live off past glories, I'd become somewhat dismissive of my older music. I only played a handful of older songs in the shows, and I would frequently speak offhand about my earlier music when asked about it during interviews. It often annoyed the fans, and for a while I couldn't have cared less, but I eventually began to understand. It looked as if I was giving the finger to songs that were important to them, and in so doing I was giving a finger to the fans who had bought those songs and still loved them. Many of them had spent years defending the very music I was now dismissing, protesting outside Radio 1, writing letters to music papers and so on. Although I had reasons for feeling as I did, the way I was handling it was foolish, and a little arrogant and disrespectful. I decided I would play the *Telekon* shows partly to apologise, partly to make it clear I would not be so dismissive going forward and partly because I still didn't want to play a lot of older stuff in my regular shows. If I could do these small retro tours once in a while, I hoped that would be enough to keep the fans who wanted the older stuff happy, and that they'd be less critical when I played tours to support a new album and played mainly new things.

The *Telekon* mini tour was a great success. The fans loved it, and I, surprisingly, found that I wasn't embarrassed by the songs I'd been dismissing for so long. The *Telekon* songs were more than twenty-five years old, and yet they actually sounded pretty good. I came away from that tour a little prouder of that album than I expected to be. But I still hated doing anything that looked backwards rather than forwards.

With that done, we headed back to Harley Street to see how Echo was doing. Mid-December was time for her twenty-week scan, and it was actually quite worrying, as it was noticed that the placenta was in the wrong place. If it stayed where it was, there was no way Gemma could give birth normally. The way out was blocked, and she would have no choice but to have a Caesarean. We were also concerned about Gemma taking the antidepressants in the latter stages, and she was advised to come off them after Christmas, which she did.

Chapter Thirty-two

2007

In late January, Gemma passed out in the bathroom and I had to call an ambulance. She was rushed to hospital, and it was discovered that her placenta-praevia condition was now grade four, the most serious. It was potentially life-threatening to both Gemma and Echo. She was told to rest as much as possible and to take things gently. It was very worrying. Taking things gently was easier said than done when you have two other young children in the house, but she was definitely a lot more cautious in the way she moved around.

Nine Inch Nails were playing in Manchester on 25 February, and, despite her condition, she was determined to go. I thought it was madness, but she's not to be reasoned with where NIN are concerned. We were ready to leave for the long drive north when Gemma decided to put a rubbish bag into the bin at the end of the garden. As she neared the gate, she passed out and fell forward onto her stomach. It was like someone had turned off a switch and down she went. She came to almost immediately, within a couple of seconds, and jumped straight up, but then she felt blood. We thought we were losing the baby. I ran inside and called for an ambulance, and by the time it arrived the blood was really bad. They put the most horrendously huge needle into her arm, placed her on a drip, loaded her into the ambulance and sped off. I followed in the car. In the hospital, they weren't able to see her straight away. I couldn't believe that someone losing a baby wouldn't just jump to the front of the queue, but I guess everyone thinks their emergency is the most urgent. When she was eventually seen, they did various checks and, much to our relief, said the baby was OK but that Gemma would have to stay in. They weren't sure if she was bleeding internally, and, in any case, she had to be monitored constantly until the baby could come out.

She stayed in that hospital for the next three and a half weeks, but we didn't want the baby born there. When we'd first found out that a Caesarean was going to be necessary, we'd made arrangements for a particular surgeon to do the operation at the Portland in London. So, when he deemed the time to be right, Gemma was transferred there by ambulance, and Echo was born at about 8 a.m. on 22 March. It was a considerably different experience to the other two. I was allowed in the room, but screens were put up so all the gory business was hidden, which I was grateful for. I was allowed to cut the cord, so three out of three for that. Echo was brought over to me before they'd cleaned her, and what a messy little thing she was. She looked for all the world like a mole peeking out of the blanket, so we nicknamed her Mole there and then. Gemma was given some time to be with her in the recovery room, but then Echo was taken, and Gemma was wheeled up to her room.

Not long after that, a nurse brought Echo into the room and laid her in the cot. It all seemed to have gone very smoothly. I was standing next to her about twenty minutes later when the nurse came in to check on things. She looked at Echo, said something I didn't catch, picked her up and rushed out. For the next few minutes, I sat there with Gemma waiting for her to come back. I thought it was something trivial, like having the wrong name-band on her wrist. But she didn't come back, and Gemma asked me to go and find out what was happening. As I left the room, the door to the room opposite was open, and there was Echo, with four or five medical staff all around her. She had tubes and all sorts of things coming out of her, and it was terrifying. A nurse came over and took me back into Gemma's room and explained what was happening. The nurse who had taken her had noticed that she wasn't breathing properly, that she was 'panting'. I hadn't noticed anything, and I was right there, so I felt terrible. She explained that Echo's lungs were sticking together, a condition called newborn respiratory distress syndrome. They'd done what they could in that moment, but she was now being taken to the intensive-care unit. Echo had been born five and a half weeks early, just like Raven, but not because she was ready to come the way Raven had been. The decision was made to take her out early due to the precarious nature of Gemma's condition, and it seemed that Echo's lungs weren't ready.

Echo stayed in intensive care for about a week. Gemma and I were allowed to go down and see her a couple of times during the day, and it was both lovely and very upsetting. She was so small, with tubes in her and monitoring equipment bleeping and wheezing around her. We couldn't even touch her, as she was inside a machine. It was the saddest thing to see her lying there like that. After the week of intensive care was over, she was put into specialist care, so we still couldn't have her with us in Gemma's room. She was under specialist care for another week, but we were allowed to see her more often, and if I remember correctly, we were allowed to feed her at times. But, thanks to the care and swift action of the staff at the Portland, she made it, and we will always be grateful. She spent a couple of days with us in Gemma's room before we were given the OK to take her home. It felt special walking out of the hospital with her safe and sound.

No sooner had we got her home, than Gemma plummeted back into depression, and it was far worse than it had been before. She became agitated, argumentative, picky. If I suggested we stop work and just go out for the day, thinking it might cheer her up, she'd have a go at me as if I'd suggested something offensive. She was erratic and spiteful, and as the months went by, I found it increasingly difficult.

Persia was enrolled at the same kindergarten school as Raven, Little Haymakers. We felt much the same as we had with Raven – that socialising with a group of children would be beneficial in a number of ways. It was a really nice place for them to be, and they enjoyed it, but I still hated dropping them there each morning, and I counted the minutes until we could pick them up again.

Ade Fenton had made a solo album called *Artificial Perfect*, and he'd asked me to sing on some of the songs. I sang on 'Recall', 'Slide Away', 'The Leather Sea' and, the first single from the album, 'Healing'. Ade made a great video for 'Healing' that I was featured in, and the album came out in April. It was a good album, and Ade's production skills seemed to me to have gone up another level. With the next Ade Fenton single, 'The Leather Sea', I was asked to do a Sky TV interview with a host who usually discussed the politics of the day. It was good promo for the song but in the first part of the interview he called it 'The

Leather Sofa'. While they were playing a clip I told him the correct title but when he was live again he called it 'The Leather Seat'. It was close enough so I left it at that.

The BBC had made an album of all three of my John Peel radio sessions called, appropriately enough, *The Complete John Peel Sessions*. The sleeve notes painted me in a very positive light, and I was rather proud of it. I felt quite honoured. A couple of weeks later, I put out yet another live album and DVD called *Jagged Live*, which contained all the live songs from that album, filmed at the launch gig the year before. I played another four-date mini tour in the UK to help promote the DVD, but they were the only live shows I played all year. Ade Fenton joined the band for this tour. I'd fallen out with my previous keyboard player not long after Echo was born, and Ade was the perfect replacement. He knew all the songs, looked great and moved well on stage.

After *Jagged*, I was struggling more than ever with motivation and, as I moved through 2007, it got worse rather than better. It wasn't so much that I was worried about the daunting task ahead of starting another album, although that was a part of it. It wasn't that I was scared of the press turning against me the way I had been after *Pure*, although again that might have been a small part of it. I just didn't feel like writing anything. I now had three children, and life was very different. I'd gone from a freewheeling, rather hedonistic, partying way of life to something totally opposite. None of the children were difficult sleepers, so luckily our nights of constantly being woken up didn't last too long with any of them. They weren't sickly or unusually difficult in any way. But it was still a totally different life, and while I welcomed it, and loved the children very much and wanted to spend every minute with them, I also missed my old life. I felt tremendous guilt over that, and I didn't know how to handle it. What made it all so much worse was that Gemma was even lower than ever. If she had been awkward and argumentative before, she was now very much worse. Ever since we had started seeing one another, we had always been able to talk openly about any problems that flared up. We had always been able to listen, to see the other person's point of view, understand it and make things better. Our entire relationship was founded on our ability to listen and to respect one another's feelings. That willingness to listen, that respect, was now increasingly hard to find. Arguments would flare up over nothing, and it was often impossible to find a reason why, so it was impossible to know what to fix. As the year unfolded, we slowly became everything I hate in a relationship: bickering, point scoring and pettiness. I understood that she was suffering. The depression she'd had around Persia seemed like a gentle warm-up for what she was going through now. The antidepressant dose was adjusted, more than once, the type of pill was changed, but at best it only made her capable of functioning. Quite often, even that seemed a struggle. Whatever her body and it's changing hormones were doing to her, it was only a part of the problem.

I've always thought she's body dysmorphic. Gemma says she has eyes, and they don't lie, and she doesn't like what those eyes see in the mirror. I think she's lovely-looking, but Gemma only sees imperfections and hates herself from top to bottom. For someone seemingly so brimming over with loud confidence and a larger-than-life personality, she's riddled with insecurities. She uses her personality as a shield against all the things she hates about herself and the way she looks. She sees it as a way of deflecting attention from her appearance. It makes little sense to me, but I've been with her a long time, and she's never wavered from that point of view. It's absolutely genuine. After Echo was born, she hated herself more than ever, and I think that made everything else she was going through so much worse. Not only that, she felt she'd lost her personality, her shield, the one thing that allowed her to be sociable and enjoy life. She was in a desperate state, and much of the anger and frustration she felt about that came directly at me. How much that played a part in my own problems is impossible to say, but as each month came and went I wrote nothing. I made excuses, replaced equipment, anything but knuckle down and write songs.

Towards the end of the summer, we decided to take a break for a few weeks, so we took Raven and Persia and went to Florida. Echo was still barely six months old, so we left her with my mum and dad, who were delighted to have some one-on-one time with her. We actually felt guilty for the entire two weeks for not taking her with us, but Mum and Dad loved it. We'd hoped that just being somewhere different, without the day-to-day routine of our life at home, might help improve things. Things did seem a little better between us while we were away, but we were still light years from being the couple we had been. Petty arguments seemed to come as easily as breathing.

It might seem as though we were falling out of love with one another, but that wouldn't be true at all. We actually still got on pretty well for much of the time, but it wasn't the same. We were both aware that Gemma was far from well, and it was becoming a little more obvious that I wasn't entirely myself either. We also knew it required patience and understanding, and love most of all, to get through it. But it's so much easier to say than to do when you feel horrible every day. When reaching for the door handle in the morning feels like the world is going to crush you if you open it. Dreading going downstairs, dreading starting the day's chores, dreading everything.

In November, I was asked to appear on *The Mighty Boosh* episode 'The Year of the Crimp'. I loved the show and watched it regularly. One of the characters was a massive Gary Numan fan, and it was a running joke throughout the series. My appearance was essentially me being in a box, I think, or a clock, and not being allowed out. It was very funny, and Gemma and I had the best time working with the Boosh team. They couldn't have been nicer. For a long time after that it was the one thing people wanted to talk about: 'What was it like working on *The Mighty Boosh*?' I honestly think that one spot with the Boosh did more for my profile than anything else I'd done for the previous ten years. Probably longer.

Chapter Thirty-three

2008

February 2008 was the thirtieth anniversary of my signing to Beggars Banquet; and although I hadn't been with them for many years, they put out a special version of the *Replicas* album called *Replicas Redux* that included the original songs, the single B-Sides and several outtakes that Steve Webbon had found in the Beggars archives – the same Steve Webbon who Paul had handed our demo to back in 1978. Steve Malins had been working closely with Beggars on all the recent re-releases of old material and had been a driving force in seeing them come out again. He'd also written all the sleeve notes, and it helped the overall situation considerably. *Replicas Redux*, for example, got some five-star reviews, and many of the re-releases were treated equally well. Just as the new music I'd been making had received several great reviews, so Steve's work with the back catalogue had been paying dividends with the way it was seen as well. Albums not particularly well received when they first came out were now being hailed as classics and groundbreaking. It all combined to keep pushing a wave of re-evaluation. The way I was seen continued to improve and evolve. Steve had a lot to do with that.

As I still hadn't written a thing since *Jagged*, it made good sense for me to go back out on tour and support the *Redux* album. Unlike the four-date *Telekon* retro tour, this would be a bigger affair – a fifteen-date tour ending at the Indigo in London's O2 Arena complex. I still hated retro with a passion, but the *Telekon* shows had worked well, and the fans seemed to genuinely appreciate them. I hoped that playing a full tour of *Replicas* would be equally well received. I made it clear that these sorts of tours would not be a regular thing.

I had my fiftieth birthday the day we played Manchester Academy, the same venue that I'd played in 2003 the day after Raven was born. The Academy seemed like a magnet for important occasions in my life. It was a great night, one I will always remember. The crowd were everything a great crowd should be – they sang 'Happy Birthday', Gemma nervously walking on with a rude cake. It made reaching fifty seem OK. But it really wasn't. I honestly thought I'd sailed through the fifty mark with no problem, but I hadn't at all. When we got back from the tour, I started to notice things. I couldn't look at old people without getting upset. I couldn't understand how they could be so old, so close to the end, and yet be walking about seemingly without a care. Old couples were the worst. It got so I couldn't look at old people without crying, without waves of sadness washing over me. I could be sitting in my car, waiting for Gemma, and by the time she came back I was a mess. At first it happened once in a while, then more often, until it was every time I stepped out the door. Even watching old people on television did it. I talked to my dad about it, but he said you just accept it. I couldn't grasp that at all.

I became obsessed about my own mortality, about getting sick, developing some horrendous condition that would ruin what remained of my life. I worried about not being there for the children. I cried at the thought of not being around them. Every headache became a possible brain tumour. Every pang of indigestion became stomach cancer. I was a nightmare. It seemed that going through fifty had changed something in me, and I was a mess. I'd heard about midlife crises, where men want to sleep with young women or buy a sports car to relive their youth in some way, but I had none of that. I just became sad looking at old people, and paranoid about getting old and dying myself.

Then I started to find it almost impossible to talk to young people. I felt like a dirty lech just having an innocent conversation with them. I think passing fifty was the moment when I accepted that I had fewer years left to live than the years I'd lived before, and I couldn't handle it at all. Now, how much of that was to do with being fifty, and how much of that was the result of the stresses of the previous few years and my faltering relationship with Gemma, I'll never know. But then it got worse, and I started having panic attacks. I would think of something, perhaps the thought of the children being older when I was gone, and it was as if I'd pushed over a domino on one of those domino cascades. As one fell, it made the next fall, then the next, in an unstoppable torrent, and that was my brain. I would feel the first one fall, and I knew I was lost. Seconds later, I would be on the floor in a ball, sobbing, screaming sometimes. Gemma was always there, helping, calming, soothing me back to reality, but it was embarrassing. I saw myself as someone who was always in control. I had always been able to wrap emotion up and move it sideways. This was a new and unnerving experience for me. It was everything I didn't want to be, didn't think I ever could be. Gemma made the point after one particularly bad moment that this was clearly something more than a midlife crisis. I needed to go and see someone.

In a way, the timing was perfect, if it can ever be perfect. Gemma had been getting better for a while. She'd been weaning off the pills slowly but surely and, in almost every respect, was close to being her old self again. I dread to think what would have happened if she'd still been suffering herself. Anyway, I visited the doctor and described the anxiety attacks, and he said that the root cause of anxiety is depression. I had no idea. I certainly didn't feel depressed – not as I understood depression, anyway. But I took his advice and went on to the same pills Gemma was just coming off. About two weeks later they started to have an effect, but it was not the one I'd hoped for.

My whole life I'd been moody. Every day pretty much, I would rise and fall with no obvious reason why. In fact, more often than not, the ups and downs would be out of sync with the experiences I was having. I could have some great news, and instead of my mood being lifted, it would plummet. Bad news could come and barely touch me at all – I'd even be happy on occasions. None of it made any sense. My moods were extreme, up or down, and yet they had little to do with my life. I often felt it change in the middle of a sentence. I could happily be talking to Gemma, and I'd feel it go, as though a tap had been turned off, and there was nothing I could do about it other than wait. I had no idea when it would happen, in either direction, and it was impossible to make it happen if I wanted to. It was as if my mind was completely disconnected from the ebb and flow of my life. My mind literally had a mind of its own, and it was very wearing. To not know from one minute to the next how I was going to feel – and the mood changes could be extreme – wore me out. But I'd always been like that. I was used to it. It was all I'd ever known. Those first antidepressants stopped the mood swings and they levelled me out. But they levelled me out at miserable. If they'd levelled me out at happy, I'd probably have stayed on them for ever.

I went back to the doctor and we tried another type. This time, after the two weeks, I felt a bit better. I wasn't stuck at happy, but I was OK. My moods didn't swing one way or the other. I was just left with an easy-going attitude that made me feel that everything was all right. Nothing really mattered. After fifty years of out-of-sync mood swings, it was truly amazing to feel the same, all day, every day. It was utterly seductive, and I couldn't imagine ever wanting to go back to the way I used to be, which would eventually become quite a problem

Still, I did do some useful things. I dusted off my non-existent carpentry skills and made the children a playhouse six feet off the ground on four huge poles with a slide. It took me all summer, but I was proud as punch when it was done and I could watch them playing on it. It was so ridiculously overbuilt, it will probably still be there long after the house is demolished.

I played some shows as well. The Mighty Boosh had their own festival that I was asked to play at, and I headlined the Wickerman Festival, and played at the Magic Roundabout festival and Bestival on the Isle of Wight, plus assorted warm-up and cool-down gigs around those festivals. By the end of the year I still hadn't written any new songs, and now, thanks to the pills, I really didn't care. Everything was OK with me.

In July, I put out a remix album of *Jagged* songs called *Jagged Edge*. I loved it. It took many of the songs into new areas, and I thought it was some of the best music I'd ever put out. It wasn't really new, and Gemma wasn't too happy. Neither was Ade, neither was Steve and neither was my dad. One of the main requirements of a recording artist is that you record, and for that you need new songs, so Gemma and Ade came up with a secret plan. They needed to find a way of getting me to re-engage with my career, so Ade came to visit and made me go through all the tapes I had of songs I hadn't released or hadn't developed. We identified about fourteen possible songs that could be worked on. Ade's idea was to make an album out of unfinished gems. To me, it seemed like an easy way out, so I said, yes, go for it.

Soon after Ade's visit, Gemma was taken to hospital with meningitis. A few years before we'd met, she'd collapsed with what looked very much like a stroke. In the hospital, they'd given her a drug that she'd reacted badly to. The spasms due to the reaction caused so much damage in her neck that it took months of traction before she was anywhere near back to normal. Unfortunately the original problem, the suspected stroke, was forgotten about as they fixed the damage caused by her reaction to the drug. That bad reaction had damaged several vertebrae in her spine, which now contributed to almost constant headaches. I'd already had to take her to emergency twice after she'd accidentally overdosed on painkillers. So, when meningitis appeared, we put it down to yet another terrible headache for the first few hours. But then she couldn't see, and other things happened, so she ended up in hospital.

The doctors told me it was a new strain of viral meningitis and that it was very serious. It was a difficult time. My mum and dad were great with the children, but, nonetheless, I felt so helpless. It took a couple of weeks, and she suffered greatly for much of that time, but thankfully she got better and was able to come home. Sadly, in a horrible coincidence, the wife of a friend of ours contracted the same strain of meningitis just days later and died soon after going into hospital. It really brought home just how lucky Gemma had been.

In September, Raven started school proper, in a school not too far from where we lived called Skippers Hill. It was lovely to see her dressed in her uniform, but I was worried about how she would fit in. She was a unique little thing and, much like me, didn't interact in the way most people would expect. In many ways, it actually went better than I'd hoped, and she made some new friends fairly quickly. The school itself was old and pretty, but it was rather academic and had a sporting history it seemed overly proud of. I wasn't entirely sure Raven would suit somewhere with high demands academically – I saw her more as a creative type – but we would find out soon enough.

Chapter Thirty-four

2009

My depression got worse. I didn't engage in anything. I just drifted in my own little cloud of indifference. I loved my wife, I loved my kids, I loved my life, I loved my house and absolutely nothing bothered me. Gemma found it increasingly worrying. I had absolutely zero drive, and I absolutely didn't care. I didn't work, didn't want to – everything was right with me and the world. I didn't know it at the time, but it was becoming quite a problem. Gemma noticed that I no longer planned and schemed. I had no idea what I wanted to do. I had no ideas about anything. No new thoughts on albums or song themes or images. Just nothing. It wasn't just the fact that I wasn't being creative or thinking ahead about career strategies. It was the fact that I didn't care about any of that. I didn't think it was a problem, but Gemma could see our hard-won new life slipping away, and I was little more than a dribbling, happy child in the corner.

Ade was hard at work on the outtake songs we'd chosen, but I was far from interested. He would send the work he'd done, and I'd barely listen. When I did bother, I'd find things I didn't like and send it back. I didn't want to sing on the songs, didn't want to write lyrics for them, didn't really want to be involved at all. I just wanted to stay floating along in my little 'couldn't care less' bubble. How he kept going, I'll never know, but he did. He put up with all of my lazy indifference and just kept at it.

In March, we flew out to Australia for a short tour, my first there in twenty-nine years. We played three shows of my own and then travelled out to play at a festival. It was my first Australian festival, and it was a good experience. The crowd were surprisingly supportive, although at one point I did see an apple come flying out of the haze. It was a perfect pitch, and a long one, and I swear it was coming directly at my face. I watched it curve inexorably towards me, and, at the last second, I just leant to one side and let it pass. I didn't miss a beat, or a word. That seemed to cement my popularity with the crowd, and it just got even better after that.

In April, I released another live album, *Replicas Live*, taken from the *Replicas Redux* tour the year before. When we got back from Australia, I played a three-show weekender in April to help it along, then another two shows in June as a warm-up for the Rabarock festival in Estonia on the 13th. In July, we played the Lovebox festival in London, more shows around the Waregem Gothic Festival in Belgium and a strange one in Folkestone called the Hevy Music Festival. The weather was appalling, and it was set up in a small car park as far as I could tell. Everything about the organisation said 'low budget' and 'we don't know what we're doing'. I was one of three main acts – the other two were Feeder and Ash, so big names at the time. The storms that ravaged the site destroyed half of it, the stage canopy leaked and water poured all over the equipment, much of which blew up. There was a tiny crowd, and it was more a comedy of errors than a rock festival.

Earlier that summer, Steve Malins got in touch with Gemma and said he'd heard that Nine Inch Nails, who had just started a UK tour, were playing 'Metal' in their set. I was still lost in La La Land thanks to my antidepressants, and Gemma knew that underneath that druggy mist my confidence was at an all-time low. She was desperate to find something that would pick me up and refire my sense of purpose. When she heard about NIN and 'Metal', she came up with another plan, one that she kept entirely secret from me. We'd been friends with NIN producer Alan Moulder for some time, so she spoke to him about it. We were also good friends with Alan Wilder from Depeche Mode, so she spoke to him about it as well. They helped provide contacts and how to word an email that Gemma intended to send to Trent Reznor. So, behind my back, knowing full well that I would have absolutely forbidden any such approach, she wrote to Trent and said something along the lines of 'what a good idea it would be if Gary got up on stage and sang "Metal" with you'. She then sat back and waited. If the answer was no, she would have kept her secret, and I'd never have known she'd even asked. But the answer was an emphatic yes. When she told me, I couldn't believe she'd had the cheek to do it, and I was annoyed she'd gone about it sneakily, but I loved her for thinking of it, and for trying something to wake me up.

Trent invited me to sing with them at their huge O2 Arena show in London. It was a huge honour. Nine Inch Nails were the band I most admired, and to be asked to sing one of my own songs at their big London arena triumph was very special. But I was terrified. I couldn't imagine that NIN fans would have the slightest interest in seeing me come on and sing a Numan song. I imagined a wide range of horrible scenarios, and, come the day, I was far from confident that it was going to end well. We arrived for the soundcheck, and it was the most friendly of welcomes, by band and crew alike, and it did much to put me at ease. That all vanished when Trent said they were also going to play 'Cars' that night. Two Numan songs! I was more convinced than ever that the crowd were going to hate me. I said to Trent, 'I don't think your fans are going to be interested in someone else singing their own songs,' but he was positive it would go well. During the soundcheck, I looked down at Gemma and saw that she was crying her eyes out. Big black lines of runny make-up were streaking down her face. I think it was one of the happiest moments of her life, and she was proud that she'd managed to make it all happen.

I watched the show from the side of the stage, and it was epic, which made me even more nervous to come on and stop all that for my two little songs. The moment came, and Trent gave me the most incredible introduction. He talked about how important and inspirational I'd been to him when he was first putting Nine Inch Nails together, how important the music had been to him. He mentioned *The Pleasure Principle*, and it was just amazing for me to stand there and listen to. I'd arrived with no confidence whatsoever, having not written any new songs for years, with little faith in my back catalogue or where I was going next . . . if anywhere. To stand there and listen to someone I truly admired saying such complimentary things changed something in me. In the seconds before I had to walk on, I thought, If he can feel like that about my older music, why can't I? If he thinks it was special and groundbreaking, why don't I? That one moment made me change my entire attitude to my earlier work.

Nonetheless, glowing introduction or not, I was as nervous as I'd ever been walking on. But if there's one thing I've learned, it's never let it show. Whatever you feel on the inside, walk on as if you own the place, as if it's the only place you should be. I did my best, but inside, for about five seconds, I was jelly, because as I walked on, the crowd erupted, and I just couldn't believe it. It stunned me. From front to back of that huge arena, arms were in the air, and the roar from the crowd was deafening. The next ten minutes were the best. I was at the O2 Arena, with a sold-out crowd, singing my own two songs, with Nine Inch Nails as my backing band and Trent Reznor on keyboards. Can it ever get any better than that? It was as uplifting a moment as you could ever wish for. Gemma's sneaky little plan had gone better than in her wildest dreams.

Soon after the O2 show I was asked if I wanted to fly out to Los Angeles and be a part of what were being talked about as the last Nine Inch Nails shows ever. Over the four nights, Trent brought on an array of celebrity guests, and he kindly filmed an interview that we would use later in a Gary Numan documentary. Each show, I would come on and sing a song of mine that Trent had chosen. We did 'Cars' and 'Metal', but also 'I Die: You Die' and, on the final night I think, 'Down in the Park'. That was an especially emotional moment for me, because he had Bowie's keyboard player, Mike Garson, play an instrumental version of the song before the rest of us came on. It was one of the proudest moments of my life.

Back in the UK, Beggars Banquet, with Steve Malins very much involved, had released a thirtieth-anniversary edition of *The Pleasure Principle*. It had a tremendous amount of extra, previously unheard material in the package, and the reviews were remarkable. The *Sunday Times* chose it as their 'Must Have Reissue of the Week' and wrote, 'Numan's reputation has been restored lately. He's finally been recognised as an important and influential figure. [His] importance lies in his ability to slap an earth-quaking hook on top of his glacial synths ('Cars' being the definitive example), and therefore join . . . the dots between Kraftwerk, Bowie and Eno on one side and the rise of synth-pop, techno and industrial music on the other.' *Mojo* gave it five stars and said, 'What makes it so successful is its perfect fusion of electronics with more traditional elements as in the beautiful melody of 'Complex' – the first ballad of electronica, a weave of violin, viola and Moog – or 'Films', its propulsive drum and electric bass figures set against washes of bleak synthetics. Much sampled, much admired, it is an album full of astonishing ideas.' And *Record Collector* wrote, 'For once, here's a much-hyped album which deserves the hype. Gary Numan's third record was the year zero of big-selling synth-pop, though 'pop' is far too light a word for a sound that scared the crap out of spotty teenagers worldwide. *The Pleasure Principle* left people chilled to the core with its deathly cold combination of Moog bass, digital bass and Numan's numb, robotic vocals. After listening to 'Cars', 'Films', 'Metal' or 'Engineers', you could well believe that guitar music was finished forever. There's not a duff track on here. Highly recommended.'

Thanks to Trent and his comments about *The Pleasure Principle*, I'd decided to celebrate rather than ignore its anniversary and announced a sixteen-date UK tour for November. Before that, though, things went very wrong between me and my parents.

We arrived back in the UK from Los Angeles and went straight to my mum and dad's house to pick up the children.

Our trip away had been extended slightly after Trent got sick and rearranged the dates, but only by a few days. Mum and Dad didn't seem happy about it, though, Dad especially. It was a slightly uncomfortable meeting back at their house, so we didn't stay long. I arrived home about an hour later to find that my dad had sent me a not very nice email. It seemed to blame Gemma for things that I couldn't see as being 'things' anyway. The antagonism had been going on for years. We'd been together seventeen years by now, married for twelve, and I think I'd just had enough of trying to walk the line between them, so I wrote a heavy email back. The next morning I got a phone call from Mum saying not to write to my dad like that – it would make him ill. She implied, or so I thought, that something was wrong with him and any extra stress was to be avoided. I immediately backed off. I wrote to my dad and made peace, saying that I hadn't been aware anything was wrong. But I then got an even nastier one back saying that Mum had said no such thing – there was nothing wrong with him. He seemed madder than ever. I was totally lost with what was going on. I said to him, 'Ask her, she just said it,' and then Mum denied it. I have no idea why. I have never been able to understand why she did that, but it caused a huge falling-out. My dad's dislike for Gemma poured out, and it was pretty unpleasant. I was accused of lying about my mum, which I absolutely didn't. I fought back equally hard, and we went from being a happy family to fierce enemies almost overnight. I would never, in all my life, have thought that we would ever fall out. A great many things happened after that, few that I will write about here, but it knocked my life sideways. Not only that, my dad pulled out as my manager after thirty years. I was dropped in the shit from the greatest of heights, and I had absolutely no idea what to do. If I was suffering from depression before, it was just about to take a nosedive to even lower levels.

I turned to the only people I knew who might be able to help: Steve Malins and Ade Fenton. Steve already managed a couple of people and, with a long history in press and PR, seemed the right sort of person to step in. Equally, Ade had long impressed me with the way he ran his own DJ career and label. The two of them together looked to be a good solution, and I felt lucky to have people already close to me whom I could turn to.

Not long after the family drama kicked off, I had a thing called an S lift. It's like a mild face-lift for beginners. I don't think it made much difference. When I came round after the op, which was done in Manchester, I felt pretty good, so Gemma and I went to the cinema. My head was bandaged up like the invisible man, and I think I was probably still off my tits a bit. I was way beyond being recognisable, so I didn't really care too much. I even appeared on *Later . . . with Jools Holland* for an interview about two weeks later when my face was still the size of a melon from most angles.

A TV documentary called *Synth Britannia* about the birth of mainstream electronic music was aired on 16 October, and I watched it more out of interest than expecting to feature in it too much. It was brilliant, and the way I was portrayed in it was better than anything the most loyal PR team could have written. Even I was impressed by me after watching that show. It made quite an impact both near and far and did much, I believe, to elevate my standing to an even higher level.

In November, I began the UK *Pleasure Principle* thirtieth-anniversary tour in Brighton. Throughout it, the family falling-out kept showing itself in different ways. I remember singing the line 'If you are my father, then love lies abandoned and bleeding' from 'A Prayer for the Unborn' in Nottingham, and it made me upset. I'd received a nasty email from my dad just before the show started, so it was quite fresh. What made it worse was Gemma thought I wasn't doing enough. As much as I hated what was happening, and as much as I thought my mum and dad were absolutely in the wrong, I still loved them. I still owed them so much. I couldn't just wash my hands of them. I had no intention of denying them time with the children, although I was accused of that, and Gemma thought I should stop all access. I was in a bad place. My mum and dad were at me for, as they saw it, siding with Gemma against my mum. Gemma was at me because I hadn't cut them off completely, which she thought I should have done. It was a fucking nightmare, and it went on for the next two years.

Chapter Thirty-five

2010

My depression only got worse. I upped my dose of anti-depressants and eased into what Gemma called my Forrest Gump phase. My 'couldn't care less' attitude to life and career reached new heights. I was the most laid-back, easy-going person you could wish to meet. No moods, no ups and downs, not much of anything, really.

With my dad no longer managing me, I also had to start looking after myself financially. The problem was, I'd never been involved in my financial affairs. I had absolutely no idea about any of it. I was in my fifties and didn't even know how to write a cheque. I didn't know about bank statements, bank accounts, loans, any of it. But I obviously had to learn, so I took over the money side of things and made it my mission to under-stand as much as I could, as quickly as possible. With that done, I cut the last string to my mum and dad, as far as my career was concerned, anyway. It was a rather strange, lonely feeling at first, but I got used to it. I was nervous about making mistakes, about doing something stupid that could hurt us, but after a while I began to enjoy it.

In the USA, a car-battery company called Die Hard were using 'Cars' as the music for an ad they were making to promote their product. Not only that, they wanted to fly me and Gemma out to Los Angeles so I could appear in the ad. We were driven way out into the desert, where twenty-four cars, some black, some white, had been arranged to look like the keys of a keyboard. I would play the riff to the song on a real keyboard inside a glowing cube of light, and the car horns would sound the tune. At some point, all the cars would then be started up using just one battery. It was all very cool and good fun. My only fear was rattlesnakes. I overheard someone say they had people out on the perimeter of the site making sure the snakes didn't come in. I found it really hard to concentrate on the notes after that. While we were in Los Angeles, we stopped at a real-estate agent and made our first tentative enquiry about buying a house there.

In April, I played a one-off show at The Scala in Kings Cross, London. It was intended as a warm-up for an appearance at the Coachella Festival in the USA the following week. During the day, I received messages saying that Adam Ant wanted to guest on stage that night. I wasn't quite sure what to say about that. I'd met Adam a few times before, and I liked him. In fact, when he'd first made it back in the '80s, I'd noticed the press giving him a really hard time, so I'd invited him out to my studio in Shepperton to show my support. But back at The Scala, I was told Adam wouldn't be able to come to the soundcheck. I politely explained that if it was going to happen, we would need to rehearse whatever he wanted to do, and I would be uncomfortable just launching into something without a rehearsal. Then I got a message saying he'd been learning the backing vocals to 'Cars' all day, and he was ready to go. But 'Cars' doesn't have backing vocals, so it was all starting to sound a bit weird. I said no, and that I'd love to do something in the future, but I'd need a little more warning and some time to work out what we would do.

He turned up anyway. Gemma told me later that she met him in the hall, while I was playing, and had to put her arm out to try and stop him coming backstage because she wasn't sure if he might just run onto the stage during the gig. When she put her arm out, he ducked under it and ran backstage anyway. It was the funniest thing. I came off after the main set and Gemma grabbed me: 'Adam Ant is here, and he really wants to do "Cars".' What to do? I found him, and he was as lovely as ever, so I said, 'OK, it doesn't have backing vocals, but I'll introduce you. I'll do the first verse, you do the second.' Which should have been simple. So, I do my bit. I introduce him, the song starts, I sing the first verse and then ease to the side to watch Adam do his thing. I'm not sure if he'd ever listened to the song, but he launched into quite an effective rap, which had new lyrics – something like 'In the back of my car, I'll fuck you up the arse'. I actually loved it – it was a real 'what the fuck?' moment. I looked out at the crowd, and I would guess half of them felt the way I did, the other half definitely didn't. It's still on YouTube if you want to check it out.

I'd been invited to perform at Coachella that year, as 2010 was the thirtieth anniversary of *The Pleasure Principle* first being released in the States. A couple of dates had been added after the festival, so that it made sense financially, and it was clearly a major opportunity. It was meant to be a prelude to going back to the USA later in the year on the back of the festival profile. Coachella was widely seen by Ade and Steve, and me probably, if I could have given a shit, as a potentially pivotal career moment. It was very important. Then the volcano in Iceland erupted and a cloud of volcanic ash formed between Europe and the Americas. Flights were grounded, plans adjusted, scrapped, adjusted again and then abandoned altogether. First, we sat at home and watched the news. Then, feeling a little optimistic, we moved to a hotel not too far from the airport, just in case. It was even suggested that we might be able to fly down to Spain or Portugal and maybe sneak by the ash and get to the USA that way. But the cloud moved faster than the flow of ideas to circumvent it. Eventually, it became clear that our flight to California just wasn't going to happen. The crushing disappointment, the loss of such a major opportunity, seemed to upset everyone apart from me. When the decision was made that the trip was off, I stood up and said, 'OK then, let's go and get something to eat.' I wasn't the slightest bit bothered, which clearly wasn't the way I should have been feeling.

My strange reaction to the disappointment of Coachella spurred Gemma, Ade and Steve to try an intervention. A few weeks later, they took me to a quiet pub not too far from Weavers, and for an hour or more gave me a lecture on what I needed to do. They explained that I'd only written a handful of new things since finishing *Jagged*, and that was years ago. They said my career was slipping away, that I was throwing away all the work I'd put in to rebuild it. They really tore into me, and every single thing they said was true, probably. At the end of it, they said to me, 'What do you think about all that.' I hadn't really taken much notice. I said, 'Sorry, I've been thinking about kittens.' Which was true, but not what they needed to hear. I was taking my pills, and in my head everything was OK.

In May, we flew to Portugal for what I thought was a festival but turned out to be a Gary Numan show instead. Hardly anyone turned up, and it was horribly embarrassing. The few people who were there made a valiant effort, but I was glad when it was over. Shows like that prove that time slows down when you're counting the seconds. After that debacle, we travelled to Barcelona and played at a major festival there called Primavera. I was flattered to see Florence Welch dancing at the side of the stage during my set.

Back home, Gemma gave me a huge talking-to. She said my lack of drive, my lack of ambition, had made me ugly. I wasn't the man she'd married, and she was disappointed. She said the Gump that I'd become was unattractive and that she didn't fancy the new me. That did it. Hearing her say things like that shocked me to my core. It was that talk, those words, that made me start to come back, but I was frightened of what I would be when I returned. I lowered the dose of the antidepressants, stage by stage, and slowly began to feel my way back to normality, whatever that was going to be like. I clearly remember, many weeks later, feeling my mood shift for the first time and it filled me with panic. But I stuck with it, and over the next couple of months I weaned myself off the tablets completely. What I was left with was better than I'd hoped. I was definitely less moody but, far more importantly, every mood change was in sync with the life I was living. If something good happened, I felt good about it. If something bad happened, I'd feel a bit down. It all made sense. It felt very much as if, much like IVF had done for Gemma and getting pregnant, the antidepressants had taught my moods how to work in harmony with life itself. That one change has made a huge difference to my life. I came out of the depression in much better mental shape than I'd ever been in before. I would say to anyone, if you are having those sort of problems, you don't need to suffer. It is a very fixable thing, and you may find, like I did, that the treatment fixes more than the depression it was intended for. But the cure can be seductive. Like me, you may want to stay wrapped in it for longer than you should. If you allow that to happen, the cure can be as damaging as the illness.

At the end of the school year, we decided to take Raven out of Skippers Hill. Gemma had seen a clip on TV about Rudolf Steiner and his Waldorf schools. She'd been very taken by what she'd seen and, as luck would have it, the original Steiner school in the UK, Michael Hall, was only a thirty-minute drive from Weavers. Raven was finding the sheer volume of work at Skippers Hill difficult, and neither Gemma nor I were happy. A full school day followed by so much homework that it took her up to bedtime to finish was not the carefree life we wanted for her or any of our children. Not only that, it followed the typical hierarchical pyramid structure that put maths and languages at the top and the creative arts firmly at the bottom. They did a play from time to time, but there was very little attention given to personal expression, and that's what we wanted. I wanted my kids to be able to express themselves through a variety of artistic outlets, to develop whatever creative impulses they had. We really didn't care about how well they did calculus. More than anything, we wanted them to be children for as long as possible. No pressure, lots of play, lots of time to just be children. Skippers Hill was the opposite of that.

We arranged a meeting at Michael Hall, and my first brush with the Steiner philosophy was a bit disconcerting. As we walked towards the main building, we passed a woman sweeping leaves, who was singing a song about the beauty of sweeping leaves. She was dressed somewhat like you would expect some-one in a weird cult to dress. We asked her directions, and she was very lovely, but she soon went back to singing. It felt odd to me. The meeting was OK but, in all honesty, I wasn't getting it. We went back for a second meeting, and I grasped a little more of what they were saying, but I still wasn't convinced. One thing they said struck me, though. In Waldorf schools they don't start to teach children how to read until they're seven. They believe that a child's capacity to fully process the words doesn't develop until that age. Raven had been reading well since she was four or five, and when I got home I asked her to read to me. She read beautifully, but then I asked her to talk to me about what she'd read, and she couldn't. She could read the words but not fully grasp the meanings behind them. I began to understand what they were getting at about child development, what they call age-appropriate learning. They also talked about the way chil-dren play. The Steiner approach frowns upon letting children watch TV or play video games – media in general, actually. It was explained that children imitate such things with play rather than use their own imaginations, and it's a child's imagination they wanted to encourage. They asked us to stop our children watching TV for a couple of weeks and observe the way they played. It was remarkable. In just two weeks, the nature of their play completely changed. They stopped re-enacting scenes they'd watched on the television, they stopped pretending to be characters they'd seen, and they started to create their own games, their own characters. Their play went from imitation to creation, and they seemed happier. The third meeting did it. I sat and listened to teacher after teacher as they explained the thinking behind the Steiner approach and what they wanted for the children. It all made sense, it was gentle and lovely, and I was completely sold. Importantly, they wanted to give the creativity within each child as much freedom as possible to flourish, and they wanted them to stay children for as long as they could, to be happy. It was all we wanted.

In July, I played at the Sonisphere festival at Knebworth, which was a big one for me. I was second from top of the bill on the second stage, before Alice Cooper, I think. Sonisphere is very much a rock festival and, although I was confident that the last few albums would suit, I was worried that my reputation as a purely electronic artist might pit the crowd against me before we even walked on. It wasn't too bad for the first song or two, but they weren't exactly going wild. But with each song, the crowd filled up, and their enthusiasm built. Near the end, we played our heaviest version yet of 'Cars', and the crowd, now vast in size, were going for it. I stood there and thought to myself how strange it was that a classic electronic song was setting the crowd alight at a rock festival thirty-one years after I wrote it. It felt great. It was one of the best festival sets we'd ever played.

A month later, we flew to Hong Kong and then took a boat out to Macao for another festival. This one was in an arena deep inside The Venetian hotel. The place was absolutely vast, and, to be honest, I hated it. It was incredibly luxurious and yet seedy somehow. Glamorous and yet dark. It was impossible to sleep. Men were openly offering women for the hour, and it was all just cold business. It wasn't for me. The festival itself was absolutely bizarre. The venue was massive, but no one came. We watched Chris Cunningham play a blinding set to us and about six others. We played to about twenty people; Unkle played to about the same. I was convinced I wouldn't get the guarantee I'd been promised, but the promoter seemed very happy with the way it had gone. It made no sense, but I found out later that a huge storm had stopped all boats arriving in Macao. Buried deep inside the Venetian we had no idea there even was a storm.

We squeezed in a holiday, to Florida once again, with all the children. We did all the usual things, but there was one interesting moment which would make a difference to my career. My involvement with, and enthusiasm for, the outtakes album Ade had been valiantly persevering with had been minimal at best. I just didn't like it. One morning, I was having breakfast before we headed off to Disneyworld when I heard Gemma playing some music from another room. Whatever it was, it was great, and I rushed in and said, 'What's that? That's brilliant. That's exactly what I should be doing.' She looked at me as though I was mad and said, 'That's you. That's what Ade's been working on, the songs you've been saying you don't like.' I couldn't believe it. I have no idea whether it was coming off the antidepressants, feeling different about life, being in a 'happy' place or what. But I listened through to everything Ade had done, and this time I loved it. The music was exactly the same as the last time I'd heard it, but my state of mind had changed, and now I could truly hear it for the first time. There was still a lot of work to do, mostly by me, but I was keen to get back and get involved.

In September, Raven, Persia and Echo started at the Michael Hall Steiner school, and we were very happy. It definitely had a hint of cult hippy about the edges, and some parents were clearly more into it than others, but we loved it. They've been a part of Steiner education ever since, and we have absolutely no regrets.

In October, we had to say goodbye to the children and fly to Orlando, Florida, for the start of the North American *Pleasure Principle* anniversary tour. We now had a lovely young woman called Sammi who looked after them while we were away, so we knew they were safe and well cared for, but it was becoming harder and harder to say goodbye to them. We'd looked at many options for touring differently, but it is what it is. I had to go, and Gemma worked beside me – we had no choice.

Despite my newfound appreciation for my own musical history, it still didn't sit too well with me to be doing a nostalgia tour in North America. But the album was now seen as a classic, one that was at the very forefront of bringing electronic music to the mainstream. I hoped I'd be able to use that credibility to secure my standing and also build a greater awareness for the new music I'd been making. Not that I'd made any for a while.

The tour was good, people loved *The Pleasure Principle* and the shows sold extremely well. During the tour, with my ties to Mum and Dad severely strained, I made the decision that Gemma had been wanting for years: we would move to California. I was now fifty-two years old, and the passing of time was a big deal for me. Every day felt precious, and I didn't want to waste a moment. I started to talk in terms of 'how long I had left', as if I was at death's door, which was silly, but I definitely felt the need to live every day as fully as possible, and to be as happy as I could be for the rest of my life. I was tired of waking up in England and looking out the window at yet another rainy day. I was tired of organising gatherings or trips for the family only to have them cancelled because of the weather. I had a boat that was hardly used because of the weather. I had a house with acres of beautiful land that, for half the year or more, was just a muddy mess. I didn't feel that I was making the most of my days, and if I was ever going to achieve that, I needed to be in a better climate. I wanted to eat outdoors, see blue sky every day, actually do the things I'd planned. I wanted to be warm, not have to wear coats and scarves for half my life. I was just fed up of sitting in my lovely English house looking out at raindrops falling into puddles. It wasn't that I didn't appreciate what I had, I really did, but my fear of wasting the years that remained to me became almost all consuming. My worries about this would come to me in the strangest ways. I would look at my dog and think, I'll probably only have two more before I die. I actually counted how many hours I had until I was eighty. Although my depression was gone, some of the fears that might have caused it were definitely still with me.

So much nonsense has been written about why I made the decision to move to California. Some claimed it was because of the riots in 2012, even though we applied for our US green cards in 2010, so it clearly wasn't that. Others said it was to avoid paying British income tax, not fully understanding that the tax system in the USA, California especially, is no better. Different, yes, but ultimately no better. I also pay income tax to the State of California as well as the federal government. So, no, avoiding tax definitely wasn't the reason. I did mention that I was tired of the little gangs of loud-mouthed teenage thugs that seemed to be hanging about in every city, town and village, and I do stand by that, but it wasn't the reason I left. Even a local vicar and a councillor, neither of whom I'd ever met, got in on the act and wrote scathing pieces about my decision to emigrate in local newspapers, talking about gun violence in the USA. I read piece after piece, email after email, post after post, all getting it totally wrong. I moved to America because I wanted my daughters to have the best opportunity to live the life they wanted. I moved to make Gemma happy. I moved so that I could live each day more fully than I was able to in England. It had nothing to do with turning my back on England. I still spend several months a year there. I still pay British tax on my UK touring income, and nearly all of my closest friends still live there. I still love it, I still think of myself as English and I enjoy being there when I am. But I have not regretted the decision to move to America for a moment.

The first people I told were the crowd at the El Rey show in Los Angeles on the last night of the tour, 4 November 2010. Two days later, we were in Mexico for my first-ever show there. I was very excited and very nervous. I had no idea if anyone knew who I was or if they knew about the music, new or old. Hector Mijangos, the promoter, was a lovely man, and meeting him helped calm my nerves considerably, but not entirely. I needn't have worried. The place was heaving, the crowd knew the songs and it was a great night.

After the show, Hector took us to a cool roof-top bar for an aftershow party. I was given a blue fruit drink that I assumed was a Mexican version of Red Bull or something like that. It was delicious, and I drank about four over the next half-hour. What I didn't know was that it had vodka in it, which I couldn't taste at all. I was fifty-two years old and had never been drunk, not once. I'd had no interest in alcohol my entire life; in fact, I was quietly against it, as I rarely liked being around drunk people. Another reason I'd steered well clear of alcohol was my firm belief that I would be a nasty drunk. I was moody and short-tempered, lacking in patience at the best of times. If you add alcohol to that, it would make for a horrible mix. But I was drunk, and I wasn't like that at all. The more drunk I got, the more I turned into a giggling buffoon. It was quite a surprise.

Back in the UK, I started to work with Ade on the outtakes album. Apart from writing the songs in the first place, it was the first time I'd really got involved since we'd chosen the final track list way back when. But now I was all in. I wrote lyrics, worked on new parts, new sounds, recorded vocals. I wanted to call the album *Resurrection*, but it had been suggested I steer away from anything vaguely connected to religion, as I'd hammered that particular theme quite heavily. So, I called it *Dead Son Rising*, which means exactly the same thing when you think about it.

Chapter Thirty-six

2011

In February, we decided to make a video for what sounded like the most obvious single on the album, a song called 'The Fall'. Paul Green was again involved in the making of the video and he'd discovered an abandoned asylum near Lincoln. It was falling apart in places, so it gave us the perfect setting for the song. It was bitterly cold. We shot the video over three days in the dead of winter, in a building with few unbroken windows and zero heating. It was a tad creepy as well. But Paul put together a video that is still one of my favourites. Gemma was in it, playing the part of a dead woman in a bath, which she did magnificently. Ade Fenton was in it too, which made perfect sense, as I'd decided to credit everything on the album as a co-write, so it was as much his as it was mine. I was very aware that it was only Ade's dogged determination to keep working on it when I didn't want to know that had made the album happen at all. Not only that, the production work he'd done was above and beyond, and it seemed only fair that he should take a larger share of it. I was all for calling it a Numan–Fenton album, but he didn't want to. As the year progressed, we carried on tinkering with it and adding parts and some new songs that were never part of the original outtake idea. By the time it was finished, it had become so much more than an outtakes album.

A song called 'Crawl' that I'd co-written with the band South Central was released as part of their album *Society of the Spectacle* in April. I'd written the lyric and melody, and sang the vocal, over their music, which was absolutely immense. It was one of my favourite collaborations.

Around that same time I finally played the Back To The Phuture shows that had been postponed from the year before. The first one, at the Manchester Academy, had Alan Wilder's Recoil project as the support, plus the band Motor. It was such an honour to play a show with Alan. I had long thought that his work with Depeche Mode had been phenomenal. In fact, hearing their *Songs of Faith and Devotion* album had been a pivotal moment for me when I was getting *Sacrifice* under way in 1994. The sound of that album, the dark atmosphere that poured out of it, was all very much to do with Alan Wilder and so, in many respects, he had unknowingly been a huge inspiration for how I'd reinvented myself. Not only that, I thought his work with Recoil post-Depeche Mode was exceptional, so his influence on me was ongoing.

The second Back To The Phuture show was at The Troxy in London. Again, I had the honour of playing with John Foxx at that show with Motor in the second support slot but Daniel Miller also played a DJ set. To play a show with John Foxx meant a lot to me. John had been such a huge influence on me when I first moved into electronic music. I'd been to see him numerous times as the original frontman for Ultravox before my own success came along. To me, he was a true visionary, a genuine pioneer. Ultravox had already made three electronic albums while I was still thinking about my first. That's groundbreaking. He was also extremely smart with an analytical view on the evolution of music that I found fascinating.

I'd been asked to tour Australia again, a short five-show run with one more added in Auckland, New Zealand. I hadn't been back to New Zealand since my unfortunate trip in 1980, so I was hoping things would be different this time. I'd thoroughly enjoyed my last visit to Australia, and I was keen to try and build a following there. It's hard, though. To fly a band and crew there is very expensive, and if you're not able to command high guarantees, the money you earn barely covers costs. The other problem was they insisted it be a *Pleasure Principle* anniversary tour, and I really didn't want to do another one. I'd done enough retro as far as I was concerned, at least for a while, but they insisted, so I went with it. However, like the UK and North American anniversary tours, I filled the end of the set, once *The Pleasure Principle* songs were over, with the heaviest of the new material. My thinking was that if people wanted to come and listen to the old stuff, it was possible they didn't even know about the new material, so I'd give them a big jolt of it before they left. In Australia and New Zealand, I added a brand-new song to the heavy section of the set. I'd started writing new songs for the album I was planning after *Dead Son Rising*, called *Splinter*. The new song was called 'Everything Comes Down to This', and I'd written it when my relationship with Gemma had been at its worst. The tour went well, the Australian dates were good, people came out to see us and we were well looked after. The support band for the tour, an Australian electronic band called Severed Heads, came out of retirement just to play on it. The final show in New Zealand was particularly exciting, and it was good to finally play there again after so many years. It was a much happier experience than it had been in 1980. Coincidentally, I released a DVD called *Decoder* that same month that had been filmed during my previous Australian tour.

I finished the vocals for *Dead Son Rising* in June, and Ade and Nathan Boddy mixed it. Sadly, I was no longer able to mix my own albums. My hearing had deteriorated to such a degree that I could no longer trust what my ears were telling me. It mattered less when I was writing the songs and recording the demos, but when it came to mixing, the days of me doing that alone were over. I have no idea how long I'd been in denial about my hearing, but it was years for sure, so I stood down on *Dead Son Rising*, and I think the album was all the better for it.

I'd written the lyrics and recorded a vocal for a song called 'My Machines' that had been written by the band Battles. They'd approached me about it earlier in the year and I'd made a bit of a mess of my first attempt. When the file arrived with their backing track for the song I made a mistake when I downloaded it and the song played at half speed. Only I didn't know that. It was the first time I'd heard the song and I just assumed that was how it went. It was slow and heavy but I really liked it. So, that's what I wrote the first vocal melody and lyric to. I sent it off to them, quite pleased with what I'd done, only to get back the most painfully polite message that was clearly trying to say it wasn't quite what they were looking for. It also mentioned it being much slower than the version they'd sent, and I couldn't figure out what they meant by that. I'd worked on the exact version they'd sent me, or so I thought. I think it was Ade that called me and pointed out my error. I downloaded it again, correctly, and found it was an entirely different animal and nothing I'd done on my original attempt worked. So I wrote a new lyric, and a new melody based very much on a guide they sent me instead of my own, and sheepishly sent that to them. Luckily they liked that one and it came out on their *Gloss Drops* album the same month Ade was mixing *Dead Son Rising*. They also released it as a single, along with a great video that they'd flown me to Los Angeles to film. I kept the lyric and vocal I'd done for the first version, though. I wrote a new song called 'A Shadow Falls on Me' for the new album I was working on, *Splinter*, and used it on that instead.

In July, I played three festivals back to back over a weekend, one in York, one in Manchester and one in London. Festivals were still hard to come by but, year by year, I was building up a reasonable amount of festival experience. They felt increasingly important to me, and it continued to frustrate me that I didn't get too many. In the absence of radio play, festivals were the next best way of reaching out and being seen by large numbers of people. If you could play enough of them, it could make a difference, but I still wasn't playing enough.

Dead Son Rising was finally released in September, in multiple formats. In some respects I never got away from the original idea of it being a stopgap outtakes album, so I made no attempt to have it released and distributed properly. It would, in essence, be sold exclusively to those fans who followed me on social media, on my website and those who used the Gary Numan online store. It wasn't really available in many places outside of the store. Looking back, I can only wonder at how well it might have done if I'd released it properly.

A number of the ideas behind the songs on *Dead Son Rising* were taken from yet another book I was writing but wouldn't get to finish. The song 'Dead Sun Rising', for example, was about the last living human beings, old and mystical, at a time near the end of the world. Their only remaining purpose was to protect a batch of human embryos from the ravages of the waking world, and the creeping dangers of the sleeping world, and in so doing keep them pure until they were born. Only then could the old die peacefully and yet keep humanity alive. The album got some great reviews. *The Quietus* said, '*Exile* is great, as is *Pure*, but it's on 2011's *Dead Son Rising* that Numan really rewired the genre's piston-powered brutality and made it his own.' And *Classic Rock* wrote, 'Now that he's been raised to the point of electronic sainthood, the releases are coming thick and fast. Rather than resting on his laurels, Numan is out there fashioning new ones.'

Chapter Thirty-seven

2012

After a long period of building a credible portfolio, thanks largely to Steve Malins, our immigration application had been presented to the US authorities. It was vitally important that, should we be approved, we be approved as a family. I didn't want the worry of the children getting to eighteen years of age, then having to apply in their own right and possibly being refused and sent back to England. We went as a family, all legal and approved from day one, or we didn't go at all. As I had no family in the USA, and no employer, the types of petition open to me were limited. In fact, I was advised that the only one that really made sense was to apply as a 'Person of Extraordinary Abilities in the Arts or Sciences', an EB-1A green-card application, which to me sounded rather like several 'extraordinary' bridges too far. But, thanks to Steve's meticulous work with our immigration lawyers, I seemed to satisfy the many demanding requirements of the petition. We were told that the first hurdle was getting the US authorities to agree that such a petition was the correct one for me. If they did accept it, then that would technically mean that they agreed with the proof contained within it regarding my meeting the criteria for immigration. So, in effect, that first hurdle was also the biggest. If they approved it, we should be OK for all subsequent approvals in the process.

Nothing was guaranteed. It was a long, long nerve-racking wait. I think months went by, but we finally heard from our lawyers, and our petition had been accepted as the correct type. So, one down – a big one, to be fair – but several still to go.

Getting that initial approval made it all seem very real, so, feeling positive and optimistic, we started to look more seriously into buying a house in California. Before we could choose a house, we had to find a school. I looked up all the Steiner schools and found one that was just 100 yards from the beach. I thought it was perfect, and we started to look online for houses in the area. Then we noticed that the school didn't teach beyond eighth grade, so we'd need to move the kids for each of their last four years. Didn't fancy that. So, we looked again and found another school in the San Fernando valley that could take them from kindergarten all the way through to twelfth grade. It would be the only school they'd need, and it looked perfect. We got in touch, explained our plans and arranged to visit the school on one of our house-hunting visits.

I did all my house research online at home. I set up my filters on various house-hunting sites for what we could afford and all the other requirements we thought we needed. I looked through all the results and picked out what I thought was suitable, printed them out and gave that pile to Gemma, who took out all the ones she didn't like. Those that were left became the ones that we would go and look at. Once a month, we would fly to Los Angeles for a long weekend looking at houses. It was fantastic. We got to learn about the different neighbourhoods, how long it would take to drive to and from the school, what the traffic was like at different times of day, all really useful stuff to know before committing to any particular house. After a number of trips, we began to zero in on one particular house. We eventually visited it three times, even went with a builder the third time, so it was almost certainly going to be the one. The only problem was it was a bit too far out, and the school run would take at least a couple of hours every day.

In March, I received some terrible news. My old drummer, Ced Sharpley, had died of a heart attack. I couldn't quite believe it. It had been some time since I'd seen Ced, but he still seemed such an unlikely man to have died so young. He was only fifty-nine. I wrote on my Facebook page at the time, 'Ced was not only a truly great drummer, he was also a gentle, fascinating and funny man to be around and he will be greatly missed.' It took me a while to grasp that he was gone, and I deeply regretted that I hadn't done a better job of staying in touch.

I released another DVD in May called *Machine Music*, a collection of twenty-one of my promo videos plus a range of rare material, including 'Cars' on *Saturday Night Live* and the Kenny Everett 'I Die: You Die' clip. It seemed to resonate with the fans, and all three thousand copies sold out quickly. I played a twelve-date tour to support it and included a Ced Sharpley tribute in the set each night when I played the Dramatis song 'Love Needs No Disguise'. The tour was a little different in that fans had been invited to submit films they'd made for certain songs, and we used them as projections at the back of the stage during the set. Some of them were amazing and added a new dimension to the show that I hadn't really expected. I began to see projection as an important part of the show in the future. I also had a band called Officers support me on the *Machine Music* tour, who I absolutely loved. The radio DJ Eddie Temple-Morris had first played me their music, and it made a big impression on me. I knew I wanted them to do the tour.

Officers wrote a song called 'Petals' that they asked me to sing on. I thought it was a very strong track. I really liked them as people, loved their music, they were great to tour with – just a great experience all round. It makes me sad when bands with so much talent struggle to get heard and recognised. Not long after the *Machine Music* tour was over, they made a cool video for 'Petals' that I appeared in.

After we played our set at the Hop Farm Music Festival in June, I took the opportunity to go out into the crowd and watch Bob Dylan. It's not every day you get to see a genuine legend doing their thing, and I was keen to witness some Dylan magic. I didn't like it at all. In fact, I barely lasted one song before I headed back to the backstage area. On my way, I was approached by a man who said he'd enjoyed my set, so I stopped for a brief chat. I told him I was working on a new album and that I was emigrating to America. He said his name was Steve Read, that he was a film-maker and that he'd like to make a documentary – one that followed our move to the States, my progress on the new album and my rather unique relationship with Gemma. I was polite and said something friendly and reasonably non-committal but, to be perfectly honest, I thought it was all talk, and I expected nothing to come of it. But I was wrong. A few days later, he got in touch with Ade and Steve, and a serious plan started to come together for a documentary that would come to be called *An Android in La La Land*.

Our house searching in the USA had pretty much narrowed down to the one likely candidate, in a place called Santa Clarita, but I was still looking. We'd put our own house on the market and had unbelievably found ourselves the beneficiaries of a bidding war. Two people really took a shine to the house, and instead of trying to beat me down on the price, started to outbid one another. When it looked as if it was all over, our estate agent rang the highest bidder and said to him, 'Is that the highest you can go?' He must have taken that as a warning that a higher offer had been placed, which it hadn't, and he promptly added another £50,000 to his previous offer. We sold it for way more than we'd been asking.

Gemma decided she wanted to get in on this online-house-hunting thing, so I gave her the parameters for the search, in particular our maximum price, and she ignored them completely. I said that it was pointless doing that. You were bound to see lovely houses, but we couldn't afford them, and it would only make the ones we were looking at, and had been happy with, seem inferior. But she did it anyway, and, sure enough, a beautiful house popped up straight away. It looked like a castle. It was huge, was wildly beyond our budget, and therefore wildly out of reach, and, just as I'd said it would, made everything we'd looked at suddenly seem like a poor option. I was not happy. It was only a five-minute drive from the school.

A few weeks later, we flew out to Los Angeles once again, met up with our two real-estate experts and viewed more houses. Those we could afford. On the second day, Gemma asked if we could just drive past the castle house. I was very reluctant, for all the same reasons: 'It will look amazing, and it will make all the other things we plan to look at seem rubbish.' But she insisted, so we did. We pulled up outside, and it was indeed quite spectacular. It was about the closest I'd ever seen to what I would consider my dream house, and I felt a little bit sick inside. Gemma started to get out, but I said no, there was no point. We couldn't afford it, and it was actually upsetting me looking at something so amazing that I knew I couldn't have. Then I noticed our two real-estate agents getting out of the car opposite, and it suddenly sank in that Gemma had arranged a viewing behind my back. The house seller's estate agent drove up and opened the tall metal gates to let us in. I whispered to Gemma, 'Whatever you do, be calm. All we can do is find as many things wrong with it as possible and put in an insultingly low offer, I wasn't even really thinking about buying it. I was only thinking how we could walk away with some dignity and not look like the chancers Gemma was clearly showing us to be. The man opened the door and, with my warning still fresh in her ear, Gemma screamed and ran off into the depths of the house. For the next ten minutes at least I didn't see her. All I could hear was her screaming as she went from one room to another, from one floor to the next. Any possible chance of being cool and finding fault with it was utterly destroyed, all bargaining power gone. It was an amazing house. Not only that, it came fully furnished, and most of the furniture was pretty special too. But we couldn't afford it, not even close. We put in our insultingly low offer, and, as expected, it was rejected. We then flew back to England and got a phone call saying that the owners had been made a better offer, which they'd accepted. I thought it was all over, but Gemma hadn't given up.

Back in England, we played at Guilfest, and Steve Read started to make his documentary. He came out to Weavers and interviewed me, Gemma and the children, who were all very cute. I liked his three-pronged idea. The first thread was to be the story of how Gemma and I got together, how we'd made a family and how we seemed to be immune from the showbiz world that often ruined so many relationships. The second one would follow our journey to a new life in America. The third would follow my progress on *Splinter*, and whether it would finally see me back in the charts. I thought it could make an interesting film. It promised to be a deep, probing look at what made me tick.

Although things with my mum and dad were as bad as ever, we did still keep in touch a little, mostly to arrange when they could see the children. During the year, they told me that Mum had developed a new cancer, in the oesophagus. Mum seemed typically unconcerned, but she always did, so that didn't mean it wasn't serious. After her breast cancer was diagnosed, she'd also developed different types of skin cancer. Her upper-chest area often looked as though she'd been in a fire after she'd been treated. She frequently had to go to hospital to have things cut out of her skin. She just took everything in her stride, and her attitude made me feel as though she was invincible. Hearing about the new throat cancer didn't fill me with horror, because it didn't seem to worry her. But it would turn out to be a hard thing to beat.

After Guilfest, we flew back to America for one last look at houses. My focus had narrowed down to the Santa Clarita house, which was quite lovely and we could afford, and the castle house, which was even more lovely but we couldn't afford. However, the agent let us know that the other offer on the castle house had fallen through, and did we want to make another? We did, but it was the same low offer we'd made before, because that really was the best we could do. It was, not surprisingly, rejected again. It was horrible, because I absolutely loved the house. I felt like a donkey with a carrot dangled just far enough in front to be enticing but always slightly out of reach. As we left for the airport to fly home, we received a message saying another offer had been put in and accepted – the full asking price. That was surely it, dream over. To add to our misery, we still hadn't been granted an interview at the American Embassy, so, despite all our school and house-buying efforts, we still didn't know for sure we would even be allowed to emigrate. It was all incredibly stressful.

Around the middle of July, our patient real-estate agents called to say that, as far as they knew, the house had sold, and we needed to think about finalising the other house in Santa Clarita. As much as I'd always thought we wouldn't get the castle house, there was always that small nugget of hope that it might happen. Gemma had always thought it would be hers, so she was devastated. We decided to go out for the day and, stupidly perhaps, took the children to Rochester Castle in Kent. It rubbed a big bag of salt into the wound, and by the end of the day Gemma and I had a huge row which lasted all the way home. I stormed in, went straight up to bed and left her to watch whatever terrible TV programme she fancied. I picked up my iPad and immediately saw a message about the castle house. I knew what it would say: 'Sold'. I was in too bad a mood to deal with that, so I ignored it. But I was still so angry I couldn't sleep, so eventually looked, and, to my surprise, it didn't say 'sold', it said 'for sale'. I went down to Gemma, all thoughts of our argument gone, and showed her the message. I said it had to be a mistake. We had been told only that morning that it had sold, but I gave them a call to check. Twenty minutes later, we got a call back saying the people buying it had lied about having the money, and, once again, it had all fallen through. They asked if we wanted to make another offer, so we did, only it was even lower than before, but this time they accepted.

It was unbelievable, although we still didn't have our green cards. I knew we had to do something to convince them we were serious and not messing them about like the previous two buyers. So, I offered them $50,000 as a sign of intent. If we didn't buy the house, they could keep the $50,000 and put it back on the market. I had no idea when our embassy interview would be, so I took a gamble and asked if they would hold the house for three months. They gave me two. If we didn't get our interview, and approval, within the next nine weeks, we'd lose the house and the $50,000.

The best thing to happen throughout all of this was the rift with my mum and dad ended. During one of their usually prickly visits to pick up the children, Gemma, without letting me know she intended to say anything, went up to my dad and simply said, 'Do you want to start again?' And that was it. All over. Two years of unpleasantness just went away.

I released yet another DVD and live album called *Big Noise Transmission Live* in August that I'd recorded at a Manchester Ritz show in 2011. It was a good one, beautifully filmed by Paul Green yet again, but it occurred to me I was probably putting out too many live albums and DVDs. Soon after, we got our interview appointment at the US Embassy in London, on 6 September, when we would find out if the answer to our dream of emigrating to the United States would be a yes or a no, and if the castle house would be ours. Unfortunately, I had a show in Reading the night before, and we were appearing at Bestival, on the Isle of Wight, on the 6th.

We played the show in Reading, got in a car that took us into London and were in bed in a hotel by about 2 a.m. Our interview was early, 7 a.m. I think, so Sleepy and Dopey found themselves queuing outside the US Embassy at about 6.30 a.m. The build-up to the interview had gone on for a long time, and the fear of rejection was enormous. I was expecting an FBI-type grilling, about my two arrests especially, but it was all a massive anticlimax. At the end of it, we weren't even sure what had happened, so Gemma had to ask, 'Are we in, then?' – we were. We ran from the embassy, because the next problem was getting to the Isle of Wight. We made it just in time to get changed, do make-up and then play the gig. It was quite a day. Unfortunately, none of it was filmed for the documentary, apart from the show itself. The real drama of the day, of our lives in a way, was missed. We had, however, managed to buy the house with just one week of our two-month holding period to go. My $50,000 bribe was safe.

Packing was a nightmare. You don't realise how much rubbish you accumulate throughout your life until you have to pack it. I actually found an old MiniMoog synth completely buried under vines that had grown into the attic space of the garage. I thought it had been stolen years before. We also had one giant problem in particular: Wilburforce, our dog. Wilbur was a 200lb English Mastiff, and getting him to the USA required much paperwork and a special crate. He would also have to fly on a separate flight, two days after us, although our two cats would be alongside him. The vet company that dealt with transporting animals came and took him two days before we were due to leave, and they set to building him a pen suitable for flying. We then got a call saying he'd eaten his way out of that one and they were having to build a heavier-duty version. We were very concerned about how he was going to handle the long flight.

Eventually, the packing was done and loaded into two forty-feet containers. Our worldly goods were to travel to California by ship, via the Panama Canal, and would arrive a week or two after we did. We gave a huge amount of stuff away and still ended up taking too much. I then discovered there was yet another chance we would be refused entry into America. When we arrived, we had to be seen by immigration officials at the airport, and they could say no. It seemed ridiculous. You need to set up your new life in advance – a house, school, bank accounts, a whole world of things – and yet having done all of that, and having sold everything you have in England, you could still be turned away after arriving in the country with your bags and family. It really is very stressful.

So, we sat in LAX for another hour or two and answered the same questions yet again. No, I wasn't part of a terrorist organisation. No, I had never committed genocide. No, I wasn't a drug dealer, nor was I connected to a crime syndicate, and so on. By the time it's all over, you're more relieved than jubilant. We stayed at a hotel that night and drove out to take possession of the house the next morning.

Before we left, I'd asked a financial company in London to make sure my business affairs were properly transferred from the UK to the USA. I had two UK companies, Machine Music Ltd and Numan Music Ltd, and I needed them to be closed down and US equivalents created. I was told it would cost

£8,000 and would be done by the time I arrived in America. It didn't, and it wasn't. About a year after we arrived, the work was finally done, and I had a bill for over £55,000. When I reminded them about their £8,000 quote, they said I'd misunderstood – the quote was for the 'advice' only; the actual work was on top. They also strongly advised me to use business-management services in the USA rather than an accountant. Business managers do your accounts, but, in theory, they do far more as well: pay bills, set up services, generally take care of the financial running of your day-to-day business. I went for it, because I didn't know any better. Emigrating was challenging enough, especially as I did it halfway through making a new album, so I readily accepted expert advice like that. It was a big mistake, though. Over the next few years, I would move through three different business-manager companies before realising that, for me at least, it was a waste of time and money. My first business manager called me up one day, about six months after we'd moved, and told me I was completely broke. This was the man supposedly 'managing' my affairs.

Back in England, at the end of 2012, I released *Dead Moon Falling*, an eleven-track album of remixes of *Dead Son Rising* songs. Some of the mixes were brilliant. It also included another song I'd written with Andy Gray called 'For You', as well as the Officers track 'Petals'. I toured that album as well, with another seven shows around the UK. The feeling at the time was that it was possibly one tour too many, as some shows didn't sell as well as we'd hoped. I was OK with it. I played two new songs destined for the forthcoming *Splinter* album, called 'I Am Dust' and 'Unforgiven', and I wanted to see how they would work in a live setting. I was already planning to undertake a much bigger, more concentrated touring effort when *Splinter* was released.

When I arrived in America, I was about halfway through writing *Splinter*. I wanted it out in late summer 2013, so, to meet that deadline, everything needed to be completed by the end of May, including mixing, mastering and artwork. That meant all the songs recorded by the end of April at the latest. However, our two containers didn't arrive from the UK until late October, so I couldn't do anything for a while. My studio was packed into lots of boxes, and even when it was delivered, it stayed in those boxes for a while as we unpacked the essentials. The property also had a small guest house in the garden, or backyard as they say here. Half of it was set up as a kitchen/lounge/bathroom, which would become my office. The other half was a bedroom, now empty, so our mountain of boxes were dumped there. That was the room I intended to be my studio, whenever I managed to find it under box mountain. But an offer came in that hurried me along a little. I was asked to write some music for the end titles of a movie in development called *Plush*. One of the many reasons I'd moved to the USA was to get involved in making music for films, so, coming almost as soon as I'd arrived, it was great news. I ended up moving boxes around for a few days, found all my equipment and wired everything up in the most basic way. There were boxes everywhere and packing materials all over the floor. I had the sound desk balanced on a tiny table, and I even sat on a box to operate the desk. It was like working in a cluttered, abandoned storeroom. The most unlikely, ugly-looking studio you'd ever see, but it worked. I wrote the song for *Plush* and then just carried on finishing off *Splinter*. Each day, I'd spend a bit of time trying to clear out the empty boxes and assorted litter before working on my music. But I finished the album in time.

When it was complete, it was clear that the majority of the songs were connected to my depression. There were songs about how it had affected my relationship with Gemma, 'Everything Comes Down To This' and 'Lost', and songs that tried to put into words how it felt, at its darkest point, to be truly depressed, such as 'Here in the Black' and more. I decided to add an additional element to the title. The album would be called *Splinter – Songs from a Broken Mind*.

Before that, we simply got used to life in America. We made modest improvements to the house, one of which meant removing the tennis court that filled most of the back garden so the kids had somewhere to play. The children quickly settled into life at their new school, Highland Hall. For a while, they were the star attraction as the only British children there. Gemma and I, every single morning, would drive to the school and joke, 'Not another clear, blue, sunny sky,' and pretend we missed the rain. We'd send photos of palm trees against the cloudless blue to Ade Fenton. We loved it. I bought a car, got my California driving licence (100 per cent score, not bragging), got our social-security numbers and just revelled in the newness of everything. You know that feeling when you've had the best holiday ever but today is the day you have to go back to the drudgery of your everyday life? Imagine being told on that very day that you've won a competition and you can stay in that paradise for a bit longer. That's how it felt every day, like a never-ending holiday, despite all the work I was doing. We even had a swimming pool that was always warm.

Chapter Thirty-eight

2013

Mum and Dad came to visit in early 2013, and we did everything we could to show them what life was like. I think I was trying to justify to them why I'd moved and taken us all so far away. We drove out to the mountains and down to the ocean. We took them to Disneyland and on star tours around all the celebrity homes in Beverly Hills. Shopping, obviously – we just crammed it all in. My mum took me to one side before they left and said, 'I can see why you left. What an incredible place for the children to grow up in,' and that meant a lot to me. I could see she was struggling. She hardly ate, and when she did, she found it almost impossible to swallow. Her doctors had inserted a radioactive isotope pellet into the centre of her tumour, the idea being it would kill it from the inside out and do as little damage as possible to good tissue.

When they got back to England, her troubles got worse. She lost almost half her weight and came close to dying. It seemed the radiation had killed the tumour but had kept on going, causing terrible damage in her throat, which had then become obstructed, making it impossible for her to eat. Even liquids would make her sick. She suffered greatly for month after month, but she beat it eventually. She said dealing with the damage from the cure was worse than having the tumour.

When I'd finished *Splinter*, we rented an RV and took a three-week break to explore as much of California as we could. Steve Read met up with us at times and filmed parts of it for the *La La* documentary. I thought it would be a trip of a lifetime, but it was mostly horrendous, mainly due to the children. They were horrible on that trip. They moaned about everything, argued and fought with each other constantly, wouldn't help, just awful. At one point, I stopped the RV, got out and walked to the back of it and cried. After all the stress of the move, and Mum's cancer, and getting the album finished, I just wanted a nice, peaceful few weeks with the people I loved most. I'd only been there a minute when Gemma walked round from the other side and joined me, in a similar state. I think that was the worst they ever were, and thankfully they've not been remotely like that ever since.

While we were camping at Lake Tahoe, Gemma got bitten on her toe. It didn't seem a big deal, but about a week after we got back from the RV trip, she came down with meningitis again. They suspected it was connected to the insect bite. The American health-care system is vastly different to the British, and luckily we'd sorted out our health insurance only two weeks before. Luckily, because the bill for Gemma's week in hospital was more than $115,000. Without that insurance, we'd have had to pay the lot. You even have to think twice about calling an ambulance, because if you do, and your insurance company decides you didn't really need to, you have to pay for it. One ambulance ride to the hospital can be thousands of dollars. It took us a long time to really grasp just how different the American health-care system is.

Gemma's week in the hospital was frightening. Surviving

meningitis once was lucky enough, being able to survive it twice seemed far from certain, and she was very ill. It was horrible, and not knowing the system made it worse. Different doctors would come and go, and neither Gemma nor I had any idea who was in charge. She was discharged but seemed far from well. I suspect, though, that her release had as much to do with her as it did the hospital. Nine Inch Nails were playing at Lollapalooza in Chicago that night, so she had to be there. We went pretty much straight from the hospital to the airport. Gemma took pills with her called Topamax, something they'd given her to help with the meningitis. In the back of the cab driving into the festival, her head fell back onto the seat, and her eyes rolled into her head. It was like something from *The Exorcist*. I thought for a minute she was fucking dying. When we arrived, she seemed to veer from vaguely OK to a mess from one minute to the next. She fell over and couldn't get up, couldn't finish a sentence, couldn't walk in a straight line – it was horrendous.

Back in Los Angeles, things improved a little but not much. The doctor who'd prescribed the Topamax wouldn't return her calls, so she went online and investigated the drug herself. She seemed to be having every side effect possible, so she cautiously came off it and mostly got better. During her stay in the hospital, MRI scans had shown brain lesions that indicated the possibility of multiple sclerosis. But it was decided they were due to her regular migraines, and, in addition, she learned that the side effects of Topamax mimic the symptoms of MS. So, for now, the MS scare was put to rest.

Moving to America had thrown up another concern for me. Trying to rebuild my career in the USA, the way I was slowly doing in Britain, was hugely important to me. I had hoped to find US management that would look after me in the States, and I'd leave the rest of the world to Steve and Ade. It would require a degree of give and take from all sides, of course. But we'd spoken about it at length and agreed that having US representation was necessary, as neither Ade or Steve had any meaningful experience there. Unfortunately, it didn't quite work out. It took a while, but I eventually found a good US management team. The problem was the friction that then flared up between that US team and Ade and Steve in the UK.

I flew to London for the *Splinter* album-sleeve photo shoot. The shoot was OK, but it turned a bit strange after that when I was told I was only allowed to choose twelve photos from the hundreds taken. Steve and Ade had done a great deal with the photographers that made the shoot cheaper than it would have usually been, but then the photo limit came in, unexpectedly, and it all became a bit testy. The photographers also insisted on doing their own photo manipulations and limited what we were allowed to do with prints, so it got very messy, frustrating and time-consuming. I learned some valuable lessons from that unfortunate experience.

The problems between the two management teams became too much for me. It was a very unhappy, stressful time for almost everyone involved, I think. An error by Townsend Music, who ran my online store, had accidentally allowed the album to leak, and the blame went backwards and forwards. I eventually got tired of it all – none of it seemed to be helping me or my career. There was a great deal that went on in the build-up to my decision to make some drastic changes. I heard snippets but it was impossible to really know what was going on – who was right, who was wrong. All I knew was it wasn't helping, and it had to stop. First, I let Steve Malins go, which Gemma was furious about, and she was probably right. Gemma felt strongly that Steve had been levered out by the gossip and that I shouldn't have listened. But Ade Fenton had become my closest friend, and I'd lost touch a little with Steve. Also, Ade produced my albums and played in the band. He had become very embedded in everything I did.

I played a short series of shows on the US West Coast and Canada in late August and early September, mostly around an appearance at the Bumbershoot festival in Seattle. I added four songs from *Splinter* to the set most nights, building up my knowledge of what worked and what didn't before the tour proper started in October.

I filmed a video for 'I Am Dust', directed by Chris Corner from IAMX. I had long been a fan of IAMX, and I knew Chris to be a great photographer and film-maker. So many of the things he'd done for IAMX had been exceptional. Not only that, he was a great songwriter and a truly outstanding singer, so he had experience on both sides of the camera. We'd become friends over the years, and, not long before, he'd moved to Los Angeles from Germany, where he'd been based for some time. The video was brilliant, probably the best video I'd ever made at that point, and it added a powerful tool to our promotional arsenal.

I had a huge surprise one day. I was watching a *CNN* news article on the TV about a mistake during a church service. Apparently one of the hymns to be sung during the service was called 'Hail Mary' and lyric sheets had been placed in the church for the congregation to sing. Unfortunately they'd printed out the wrong lyrics, using those from the Tupac song of the same name by mistake, which were very, very different. For example, it had the line 'Revenge is like the sweetest joy next to getting pussy' and on it went. This was such a big deal it had made the news. I didn't care too much one way or the other but they showed a tiny snippet of the promo video for the Tupac song and, just for a second, it looked like the inside of my house. I called Gemma and we searched for the video and, to our huge surprise, found that it was our house. At some point, long before we bought it, they'd made a Tupac video inside the house. I had no idea.

Splinter was to be released in September but slipped a little, eventually coming out on 14 October. It was the first release credited to Machine Music USA Inc., the name of my US company that would now handle all future releases. To launch the album, we played a couple of shows at the Hollywood Forever Cemetery – in the Masonic Lodge to be exact. I played nine songs from the album each night, plus a variety of recent and older songs. For the first time in years, Richie Beasley wasn't on drums. Something had come up that he couldn't get out of, so we were joined by Frank Zummo, who did an amazing job. A week later, we set off on the first dedicated *Splinter* tour, starting in Atlanta, Georgia, where Robin Finck guested on guitar for 'Metal'. It wasn't too long – just six shows, including two supporting Nine Inch Nails on their arena tour, and the Mountain Oasis festival in Asheville, but it was only the start of a much bigger campaign.

The second of the two Nine Inch Nails support shows was sadly, and unexpectedly, far more stressful than I'd anticipated. Not long after we arrived at the huge venue my guitar player Steve Harris got a message that his dad had been taken seriously ill and was fighting for life. Steve had to leave the tour immediately to try and get back to the UK in time. It was horrible for Steve and I had no doubts about his need to leave the tour there and then. In the few hours that were left to the rest of us we came up with the only plan that could possibly work to save the show that night. One of my US management team at the time was a man called Marc Sallis, who was also a great bass player. As luck would have it Marc was with us that night and so he stepped in to play bass, and Tim Muddiman moved over onto guitar. Steve showed him what he could before he left and so, with that horribly rushed and hopelessly unprepared line up, we played the show. It was nowhere near the disaster that it could have been.

The album entered the UK album chart at number 20, which just meant the world to me – but only for a moment. It was the first time I'd had a studio album in the Top 20 for thirty years. The reviews were exceptional, the fans loved it and I felt I'd taken another important step back up the ladder. But it was only a step. Gemma read me a glowing review of the album as we were driving somewhere, and all I could think about was what comes next. I barely smiled at the review, which made her angry. She still couldn't understand why I wasn't able to just enjoy the moment. Neither could I, to be honest. I've thought about this a lot, why I'm not able to savour good things as much as I should, and I think it's because I'm looking further ahead. It's like an obstacle course, with lots of things to overcome before I get to where I want to be. The success of *Splinter* was a big deal, but there were plenty more obstacles still to come, and my thoughts turned to those about two minutes after I heard the chart position.

The tour picked up again in the UK when we played eleven shows, including one in Dublin, Ireland. I also finally lifted myself up a level when we played The Roundhouse in London instead of the Empire. It was a small but significant step for me. The vibe around the album and the tour was really quite exceptional. Some reviews said it was the best thing I'd ever done – a lot of fans said the same. It was the first album I'd made since 1979 whereby I genuinely felt I'd finally moved out from under the shadow of the early success. That feeling helped in many ways. Although I was no longer negative about my older songs, I'd still felt the need to prove myself as an ongoing, viable artist. *Splinter* finally did that for me. It gave me a sense of real pride in what I'd achieved. But, like I said, it was still just a step.

After the tour, I took another step, this time to do with my interest in writing music for film. Ade and I were asked to write the music for a full-length animated movie called *From Inside*, a dark and unusual story about a mysterious girl traveling on a train through an apocalyptic world. The movie had already been released with a score, a good one, but they wanted to re-release it with new music. It was a perfect opportunity for me and Ade to dip our toes into the world of movie scores without all the high pressure that can so often accompany it. As Ade lived in the UK, and I was now in the USA, sitting side by side and writing together wasn't an option, not that either of us would have wanted to work that way even if it was. Nor did we want to swap ideas backwards and forwards, as that would be a much slower process. So, we decided that I'd write music for the first half and Ade the second. There was a small amount of sharing and exchanging of ideas, but in the main we wrote our halves in isolation. It was a most enjoyable experience. Working on music for each particular scene in the film, trying to find the emotion that would dominate or underpin the pictures, was a new challenge and one that I loved. When it was all done, Ade flew over, and we made some final adjustments before the film's creators came to listen. They sat in my small studio, and we ran through the film and score from start to finish. I have to admit, I was surprisingly nervous, but at the end of it they were very happy, and I was both relieved and proud.

Chapter Thirty-nine

2014

My relationship with Ade Fenton was changing, although I couldn't quite put my finger on how or why. It seemed to have become more businesslike – nothing wrong, nothing unfriendly, just not quite the same. I put it down to him now being in the band and doing non-US management duties. I assumed it added a lot of pressure. We had two shows in Tel Aviv, Israel, the first time I'd ever played there, and they went well. However, when we'd arrived at the airport to fly out to Tel Aviv, the tour manager I was expecting wasn't there, another man was. Not being told about that up front annoyed me. The day after Tel Aviv, we were due to fly to Belgium to start the European leg of the tour. As we arrived back at the hotel, Ade told me that our tour manager for Europe was still unwell and wouldn't be able to do the tour, which started in just over thirty-six hours. That tour manager was also the lighting designer, so it was quite a bombshell. Ade said he would take over tour-manager duties and a standby lighting man was ready to go, but this would be my first European tour in eight years, and it was important to me that it was successful. It was unsettling news, to say the least, and I was unhappy that I hadn't been made aware of all this long before.

We arrived in Belgium and met Luke Edwards, the new lighting man. Gemma said he looked like a child – a very big child, to be fair – so she instantly named him 'Lighting Child', which stuck. The tour was so much better than the previous European tour in 2006. The venues were selling out, the crowds were loud, younger, enthusiastic. It was a completely different experience, and I was greatly relieved.

A few days after that tour finished, we were back in the USA for a second, much bigger, tour of North America. It was interesting. We played Solano, Los Angeles, Las Vegas and Phoenix, where I had my fifty-sixth birthday, and then travelled on towards Austin, Texas, where the South by South West (SXSW) festival was in full swing. We played six shows in three days at SXSW, including three on the 15th alone. Our last show of the day was on the Moog stage, and they presented me with a beautiful Moog Voyager synth. Then we drove to Nashville where Gemma and I visited Jack White who gave us a tour around his incredible facility. The tour was hectic but a lot of fun. The shows sold really well, people knew all about the album and for possibly the first time in the USA the new songs were getting a bigger reaction than the older stuff, even 'Cars'. The only downside was that my relationship with Ade Fenton came to an end. He'd been increasingly distant as the tour progressed. He actually made it very clear that he didn't want to be around Gemma or me but didn't say anything, so there was never a good opportunity to thrash it out. When the tour was over, I wrote to him and said we were done. No more managing, no more band, no more production. A few weeks later, we flew out to New Zealand for the Australia and New Zealand leg of the *Splinter* tour, and Ade wasn't with us. Neither were Tim Muddiman or Richie Beasley, so it was quite a different line-up. Frank Zummo was back on drums,

Tim Slade was on bass and another American, Josh Giroux, had joined on keyboards.

I have a very hard line with ex-friends. Once they're gone, it's as if they all but cease to exist for me. Something is switched off and that room becomes forever dark. So it was with Ade Fenton. Unusually, though, something would happen that would switch that light back on. But not for a while.

The Australia and New Zealand tour was good, and I was glad we played in both countries, but it was hard. We actually had some fantastic promo opportunities thanks to the promoter, the best I'd ever had for Australia, but I still struggled to sell the shows. It didn't feel as if the album itself had been pushed there the way it had in other parts of the world. I didn't see one record-company person throughout the entire tour, for example. It felt as if there was no label interest or support for the album at all, or the tour, and without that it was questionable whether it made sense even to have gone. I'd expected more, to be honest.

Three weeks later, we were back in the UK for a second UK *Splinter* tour. Actually, the first show was a cool little festival in Ireland, where a laptop failure just as we started almost ruined it. Luckily, Josh fixed the problem in seconds, and we got through the next hour without any more problems. After that, we played another ten shows, ending at the Sonisphere festival in Knebworth. I firmly believed that the constant touring helped the album. Each time we went out it seemed to create another little boost in interest and just kept extending the life of the record.

In October, we played a third US *Splinter* tour, which might have been one too many. Some of the gigs sold well, but it didn't quite have the vibe of the previous tour. In Vancouver, we played at the Rickshaw Theatre, positioned squarely in the middle of the drug centre of the city, and it was truly unnerving as we drove in. Everywhere you looked, people were like zombies, and I do mean that. It was actually quite distressing. These poor people, brains addled by meth for the most part, wandered around aimlessly. They looked awful, ravaged, and you could only wonder at what their future would be like. That evening, as we waited outside the stage door to go on (the dressing rooms were so disgusting we all got changed on the bus), we noticed syringes on the floor and rats scurrying around. It really was quite unpleasant. Great gig, though, strangely enough. In Saskatoon, about ten people turned up. I rang the management team and grumbled long and loud, but it really wasn't anyone's fault. I obviously wasn't popular in Saskatoon. Then we played in Winnipeg, which was better, but then dropped back down into the States to Iowa City, which was even worse than Saskatoon, I think. The last show of the tour was the Fun Fun Fun festival in Austin, Texas. Thankfully, that was epic, so we ended on a high.

We had one more show to do, the seventieth of the year. I was proud to be going back to the Hammersmith Odeon, or the Eventim Hammersmith Apollo as it was now called. It was another small step up, but it meant a great deal to me. It was a big moment for me to be back there, and I wanted it to be perfect. Amazingly, the legendary Gang of Four wanted to do the support slot, which was just perfect. We had a special LED Light Panel system going in just for that show. It was going to be a huge, fitting triumph to end the *Splinter* campaign. In the days leading up to the show, we rehearsed the lights in a cold, damp warehouse. My US management had put a lighting man of their own in place for the show, so Luke Edwards was stood down. I was not comfortable with that at all, but this new man was, apparently, highly regarded, and I was persuaded to accept him. For the final day of rehearsal, we moved to a larger room, where the entire rig was put up. As the day progressed, my heart sank. First of all, I was coughing and spluttering, and my throat was tight. I'd clearly picked something up in the damp environment. Mostly, though, my heart sank because this highly regarded lighting man didn't seem to have a fucking clue. He didn't know the songs and didn't really seem to know much about lighting. By the end of the day, which was a constant battle, I was desperate but totally powerless to do anything about it. I was assured, many times, that come the gig he'd have it all together, so I hoped for the best.

On the morning of the big show, I woke up and had no voice whatsoever. Absolutely nothing. I couldn't sing – couldn't even talk softly. It was one of the biggest feelings of disappointment I think I've ever known. I'd waited years to get back to the Apollo. The show was to be a crowning glory, not only for *Splinter*, but for the recovery of my entire career. It was to be a celebration of the long fight back. I was genuinely devastated, and I didn't know what to do. Should I wait and see if it got better throughout the day? Should I cancel the show? I knew fans were flying in from all over the world – from America, Canada, Europe, even as far away as Australia. It was a big deal to a lot of people. So, I just hung on and sucked a million and one lozenges, which made me feel sick, but nothing helped. I didn't even try to sing during the soundcheck. I did a meet and greet with the fans without speaking, and I felt like I was floating through a disaster of my own making. Still, at least it took my mind off the lights.

Someone mentioned a steroid injection that had been known to help, so a local doctor was contacted. I waited two hours and still no sign. The crowd were in, Gang of Four had nearly finished their set and still I waited. When he finally arrived, we went to an upstairs dressing room, and I saw him pull out the mother of all needles. It had to go in my backside, and I could have sworn it went right through and out the other side, pinning me to the table. Perhaps not, but it was a looooong needle, and it hurt. The doctor explained that for some people it helped a lot, for others not at all. For me, it would turn out to be somewhere in between.

With the injection done, I had about twenty minutes left before show time. We could hold a little, but I would have to be onstage in thirty minutes regardless, so I used the time to explore which parts of my voice were coming back. I found a small room, away from everyone, and began to sing sections of songs in the set and so figure out which ones were acceptable, where I would struggle and what was hopeless. Over the thirty minutes, I did see an improvement in a number of areas, but I was a long way from where I needed to be. But we had a sold-out crowd, and it was the Hammersmith Apollo, so all I could do was get out there and try my best.

I arranged with the band that we would do the first song and then, rather than go straight into the next, stop. I wanted to apologise for my voice and to let the fans know how badly I felt about letting them down at such a moment. When I finished my little apology, the roar of support was indescribable. It was a heart-melting moment, and my feelings of gratitude over-flowed. It was a remarkable moment of bonding. Many of these people had been with me from the very beginning, had stayed with me through all the ups and downs, and were here to enjoy this moment with me. I think, for many of them, they felt as proud as I did of their own contribution to my renaissance. It was a shared moment of triumph but with a glitch. For the next two hours, they sang with me, even sang for me on occasions, and lifted me up constantly. It was a remarkable evening, one that I will always treasure. It really was a colossal victory snatched from the jaws of defeat, and it felt all the better for that. No one even seemed to care that much that the lights were terrible.

I took some time off after that. It was nice just hanging around the house with Gemma and the kids with not much to think about as far as music was concerned. I wanted to take a break so that I could empty my head of all the things I'd been doing, the way I'd been thinking. When I started the next album, I didn't want it to just pick up where *Splinter* had left off. I wanted a head full of new ideas, not lingering remnants of what was in there before.

Chapter Forty

2015

I was asked to play a one-off show at the Royal Festival Hall in London in March 2015 as part of the curated Convergence event (a series of events focusing on musicians who use technology in new ways). I wouldn't usually fly to the UK, rehearse and play just one show, but I could use the opportunity to see friends and family back in England. It was actually a fantastic show, and I was pleased I'd agreed to do it. I played quite a different set, with more older songs than usual, and I chose several ones I didn't usually play. It went well and got some good reviews.

I'd also very reluctantly agreed to an idea pushed hard by the US management team where I would do a three-night residency in Los Angeles and another in London. Each night, we would play one of my three most-successful albums: *Replicas*, *The Pleasure Principle* and *Telekon*. I really wasn't sure, on a number of levels, that it was the right thing to do. There was a lot of backwards and forwards before I agreed to it, but, having done so, the two residencies were set up for later in the year. I was more worried about them than excited.

Meanwhile, the *Android in La La Land* documentary had taken an unfortunate turn. I can't remember exactly when I saw the first edit, but I absolutely hated it. I'd had a few misgivings while it was being filmed, but I was entirely unprepared for the view of me that the first edit presented. It seemed as if it had been filmed with the express purpose of making me out to be a deeply troubled soul. A strange, angry, bitter man who complained constantly. The questions I'd been asked seemed to dwell way too much on the more unpleasant side of things – my early troubles with the press, for example. Gemma was unhappy, because at no time (bar once I think) did they want us to be interviewed together at the house, and all they wanted to know from her was how often I was angry, what made me difficult to be with, things like that. Almost everything was negative. I even had fans sending me messages saying much the same. When they had been interviewed for the film, the questions were always looking for statements about how weird I was. They asked me a lot about the falling-out with my dad until I'd get upset and shed a tear or two. Towards the end, an interview took place that seemed to deliberately push me into losing my temper, the reason for that seemed more obvious when I saw that first draft.

It was so upsetting that I have never let anyone see it apart from Gemma and the US management. I watched it once and never again. It also made me out to be a horrible dad, and that bothered me more than anything, so much so that Gemma had to talk to me at length in the days that followed to convince me I wasn't the way I'd been shown in the film. It really did affect me quite badly. I honestly believe it was about as warped a view of me as you could possibly create, and it would have ruined my career. So, I said no, it was entirely unacceptable.

They did a second edit, which was only slightly better, then a third, I think, but as they took out more of the negativity, it seemed they had little to replace it with. It looked to me as if so much effort had been put into gathering the 'weird' and 'angry' stuff they had little else. Unfortunately, it then got a bit unpleasant. They threatened legal action, I dug my heels in and then it went quiet for a long time.

During the last UK tour I'd received a message from Jean-Michel Jarre, asking if I would be interested in collaborating with him on a song. He was planning an album of collaborations with people who he thought had been important in electronic music so I was honoured just to be asked. In May he was in Los Angeles on business and came over to the house to talk more about the project. I was a little in awe to be honest. Jean-Michel is a true legend, and hugely successful, but he could not have been nicer. I doubt you could ever meet a more easygoing, charming, entertaining man. He had us absolutely hanging on to his many stories throughout the evening. At one point he was rolling around on the floor with 200lb Wilbur slobbering all over him. He is a lovely human being.

Meanwhile, the business manager idea just wasn't working for me. I consistently lost track of what was coming in and out and I found it impossible to get a feel for our financial state. People like me don't earn a regular amount of money each month. It's highly unpredictable, so you need to be cautious, but we seemed to be forever standing on the cliff edge of ruin, and the constant worry and uncertainty about money was ruining my life. I was snappy much of the time; I wasn't sleeping properly. It was a never-ending nightmare, and it certainly wasn't being 'managed'. The business-management service was also horribly expensive, so that was the first thing that had to go. The only way I could truly grasp what was going on was to take back control of the money and look after it myself, but it was a lot of work. I hired an accountant who would mainly look after my taxes and got to work unravelling everything so I could understand it and look after it. Although the workload was significant for a while, it made me feel far more comfortable. I could map out the next twelve months and see where the potential problem areas were, and, knowing that, I could do something about it. Doing it myself allowed me to see the big picture, and it made all the difference in the world. We haven't had a single problem since, and I always know exactly what's going on.

The thing that finally encouraged me to make that big decision was finding out I was broke yet again. When I took back control of the accounts, I looked carefully at the figures, trying to understand why it kept going wrong. More than that, I attempted to see what changes I could make that would move us away from that seemingly permanent financial cliff edge. I could see lots of changes that would make a difference, but it was pretty clear that one of the biggest outgoings was management. I had no problem with them whatsoever, neither as people nor as managers, and I was grateful for everything they'd done. But it was painfully obvious to me that I simply couldn't afford to have them. I was frightened. The thought of taking over my own management for the first time in my thirty-seven-year career was massively intimidating. I had no idea how to negotiate, how to do anything, really. I spoke to several people about it, and to hear them speak you'd think artist management was some kind of high-level sorcery, way beyond the wit of a mortal man. Soon enough, I found myself with no official management at all.

I had often questioned how much of any management function was simply making yourself the point of contact and then doing little more than answering the phone. You hear stories of powerful, influential managers moving mountains for certain artists and generating million-dollar deals, but I suspect those mega deals are few and far between, and mostly for people already making millions of dollars. I had questioned at times, when someone had come to me and said, 'I've worked hard and got you this great opportunity,' whether that was really true? Or did they just answer the phone and take the call from the person making the offer? I suspected the latter. So, armed with my suspicions that I was unlikely to miss out on too many opportunities by managing myself, I set to it. I would work as a team with Gemma and her winning personality. I already knew that she was more than capable of cutting quickly to the heart of a discussion. I'd never seen her intimidated by anyone, except Siouxsie Sioux, and as I did very little without talking to her first, it made perfect sense.

I didn't entirely shut the door on outside management, though; it seemed foolish not to at least talk to people who were interested. However, I wasn't looking for management, and I made that perfectly clear. But we did have a number of meetings with people who said they wanted to manage me. Gemma and I would meet with these people, all very charming and enthusiastic, and listen to them talk a great deal and yet say absolutely nothing. A favourite word of theirs used to be 'synergy' as I remember. When they left, we would go over the conversation and see if we could remember one single meaningful idea or suggestion they'd made. We rarely could think of any at all, just way too many cool-sounding words that didn't actually mean anything. It was all sparkly noise, huffing and puffing, with zero substance. After a while we stopped talking to them.

I would never claim to be a proper manager. I just look after my own career, but I enjoy it, and I've grown comfortable doing it. At first, it seemed like a twenty-four-hour-a-day job, but I got better at knowing what to focus on and what to ignore. I'm no longer frightened of making a wrong decision or missing a big opportunity. The phone keeps ringing. The thing that encourages me most, and makes me feel confident that I made the right decision, is the fact that I'm doing better now than at any time since 1980. I can't claim all the credit for that, of course, far from it, but I can certainly claim some of it.

I played a festival in Long Beach, California, called Ink-N-Iron in June. The stage was set up in front of the old ocean liner the *Queen Mary*, which made the most stunning backdrop ever. Peter Murphy was the headliner, and I was on before him. They had allocated some of the rooms on the ship as dressing rooms, and I loved it. We went back to the ship a few months later – it's actually a floating hotel – and stayed in Winston Churchill's old state room, which, according to rumour, he now haunts. Around Halloween, the ship is used as a home for various horror mazes. Halloween is a much bigger thing in America than it is in the UK, and it's just so much fun. They create areas in the lower decks of the ship where people, dressed and made up very convincingly to look like zombies or other horrific creatures, hide in dark areas and leap out at you. As well as the lurking monsters, there is noise, music, smoke, lights – it's all highly orchestrated, and you can hear the screams for miles. The first time we ever went was with Trent Reznor, Josh Homme from Queens of The Stone Age and a group of their friends. I embarrassed myself by using Gemma as a human shield every time we went past a dark room or around a corner. It's properly scary.

At the Q Awards in London that October, I was given the award for Innovation in Sound. It was presented to me by Jean-Michel Jarre, which made it even more special. Getting that award meant a lot to me, and I was proud to receive it. I've been at award shows many times where the people being given awards don't seem to care. I even saw somebody collect his award once and then throw it onto the floor. I don't understand that. Perhaps they get so many they lose meaning, or perhaps they're just too full of themselves to appreciate it.

It was in 2015 that my parents told me that Mum's cancer had returned once again. This time it was in her bones, and there was no meaningful treatment. They could do things that would hopefully help to slow down its advance, but they couldn't get rid of it. My mum was her typical self yet again, with all bad news seemingly taken in her stride. I sometimes wonder how much more of her true feelings she revealed to my dad. The fear must have been enormous, and she'd carried that fear for so many years. To me, though, and to John, and anyone else who wasn't my dad, she was a tower of strength and resilience. Through all the treatments and the drugs, and the pain and the fear, she didn't waver. She was seventy-seven years old, and I just assumed that she would be able to beat it for the rest of her life. I was so guided by her belief that she would die of old age, not cancer, I honestly didn't think it was too serious.

For part of the year, Chris Corner from IAMX stayed with us. He'd found himself between houses for a month or so, and as we have spare rooms, it made sense for him to come and be with us while things were being sorted out. Chris has been a friend of ours for a long time, and along with Janine Gezang, his bandmate in IAMX, has a great deal of experience in areas I was particularly interested in at that time, self-management being one. I spent much of the time picking their brains. The thing I was most interested in, though, was the two campaigns IAMX had run with Pledge Music. I listened intently to everything they had to say, asked as many questions as I could think of and decided I wanted to give it a try. I made contact with people at Pledge, had a meeting at Soho House in Los Angeles and put the wheels in motion.

The idea for my Pledge campaign was to give fans a window of sorts into the ups and downs of making an album. However, the idea of putting a camera in the corner of the studio and letting it run 24/7 was never the idea, although I suspect some people thought it was when they joined. The truth is that songwriting is not exciting or fast – not to watch, anyway. I often spend hour after hour going over the same simple phrase, trying to think of how it can be improved. Adding a note, taking it away, trying another, taking it away again, hundreds and hundreds of times until you find the notes that work best. It's about as exciting for a spectator as watching grass grow. What I wanted to offer instead, through a series of video and text updates, was a sense of how the songs progressed from the first note as an idea came to mind, all the way through the many stages to the finished item. People would see edited updates that showed how that first note developed into a full tune, or how a piano arrangement would become the frame upon which the rest of the song was built. They would then see how I added layers of sound to build upon that framework, how the vocal ideas were arrived at, and how those rough versions guided the lyrics and the final, accurate vocal. Also, how the production work came into play and how that changed the songs, early artwork ideas for the sleeve and how they evolved, and a first look at photos before they were added to the artwork. The campaign offered signed lyric sheets and various bits of old equipment that had been used on previous albums – even the microphone that was used to sing the vocals was sold off when it was finished. Essentially, though, it was just a pre-order campaign for the new album but on steroids. If enough people got involved and pre-ordered the album, hopefully because they liked what they heard, those orders would all count as part of the week-one sales when the album was released and could help the initial chart position. It would give the fans a genuine opportunity to get involved, support the album at an early stage and actually make a real difference.

I launched the campaign on 9 November, and from the first moment it was exciting. It broke through the initial target level in about two hours, and I watched as the technical team at Pledge repeatedly adjusted the target to allow for the demand. It was incredibly successful. I discovered that the extra work involved in servicing the campaign commitments was far more than I'd anticipated, but it was OK – the fans were engaged, and it was doing everything I'd hoped and more.

A few days after I launched the Pledge campaign, terrorists attacked the Bataclan club in Paris. It was particularly shocking to me and hit home especially hard, perhaps because it was a live venue and I knew people there. Ten days later, Gemma, the girls and I flew to London, got on a train and went to Paris. It was a small thing, I know, but we felt a need to visit and show support to the French people in our own small way. We had lunch with Jean-Michel Jarre, visited the Eiffel Tower, the catacombs, Notre Dame. We had an argument with a rude waiter, but then what trip to Paris is truly complete without arguing with a French waiter?

Back in Los Angeles, I had to admit that managing myself, writing the new album, running the Pledge campaign and looking after the day-to-day accounting, as well as being a dad to three young children, was getting to be a bit too much. So, we took on a bookkeeper, Michelle. She is actually an actress above all else, and, as much as I want her to do well, I dread her getting that big part that takes her away from us. What started out as simply paying bills and keeping the books straight has become so much more, and Michelle has become an indispensable part of our little team.

Towards the end of the summer we took a few days break and rented a small house in a place called Three Rivers, not too far from the Sequoia National Park. The house was a bit smelly to be honest and a major wildfire in the region was laying a thin blanket of smoke onto the air. The smell of the house, and the smell of the fire, didn't exactly add to the charm of our little getaway but it wasn't too bad. A small babbling river was on the doorstep and the children took their floaty rings and spent some happy time drifting along through the mini rapids. It was all very relaxed, and slightly boring to be honest, until we went to a restaurant on our last night. Near the end of the meal I noticed that Gemma and the girls were looking at something behind me very intently so I looked round, only to see a huge snake making its way along the floor, inside the room we were in. I may have mentioned already that I love snakes, but only at a distance, and a much greater distance than this thing was at. It was fast, and seemed to be on a mission. At one point it left our room into what I think was the kitchen, only to reappear a few seconds later, heading in my general direction. That was enough for me. With as much bravado and dignity as I could muster I gave the order 'every man for himself' and made a run for it. I assumed that Gemma and the kids would have the good sense to follow me and so saw no reason to wait around to check. I found one of the staff, told them about the snake and was amazed to find that they weren't bothered in the slightest. They took a half interested look at it, said something about it being a good thing as it was a King snake, and that doesn't attack humans but does eat rattlesnakes, as though that was somehow comforting. I decided to skip dessert and drove back to the smelly house.

Just before the year was out, I got a message from a man called Alistair Norbury, who had heard about the ongoing success of the Pledge campaign and was interested in my plans for the new album. He said that in the new year he was moving to the record label BMG, and he would be interested in talking to me again once he was in and settled. At that time, two things stopped me from being as interested as I would otherwise have been. First of all, I had all but decided that I didn't want to get involved with a record label again, in any way at all. I'd convinced myself that self-releasing albums in the future was the way I should go. I'd become used to manufacturing my own albums and DVDs by then, and my dislike and mistrust of labels had grown considerably. The second reason was that I remembered experiences years before when new people joined a label and tried to foist their favourite projects onto a team that didn't share their enthusiasm. I thought that was the case with Alistair, and I didn't want to end up on a label that essentially didn't want me apart from one person. I didn't fully appreciate at that point the position Alistair was taking up at BMG. Anyway, I didn't follow it up, it all went very quiet and I thought no more about it for another year or so.

Chapter Forty-one

2016

I thought that the LA and London residencies I played in 2015 would be the end of my little dip back into retro for a few years. However, I was asked to do the same thing at the Moog Festival the following May, which led to three more residencies being planned in New York, Chicago and Toronto for the same period.

Not long after we moved to California, I'd taken a test, got my firearm license and bought a handgun, the reason being our burglar alarm went off one night. It turned out to be a false alarm – I think one of the children had opened a door they shouldn't have – but it made me think about what would happen next? It's all very well having an alarm that lets you know you have intruders, but what if they don't run away? It occurred to me that just knowing they were in the house didn't really make us any safer, so I bought the gun – not with the intention of going downstairs in the middle of the night and confronting someone, but as a last line of defence should that intruder be coming for us rather than our things. I am by nature a person who always tries to think ahead as to what dangers might be lurking for me and my family. I think I've watched way too many films of bad things happening to unsuspecting people. On one occasion, Gemma had an operation in San Diego, and one of the many highly unlikely scenarios I was concerned about was breaking down on the way there and finding ourselves stranded and vulnerable, so I took my gun as a precaution. We arrived at the hotel having miraculously escaped attack by marauding bandits on the busy freeway, so I put the gun, in its case, inside the room's safe. When we left the hotel a few days later, Gemma was not doing well and needed to go back to the doctor quite urgently. I was panicking a little and forgot the gun was in the safe. I remembered about an hour later, called the hotel, but it was already too late. The maid had found it, and it had been handed in to the police. I wasn't in trouble – it was all perfectly legal – but to get it back the first question on the form asked for the serial number of the gun. It was only then I realised I hadn't ever written it down. That was that. No more gun.

The four retro residencies came along soon enough, and in May the band flew in to Los Angeles for a couple of days of refresher rehearsal. With that done, we flew to New York and the shows began. Much like before, we did the same three albums across the three nights. After New York, it was Chicago, then on to MoogFest in Ashville, where I was also presented with the Moog Innovation award. I was particularly pleased to get that. The name Moog was synonymous with electronic music, and to be recognised by them was rather special. We then drove into Canada for the final residency in Toronto. When we arrived, I received a message from my dad saying Mum was in hospital with severe pain. This was a surprise. Mum wasn't ever one to complain about pain, so if she'd gone to hospital, I could only imagine how bad it must be. But a few days later, she was out and talking as if it was all nothing, and I went back to thinking she was invincible.

I was given a beautiful guitar after one of the Toronto shows. A man had hand-made it especially for me and it was a work of art, absolutely beautiful. I was able to use it during the show the following night and it played every bit as beautifully as it looked. It now sits proudly in my studio.

Back in Los Angeles, we had friends visiting from England and spent some time showing them around. But then I got another call saying Mum was back in hospital. Both Mum and Dad were keen country-music dancing enthusiasts, and for many years it had been a big part of their lives. They would regularly travel to events, sometimes camping in their caravan or staying in hotels, and they loved everything about it. On this occasion, they'd arrived at their favourite event of the year but had to leave as Mum was in so much pain. It got so bad that instead of driving home they diverted to the hospital and Mum was admitted. I started to get regular messages each day about how she was doing, and at first it seemed like no big deal. I was under the impression they were just working on what cocktail of drugs would work to stop the pain and things would carry on as before. Then things became more worrying, and I can't remember why I thought this or what was said to me, but I came to the opin-ion that she might not have much more time left to her after all. That was a horrible shock.

She was expected to leave the hospital that weekend, and I'd arranged to fly over and see her the following week. She left the hospital as expected, but her condition didn't sound too good, and it seemed to be changing by the day. On the Sunday morn-ing, I got a call from my dad saying that if I was going to come, I should come as quickly as possible – she probably wasn't going to make it more than a day or two. It just threw my world completely upside down. A few days before, I'd thought she would live for ever, then I was told it might only be a couple of years, and now it was a couple of days at best. I found a British Airways flight that left in a few hours. We grabbed the kids, packed enough clothes for a few days and hurtled off to the airport. When we arrived at Heathrow, John was there to meet us. I went with him to my mum and dad's house, where Mum was, and Gemma took the children to sort out a hotel and wait for news.

As soon as we were away from the children, John warned me what to expect – that Mum didn't look good, and he'd found it quite upsetting at first. It was that and more. Seeing her for the first time took my breath away. She looked awful, and the sound of her breathing is something I will never forget. I spoke to her, and although I will never know for sure if she heard, I think she did. Gemma and the children came over later, and we all sat with her. I held her hand and marvelled at how hard she'd fought for so many years, but she looked so battered now. Bruised and gaunt and so very tired. It looked as if all the marks of damage from her long fight with cancer had appeared all at once, and it broke my heart. That such bravery should be rewarded with such an end seemed so unfair. The next day, on 7 June, that awful breathing changed slightly, just for a moment, and then with one last gasp it stopped altogether, and she was gone.

That night, I was sitting in Mum and Dad's 'best' room, thinking of words to say at the funeral. I was very upset, crying a lot, when I felt a tingling in my toes. It flowed gently up and through my entire body and seemed to burst out the top of my head, and I was left with the most beautiful feeling of calm. It felt like a goodbye, so I smiled and said, 'Bye, Mum.'

The funeral was sad, of course, like all funerals for people you love deeply. We'd been allowed to visit her in the funeral home, which we all did, but I didn't find the experience comforting at all. I looked at her body, but she wasn't there. Gemma and the girls left me alone in the room, but I didn't want to stay and left quickly. During the service, I read out a little tribute, not just to my mum but to my dad as well. In many ways, he had suffered right along with her for decades. Cared for her, helped in any way he could, always at her side. The quality of life she managed to enjoy despite her illness had much to do with her own strength but was helped immeasurably by my dad's constant and resolute support. I wanted him to know I was aware of that, and I wanted everybody there to know what he'd done. I thought my mum would have wanted that as well.

This is the tribute I read out:

On 7 June 2016 my mum died. It cannot be possible that a better mother has ever existed. I have been wrapped in love, care and kindness since the second I was born. It never wavered, not once, no matter what I did, or how often I let her down. It was absolute and unconditional. Beautiful.

She has guided and helped my brother John and I through every stage of our lives, from tiny babies to the men we are today. Through triumphs and disasters, successes and failures, great things and shameful things. She has been there to lift us higher, or help get us back on our feet. Throughout my entire life there was nothing she wouldn't do if she thought it would help either one of us, even if it was just to make us smile. She made us feel anything was possible, that we could do anything, be anything, and she gave us the courage to try.

I have only good memories. My childhood is one long, happy memory of feeling like we were the most important things in the world, in her world. Always safe, always secure and always loved. That blanket of love, that cocoon of protection and support, gave me a start in life that I was never able to repay, and it has comforted me every day of my life. She made us laugh, kept our secrets, joined our battles and surrounded us with warmth and never-ending affection.

She was remarkable, unique, and so I find myself standing here, filled with a sadness that constantly overflows. Shocked at the speed at which it all came to an end. I love her so much, I have so much to be grateful to her for, so much to be thankful to her for. It's impossible to truly grasp that I will never see her again, that I will never talk to her again. As a family, I know we have a lot of pain still to come, but it will be a good pain. Because every tear will be a witness to the love she earned, the love she deserves. Every sob will be a celebration of the never-ending love she leaves behind.

Her long, defiant battle against many forms of cancer has been a shining inspiration, not just to me, but to so many other people that she helped along the way. She seemed genuinely indestructible. So much so that I think sometimes the true horror of what she was fighting, and the enormous suffering she endured, seemed almost as nothing. She bore it all with such incredible courage that she made it seem far less than it really was. Where others have succumbed to this horrific disease at the first hurdle, she has run countless marathons and more, for decades, and literally fought to the very last breath.

Not only did she never complain, as breast, skin, throat and bone cancers attacked her relentlessly, she laughed, for year, after year, after year. I have never seen bravery like it.

But, a word also about my dad. I have always admired my dad beyond all other men. I'm not sure even to this day if he's aware of this, but he is the man that set every standard for me to aspire to, in all those areas that are truly important. Loyalty, integrity, courage, kindness and generosity, to name but a few. Before I had a family of my own his praise, and my mum's, was the only praise that mattered to me, and it's still hugely important. He is a good man, and the best father I could ever wish for.

But, if I loved him absolutely before, and I did, I love him far more now. The love and care that he gave my mum in her final days was nothing short of incredible. No matter how sad, it was a beautiful thing to witness. Such total love and devotion is a very rare thing. After sixty-two years together they still laughed and played like love-struck teenagers, sharing every moment in a bond never broken. Through every agonising stage of my mum's long, long battle, he has been right there by her side, doing whatever needed to be done, and doing so much more. She could not, would not, have survived all these years without him. What he has gone through these last few weeks I can't begin to imagine. But he has done it with a strength and composure that I can hardly believe. I didn't think my admiration for him could be any higher, but I was wrong. What a fantastic husband he has been to my mum, what a fantastic father he is to John and I. He is a phenomenal, remarkable human being, and I stand humble but proud in his shadow.

What a couple they have been. What an example to the world. As husband and wife, as parents, as grandparents, they have been truly exceptional.

But now my mum has gone, and I miss her, and life will never be the same.

Bye bye Mum. Until I see you again xxxxx

Gemma had found a place for us to stay while we were in England. We had a small cottage in the grounds of Coworth Park Hotel, and while I'd been with my mum, Gemma had met the singer Tom Jones, who was staying in the next cottage along. After Mum had died, we were sitting outside the cottage having breakfast when Tom came over and sat with us for quite a while. He'd recently lost his wife and was still visibly upset by it. It was a very warm, if somewhat emotional, conversation, and I liked him a lot. People are people, no matter how legendary or rich they might be, and they all hurt just the same.

To take the children's minds off all the sadness, Gemma took them horse-riding around the hotel grounds. After the ride, as they were walking back to the cottage, a car coming along the hotel road slowed down as it approached them. As it drove slowly by, the window rolled down, and a smiling Prince Harry waved to them. It made their day, and I have had a soft spot for Harry from that day onwards. That kind gesture brought a lot of joy to three little girls at the saddest time of their young lives.

While I was there, I received a very lovely message from Ade Fenton about my mum. It had been around two years since we'd communicated at all, and usually I'd have had no interest in reading it whatsoever. I think it came at just the right moment, though. I was obviously sad because of my mum, and very emotional, and I had no interest in fighting or being difficult with anybody. With that message, the cold ice was broken, and the first baby steps of rebuilding our friendship were taken. I didn't know at the time, but Gemma had been in touch with Steve Malins and Ade for a while, keeping the remnants of a bridge between all of us hanging together.

I was worried about my dad for a while. I had a feeling that he could go either way. He'd either battle through the grief and come out the other side, or he'd crumble and fade away. He battled through. He decided he would clean out their house, sell it and move somewhere smaller, where he could be close to friends. It was the best thing he could have done.

Long before my mum's downturn, we'd booked a rather special holiday. We'd planned to spend a couple of weeks exploring New Zealand, and then one more week in Bora Bora. Now, though, going on holiday so soon after my mum had died felt very wrong. I spoke to my dad about it, and he thought it was exactly what we should do. He said it would be good for me and especially good for the children. So, we went on holiday, but I felt very awkward about it. Our two weeks of adventuring around New Zealand was a mix of great experiences and a few disappointments. We took a helicopter up a mountain and landed at the top of a glacier. That was truly awe-inspiring. We rode in a jet boat at ridiculous speeds through rocky canyons, where every second it seemed like you were going to die. We took quad bikes out into a rainy wilderness and a light aircraft through the mountains to a fjord, where we caught a boat filled, unexpectedly, with Chinese tourists. We visited Hobbiton for the second time, went whale watching and took a train ride advertised as one of the most stunningly beautifully in the world, but it really wasn't. Saw more *Lord of the Rings* movie sites than I could count. Gemma threw herself of a mountain clipped to a bungee. One of our guides also took us to a sock museum, so it wasn't all high excitement.

But Bora Bora was everything I'd dreamed it would be. It was every picture of a Pacific paradise you've ever seen, with the turquoise lagoon curving around an extinct volcano. Outside the tiny airport terminal, boats waited to take you to your respective hotels, almost all of which were a series of thatched houses built on legs out over the water. From our bedroom, you simply walked down some steps and jumped in to the warm, waist-high sea. From time to time, stingrays would swim lazily past on their way to feed. We took a boat tour and found ourselves swimming with sharks just outside the lagoon entrance. It was pretty amazing but all over way too soon.

Unexpectedly, I got another message from someone at BMG asking about the new Pledge campaign album. I wrote back and asked if it was a follow-up enquiry to Alistair's message from before. Much to my surprise, the man didn't know anything about that – his was a new enquiry. That made quite a difference to my thinking. I now had two different people from BMG independently showing interest in the new album, and that felt so much better. I explained about the original enquiry and things began to move from then on.

At the end of July, I put out a documentary DVD called *Reinvention*. The film had been made by another company and had first been seen on TV in 2011, but the deal was that after so many years the rights would revert back to me. Things had been a bit busy since then, what with emigrating and self-managing and so on, and I'd forgotten all about it. I came across it one day and thought I should look into it. Sure enough, it should have reverted to me a while back. Not only that, they had never paid me my share of the money it had made. I got in touch, and after lots of rather blatant ducking and diving on their part, I managed to get it back and release it myself.

We also visited my dad, showed the kids some English history to remind them where they came from – Warwick Castle, Stratford and all things Shakespeare – and then we flew to Geneva. Gemma had long wanted to visit the H. R. Giger museum in Gruyères, just a couple of train rides from Geneva, Giger being famous for his biomechanical creations as seen in the *Alien* films. On this trip, Gemma and I also went to the BMG offices in London and had a chat about how things might work out between us. There were a few areas of concern at first that Gemma immediately picked up on, but, by the end, I felt very confident that licensing the new album to BMG would be the smart move. I didn't want to be signed as an artist, but I did recognise the clout and expertise that BMG would bring to the table. By licensing the album, I could keep some control and, ultimately, ownership of it. It was all very exciting, and I was very happy to be with BMG.

The *Android in La La Land* documentary dispute had been settled at last, and the official release of the film was in August. They had eventually done one more edit, and it had been worth it. For me, the film didn't live up to the deep, in-depth look at my life I'd expected it to be, so I was a little disappointed. But it was no longer negative, and, all things considered, I had nothing to grumble about. British Airways would eventually show it as part of their in-flight entertainment, and I spoke to many people who saw it that way. Every comment I got back was positive, so I had to admit that, even though it wasn't what I thought it would be, and even though it was a difficult battle to get there, the finished film did me nothing but good.

In September, I played a full UK tour of classic-album tracks. The reaction to the London residency gigs I'd done had been overwhelmingly positive. The trouble was, they'd actually caused some ill feeling with the fans who hadn't been able to get to see them. I'd only done the three London shows, one in Manchester and one in Cork. People were not happy, to say the least. So, to make amends, I'd arranged the *Classic Album* tour, where we would play songs from those same three albums and a few other old rarities. Before the tour started, I finally arranged to meet up with Ade Fenton. We would meet on neutral ground, at Richie Beasley's house in Reading. It was good. We talked for a while, gave our sides of everything that had happened, found out some things that made the other's behaviour more understandable and slowly worked our way towards a peace. I was glad. Not only did we sort out our differences, we agreed to work together again.

As for the tour, the first night in Sheffield got off to an interesting start when our smoke machines set off the fire alarms, and we had to evacuate the building. The tour was sold out, and I asked my agent to try and add a couple of small shows in London when the main run was over. The new album would be called *Savage*, and I'd written one new song that I was happy with called 'Bed of Thorns' that I wanted to play, but I didn't want to add it to the retro set. I was itching to play some shows that weren't all nostalgia, which I was absolutely done with by now. The first extra show was in Shepherd's Bush, and I added six of the more recent catalogue songs to the set, but I wasn't able to get 'Bed of Thorns' right in the soundcheck, so I didn't play it that night. The next night I did, at The Electric in Brixton, and that was the first time any fan had heard a *Savage* song live. All I needed now was about fourteen more. When I got home from the *Classic Album* tour, I sent Ade all the work I'd done on the new album so far, and we started to work on it together.

In October, our lovely gentle giant Wilbur died, and we were crushed by guilt with the way it happened. It was a very windy day but still hot. We had gone out for something with Wilbur, come home, unloaded the car and gone indoors. He was quite a farty boy that day, so I left one of the back doors open to air the car. Not too long after, it was time to get the kids from school, so we went out to the car and found Wilbur inside it dead. We still don't know what happened for sure, but we suspect that during the backwards and forwards of unloading the shopping he may have slipped out the front door of the house, perhaps hoping to steal some food from a bag, but we didn't see him. We think he must have jumped into the car through the open door and then either the jolt of that caused it to shut, or perhaps it was the wind, but he was trapped inside. By the time we found him, he was already gone. I cannot adequately put into words the guilt we felt. It was, without a shadow of a doubt, one of the worst moments of my life, and I know it was for Gemma as well. How could we not have noticed that he wasn't in the house? But it's a big house, and he often slept upstairs or out in the garden in the shade. We didn't see him for hours sometimes. But it was a terrible thing, and it bothers us both to this day.

A local animal-rescue centre had a big St Bernard who needed a home. It hadn't been too long since Wilbur had died, and none of us were in any hurry to get another dog just then, but we went to see him anyway. They told us that he had been there for two months and not one person had asked about him or been to see him. He had belonged to a family in which the husband beat the wife and she'd left. The dog was left with the abusive husband who didn't want him so sent him to the shelter, where he'd stayed ever since, unwanted and unloved. He was so lovely, and so friendly, it was hard to imagine anyone giving him away. We couldn't understand why he hadn't been snapped up straight away. He was really big, so that might have had something to do with it. He also had a bit of a breathing issue but nothing too bad. He walked a bit strangely, with kicky-out back legs, but you could hardly notice that. The next day, they brought him over to the house to see what he made of it. He got out of the van, ran into the house and never went back. The centre had called him Andre, which we didn't like, so, in a terribly unimaginative moment, we called him Bernard. He was really quite special.

It was about then that I started to make a late but determined effort to get *Savage* written. I had 'Bed of Thorns', which, appropriately, was about my fear of starting a new album after the success of *Splinter*, but little else substantial after that other than a long list of bits and pieces. So, to get under way, I borrowed some ideas from yet another book I had started to write. The book had the working title of *Ruin*, and the story was set in a far-distant future, long after the world had overheated due to climate change and all but destroyed humanity. Survival was hard, people had settled into tribes and fought constantly for what little there was. In the story religion had all but vanished until, quite by chance, a fragment of a bible is discovered far away. The tribe that find the fragment had no knowledge of what a bible is or a belief in a God, until now, and now they believe they are special. After all, the words came to them, and the words speak of a God, and so they must be chosen. They come to believe the words are not only a command on how they should live, but how all people should live. They become a wandering band of brutal missionaries, calling themselves The Righteous. They roam the desert lands of the scorched earth with the sole intention of conversion or death. But, like all religions, as time goes by they gradually reinterpret the words they follow to suit their evolving aims, which begin to include rape, abduction and slavery. And so they find themselves at the home of the man who will become known as Ruin. They kill his wife, take his child and leave him for dead. The story then is essentially his recovery and long search for his daughter, and the things he has to do in order to find her. Things so terrible he becomes known as the bringer of Ruin, and so earns his new name. By the time he finds his daughter the decision he must then face is stark; is he now any better than the men who took her?

I borrowed some ideas from the book and wrote a couple of songs about this possible future earth. That exact same week, I heard Donald Trump's opinions on climate change for the first time, and his desire to withdraw the USA from the Paris Accord. I was horrified by that. The sheer ignorant stupidity of it was stunning, which made me want to write more songs about my future world. So, I went back to the book again and again. Soon enough, the album became devoted almost entirely to ideas from the book, and *Savage* became a very small contribution to the thunder of voices speaking out about the dangers of global warming. I also added a subheading to the album title, much as I'd done with the *Splinter* album before. Now it would be called *Savage – Songs from a Broken World*.

Earlier in the year, I'd been asked by renowned record producer Nick Launey if I wanted to record a guest vocal for a Mexican band called Titan he was working with. Nick had become a friend after I'd written the *Plush* outro music a few years before. Nick had written the main score of the film. I liked the Titan music for the song, so I came up with the vocal melody, wrote the lyric, named it 'Dark Rain' and recorded the vocal at my home studio. They released the track as a download single in Mexico in October, and in November they asked me to be in the video for it, so Gemma and I flew down to Mexico City. We spent a few days seeing the sights, making the video and hanging out with the band. It was a really good trip, and I enjoyed working with them. The Titan song was the fifth collaboration I'd done in 2016. In April, I'd worked with The Duke Spirit on a song called 'Blue and Yellow Light', I did one with John Foxx and The Maths when I sang on his track 'Talk (Are You Listening to Me?)'. In October, I'd also worked with the band Dusky on a song called 'Swansea', and I sang on a track called 'Within the Deepest Darkness' for The Mission that appeared on their *Another Fall from Grace* album, released in November.

The last event of the year was the release of my *Obsession* live CD and DVD. *Obsession* had been filmed and recorded at the Hammersmith Apollo show the year before and captured the evening perfectly. It was a perfect final piece of the *Splinter* campaign. I dedicated the album to my mum, as it was the last Hammersmith show she ever saw me play.

Chapter Forty-two

2017

As 2017 got under way, I was still hard at work on writing music for *Savage*. I'd also been talking with photographer Joseph Cultice about ideas for the sleeve. As the album had a consistent setting of a windswept apocalyptic desert landscape throughout, I wanted that to be the backdrop for all the photos. For my look, I initially had an Assassin's Creed vibe in mind, and we even ordered a number of items of clothing to go along with that. It would have worked, I think, but it wasn't really what I was looking for. I wanted something almost military-looking but not. Something that looked battered and worn out but not rags. Something that you could imagine a violent desert dweller actually wearing to survive in a windswept hell.

Jean-Michel Jarre asked me to take part in a panel he was putting together that would discuss music as part of the promotion for his electronica collaboration project. It took place in February in Los Angeles, and on the panel were a number of artists, including Jean-Michel, Little Boots, Moby, Hans Zimmer and me. It was quite a gathering. An audience was invited, and the questions were asked by Nic Harcourt. It was a good evening, with plenty of interesting opinions being discussed.

A few days after that, something went wrong with me. I had been under a great deal of stress for some time, but on the day in question I'd had a good day in the studio. In fact, that was the day I'd come up with the 'My Name Is Ruin' song, so I was pretty pleased with myself when I locked the studio. As I walked into the house, I went very giddy, my arms and face began to tingle, then they went numb and then I found I could barely stand. I tried to stay calm, but I was frightened. Gemma and the kids were talking to me, but I couldn't really concentrate on what they were saying. I knew those symptoms, or so I thought. Many years ago, I saw the model Vivien Neves for a while, and she had multiple sclerosis. I remember her telling me what it felt like, and that was exactly the feelings I had. My head took an enormous leap and landed squarely in the 'Fuck, you have MS' circle, a bit like adding up two and two and thinking it makes 107. But I was genuinely terrified. Over the next seven days, it slowly went away, and my fears slowly subsided with it. It was such a ridiculous overreaction, I'm embarrassed even writing about it now. But on the seventh day, it came back worse than ever, and off I went again: 2+2 = 107. I could barely function. I said to Gemma I wasn't sure what was going to happen next, as my body seemed to be losing control of itself – perhaps we should call an ambulance. Gemma said to take a Xanax and wait a little bit, so I did, and like a miracle it had completely gone only twenty minutes later. Not MS after all, then. I felt pretty ashamed of myself for panicking so badly. The next day, I went to the doctor, and he told me it was stress-related. He gave me some pills for any future emergencies of that nature, along with dire warnings about not using them casually, and sent me on my way. How my mum got through the stress of all those years of having cancer I will never know. I do not have a fraction of her strength.

The new image problem was solved when Gemma found the perfect clothes for the *Savage* sleeve. After weeks of painstaking searches, she simply typed into Google something like desert-apocalypse clothing, and a designer came up with a range of clothes that fitted our needs perfectly. In the meantime, Joseph had also found the perfect location: the rim of an old volcanic crater halfway between Los Angeles and Las Vegas.

Gemma heard about a man who rescued English Mastiffs about a four-hour drive north of us. When she called him, he happened to have a couple of older puppies, which is pretty unusual, so we arranged to drive up to his place and take a look. That's how we got Mildred. Mildred is almost fully grown now and isn't anywhere near the size that Wilbur got to, but she's still a giant at around 150lb.

Towards the end of March, I had a studio photoshoot with Joseph Cultice for the shots I would need for press. Some of them were also used for promo shots, but for the main sleeve artwork I really only wanted to have photos in the desert. So, in early April, Gemma and I drove out to the volcano rim and met up with Joseph with a box full of desert-style clothes. For the rest of the day, we created a range of different but connected shots that would serve for all the formats that would be made available, including booklets, singles, EPs and anything else we could think of. When we arrived at the site, there was an actual dust storm swirling about. It was perfect. The wind was powerful, with dust and sand spiralling up through the air, but all under a bright, blazing sun. I couldn't have asked for more perfectly hostile conditions, and we got everything we needed.

After the photoshoot, we drove straight to Santa Barbara, where I was booked in to have a face-lift – a full one this time, not the little tuck I'd had in Manchester a few years before. I'd been with Gemma many times when she'd gone in for her various ops, so I knew what to expect. I wasn't prepared for how I felt when I came round afterwards. It was horrendous. It was like I was having a really bad acid trip, and I felt truly awful. I recognised Gemma through the mind-bending haze and was able to say something like, 'This is the worst I've ever felt in my life,' and rather bizarrely blamed her for it. We were staying at a nearby hotel, and a nurse was going to stay with us for the first twenty-four hours. She drove, and I threw up as soon as the car started moving. I have been horribly drunk only once or twice in my life, when you can't walk, and this was like that, but with what felt like half a gallon of LSD thrown in just to make it all a tiny bit weirder. It really was the worst I've ever felt.

Back at the hotel, after a few hours, it began to back off a bit, and I was able to take a look. I couldn't see too much, as my face and head were wrapped like a newborn in a snowstorm. My eyes were almost closed, but what really freaked me out was the three blood drains coming out of my face. I had one coming out each side of my neck, and one in my forehead, all the tubes ending in little plastic bottles full of blood that had to be emptied regularly. It was pretty grim.

The painkiller I was on made me dream in a weird way, in that it merged nightmares with real life. I would have the most horrible dreams, and then the room I was in, and the people in the room, became a part of the nightmare, and I would slowly start to wonder if I was no longer dreaming at all. Then it would start to get really weird again, and I would return fully to the nightmare. It was so horrible that I only lasted a day and a half before refusing to take any more. I preferred the pain to the way those painkillers made me feel.

It sounds a tad gruesome, but you are stitched and stapled in a variety of places. I went into an oxygen tank for an hour each day, as it supposedly helps you to heal faster. After four days, I think I was allowed home, and by then I felt OK. I even drove the car back to Los Angeles. I got a thing the doctor called noose neck for a while, where it feels like you have a rope tightening around your neck – that was pretty unsettling but very common, apparently. I was dreading having all the stitches and staples taken out, but it wasn't too bad. I can honestly say, apart from the first few hours after recovery and the weird nightmares, it was all fairly painless and trouble-free. You get what feels like tiny electric shocks in your face from time to time for the first few months, which I think is a sign the nerves are reconnecting, but, generally speaking, it was surprisingly lacking in drama.

Joseph sent me the photos, and I got to work creating the artwork for the *Savage* album formats. I did everything, every last Photoshop tweak on the Arabian font down to the catalogue number on the spine of the vinyl, even the labels. I wanted everything to be as perfect as could be, and I spent a great deal of time going over every tiny detail. When the proofs came back, I was very happy. The entire album was exactly what I'd hoped it would be – the music, the production (thanks to Ade), the lyrics, the image (thanks to Gemma), the photography (thanks to Joseph), the sleeve, everything. I was very, very proud of that album.

I'd been told that my face would look pretty normal after six weeks. This was important, because it had been announced that

I was to receive the Ivor Novello Inspiration award for song-writing on 18 May, exactly six weeks after the op. To get the award, I had to attend the ceremony in London in person. I'd actually been awarded it the year before, but I wasn't able to go because of the residency shows, so, luckily for me, they'd put it back a year and still allowed me to be a recipient. Getting the Ivor in 2017 was so much better, as it made for a great build-up to the album release a few months later.

An Ivor Novello award is hugely prestigious for a songwriter. But to get the award for Inspiration in songwriting was, for me at least, the most prestigious of them all. Gemma and I flew to London a few days before, and sure enough my face did look absolutely normal again, just less baggy. I went to see Ade and Nathan Boddy first of all, and we worked on the final mixing tweaks for *Savage*. On the 15th, I signed the deal with BMG in their London offices, then did some more mixing and then went to the awards on the 18th.

I've been to many awards ceremonies, both to present and to receive, and I do find them quite daunting. For a start, the arrival with all the photographers is not my favourite thing. But then watching all the presenters and winners ahead of you get up and give their speeches is hard. So many of them are in their element. Confident, witty and often with a lot to say, all taking it very much in their stride. I'm not like that. I'm a big bag of nerves waiting to get my award, and the Ivors were worse than ever because it's such a big deal. I'd asked my friend Alan Moulder to present mine. Alan has himself received countless awards, including multiple Grammys, so he has world-class standing. I thought that would calm me, but it didn't. Winner after winner went up onto the stage, and I felt less and less

444

deserving as each one came and went. These really were the best of the best, and I was in awe of so many of them for what they'd achieved. My songs didn't seem worthy of standing in their shadow. But my turn came, and they played a most flattering film by way of introduction that made me look far better than I deserved. Alan gave his speech, which was equally flattering, and I walked up and collected the Ivor. It really was one of the highlights of my life. I do not take any award lightly, I am always grateful, but that was extra special.

After the ceremony was over, I went straight to the studio to meet Ade and Nathan, and we spent the rest of the night putting the final touches on the *Savage* mix. The next day, we mastered the album, with four fans from the Pledge campaign in attendance, and it was done, eighteen months since I'd started it.

Everyone at BMG thought that 'My Name Is Ruin' should be the first single, so in June I drove out to the Joshua Tree area to meet up with Chris Corner. Chris had agreed to make the video for 'Ruin', which was a huge relief for me. I had a great deal of faith in Chris's vision and his ability to create a visual setting that would make sense of the song. My daughter Persia had sung on the track, so I persuaded her to take part in the video as well. As bad luck would have it, the day we chose to film was also the hottest of a short but intense heatwave. A heatwave in the desert is like no other, and it was shockingly hot. The cameras were wrapped in ice packs and still constantly overheated. But it was a great day for filming the sort of landscape and conditions the song demanded. Persia, who had never done anything like it before, was an absolute star. Chris came up with the idea of putting a white cross on her forehead, which made perfect sense, as in the story she'd been abducted by 'The

Righteous', a group of religious fanatics. That white cross became a symbol for much of what followed, both with my onstage image, tour posters and more. I'd taken my drone to the shoot, and Chris was able to get some amazing footage with it that was put into the finished video. My favourite video up until then had been 'I Am Dust', also directed by Chris, but now the 'My Name Is Ruin' video eclipsed even that.

I was booked to play the Standon Calling festival in Hertfordshire in late July, so I added three warm-up shows before it. I wasn't ready to reveal the full *Savage* image just yet so went for a fairly non-revealing look, with just a hint of some of the things to come. The first show was in Liverpool, at the Exhibition Centre, and it was the first major live show they'd put on there. When we arrived, the seating layout was clearly a disaster. They were spread so wide that people at the end of the front row were a long way from the stage, and their view was obscured by the PA system. Not only that, people with standing tickets, expecting to be at the front, were put in a standing area at the back of the hall. We argued with the staff all day to rethink what they'd done, but they would have none of it. As soon as the fans started to arrive, the complaints began.

The guest support for the show was intended to be John Foxx, but he was unable to do it, so Gang of Four stepped in at short notice and played instead. The biggest thrill for me was Persia coming on stage to sing 'My Name Is Ruin' with me. She was just twelve years old, as nervous as can be, and we had more than three thousand people in the venue that night. She'd never sung through a microphone, never been on a stage outside her school, never used in-ear monitors. Every part of it was new to her, and she must have been terrified. But she came out, sang beautifully, said thank you to the crowd at the end and left a hero in my eyes. For someone so young to have overcome that fear, in such an overwhelming environment, and performed flawlessly, I thought was remarkable. She did it again the next night in a very different type of venue, again the night after that, and then once more in front of a huge festival crowd. She was absolutely brilliant.

I started an intense few weeks of promotion to support the album and single. Countless radio interviews, TV spots, press interviews and photo sessions followed. It was encouraging to see so much interest, and the team BMG had put together was clearly doing a great job. Persia even did her first radio interview with Eddie Temple-Morris on Virgin Radio. It was exactly what the album needed – a lot of attention.

Back in the US we took a road trip up to Oregon to view the solar eclipse and spent as much time with the children as we possibly could. The touring schedule for *Savage* was shaping up to be the biggest campaign I'd ever done. We would be away from home a lot in the next eighteen months.

Part of the Pledge campaign offer had been for people to join us for an album listening party before it was released. A sneak preview if you like. To make it more of an event, we'd hired a big boat, much like an old Mississippi paddle steamer, in the beautiful Newport Beach area, and we cruised up and down the water there for a few hours. Fans could eat and drink, listen to the album, chat with me or just enjoy the cruise. We did the same thing on the River Thames in London a week or so later.

Hello! magazine came to the house for a chat and photoshoot with the family. They brought a make-up artist and stylist, so the girls were all made up and dressed rather glamorously. It was the first time we'd been in *Hello!* since they were babies, and I was very proud of them all. But that was about the last thing we would do with them for a while. A few days later, Gemma and I flew to New York for another round of promo work, and then it was on to the UK for the release of the album.

The first thing I did was go to the Pledge offices and sign thousands of albums. I think it was about 2,500 or thereabouts. It was a long day. More promo followed, more press, more radio, more photos. Gemma and I appeared together on the *Loose Women* TV show, then Soho Radio with Eddie Temple-Morris, and it just kept coming. I was grateful to have so much media interest, the most of any album since 1979 by far, but it was exhausting. I received the *T3* magazine award for being a Tech Legend and even appeared on the political TV show *This Week* with Andrew Neil.

When the album was released on 15 September, a series of daily chart positions began. At first, it went to number 2, which was extraordinary. But I said to Gemma that it couldn't possibly stay that high. I'd had high chart positions before on day one of a release, only to see them drop out of the chart completely by the end of the week when the final position was announced. I'd said all along, if it did better than *Splinter*, so higher than number 20, I'd be happy. The next day it was still at 2, and the next, and the next. Even the day before the final announcement it was still at number 2. On the day itself, BMG had asked if I wanted to go into their offices and sit with them to wait for the final chart position, but I couldn't. I was too nervous. The thought of sitting with everyone only to hear it had gone down would have been crushing. I now found myself in the strange position of knowing that I would feel disappointed if it dropped lower in the Top 10. The number 2 was so close now, everything else, great though it might be, would feel like a let-down. I really didn't want to feel like that, but it's human nature, I suppose. So, I sat with Gemma in our hotel room and waited for the phone to ring. When it did, Gemma answered and seemed to not be excited at the news and my heart sank. Then she very calmly said, 'Number 2,' and nearly forty years of longing, and hoping, and battling, and setbacks, all came out at once, and I cried like a baby. I had no idea the emotion was there, waiting to come out. No idea at all. I didn't expect it, but it was instant. It caught me by surprise, and I didn't know what to do with it other than just sit there, with my head in my hands, and wait for it to stop. It was quite possibly the greatest career moment of my life.

People assume that it couldn't compare to when I was number 1, but they don't see it the way I do. It's not just about the chart position – it's about knowing you've finally got back to a point that is undeniably successful. That number 2 was the end result of a thirty-five-year struggle, and it honestly meant more to me than all the number 1s. They'd come easy – this had taken more than half of my life. I'd been all but dead and buried, written off more than once, vilified, ridiculed, dismissed, and yet here I was again. More than that, here I was with an album that was heavy and uncompromising, relevant and contemporary. Whereas most other people with long careers fade into bland middle-of-the-road mediocrity, I was still out there, pushing forward. I promise you, it was the most satisfying, rewarding moment of my career. So far.

A strange thing happened in the USA. In the Billboard dance/electronic chart, *Savage* went to number 1. It was an amazing result, but then I started to get calls asking how much of the album was actually electronic. It was almost entirely electronic, far more so than those two 'classic' electronic albums *Replicas* and *The Pleasure Principle*, in fact. But the powers-that-be at Billboard decided it 'wasn't electronic enough', and the album was disqualified from the chart completely. It was the most ridiculous thing but, when objections were lodged, they said that the decision was made and, pretty much, told us to piss off. You don't expect something like that from such a lofty organisation as Billboard. Rumours began to float back that they saw it more as a dance chart and didn't want any non-dance albums in there. But it's labelled as dance/electronic, and of all the people in the world who could justifiably claim to be electronic, I think I would qualify.

With the album released, the touring started in earnest. I'd been taken on by SJM, a major promoter, and the difference was immediately noticeable. Better money, better sales, better everything. The shows were selling out, the crowds were amazing and it just went from strength to strength. We went back to Europe, and the same thing was happening there. I even received an award in Poland for 'Visionary and Pioneering Solutions in Production'.

In the USA and Canada, we played a long thirty-date tour, and, again, the sales were fantastic. With the exception of Aspen, strangely enough, where I think about fifteen people turned up. At the end of the tour, the last show being in Salt Lake City, Utah, the band decided to fly straight back to the UK. The rest of us, including the children, who had come out to join us, decided to stay with the bus and drive back to LA but via Las Vegas. We got back to LA just three days before Christmas.

Chapter Forty-three

2018

It was Gemma's fiftieth birthday on 12 January, and she wanted to do something special but couldn't think what exactly. I really should have come up with a lovely surprise, but I was as useless as always and failed dismally. At the last minute, she decided she wanted to go to Alaska, so we bought some tickets and headed off to the airport. Next stop Anchorage. Alaska was cold but interesting. We flew over a glacier in an old ski-equipped aeroplane, and then landed on a frozen lake and got out. We saw bears, caribou and some of the most spectacular scenery I've ever seen. Unfortunately, I almost got caught up in a fight with a drug-addled man, which freaked Raven out a bit.

I'd been talking with my agent for some time about touring Australia and New Zealand with *Savage*. The best deal they could come to really wasn't very good, and a tour could have possibly lost me a considerable amount of money. But if the album was out over there, and a tour would give it a push, I was willing to risk it. I spoke to BMG and explained the situation and was told not to bother. I found that a little disheartening. But with no label support, it made the tour impossible. It was very disheartening to have to cancel that tour before I'd even announced it.

The next leg of the *Savage* tour kicked off in Stockholm, and we played eight shows through Scandinavia and Europe. I had my sixtieth birthday in Antwerp, which I hadn't been looking forward to at all. My birthday that is, not Antwerp. I'd done my best to ignore it and definitely didn't feel like celebrating. I saw nothing to celebrate about being sixty years old. During the day, it was all fairly low key, and by the time I was playing the show, I'd actually forgotten all about it. But then the band stopped playing, made an announcement, the crowd sang happy birthday and it was all very lovely. A giant card was brought on stage that had apparently been set up in the foyer and hundreds of the fans had signed it as they came in. The best bit was when the LED screens at the back flickered into life and a film came on of Raven, Persia and Echo wishing me a happy birthday. That was just too much, and I got quite emotional. It really was a quite special moment. Back on the bus after the show, I found it had been decorated and turned into a birthday-party bus. The day I'd been dreading turned out to be one of the best birthdays I'd had in years. But the next day wasn't a party, and I was still sixty.

The bus left Germany, and we drove to the docks, got a ferry and made our way to Portsmouth. We played another twelve-date tour of the UK and then got another ferry across to Ireland, where we ended the tour with a show in Dublin at the Olympia Theatre. The Olympia had once seen the likes of Charlie Chaplin and Laurel and Hardy perform on stage. It was a great place to end that leg of the tour, and one of the best crowds we'd had since the *Savage* shows began. With that, we flew back to the USA, because Gemma had the mother of all ops planned.

This time she was going for a full body lift, which is pretty major. When I saw her afterwards, I found it hard to believe that anyone could survive such a thing, and yet, later that afternoon, she was back in the hotel complaining about the exact position of one of half a dozen pillows. It really is quite incredible. When I was little, I could barely look at so much as a cut finger. Now, thanks to the things I've been forced to witness with Gemma, I feel I could cope with almost anything. Once, after she had a boob job back in England, it all just came undone. I had to pull it together and tape it so that it would hold long enough to drive her back to the doctor.

Unfortunately, a few days after the body lift, an area started to go black. When they mentioned leeches, I thought they were joking, but oh no, leeches were brought to the hotel room, and for the next few days they attempted to fix the problem by having them suck out the blood. Now, I can't begin to tell you how scared Gemma is of all things wriggly, so having leeches sucking on her was asking a lot. She did it, though. In fact, when the leeches were finished with, she made sure they were taken to a nice stream and released rather than killed. She even had someone video their release to prove they'd done it kindly. Unfortunately, she wasn't well enough to travel at the end of the month, so I had to fly to Mexico to play at the Cntrl F festival without her. I think she's only missed a couple of shows since we've been together, and it feels like half of me is missing.

Bernard, our lovely St Bernard, had come to us with a breathing problem, and over time it had slowly got worse. One day, he collapsed on one of his walks. The vet recommended an operation that was risky, but without it he would certainly die, so we gave the go-ahead. He came through the op OK, went into recovery for a few days and we were given a time to pick him up. Then we got a phone call to say that he'd taken a bad turn unexpectedly and despite all their efforts to save him he had died that morning. That hurt us all very badly. When I could, I wrote a song for him called 'If We Had Known' and put it on *The Fallen* EP that came out that year.

Two weeks later, we got a phone call from the same rescue home that Bernard had come from. They'd heard about Bernard and wanted us to know that another St Bernard had just been brought in. Gemma explained that we were still upset and weren't ready for another one, but then the rescue lady said, 'But he is.' We hadn't thought of it that way at all. We were so wrapped up in our own feelings, we hadn't stopped to think how this poor dog must be feeling. Newly abandoned by a family he loved, lost and bewildered, locked in a place he didn't know. We drove straight there and so met Ronnie. The first thing Ronnie did was roll onto his back and wait for fuss. He was as lovely a dog as you could ever wish to meet, and he needed a home and a loving family, and that was us. We brought him home the next day.

I'd long wanted to play shows in South America, but it had never come together. In early 2018, an offer came in that would finally change that. We were asked to play two shows in Santiago, Chile. That was exciting enough, but we flew out to Chile a week before the shows and took another flight to Rapa Nui, or Easter Island. Rapa Nui is the most isolated inhabited island in the world and has a unique history. It's where the famous statues of giant heads stand facing out to sea. The flight from Santiago to the small island took another six hours, all over ocean, so it really is a long way from anywhere. It's an incredible place, the sunsets are spectacular and the walk around the huge volcano was stunning. Persia and Echo had their first-ever tattoos, on their feet.

We spent six fascinating days in Rapa Nui before flying back to Santiago for the two shows. The first was in a club and was hot, loud and very exciting. The second was in an arena about an hour's drive out of the city and, if anything, was louder and even more exciting. The media interest was surprisingly good – front pages of newspapers, featured guest on radio shows. It was all very unexpected, having never been there before, and it was one of my favourite trips of the year. As a first step into South America, it couldn't have gone better.

The tour continued in North America, and we meandered our way across the vastness of the United States, including a set at the Riotfest festival in Chicago. Beck was headlining and asked me to join him for a version of 'Cars' during his set. When we played in Cleveland, the tour bus arrived quite early, so we decided to visit the Rock and Roll Hall of Fame. We were given a tour of the archives not usually seen, which was quite fascinating. With that done, the bus headed into Cleveland for the show that night. Sadly, tragedy was just around the corner. At a junction in the city, the bus waited to turn, and when the way was clear, it moved slowly around the corner. But, completely unseen, an old man had carried on across the walkway, and the bus pulled across him, knocking him down and killing him. It was a horrible accident. The police arrived and looked at security footage and were satisfied that our driver was not to blame. But, nonetheless, it was devastating for him and for everyone on the bus. Most of all, though, for the family of the poor man who was killed.

The show that night was cancelled, and later in the evening we all met to discuss what we should do. There were a lot of very different feelings, as the shock of what had happened worked its way through people in different ways. Eventually, though, it was decided that we would carry on, but it was a very sad and sombre bus that drove away the next morning. At each venue after that, we were greeted with considerable sympathy and understanding by venue staff and fans alike, and we were grateful for that. But, for some in the team, the shock was so great that it would take a long time to come to terms with, and for a few it would require professional counselling. When the tour was over and we were back in our homes, I know for sure we all relived it again and again, both awake and asleep.

As part of my *Savage* deal, I was expected to supply fifteen songs to BMG. But I only had twelve done in time for the album. So, whenever I had gaps in between tours, I was working in my studio. The three songs I came up with were 'It Will End Here', 'The Promise' and 'If We Had Known', and they were put on *The Fallen* EP in November.

When *Savage* was first released, I did a great deal of promotional work for it, and I mentioned more than once in interviews about one day wanting to work with an orchestra. Then I received a message from a man called Simon Robertshaw who said he had one, the Skaparis Orchestra. That started a long period of negotiation and work which would ultimately lead to one of the most enjoyable onstage experiences of my life. Simon put in an extraordinary amount of effort to make the orchestra shows happen. His talent, experience, commitment and enthusiasm carried the project along until, on 12 November, the band and I took to the stage in Cardiff with the Skaparis Orchestra behind us. It was everything I'd dreamed it would be. My songs took on the feel of cinematic epics, and I don't think I have ever been more proud of my own music as I was then. I'd expected the orchestra players to be old, jaded and not interested in the music they were playing. I was actually anticipating, months ahead of the shows, the arguments I was likely to have as they constantly looked at their watches eager for their next break. But it was nothing like that. The Skaparis players were young, full of enthusiasm and great fun.

As good as all the shows were on the orchestral leg of the tour, seven in all, the pinnacle was the Royal Albert Hall. All five thousand tickets sold out in a few hours, my biggest Numan crowd since Wembley in 1981. If the Hammersmith show at the end of the *Splinter* tour had been a triumphant return, this was more. It was an emotional, overwhelming evening, and I cannot think of a time, in my entire forty-year career, where I ever felt more loved and supported. It almost made the Hammersmith show feel like a rehearsal. It was absolutely magnificent, and if that had been the last show I ever played, I would have been content for the rest of my life. Luke Edwards, the lighting designer, had come up with an incredible spectacle, and I had thrown as much money at it as he needed. It was a stunning light show. Dave Dupuis did his usual magic with the front of house sound, the orchestra were flawless and the band seemed to feed on every bit of energy coming at us from all directions in that huge hall. At one point, I just stood and listened, soaking everything up. It was incredibly emotional. My children were there, Gemma, my dad, my brother, and I'm sure Mum would have found a way to be there as well. If the album success had felt like the culmination of a very long journey, that show felt like we'd gone one step further.

The last full tour of the *Savage* campaign took us back to Europe. Although there were parts of Europe that I still needed to work on, things were very much better overall. We played another ten shows, ending in Helsinki, Finland. Mike, one of the crew, had been feeling unwell for several days and in Oslo had turned a kind of grey colour. Dave Dupuis insisted he go to hospital, which probably saved his life. At the hospital, it was discovered that without an emergency operation he wouldn't have survived the night. To get from Oslo to Helsinki involved a long journey on a ship. If Mike had boarded, he almost certainly wouldn't have got off it alive. That close call shook all of us.

Chapter Forty-four

2019

The one-hundred-and-thirtieth and final, *Savage* show was at the Rockaway Beach festival in England. It was a very strange feeling to see it all come to an end. I'd played more live shows for *Savage* than for any other album in my career. The success of the album, the tours, BMG, the entire campaign, in fact, had been a truly epic experience, and it felt almost as if we'd lost something for ever when it was finally over. But it meant I could now start to put into action all the other ideas I'd been working on.

The first of which was a couple of *In Conversation* shows that I'd planned with Steve Malins, who had thankfully forgiven me for letting him go a few years earlier. *In Conversation* was simply me and Steve having a conversation about me and my career in front of an audience. Around the stage behind us I had arranged a few significant items of memorabilia, including my SunBurst Gibson Les Paul guitar, my *Savage* album-sleeve outfit, the *Telekon* car, the bass guitar I wrote 'Cars' on and some others. We did one night in Manchester and one night in London, and as an idea it worked very well. I've thought about doing a lot more, but I'm not sure it's something that would work too often. I will occasionally do more in the future.

Pledge Music, the company that had so successfully handled my *Savage* pre-order campaign, had gone bust soon after my campaign had finished and were no longer around. But I very much wanted to do a similar thing with the next album I was planning, *Intruder*. Townsend Music, who had looked after my online store for many years, were keen to start something similar to Pledge called Making Music, so my *Intruder* campaign became their first foray into that area. Much like with *Savage*, the Making Music campaign for *Intruder* offered a behind-the-scenes look at the album being made, signed lyric sheets, used equipment and a range of other things, including fans coming to the mastering and launch parties in the USA and the UK. The campaign launched and almost straight away I ran into some quite serious teething troubles.

For a number of years, I'd used a Pro Tools system to record my albums. But as soon as I started to work on *Intruder*, a series of problems made me decide I should switch over to another system called Logic Pro. It sounds quite minor, but it was anything but. The sound desk that I used to operate Pro Tools wouldn't work with Logic, so that also had to be replaced, which meant replacing the huge wooden frame the desk sat in, and on and on it went. As each thing was retired, so another thing needed to be replaced that supported the first thing. The simple task of moving from one bit of software to another actually closed down the studio for several months – it was a disastrous start. Eventually, everything was in place, including a new touch-screen desk, coincidentally called a Raven, and Ade Fenton came over to talk about new ideas and to give me a crash course in Logic. Ade had used Logic for years, and it made sense for us both to be using the same system.

Intruder was, in some respects, going to be a further exploration of ideas around the impending catastrophe of global warming. However, where *Savage* had been a series of fantasy stories set in a future Earth devastated by climate change, *Intruder* would be written from the Earth's point of view. If the planet could speak, and voice its feelings, what would it say? Would it be angry and hurt? Would it feel betrayed? Would it want to fight back? Had it already begun? With the new studio installed and working, I once again got down to writing new songs.

That summer I received a Nordoff Robbins 02 Silver Clef Icon award, presented by Virgin Radio DJ Eddie Temple-Morris. Eddie did me a great favour, actually, as he was still on air when the awards started. He finished his show, came straight to the ceremony and arrived just in time to present my award. The children got to meet Dua Lipa, so they were happy.

I posted a little video on my socials of me driving around in Echo's toy electric car in May, and the result was surprising. It was, by far, one of the most popular posts I'd ever put up, and it made me aware of something I hadn't really noticed before. Whereas I'd always thought people would be most interested in news about tours or new albums, the things that got the biggest response were the behind-the-scenes, private moments, well away from work. I knew a number of friends who were running Patreon sites – Chris Corner had a particularly impressive one, for example – so I started to think about if it would be worthwhile to start my own. It took many months of careful planning and study before I decided to go for it, not least of which was working out how much extra time it would take to create the things I wanted to offer. I don't have a great deal of spare time, and what little I do have I like to keep for the family. It's the only way we can have a life together and give the children as much normality as possible. It was clear that running a Patreon site was going to take a great deal of time beyond the work I was already doing as a self-managed recording and touring artist. So, it would be an experiment. I would do my best, but if it became too much, I would close it down. I spent the next few months fine-tuning the idea and getting it ready to launch later in the year. It would be called *Ghost Nation*.

Gemma had organized another boat holiday for us all in Croatia but, a few days before we were due to leave, she became quite ill. The doctor said it was probably the tail end of the flu and was nothing to worry about, but she was in a bad way. But not much gets in the way of Gemma and a holiday, so we boarded a plane to London and hoped for the best. Unfortunately it did not go well. In the plane she was worse than ever and, even to me, looked like a junkie in withdrawal. I was extremely worried. By the time we landed the crew had called ahead and a wheelchair was waiting. We were even prioritised at immigration to get her to a doctor as quickly as possible. It turned out she didn't have flu, she had pneumonia. The doctor in London was fantastic, a Gary Numan fan as it turned out, which may have helped, and he prescribed her some medicine that worked wonders. The next day we flew to Croatia but it took another week before she felt good again.

In 2019, we celebrated the fortieth anniversary of my break-out year in the UK, when the 'Are "Friends" Electric?' and 'Cars' singles, and the *Replicas* and *Pleasure Principle* albums, had all gone to number 1. I wanted to mark that with some live shows, so we put together a twenty-five-date UK tour for the autumn called *(R)evolution*. Rather than being a celebration of 1979 I wanted it to be a celebration of the entire forty years since. To that end, we rehearsed a huge number of songs from across the entire span of my career and were able to play a different set almost every night. I wanted to show two things: how revolutionary electronic music was when it first came along, and how I'd evolved in the forty years since, hence *(R)evolution*. During the tour, David Brooks had to leave, as his father became very ill, and Ade Fenton stepped in at very short notice for a few shows. I was even given an award by the Rock City venue for playing there fifteen times. They'd replaced the wooden floor of the venue and engraved some of the old tiles into awards. It made my day.

While the tour was under way, I finally announced and launched the *Ghost Nation* Patreon project. From the outset, I knew it was only going to appeal to the hard-core fanbase, so that's who I made it for. What *Ghost Nation* does is add something new to all the other things I do. It offers a peek into my private life, my family time, something I've kept largely separate from my career in the past. But, just like making albums, or touring, it takes a lot of time, and that time has a value. So, *Ghost Nation* is a four-tier paid membership service. Some people seemed to be upset by that, but this is how I earn my living. I create things, and I sell them. That's my business. It's actually the fan who has total control over all of this, because it's the fan who chooses whether to buy something or not. I have no leverage at all to make people do anything. All I can do is try to think of things that people might enjoy so that I can continue to earn a living. It's in my interest to try and come up with ideas that add to the fan experience, to find things that fans want. The meet and greets, for example – people seem to like them. After that, I added Rehearsal VIP experiences, where fans can come and sit in on the rehearsals. They have been extremely popular, and I continue to look for other ideas, things that I can do that might be of interest to my fans – new experiences and opportunities, things that allow them to see, or be a part of, something that wasn't available before. *Ghost Nation* is just another idea along the way that I hope people will like.

Chapter Forty-five

2020

So here we are, in the most bizarre year of all. Before the COVID-19 pandemic brought the world to a halt, it had already been busy for me. We spent some in Florida, flew up to Oregon and stayed at the Timberline Lodge (of *The Shining* fame) for Gemma's birthday, where we almost got trapped on the mountain in a blizzard. Mark Ronson came to the house, work on *Intruder* continued and we became US citizens, or, to be more exact, joint British and US citizens. Gemma was told that she did have MS after all, only for it to be dismissed once again. That was a truly unsettling few weeks. I was then invited to be a guest speaker at Cornell University as part of their *When Machines Rock: A Celebration of Robert Moog and Electronic Music* event. Shortly after, we were put under lockdown and everything changed.

I've taken the virus very seriously. I do not think it's part of a world conspiracy to either control us or kill off the weak. I think it's a disease that got out of control. I do not think masks are an invasion of my civil liberties – I think they might just save my life, and yours. I absolutely do not want to get sick. If you're lucky, the virus doesn't bother you much at all; if you're not, it can be a horrendous experience and may kill you. This is an extraordinary time to be alive – it already was before the virus came along, but there is absolutely no doubt about it now. The live music industry, the industry that I largely rely on for my living, is in terrible trouble. Industry friends of mine have lost their businesses, many have lost their jobs, venues are closing down and we are all anxious about what the future holds.

With this book I realised it had to be in my words or not at all so I abandoned previous drafts and wrote the whole thing from scratch. It took seven weeks, which made the *Intruder* album late, so the pressure is now pretty intense. I'd come up with an idea to make two *Intruder* albums instead of one. BMG liked the idea, so that's the way it will be – one to be released in early 2021 and the other in late 2021. I've not done that before, so it will be interesting to see how it works out. Most importantly, though, it looks as though I'll be going back to Wembley Arena as part of the *Intruder* tours. For me, that really will be the final, glorious piece of the jigsaw I've been putting together since 1981. It's been a long time coming, and yet I can't help wondering what will come after that.

Acknowledgements

I would like to thank Gemma and Steve Malins for helping colour the many grey areas of my memory. Also, many thanks to James Hogg.